D1640227

'18 Phil   €47,-

Order Ethics: An Ethical Framework for the Social Market Economy

Christoph Luetge · Nikil Mukerji
Editors

Order Ethics: An Ethical Framework for the Social Market Economy

MÄNGELEXEMPLAR

Editors
Christoph Luetge
Chair of Business Ethics
Technical University of Munich
Munich
Germany

Nikil Mukerji
Faculty of Philosophy, Philosophy
 of Science, and the Study of Religion
Ludwig-Maximilians-Universität München
Munich
Germany

ISBN 978-3-319-33149-2   ISBN 978-3-319-33151-5 (eBook)
DOI 10.1007/978-3-319-33151-5

Library of Congress Control Number: 2016942011

© Springer International Publishing Switzerland 2016
This work is subject to copyright. All rights are reserved by the Publisher, whether the whole or part of the material is concerned, specifically the rights of translation, reprinting, reuse of illustrations, recitation, broadcasting, reproduction on microfilms or in any other physical way, and transmission or information storage and retrieval, electronic adaptation, computer software, or by similar or dissimilar methodology now known or hereafter developed.
The use of general descriptive names, registered names, trademarks, service marks, etc. in this publication does not imply, even in the absence of a specific statement, that such names are exempt from the relevant protective laws and regulations and therefore free for general use.
The publisher, the authors and the editors are safe to assume that the advice and information in this book are believed to be true and accurate at the date of publication. Neither the publisher nor the authors or the editors give a warranty, express or implied, with respect to the material contained herein or for any errors or omissions that may have been made.

Printed on acid-free paper

This Springer imprint is published by Springer Nature
The registered company is Springer International Publishing AG Switzerland

Contents

Part I Theoretical Foundations of Order Ethics—Fundamentals

Contractarian Foundations of Order Ethics 3
Christoph Luetge

The Ordonomic Approach to Order Ethics 19
Ingo Pies

Theory Strategies of Business Ethics 37
Karl Homann

Part II Theoretical Foundations of Order Ethics—The Economic and Social Background

A Critique of Welfare Economics 57
Martin Leschke

Order Ethics—An Experimental Perspective 67
Hannes Rusch and Matthias Uhl

Order Ethics and Situationist Psychology 79
Michael von Grundherr

Order Ethics, Economics, and Game Theory 93
Nikil Mukerji and Christoph Schumacher

Biblical Economics and Order Ethics: Constitutional Economic and Institutional Economic Roots of the Old Testament 109
Sigmund Wagner-Tsukamoto

Part III Theoretical Foundations of Order Ethics—The Philosophical Background of Order Ethics

Order Ethics and the Problem of Social Glue 127
Christoph Luetge

Rawls, Order Ethics, and Rawlsian Order Ethics 149
Ludwig Heider and Nikil Mukerji

Boost up and Merge with. Order Ethics in the Light of Recent Developments in Justice Theory 167
Michael G. Festl

Deconstructive Ethics—Handling Human Plurality (Shaped) by Normative (Enabling) Conditions 181
Tatjana Schönwälder-Kuntze

Contrasting the Behavioural Business Ethics Approach and the Institutional Economic Approach to Business Ethics: Insights from the Study of Quaker Employers 195
Sigmund Wagner-Tsukamoto

Part IV Problems of Business Ethics from an Order Ethics Perspective

The Constitution of Responsibility: Toward an Ordonomic Framework for Interpreting (Corporate Social) Responsibility in Different Social Settings 221
Markus Beckmann and Ingo Pies

Companies as Political Actors: A Positioning Between Ordo-Responsibility and Systems Responsibility 251
Ludger Heidbrink

Is the Minimum Wage Ethically Justifiable? An Order-Ethical Answer. 279
Nikil Mukerji and Christoph Schumacher

Sustainability from an Order Ethics Perspective. 293
Markus Beckmann

An Ordonomic Perspective in Medical Ethics. 311
Nikolaus Knoepffler and Martin O'Malley

Ethics and the Development of Reputation Risk at Goldman Sachs 2008–2010. 329
Ford Shanahan and Peter Seele

Executive Compensation 349
Christoph Luetge

Index 363

Introduction

The past few decades have confronted businesspeople, politicians and citizens with many moral issues of great concern. The worldwide financial crisis that followed the collapse of the American subprime mortgage market is merely one prominent example. The complex problems that are given rise to by hunger and poverty, global warming, corruption and international crime are others. These issues raise ethical questions that affect society as a whole and the way in which we organize it. Many people look towards economic and business ethics to find answers. The conception of Order Ethics, to which the present volume is devoted, seeks to organize such answers in a systematic way that is consistent with both economic and philosophical theories.

What is Order Ethics? Order Ethics ("Ordnungsethik" in German) originated as a theory in the German-speaking debate on business ethics during the 1980s and 1990s. Karl Homann, who held the first chair of business ethics in Germany, was its main proponent. Since then, Order Ethics has developed and widened its scope. But since its beginning, the concept of the market's order framework, or framework of rules, has played a central role.

This will be elaborated in the contributions contained in this volume. As Wittgenstein remarked, the meaning of a term is the way in which it is used, so accordingly, those who are interested in learning more about Order Ethics should look towards the contributions collected here. In a nutshell, however, the Order Ethics approach can be summarized in the following way.

Order Ethics—An Ethical Approach for the Social Market Economy

The main thrust behind Order Ethics can best be described by pointing to a feature that sets Order Ethics apart from many (though certainly not all) other views of economic and business ethics. Many approaches to business ethics tend to blame ethical problems on unethical individuals. Accordingly, theorists who subscribe to them usually propose to solve these problems through interventionist measures, i.e. *against* the market. In their view, the main task of an ethicist is to identify the moral shortcomings of the market and find individual culprits. Order ethicists have adopted a different strategy. They aimed to devise ethical systems *for* the market. This strategy stresses the importance of the social order where markets work in a way that is analogous to the German concept of Order Politics (or "Ordnungspolitik", which is the German term). The idea behind Order Politics is not to intervene directly into the market, but to provide a regulatory institutional framework in which markets function properly and for mutual benefit. Similarly, Order Ethics asks how markets can be regulated in order to bring to fruition moral ideals. This feature of the order-ethical approach is worth stressing. As the contributions that are contained in this volume illustrate, it opens up new perspectives on ethical problems that are blocked in many conventional views of economic and business ethics.

An Overview of the Book

The volume falls into two sections: The first section on theoretical foundations addresses fundamental questions of Order Ethics, the economic, social and philosophical background.

A. Theoretical Foundations of Order Ethics

Fundamentals

Christoph Luetge opens up the subsection on fundamentals. In Chapter "Contractarian Foundations of Order Ethics", he investigates the philosophical foundations of Order Ethics. Luetge connects Order Ethics to the social contract tradition in philosophy. He discusses the relation to other contract-based approaches as well as the historical and systematic conditions of the Order Ethics approach. In particular, he points to the role of competition as a mechanism that serves ethical purposes.

In Chapter "The Ordonomic Approach to Order Ethics", **Ingo Pies** takes a closer look at the economic basis of Order Ethics. Homing in on a contrast between Order Ethics and a traditional ethics, Pies explains that—from an economic perspective— the latter focuses on individual motives of action and needs an ethics of the institutional order that provides a moral analysis of the framework of rules. One aspect that looms large in Pies' analysis is the problem of incentives. He argues that traditional ethics neglects the incentive properties of the social order and that there is a need for an Order Ethics, which fills this void. Pies then introduces a narrower version of Order Ethics—the ordonomic approach—before he illustrates its application through a number of case studies.

Karl Homann discusses theory strategies in business ethics in Chapter "Theory Strategies of Business Ethics". He diagnoses a general lack of methodological reflection in the discipline as a whole and thus finds it worthwhile to back up and consider the methodology problem in more detail. He distinguishes between two fundamental strategies that one can adopt in business ethics. The first regards ethical and economic thinking as being fundamentally opposed to one another. It insists on the primacy of ethics over economics and calls for a "disruption" of the economic logic. The second, which in Homann's view ultimately leads to an endorsement of Order Ethics, regards the two realms as reconcilable. After introducing these two views, Homann addresses their respective strengths and weaknesses. He argues that there are advantages and disadvantages on both sides, but ultimately argues for the second strategy because only this second strategy allows us to implement ethical norms in modern societies.

Economic and Social Background

The subsection on the economic and social background of Order Ethics begins with the Chapter "A Critique of Welfare Economics" by **Martin Leschke**, who presents a critique of welfare economics. Historically, welfare economics started out within a classic utilitarian system of thought, which aimed at evaluating how the allocation of goods and resources through market systems affects the well-being of individuals. Modern welfare economic analysis, however, has dropped certain utilitarian tenets, most importantly the idea of cardinal utility and interpersonal unit-comparability. This has made it less objectionable. Nowadays welfare economists tend to share with most order ethicists the idea that social welfare should be measured and compared in terms of the Pareto criterion. If at least some are made better off and nobody is made worse off, then this constitutes a social improvement. Nevertheless, Leschke criticizes welfare economics. After a short discussion of the Pareto criterion and its problems, Leschke focuses, in particular, on welfare economics' neglect of regulatory aspects. Welfare economics, Leschke argues, does not take into account how the rules that constitute the market system come into being. This, he believes, constitutes a blind spot worthy of criticism.

In Chapter "Order Ethics—An Experimental Perspective", **Hannes Rusch** and **Matthias Uhl** approach Order Ethics from an experimental perspective. They highlight an aspect of Order Ethics that is generally emphasized by its adherents, viz. the question of how moral rules can be implemented. This aspect of Order Ethics, as Rusch and Uhl argue, makes it particularly amenable to empirical considerations. They support their claim by a number of examples that they draw from investigations in experimental economics. As they explain, these studies can answer certain questions related to the implementation of moral norms. Rusch and Uhl insist that Order Ethics is not at odds with experimental findings. Instead, it benefits from and contributes to them.

Chapter "Order Ethics and Situationist Psychology" by **Michael von Grundherr** also focuses on how empirical findings affect Order Ethics. Unlike Rusch and Uhl, however, he focuses on a specific issue, by considering research in social psychology that deals with "situations". Situationism is an empirical psychological theory that seeks to explain human behaviour. As Grundherr points out, we tend to view character traits as the main determinants of behaviour. Whenever someone acts in a morally reprehensible way we ascribe this to their flawed character. Situationism, however, claims that aspects of the situation play a much greater role than individual character traits. Grundherr reviews the empirical findings underpinning situationism (by Milgram, Zimbardo, Isen/Levin and others) and argues that they lend support to Order Ethics.

In Chapter "Order Ethics, Economics and Game Theory", **Nikil Mukerji** and **Christoph Schumacher** offer a concise introduction to the methodology of Order Ethics and highlight how it connects aspects of economic theory and, in particular, game theory with traditional ethical considerations. Their discussion is conducted along the lines of five basic propositions, which are used to characterize the methodological approach of Order Ethics. Later on in the volume (Chapter "Is the Minimum Wage Ethically Justifiable? An Order-Ethical Answer"), they illustrate how their proposed methodology can be applied to a practical ethical question, viz. whether minimum wage laws are morally justifiable.

Chapter "Biblical Economics and Order Ethics: Constitutional Economic and Institutional Economic Roots of the Old Testament" by **Sigmund Wagner-Tsukamoto** concludes the subsection on the economic and social background of Order Ethics. It analyses order-ethical concepts like the idea of a dilemma structure or the homo-economicus model against the background of Old Testament stories. He concludes that these stories can, in fact, be interpreted as containing many of the ideas that order ethicists routinely work with. And he argues that they add to the credibility of Order Ethics.

Philosophical Background

The subsection on the philosophical background of Order Ethics begins with the Chapter "Order Ethics and the Problem of Social Glue" by **Christoph Luetge**. Luetge discusses in detail the philosophical background of Order Ethics in relation to prominent philosophical theories, in particular, those of Jürgen Habermas, John Rawls, David Gauthier and others. Luetge's article is devoted to the central question of whether societies in the globalized world need some kind of social glue to remain stable. He argues that from an Order Ethics perspective mutual benefits suffice.

The two ensuing chapters take on the issue of justice. In Chapter "Rawls, Order Ethics, and Rawlsian Order Ethics", **Ludwig Heider** and **Nikil Mukerji** discuss how Order Ethics relates to justice. They focus on John Rawls's conception of "Justice as Fairness" (JF) and compare its components with relevant aspects of the order-ethical approach. The two theories, Heider and Mukerji argue, are surprisingly compatible in various respects. They also analyse how far order ethicists disagree with Rawls and why. The main source of disagreement, they believe, lies in a claim that is central to the order ethical system, *viz.* the requirement of incentive-compatible implementability. It purports that an ethical norm can be normatively valid only if individuals have a self-interested motive to support it. This idea conflicts with the Rawlsian view because there are cases where it is not clear, from the standpoint of self-interest, why everybody should support its moral demands. If the claim of incentive-compatible implementability is, in fact, correct, then a proponent of JF would have to reform her views. Heider and Mukerji suggest how she could do that while salvaging the heart of her normative system as a "regulative idea". The conception that would result from this reformation may be seen as a new variant of Order Ethics, which the authors propose to call "Rawlsian Order Ethics".

In Chapter "Boost up and Merge with: Order Ethics in the Light of Recent Developments in Justice Theory", **Michael G. Festl** discusses Order Ethics against the background recent developments in justice theory. He diagnoses that a new paradigm is emerging in justice theory, which he attributes mainly to recent work by Amartya Sen and Alex Honneth. Their views depart from what Festl calls the "Rawlsian Standard Approach", which proposes to deduce and then to apply principles of perfect justice—an approach that has come to be known as "ideal theory". In contrast, Sen, Honneth and Festl himself seek to identify injustices based on norms that are already implemented through social practices. Festl believes that these ideas bear a striking resemblance to certain aspects of order ethicists and suggests how they may be combined with what Festl considers the driving idea behind Order Ethics.

In Chapter "Deconstructive Ethics: Handling Human Plurality (Shaped) by Normative (Enabling) Conditions", **Tatjana Schönwälder-Kuntze** references Order Ethics back to the Continental European tradition in philosophy, in particular, to Nietzsche and to French philosophers (such as Foucault and Sartre). Her aim was to ground Order Ethics in a much deeper rooted tradition of philosophy.

In Chapter "Contrasting the Behavioural Business Ethics Approach and the Institutional Economic Approach to Business Ethics: Insights from the Study of Quaker Employers", which concludes the subsection on the philosophical foundations of Order Ethics, **Sigmund Wagner-Tsukamoto** contrasts the order-ethical view (which he refers to as an "institutional business ethics") with behavioural models of business ethics. His main claim is that Order Ethics, which is informed by economic insights, is more promising. Though the behavioural approach can work in certain institutional environments that incentivize it, it must fail in others. Wagner-Tsukamoto illustrates this using the example of Quaker ethics. According to him, Quaker ethics can be seen as an instance of a behavioural ethics, which largely ignores the economic determinants of human behaviour. Quaker employers found that the implementation of their behavioural ethics approach worked in some instances, but not in others, which can be explained by an economic inquiry into the underlying incentive structures. This analysis shows that Quaker ethics failed when it was ill-aligned with the economic determinants of human behaviour, which is anticipated by Order Ethics.

B. Problems of Business Ethics from an Order Ethics Perspective

The second section discusses Order Ethics against the background of a number of examples from business ethics, starting with the Chapter "The Constitution of Responsibility: Toward an Ordonomic Framework for Interpreting (Corporate Social) Responsibility in Different Social Settings" by **Markus Beckmann** and **Ingo Pies**. They address the concept of responsibility and argue that the term is usually used in a problematic way. Therefore, they seek to explicate responsibility using the means of constitutional economics and ordonomics (which, as Pies has argued in the third chapter, is a special version of Order Ethics). From a constitutional economic perspective, as Beckmann and Pies explain, responsibility can be divided into "within-game responsibility" at the sub-constitutional level and "context-of-game responsibility" at the constitutional level. The ordonomic perspectives yield further differentiations. Beckmann and Pies suggest the notion of "context-of-game responsibility" to comprise both a "governance responsibility" (related to institutional reform for mutual advantage) and a "discourse responsibility" to explore shared interests and the potential for reforms that benefit all. Finally, Beckmann and Pies stress that responsibilities at the constitutional level do not rest on the shoulders of government actors only, but also on those of corporations and NGOs.

In Chapter "Companies as Political Actors: A Positioning Between Ordo-Responsibility and Systems Responsibility", **Ludger Heidbrink** picks up where Beckmann and Pies left off. He addresses companies in their role as political agents and likewise considers them from a responsibility perspective. He asks which consequences are entailed by the increased shift of responsibility from governmental agents to non-governmental agents (i.e. companies) and to which extent it is legitimate for companies to adopt them. Like Beckmann and Pies, Heidbrink thinks that companies have a "within-game responsibility" and a "context-of-game responsibility". However, he believes that the ordonomic perspective, from which these types of responsibility derive, is insufficient. He believes that companies possess, in addition, a "systems responsibility" for maintaining the conditions of the social system they act in, which the ordonomic perspective is unable to account for. Companies should accept a systems responsibility too, Heidbrink argues, because it is in their long-term interest, not only to secure economic benefits through mutually beneficial rule changes, but also to avoid social crises.

Nikil Mukerji and **Christoph Schumacher** take on the issue of minimum wage legislation in Chapter "Is the Minimum Wage Ethically Justifiable? An Order-Ethical Answer". They ask whether the minimum wage is ethically justifiable and attempt to answer this question from an order-ethical perspective. To this end, Mukerji and Schumacher develop two simple game-theoretical models for different types of labour markets and derive policy implications from an order-ethical viewpoint. Their investigation yields a twofold conclusion. First, order ethicists should prefer a tax-funded wage subsidy over minimum wages if they assume that labour markets are perfectly competitive. Second, Order Ethics suggests that the minimum wage can be ethically justified if employers have monopsony power in the wage setting process. Mukerji and Schumacher conclude, therefore, that Order Ethics neither favours nor disfavours the minimum wage. Rather, it implies conditions under which this form of labour market regulation is justified and, hence, allows empirical knowledge to play a great role in answering ethical questions that arise in the context of the minimum wage debate. This, they argue, illustrates one of Order Ethics' strengths, *viz.* the fact that it tends to de-ideologize the debate about ethical issues.

In Chapter "Sustainability from an Order Ethics Perspective", **Markus Beckmann** addresses issues of sustainability and examines them with a view on their societal relevance from an Order Ethics perspective. He argues that there are considerable commonalities and overlaps between the idea of sustainability and the order-ethical framework and that the notion itself can best be understood if one adopts an order-ethical view of it. Furthermore, Beckmann argues that fleshing out the sustainability concept in terms of Order Ethics casts new light on Order Ethics itself and provides valuable insights.

Nikolaus Knoepffler and **Martin O'Malley** address the problem complex of medical ethics in Chapter "An Ordonomic Perspective in Medical Ethics", by going through a number of classical approaches to medical ethics—the Hippocratic Oath, the Christian tradition, the 4-principles approach, utilitarian ethics and human rights views. As the authors explain, all of these address themselves to individual moral agents and focus on their individual moral choices. This makes them to some extent inadequate as approaches to medical ethics because they have to rely on moralistic rules and individual blaming. Knoepffler and O'Malley argue that an Order Ethics or ordonomic perspective on medical ethics is more adequate and illustrate this using a number of practical and highly relevant examples (e.g. the allocation of organs and scarce resources in the healthcare sector). These examples bring out the importance of institutions and incentives scheme in the resolution of these ethical problems. Nevertheless, Knoepffler and O'Malley believe that an integrated approach between the ordonomic view and conventional individual-focused moral conceptions is viable as an approach to medical ethics.

Chapter "Ethics and the Development of Reputation Risk at Goldman Sachs 2008–2010" by **Ford Shanahan** and **Peter Seele** analyses, by the way of a case study, how ethical misdemeanour can affect the reputation of a company and constitute a considerable business risk. The authors focus on Goldman Sachs in the years 2008–2011. They think that ethics is an important factor, which can considerably affect corporate performance. According to them, ethics violations can, furthermore, threaten the survival of a company. In particular, Shanahan and Seele have the issue of trust in mind, which is, of course, of utmost importance in the financial section. As they explain, allegations according to which Goldman Sachs misled investors and governments in their business dealings hurt them in two ways: First, they led to substantial financial settlements and, second, they damaged the company's reputation in the eye of the public.

In the final Chapter "Executive Compensation" **Christoph Luetge** addresses a topic that regularly sparks public uproars, *viz.* executive compensation. He examines a number of arguments for high executive compensation and discusses both good and bad ones. He concludes, tentatively, that there is, in general, a justification for high executive compensation as long as certain conditions obtain (e.g. no fraud or breach of fiduciary duties).

The conclusions put forward in this volume will certainly not be unanimously accepted. However, we rejoice at a wealth of viewpoints and welcome new views particularly if they conflict with received wisdom. For it is only if divergent theses collide and get submitted to rigorous scrutiny that we can hope to find truly promising answers to the pressing moral questions that we face today. We hope that the papers we are presenting herewith will be greeted in that spirit.

Acknowledgments

We would like to thank two anonymous referees for their helpful comments and constructive criticisms.

Munich, Germany   Christoph Luetge
November 2015   Nikil Mukerji

Part I
Theoretical Foundations of Order Ethics—Fundamentals

Part I
Theoretical Foundations of Code of Ethics—Einglantianople

Contractarian Foundations of Order Ethics

Christoph Luetge

1 Introduction

The conception of Order Ethics (cf. Homann and Luetge 2013; Luetge 2005, 2012, 2014, 2015, 2016 and Luetge et al. 2016) is based on the social contract tradition that includes authors like Hobbes (1651/1991), Locke, Spinoza, and Kant. The idea of embedding business ethics in a contract-related context has been explored by a number of authors over the past decades, such as Donaldson and Dunfee (1999, 2000, 2002), Keeley (1988), Rowan (1997, 2001), Wempe (2004, 2008a, 2008b) and Werhane (1985). I will discuss the contractarian foundations of Order Ethics in this article.

2 Contractarianism and Contractualism

Many authors [such as Wempe (2004); Oosterhout et al. (2004); Heugens et al. (2004) or Heugens et al. (2006)] distinguish between contractarianism and contractualism:

Contractarianism, as understood here, is a philosophical position which regards the consent of actors as its only normative criterion. In particular, it assumes that actors are self-interested and give their consent to norms or rules only if they regard

---

This chapter reproduces material that has previously been published in C. Luetge, "The Idea of a Contractarian Business Ethics", in: C. Luetge (ed.), The Handbook of the Philosophical Foundations of Business Ethics, Dordrecht: Springer 2013, 647–658. We thank Springer Science+Business Media B.V. for their permission to reproduce it here.

C. Luetge (✉)
Chair of Business Ethics, Technical University of Munich,
Munich, Germany
e-mail: luetge@tum.de

this as beneficial for themselves. This is different from a position that takes the consent of actors after deliberation as its main starting point (i.e., discourse ethics).

Contractualism presupposes an internal morality of contracting: it assumes that contracting parties must have certain moral capabilities in order for the contracts to work. For example, Rawls (1993) postulates a sense of justice (cf. Luetge 2015b). Contractualists usually regards actors not as predominantly self-interested, but rather as being embedded in a more general frame of commitments. In this sense, contractualism is at least in some regards closer to discourse theory and discourse ethics.

3 From Buchanan to Game Theory

Order Ethics, however, draws mostly on the contractarianism of Buchanan (1990, 2000), Brennan and Buchanan (1985); for the ethical dimension of Buchanan's work cf. Luetge (2006). Buchanan's approach differs from philosophers in the tradition of Nozick (1974) in that rights themselves must be granted to each other via a constitutional contract. In general, Buchanan's objective is to "explain how 'law,' 'the rights of property,' 'rules for behavior,' might emerge from the non-idealistic, self-interested behavior of men, without any presumption of equality in some original position—equality either actually or expectationally" (Buchanan 2000: 71). Rawls's project draws importantly on the veil of ignorance both in "A Theory of Justice" (Rawls 1971) and "Justice as Fairness" (Rawls 2001), whereas Buchanan describes his efforts in "The Limits of Liberty: Between Anarchy and Leviathan" (2000) as simultaneously more and less ambitious than those of Rawls. Buchanan's approach is more ambitious in that he does discuss the critically important bridge between an idealized setting and reality, in which any discussion of basic structural rearrangement might, in fact, take place. He also tries to examine the prospects for genuine contractual renegotiation among persons who are not equals at the stage of deliberation and who are not artificially made to behave as if they were, either through general adherence to internal ethical norms or through the introduction of uncertainty about post-contract positions. This point is critically important for the application of Order Ethics because it gives Order Ethics distinct tools for problem solving.

In another respect Buchanan's efforts are less ambitious than Rawls's. Rawls identifies the principles of justice that he predicts to emerge from his idealized contractual setting, but Buchanan takes no such step. He does not "try to identify either the 'limits of liberty' or the set of principles that might be used to define such limits" (Buchanan 2000: 221). The Order Ethics approach highlights the relevance of Buchanan's normative economics to ethical questions. It does not separate between normative political philosophy or normative economics on the one hand and ethics on the other, but makes normative economics applicable to issues that business ethicists have previously considered as outside the realm of political philosophy.

Another important author in this field is Binmore (1994, 1998), who develops a contractarian theory of the evolution of social norms using methods of game theory. While Order Ethics does not depend on the evolutionary accounts Binmore gives, his way of introducing morality based on self-interest is clearly in accordance with Order Ethics in many respects (see Luetge 2015). In Binmore's approach morality provides us with a way of choosing between multiple equilibria in social or economic life. But only *equilibria* can be chosen, and this is almost identical to what Order Ethics holds: Only incentive-compatible rules can be actually implemented—and that is what matters in ethical as well as in other ways.

4 Ethics or Political Philosophy?

Two remarks should be added here: First, I understand Order Ethics as a contribution to a contractarian business *ethics*, not to *political philosophy*. The line between political contractarianism and what might be termed 'moral contractarianism' (Herzog 2013) is however blurry. Political and ethical considerations go hand in hand. Rules that Order Ethics aims at can be found both at the level of laws, as well as on informal levels of social norms (cf. Luetge 2012, 2013; Luetge et al. 2016).

Second, deriving morality from interests (and, in a theoretical sense, with the help of economics) is a project that is especially fit for an ethics of modern *business*. As the philosopher of economics Wade Hands put it: "For economists, unlike for most others in modern intellectual life, the ubiquitousness of narrow self-interest in science or elsewhere, does not necessarily initiate a wringing of hands or lamentations about lost utopias; it only initiates a conversation about proper prices, compatible incentives and binding constraints." (Hands 1994: 97). In the same vein, contractarians, rather than lamenting interest-driven societies, would prefer channelling those interests via rules and the order framework.

A fully-fledged contractarian business ethics, in this sense, has not been yet been presented in detail, but at least some central elements have been developed over the past years. I will try to give an overview of some of these elements, and then proceed by outlining the approach of Order Ethics, which tries to spell out the idea of a contractarian business ethics. One preliminary remark is necessary for this task, however: The concepts of utility, benefits and advantages must be seen as "open" concepts in the sense that they are not limited to narrow 'economic', material or monetary utility, benefits and advantages, but rather as including—in the sense of Becker (1993)—all that actors *regard* as utility, benefits and advantages.

Before turning to Order Ethics proper, I will—for contrasting purposes—outline some basics of Integrative Social Contract Theory, which is arguably the most well-known contract-based theory in the field.

5 Integrative Social Contract Theory

The internationally most well known approach to business ethics that makes use of social contract theory is the *Integrative Social Contracts Theory* (ISCT) of Donaldson and Dunfee (1995, 1999). Donaldson and Dunfee, interestingly, are dissatisfied with the general ethical theories offered by philosophy and therefore develop a theory of their own which takes its origin not from abstract philosophical problems, but from concrete problems of business (like Order Ethics, they see contractarianism as avoiding several problems that standard theories of ethics face).

These concrete problems lie mainly in the nature of contracting which, in the globalised world, is subject to many different standards and norms. ISCT is meant to explicitly allow for such a variety of norms—within limits however. The contractarian idea is used to conceptualise both of these intentions, in the following way:

First, the authors conceive a *macrosocial contract* which all boundedly rational human beings would consent to. This contract is to regulate the process of norm-finding on lower levels. According to Donaldson and Dunfee, the contractors on the macro level will—implicitly more often than explicitly—consent to a contract that allows for significant 'moral free space' on the lower levels of communities, corporations and individual actors.

Second, *microsocial contracts* are generated within the framework of the macrosocial contract, between (mostly smaller) communities and corporations. Here, communities can accept quite different norms and standards, and immediately the question arises whether *any* such norms and standards can be ethically acceptable. Donaldson and Dunfee (try to) solve this problem by using the concept of *hypernorms*: Hypernorms are meant to be universal, overarching ethical principles which "are sufficiently fundamental that they serve as a source of evaluation and criticism of community-generated norms, and may include not only rules specifying minimum behaviour, such as the rule against the killing of innocents, but imperfect duties such as virtue, beneficence and decency" (Donaldson and Dunfee 1995: 96). Hypernorms are to express principles "so fundamental to human existence that one would expect them to be reflected in a convergence of religious, political and philosophical thought" (Donaldson and Dunfee 1995: 96). They are not explicitly seen as being subject to a contract themselves. Rather, they are to set the boundaries of the moral free space, together with the consent required from the members of the community and certain rules of thumb for dealing with the inevitable norm conflicts between communities. These 'priority rules' are the following:

1. "Transactions solely within a single community, which do not have significant adverse effects on other humans or communities, should be governed by the host community's norms.
2. Existing community norms indicating a preference for conflict of norms should be utilized, so long as they do not have significant adverse effects on other individuals or communities.

3. The more extensive or more global the community that is the source of the norm, the greater the priority that should be given to the norm.
4. Norms essential to the maintenance of the economic environment in which the transaction occurs should have priority over norms potentially damaging to the environment.
5. Where multiple conflicting norms are involved, patterns of consistency among alternative norms provide a basis for prioritization.
6. Well-defined norms should ordinarily have priority over more general, less precise norms." (Donaldson and Dunfee 1999: Ch. 7)

Critics have highlighted the vagueness inherent to these priority rules. However, ethical theories are not meant to provide ready-made recipes, but yardsticks—and as such, the priority rules certainly are good candidates to start with.

The theoretical discussion on ISCT has been continued by authors like Wempe, Oosterhout and Heugens (Wempe 2009; Oosterhout and Heugens 2009), who highlight especially the concept of "extant social contracts" and reconstruct ISCT as spelling out the details of the (necessary) internal norms of contracting. In this sense, ISCT is a contractualist rather than a contractarian approach. Boatright has criticised this enterprise by arguing (among other points) that while such an internal normativity might be desirable and even profitable, however contracting is not necessarily dependent on it and can take place without it (if less amicably) [Boatright (2007); cf. also the response by Oosterhout et al. (2007)]. Moreover, morality cannot be deduced from internal norms, but would have to be derived from other reasoning.

I agree with this criticism, in principle, and find ICST—at least in this regard—theoretically unsatisfying. To start a contractarian business ethics merely from an internal morality of contracting is quite limiting. In particular, it disregards the moral benefits produced not by individual corporations or individual actors, but by the entire system of the market economy (within rules and institutions). Order Ethics takes up this idea, and uses it to derive the internal morality of contracting in a more systematic way, employing the concept of incomplete contracts.

Nevertheless, ISCT is a major and fruitful approach to a contractualist business ethics. It allows for pluralism of ethics, it is closely oriented on business problems, and it takes empirical issues seriously, such as the "extant social contracts". Some of its systematic deficits may, however, be cured by the approach discussed in the next section.

Finally, another contract-based approach has been introduced by Sacconi (2000, 2006, 2007); see also the discussion by Francé-Gómez (2003) and Vanberg (2007). Sacconi develops a social contract theory of the firm inspired by Buchanan's constitutional and post-constitutional contract ideas. This theory is in several ways similar to the Order Ethics approach in that it relies heavily on economics and economic methodology, though some of its conclusions differ.

I will now turn to Order Ethics as a philosophical and contractarian approach.

6 Order Ethics

Order Ethics ("Ordnungsethik") can be regarded as the complement of the German conception of 'Ordnungspolitik', which stresses the importance of a regulatory framework ("Ordnung") for the economy. Order Ethics relies heavily on the Buchanan-type contractarianism, taking up its basic idea that society is a cooperation for mutual self-interest. The rules of a society, and of its economy, are agreed upon by the participants, in a situation like Rawls' *original position*. Here, Order Ethics also relies on Rawls: In accordance with his principles of justice, it will be in the mutual interest of all to devise rules that will in principle allow to improve everyone's position, and in particular, that of the least well-off. This idea is taken up in Order Ethics: the order framework of a society is regarded as a means for implementing ethics.

I will present the basic logic of the Order Ethics approach, starting with its account of modern, competitive societies. Second, I will explicate the distinction between action and rules, and third, the role (mutual) advantages play in its treatment of ethical norms. After that, the role of incomplete contracts will be looked at, in order to account for the role of rules below the level of the legal order framework.

7 Competition as a Social Condition

Order Ethics takes its start not from an aim to achieve, but rather from an account of the social conditions within which ethical norms are to be implemented: modern societies differ strongly from pre-modern ones. Pre-modern societies were "zero-sum societies" [the term has been popular in a slightly different sense by Thurow (1980)], in which people could only gain significantly at the expense of others. This view is concisely expressed in the words of the successful 15th century Florentine merchant Giovanni Rucellai, written around 1450: "by being rich, I make others (which I might not even know) poor".

Modern societies, by contrast, are societies with continuous growth, made possible by the modern competitive market economy. In this system, positive sum games are played. Many types of ethics, however, are still stuck with the conditions of pre-modern societies and lag behind: They ignore win-win-situations when distinguishing sharply between self-interest and altruistic motivation, and when requiring people to be moderate, to share unconditionally and to sacrifice. These attitudes, which make self-interest something evil, would have been functional in a zero-sum society, but they are inadequate for modern societies.

In a situation of zero-sum games, it was necessary to call for temperance, for *moderate* profits, or even for banning interest. But in a modern society, self-interest in combination with the order framework promotes morality in a much more efficient way: Morality is implemented on the level of the order framework which governs the market. Via competition on the market, the position of each individual can be improved, resulting in win-win situations. These are of economic as well as of ethical value, resulting in innovative products at good value for money, of jobs, of income, of taxes—or in the promotion of diversity and pluralism (McCloskey 2006, 2010). Within the positive-sum games of modern societies, the individual pursuit of self-interest is compatible with traditional ethical ideas like universal solidarity.

Competition is central to this conception (cf. Luetge 2014): Order Ethics emphasises the importance of competition in a modern society, which fosters innovation (Hayek 1978), the spreading of new ideas and the tendency of (unjustified) positions of power to erode (for example, those of former monopolists).

Competition, however, has negative aspects, too: in competitive situations, morality is constantly in danger of getting crowded out. The prisoners' dilemma or the stag hunt game are classic models for such situations which can be detrimental to morality if the incentives set by the rules thwart what is deemed ethical [Axelrod (1984); for the systematic use of the stag hunt game cf. Binmore (1994, 1998, 2005)]. As an example, if corruption is seen as unethical, then rules which allow for corruption (for example, allowing bribes to be deducted from tax) will promote unethical behaviour—no matter how many public calls for morality are being launched. Therefore, Order Ethics aims at changing the order framework of a society rather than at appealing to moral behaviour. This does not imply that people cannot behave ethically, but rather that ethical behaviour should not get punished by (counter-productive) incentives. The role of rules will be made more explicit in the following section.

8 Actions and Rules

The Order Ethics approach to business ethics is based on three aspects which in turn rest on the distinction between actions and rules, as outlined by Brennan and Buchanan (1985):

(1) Only changes in rules can change the situation for all participants involved at the same time.
(2) Only rules can be enforced by sanctions—which alone can change the incentives in a lasting way.
(3) Only by incorporating ethical ideas in (incentive-compatible) rules can competition be made productive, making individuals' moves morally autonomous in principle. With the aid of rules, of adequate conditions of actions, competition can realize advantages for all people involved.

For the Order Ethics approach, it is important that rules and actions do not conflict with one another. Ethical behavior on the level of actions can be expected only if there are no counteracting incentives on the level of rules. In the classic model of the prisoners' dilemma, the prisoners cannot be expected to cooperate because the conditions of the situation (the 'rules of the game') are such that cooperation is punished by defection on the part of the other player. Morality thus gets crowded out—and moralizing conceptions will not work. This is a decisive difference between the ISCT approach and Order Ethics. ISCT tries to solve genuine moral conflicts between two parties with reference to a third norm (hypernorms). Order Ethics, in contrast, will look for a (formal or informal) rule change, which benefits both parties (Luetge 2013). This extends the range of application of Order Ethics without introducing norms that are not compatible with the consent criterion.

It is much easier to come to a consensus on rules than on actions, i.e., on rules of distribution rather than on an actual distribution of goods. Nobody knows in advance what effects a certain rule will have in each individual case. It is principally easier to consent to rules that aim to achieve mutual benefits. The more abstract a rule is, the less it says about concrete results, and the more plausible it is that rational individuals will consent to it. Hence Buchanan distinguishes between constitutional and post-constitutional rules (Buchanan (1990, 2000) also calls the latter "subconstitutional" rules): The former are rules which prescribe the mechanisms of how the latter are established, by defining voting procedures or majority rules, among others. [Examples of such rules regarding tax laws, for instance, those involving wealth redistribution, can be found in Brennan and Buchanan (1980), and Holmes and Sunstein (2000)].

Order Ethics equally distinguishes between the constitutional and the post-constitutional levels. But Order Ethics can be—and indeed, has been—expanded to social problems and issues that cannot readily be solved on the constitutional or post-constitutional level. These issues concern, for instance, global trade where international law is still insufficient and sometimes completely missing, and where the concomitant rules within companies are often incomplete. In the following section, we provide a short overview of how Order Ethics has conceptually expanded its theoretical means to tackle the problem of insufficient legal orders and incomplete contracts [for another important and in many ways compatible approach, see Ostrom et al. (1994)].

This way of framing the central problem of business ethics is also related to Boatright's (1999) distinction between a *moral manager model* and a *moral market model*: While the first one focuses on making individuals (managers, officials, trade unionists etc.) more moral, the second one—Order Ethics—aims primarily at changing the institutional framework and indirectly inducing ethical behaviour.

9 Implementation and Advantages

Order Ethics does not require people to *abstain* completely from pursuing their own self-interest. Actors will abstain from taking (immoral) advantages only if their behaviour can be seen as an investment, yielding ultimately greater benefits in the longer run than defection in the particular single case. By adhering to ethical norms, an actor may become a reliable partner for others, which may open up new forms or ways of cooperation and of win-win situations. So an ethical norm that constrains one's actions may simultaneously expand one's options in *inter*actions.

While not requiring people to abandon their self-interest, Order Ethics rather suggests *improving* one's calculation, by calculating in a longer run rather than in the short run, and by considering the interests of others (e.g., the stakeholders of a company), as one depends on their cooperation for future interactions, especially in the globalised world (Homann 2007).

Order Ethics therefore does not equate altruism with moral behaviour nor egoism with immoral behaviour. The demarcation line lies elsewhere, between unilaterally and mutually beneficial action: In order to act in an ethical way, an actor should be pursuing her advantage in such a way that others benefit as well.

10 Order Ethics and Incomplete Contracts

Order Ethics does not deal only with those rules that are incorporated in the law, but with rules on other levels as well. This includes, in particular, agreements at branch level and also self-constraining actions of individual corporations, and leads into the area of Corporate Citizenship and Corporate Social Responsibility (CSR) (Crane et al. 2009). The underlying idea of mutual advantages, however, stays the same: To aim for a win-win situation.

Corporations are in fact doing much more than merely maximising their profits within the order framework: They are providing social welfare, they are engaging in environmental protection, or in social, cultural and scientific affairs. The stakeholder approach explains these observations by insisting that a corporation has to take into consideration not only shareholders, but other groups as well. From an Order Ethics perspective, however, one has to justify why the claims of stakeholders, which are already incorporated in the formal *rules*—as taxes, salaries, interest rates, environmental and other restrictions—should be incorporated a second time in the *actions* of corporations. This is not to say that corporations should not account for stakeholder interests at all, but rather that the *justification* given is not strong enough.

A suitable justification for a greater political role of corporations can be developed along the lines outlined in the rest of this section. It is consistent with the conception of Order Ethics, especially in view of two points: Ethical norms must (1) be implemented in an incentive-compatible way and (2) they should be built on (expected) advantages and benefits.

Order Ethics proceeds by extending the concept of 'order' to other, less formal orders. It therefore introduces another contractarian element: the theory of *incomplete contracts*.

In reality, contracts are most often not completely determined by rules. They are not entirely fixed in terms of quality, date, or content, for any possible circumstances in the future, and they are not resistant to any difficulties in enforcing these contracts. In more detail, it can be said that incomplete contracts are contracts in which one or several of the following conditions apply (cf. Hart 1987; Hart and Holmström 1987):

(1) The obligations of each party resulting from the contract are not specified exactly, in view of changing conditions such as flexible prices of raw goods.
(2) It is difficult and/or expensive to determine whether the contracts have been fulfilled. External consultants have to be employed.
(3) The enforcement of the contract is very difficult, very expensive, or even downright impossible, due to insufficient systems of law in a number of countries.

The globalised world is full of such incomplete contracts, like work contracts, long-run cooperation contracts, insurance contracts, strategic alliances and many others. In dealing with these contracts, there is a major problem of interdependence of the partners' actions: A partner that is honest and fulfils her part of the contract cannot automatically be sure that the other partner does the same. The other one might point to gaps within the contract, may propose differing interpretations, or it may be too expensive to enforce a claim.

A rational actor faced with these kinds of contracts would rather not sign them, especially when being risk-averse. However, if these contracts promised high benefits, the actor could try to rationally deal with the incompleteness.

Making incomplete contracts complete is no way to go: Not only is it impossible to specify all scenarios in advance, but this would also greatly reduce the flexibility which is the main advantage of the incompleteness. Incomplete contracts can be made quite productive, as the parties involved can adapt their agreements to different frameworks more easily. In order to exploit the benefits of incomplete contracts, however, trust, fairness, integrity, and good will are needed, in short: ethics. If contracts are becoming increasingly incomplete, both an ethics for the interior relations of the company (workers and management) as well as an ethics for the exterior relations to customers, banks, suppliers, and the public, become a necessity. It is rational for a company to *invest* in these ethical categories, as it contributes to the company's success in a way that directly affects shareholders.

In the globalized world, multinational corporations face a number of risks: traditional business risks like financial risks (loans), risks concerning primary products, risks due to intensified competition, or in some industries weather risks. Next are political risks, such as the introduction of new tariffs, a breakdown of trade relations or a fundamental change in a country's political structure. Moral risks, which can be increasingly found alongside the classic economic ones, have an economic dimension, too: corruption in business relations, discrimination, child labor, or questions of job safety, to name just a few. These factors have always been ethically problematic but, in the era of globalization, they develop into serious economic issues for two reasons. First, there are important changes in regulatory laws, such as the U.S. Sarbanes Oxley or the Dodd-Frank Acts. The ongoing financial crisis will probably lead to further regulation. Second, corporations are increasingly being watched over by nongovernmental organizations (NGOs). NGOs can be seen as a new element of control—even a balance-of-power component in business—which adds to legal control. The important point to learn from this is that, because of these risk structures, it will become much more important for corporations to invest in their ethical capital. From an Order Ethics standpoint, therefore, refinement of the legal framework takes priority but does not suffice alone. The legal framework can never be refined enough to cover all possible situations and outcomes as it leaves corporations with not just one, but a number of possibilities to pursue their own interest. Institutions should be built that encourage ethical behavior, and to invest in such institutions is in the interest of companies, whether they already know it or not, as outlined below.

So if rules are incomplete or if there are no rules for a specific situation, contractarianism suggests relying on substitutes: Corporations, as partners in interactions, have the opportunity to commit themselves to certain policies, to mechanisms of trust and fairness, for example. This commitment has to be made credible through organizational measures and must be signalled to others. In this way, actors create by themselves the very reliability that would normally be expected from formal rules. They create a *reputation*, which especially under conditions of globalization is a necessary prerequisite for success in the long run. This commitment must be signalled, and thus becomes an asset for the company. Corporate responsibility rankings have become increasingly visible in the past few years. Corporations, as partners in interactions, have the opportunity to commit themselves to certain policies, to mechanisms of trust and fairness. The willingness to trust each other is strongly influenced by the institutional framework and the social conditions of the situation.

So from a theoretical perspective, Order Ethics provides an integrative contractarian view on both situations, those with well-established and those with incomplete rules. In both cases, incentives and sanctions are key issues. In the first case, incentives are set by formal rules, while in the second case, this role is taken up by informal rules in the shape of 'soft' factors like ethics and reputation.

From another perspective, CSR measures can also be regarded as making ethics another production factor. Ethics is, in this way, complementing the classic production factors of labor and capital.[1] It is not an external restriction placed on corporations from the outside, but is in their own immediate interest. However, this does not entail that ethics (in the form of reputation etc.) can be reduced to just an instrumental tool for companies. That would be a misunderstanding of Order Ethics. Measures taken by companies must have more than narrow instrumental value in order to be called ethical. They must be in the interest of others, of other groups or stakeholders, i.e., they must create win-win situations.

---

[1] Interestingly, Buchanan already applied simple capital and investment theory to morals (Buchanan 2000: 159).

11 Philosophical Elements in Order Ethics

The main philosophical elements of Order Ethics can thus be summarised as follows:

First, Order Ethics is a consequentialist ethics. It aims for best consequences, for mutual benefits and win-win situations. Unlike many versions of utilitarianism, however, it regards the individual actors as the only source of normativity: The consent of all people involved is a contractarian legacy which makes Order Ethics differ strongly from utilitarian ethics. In this way, Order Ethics avoids a number of problems which keep riddling other consequentialist theories, in particular, utilitarianism: It avoids the anti-individual consequences and the danger of suppressing minorities.

For a contractarian business ethics, these ideas imply that business ultimately has to fulfil the needs of the individuals, and that economic efficiency cannot be a stand-alone criterion. In the modern globalised world, there is a good chance that competition, the market and other international actors like NGOs will help considerably in achieving this aim.

Corporations should, in this picture, not be seen primarily as collectives with no responsibilities beyond the responsibilities of their members. Rather—as recent work in analytical philosophy (List and Pettit 2011) suggests—can organisations be regarded as having duties in their own right, provided they fulfil a number of criteria, such as being sufficiently structured for meeting their responsibilities.

Second, Order Ethics can be seen as a naturalistic variant of ethics, as it makes extensive use of the methods and results of other disciplines [this is the version of naturalism espoused by P. Kitcher and others, cf. Kitcher (1993) and Luetge (2004)]. In particular, economic theory is a major resource for Order Ethics: For identifying incentive-compatible rules, economic analyses are pivotal, both on the macro-economic as well as on the company or branch level. Beyond economics, evolutionary biology and game theory are becoming key resources for ethics, too [cf. the work of Binmore (1994, 1998, 2005)].

12 Conclusion

The key contribution of Order Ethics is to apply the contractarian logic to business ethics against the backdrop of economic factors and incentive compatibility of ethical rules. In modern societies, incentive-compatible rules and institutions can fulfill those tasks that were, in pre-modern times, fulfilled by moral norms, which in turn were sanctioned by face-to-face control. Norm implementation in modern times thus works by setting adequate incentives to prevent the erosion of moral norms, which we can expect if 'moral' actors were systematically threatened with exploitation by other, less 'moral' ones [this has been confirmed in experimental studies such as Gürerk et al. (2006) or Andreoni (1988)]. In our view, business ethics (and ethics in general) should focus not only on how moral norms come into being in the first place, but on how they can be kept *stable*—which will be a much harder task, especially in competitive market scenarios. Companies and actors who systematically ignore their own interest will be singled out. In general, Order Ethics thus agrees with Heath et al. (2010) and Moriarty (2005) that questions of business ethics need to be discussed in a wider framework of political philosophy and economics, if we take the challenge of pluralism seriously.

References

Andreoni, J. 1988. Why free ride? Strategies and learning in public goods experiments. *Journal of Public Economics* 37: 291–304.
Axelrod, R. 1984. *The evolution of cooperation*. New York: Basic Books.
Becker, G.S. 1993. Nobel lecture: The economic way of looking at behavior. *Journal of Political Economy* 101(3): 358–409.
Binmore, K. 1994. *Game theory and the social contract: playing fair*, Vol. 1. Cambridge, Mass., London: MIT Press.
Binmore, K. 1998. *Game theory and the social contract: just playing*, Vol. 2. Cambridge, Mass., London: MIT Press.
Binmore, K. 2005. *Natural justice*. Oxford: Oxford University Press.
Boatright, J. 1999. Presidential address: Does business ethics rest on a mistake? *Business Ethics Quarterly* 9: 583–591.
Boatright, J. 2007. Is there an internal morality of contracting? *Academy of Management Review* 32: 1.
Brennan, G., and J.M. Buchanan. 1980. *The power to tax: Analytical foundations of a fiscal constitution*. Cambridge: Cambridge University Press.
Brennan, G., and J.M. Buchanan. 1985. *The reason of rules: Constitutional political economy*. Cambridge: Cambridge University Press.
Buchanan, J.M. 1990. The domain of constitutional economics. *Constitutional Political Economy* 1: 1–18.
Buchanan, J.M. 2000. *The limits of liberty: Between Anarchy and Leviathan*. Indianapolis: Liberty Press.
Crane, A., et al. (eds.). 2009. *The Oxford handbook of corporate social responsibility*. Oxford: Oxford University Press.
Donaldson, T.D., and T.W. Dunfee. 1995. Integrative social contract theory: A communitarian conception of economics ethics. *Economics and Philosophy* 11(1): 85–112.
Donaldson, T.D., and T.W. Dunfee. 1999. *Ties that bind: A social contracts approach to business ethics*. Boston, MA: Harvard Business School Press.
Donaldson, T.D., and T.W. Dunfee. 2000. Book review dialogue: Tightening the ties that bind—defending a contractarian approach to business ethics. *American Business Law Journal* 37: 579–585.
Donaldson, T.D., and T.W. Dunfee. 2002. Ties that bind in business ethics: Social contracts and why they matter. *Journal of Banking & Finance* 26: 1853–1865.
Francé-Gómez, P. 2003. Some difficulties in sacconi's view about corporate ethics. *Journal of Business Ethics* 42(2): 165–180.
Gürerk, Ö., et al. 2006. The competitive advantage of sanctioning institutions. *Science* 312: 108.
Hands, W. 1994. The sociology of scientific knowledge: Some thoughts on the possibilities. In *New directions in economic methodology*, ed. Roger Backhouse, 75–106. London: Routledge.
Hart, O. D., 1987. Incomplete contracts. In *The New Palgrave: A dictionary of economics*, ed. J. Eatwell et al., Vol. 2, 752–759. London, Basingstoke: Macmillan.

Hart, O.D., and B.R. Holmström. 1987. The theory of contracts. In *Advances in economic theory*, ed. T.F. Bewley, Ch. 3. Cambridge: Cambridge University Press.

Hayek, F.A.v. 1978. Competition as a discovery procedure. In *New studies in philosophy, politics and economics*, ed. F.A.v. Hayek. Chicago: University of Chicago Press.

Heath, J., J. Moriarty, and W. Norman. 2010. Business ethics and (or as) political philosophy. *Business Ethics Quarterly* 20(3): 427–452.

Herzog, L. 2013. The modern social contract tradition. In *Handbook of the philosophical foundations of business ethics*, ed. C. Luetge, 631–645. Dordrecht: Springer Netherlands.

Heugens, P., Kaptein, M., Oosterhout, H.v. 2004. Ties that grind? Corroborating a typology of social contracting problems. *Journal of Business Ethics* 49(3): 235–252.

Heugens, P., Oosterhout, H.v., Kaptein, M. 2006. Foundations and applications for contractualist business ethics. *Journal of Business Ethics* 68(3): 211–228.

Oosterhout, H.v., Heugens, P., Kaptein, M. 2007. Contractualism vindicated: A response to Boatright. *Academy of Management Review* 32(1): 295–297.

Hobbes, T. 1651/1991. *Leviathan*, ed. R. Tuck. Cambridge: Cambridge University Press.

Holmes, S., and C.R. Sunstein. 2000. *The cost of rights: Why liberty depends on taxes*. New York: Norton.

Homann, K. 2007. Globalisation from a business ethics point of view. In *Globalisation and business ethics*, ed. K. Homann, P. Koslowski, and C. Luetge, 3–11. Aldershot/London: Ashgate.

Homann, K., and C. Luetge. 2013. *Einführung in die Wirtschaftsethik*. 3rd ed. Münster: LIT.

Keeley, M. 1988. *A social contract theory of organizations*. Notre-Dame, IN: University of Notre-Dame.

Kitcher, P. 1993. *The advancement of science: Science without legend, objectivity without illusions*. Oxford: Oxford University Press.

List, C., and P. Pettit 2011. *Group agency: The possibility, design, and status of corporate agents*. Oxford: Oxford University Press.

Luetge, C. 2004. Economics in philosophy of science: Can the dismal science contribute anything interesting? *Synthese* 140(3): 279–305.

Luetge, C. 2005. Economic ethics, business ethics and the idea of mutual advantages. *Business Ethics: A European Review* 14(2): 108–118.

Luetge, C. 2006: An economic rationale for a work and savings ethic? J. Buchanan's late works and business ethics. *Journal of Business Ethics* 66(1): 43–51.

Luetge, C. 2012. Fundamentals of order ethics: Law, business ethics and the financial crisis. *Archiv für Rechts- und Sozialphilosophie Beihefte* 130: 11–21.

Luetge, C. 2013. The idea of a contractarian business ethics. In *Handbook of the philosophical foundations of business ethics*, ed. C. Luetge, S. 647–658. Dordrecht: Springer Netherlands.

Luetge, C. 2014. *Ethik des Wettbewerbs: Über Konkurrenz und Moral*. München: Beck.

Luetge, C. 2015. *Order ethics vs. moral surplus: What holds a society together?*. Lanham, Md.: Lexington.

Luetge, C., 2016. Order ethics and the problem of social glue. *University of St. Thomas Law Journal* 12(2): 339–359.

Luetge, C., Armbrüster, T., and Müller, J. 2016. Order ethics: Bridging the gap between contractarianism and business ethics. *Journal of Business Ethics*, forthcoming.

McCloskey, D. 2006. *The Bourgeois virtues*. Ethics for an age of commerce. Chicago: University of Chicago Press.

McCloskey, D. 2010. *Bourgeois dignity: Why economics can't explain the modern world*. Chicago: University of Chicago Press.

Moriarty, J. 2005. On the relevance of political philosophy to business ethics. *Business Ethics Quarterly* 15(3): 455–473.

Nozick, R. 1974. *Anarchy, state, and utopia*. New York: Basic Books.

Oosterhout, H.V., B. Wempe, and T.V. Willigenburg. 2004. Contractualism and the project for an integrative organizational ethics. In *IABS proceedings. the fifteenth annual conference*, ed. S. Welcomer. Wyoming: Jackson Hole.

Oosterhout, H.v., and P. Heugens. 2009. Extant social contracts in global business regulation. Outline of a research agenda. *Journal of Business Ethics* 88(4): 729–740.
Ostrom, E., R. Gardner, and J.M. Walker. 1994. *Rules, games, and common-pool resources*. Ann Arbor, MI: University of Michigan Press.
Rawls, J. 1971. *A theory of justice*, Revised, 1999 ed. Oxford: Oxford University Press.
Rawls, J. 1993. *Political liberalism*. New York: Columbia University Press.
Rawls, J. 2001. *Justice as fairness: A restatement*. Cambridge, Mass. [u.a.]: Belknap Press of Harvard University Press.
Rowan, J.R. 1997. Grounding hypernorms: Towards a contractarian theory of business ethics. *Economics and Philosophy* 13: 107–112.
Rowan, J.R. 2001. How binding the ties? Business ethics as integrative social contracts. *Business Ethics Quarterly* 11: 379–390.
Sacconi, L. 2000. *The social contract of the firm: Economics, ethics and organisation*. Heidelberg: Springer.
Sacconi, L. 2006. A social contract account for CSR as an extended model of corporate governance (i): Rational bargaining and justification. *Journal of Business Ethics* 68(3): 259–281.
Sacconi, L. 2007. A social contract account for CSR as an extended model of corporate governance (ii): Compliance, reputation and reciprocity. *Journal of Business Ethics* 75(1): 77–96.
Thurow, L.C. 1980. *The zero-sum society: Distribution and the possibilities for economic change*. New York: Basic Books.
Vanberg, V. 2007. Corporate social responsibility and the 'game of catallaxy': the perspective of constitutional economics. *Constitutional Political Economy* 18(3): 199–222.
Wempe, B. 2004. On the use of the social contract model in business ethics. *Business Ethics: A European Review* 13: 332–341.
Wempe, B. 2008a. Contractarian business ethics: Credentials and design criteria. *Organization Studies 2008/29* 29: 1337–1355.
Wempe, B. 2008b. Four design criteria for any future contractarian theory of business ethics. *Journal of Business Ethics* 81(3): 697–714.
Wempe, B. 2009. Extant social contracts and the question of business ethics. *Journal of Business Ethics* 88(4): 741–750.
Werhane, P. 1985. *Persons, rights and corporations*. Englewood Cliffs, NJ: Prentice Hall.

The Ordonomic Approach to Order Ethics

Ingo Pies

Abstract The ordonomic approach to order ethics contains four elements: (a) a diagnosis of modernity, which identifies the core problems and directs the research strategy to solving them; (b) a rational-choice analysis of social dilemmas, i.e., positive theorizing which informs about the un-intended consequences of intentional inter-action; (c) the idea of orthogonal positions, i.e., normative theorizing that aims at providing reform orientation while at the same time systematically avoiding controversial value statements; (d) a scheme of three social arenas that helps to understand the interplay between institutions and ideas in societal learning processes.

Keywords Ordonomics · Order ethics · Institutional ethics · Individual ethics · Orthogonal position · Social dilemma · Modern society · Growth

Schlüsselwörter Ordonomik · Ordnungsethik · Individualethik · Institutionenethik · Orthogonale Positionierung · Soziale Dilemmata · Moderne Gesellschaft · Wachstum

The first section explains why the dominant form of traditional ethics with its focus on individual motives of action needs to be complemented by an ethics of institutional order—in short: order ethics—that concentrates moral analysis on the framework of rules and their incentive properties. The second section introduces a special version of order ethics: the ordonomic approach. It consists of four analytical elements and their systematic interplay. The third section discusses several applications of the ordonomic approach to order ethics and thus illustrates its heuristic power and problem-solving capacity.

I. Pies (✉)
Chair of Economic Ethics, Martin Luther University Halle-Wittenberg,
Halle, Germany
e-mail: ingo.pies@wiwi.uni-halle.de

1 The Need for an Ethics of Institutional Order

(1) The Western tradition of Ethics, conceived of as moral theory (=theory of morality), has a long history that dates back to antiquity. There are both religious as well as secular sources that have stimulated this tradition. Among the former are the monotheistic religions—Judaism, Christianity, and Islam. Among the latter are the philosophical schools of thought in ancient Greece and Rome. Taken together, the former constitute a spiritual version, the latter a civic version of ethical reflection on morality.

Both versions have in common that they focus their ethical perspective on the behavior and character of individual persons, whether they use the idea of god and the according divine rules or the idea of a good life and the according virtues. Both versions aim at helping the individual person to reflect her moral standards and to improve her moral practice, and they do so by drawing attention to one's good or bad intentions: they focus on individual action and the underlying motivational structure.

Despite their pre-modern origin, both sources of the tradition of ethics are still influential in modern society. On the one hand, this is quite understandable since all human beings who (want to) develop a moral integrity of their own, i.e., become persons, have to solve problems for which time-proven answers might provide valuable orientation, especially if they advise to have consideration for neighbors or to consider the future consequences of today's action on oneself. In general, many of such moral recommendations can be reconstructed as prudent advice: they enlarge the horizon of self-interested behavior in both the social as well as the time dimension.

(2) On the other hand, this influence is somewhat surprising because in a modern society there is an abundance of moral problems that cannot be adequately addressed by focusing on the good or bad intentions of individual actors. This is especially true with regard to the results of competitive processes. Markets are a case in point.

To illustrate: demanders in markets have an interest in low prices. They want to buy cheap. Suppliers have the opposite intention. They prefer to sell at high prices. Now assume an increase in demand. What will happen to the initial equilibrium? For sure, the price will go up. But it will not rise because the suppliers *want* it to rise. Instead, it will rise although the demanders do *not* want it to rise. Indeed, it is the demanders who cause this price rise through their very own behavior. That demand pressure raises prices is a phenomenon which is un-intentionally and even counter-intentionally produced by actors who are interested in low prices. In this sense, competitive markets are subversive to the intentions of market actors.

Against this background, it is an intellectual mistake—an "intentionalistic fallacy"—to conclude good market results from good intentions or to conclude bad market results from bad intentions. Market results are primarily driven not by individual motives but by institutional incentives, which canalize and coordinate the un-intended social consequences of intentional action. If one is interested in understanding—and, where appropriate, in improving—market results, it is of vital importance to draw attention to the institutional order. Hence, there is a need for order ethics, i.e., a theory of morality whose perspective is focused on the moral quality of the formal and informal rules that guide the competitive interplay of actors.

Order ethics is needed not to replace but to complement traditional ethics. The underlying reason is that different contexts cause different problems, which require different perspectives in order to find adequate solutions. While traditional ethics concentrates on individual *action*—especially on the motive structure of individual action—, order ethics concentrates on individual *inter-action*—especially on the incentive structure that canalizes how different actors work together or against each other. The perspective of traditional ethics is focused on (im-)moral motives, while the perspective of order ethics is focused on (im-)moral phenomena that are primarily driven by incentives. Traditional ethics is concerned with—and concerned about—determinants of action that are inside the individual, while order ethics concentrates on determinants of (inter-)action that are outside the individual. Hence, the psycho-logical focus of traditional ethics is different from, but in general complementary to, the socio-logical focus of order ethics.

The seminal author on order ethics is Karl Homann, a German scholar who was reared in the tradition of (a liberal understanding of) the Hegelian philosophy of right. Later he became an economist (heavily influenced by the works of Walter Eucken and James Buchanan). After two dissertations and his habilitation, like much of his later work addressing the borderline of philosophy and economics, he was appointed in 1990 to hold the first chair in Economic Ethics and Business Ethics in Germany. Among his numerous disciples, similar but still distinctively different strands of thought have developed. The following analysis sketches the ordonomic approach to order ethics.

2 The Ordonomic Approach to Order Ethics

The ordonomic approach contains four elements: (a) a diagnosis of modernity, which identifies the core problems and directs the research strategy to solving them; (b) a rational-choice analysis of social dilemmas, i.e., positive theorizing which informs about the un-intended consequences of intentional inter-action; (c) the idea of orthogonal positions, i.e., normative theorizing that aims at providing reform orientation while at the same time systematically avoiding controversial value statements; (d) a scheme of three social arenas that helps to understand the interplay between institutions and ideas, which is of vital importance for the (mal-)functioning of societal self-governance, i.e., the diverse processes of self-enlightenment and self-rule in modern society.

2.1 A Diagnosis of Modernity

(1) From the ordonomic point of view, the defining criterion of a modern society is its continuous economic growth, which leads to rising per capita incomes. In historical perspective, sustained growth is a relatively new phenomenon that simply did not exist before 1800. The underlying reason is that, for several thousand years before 1800, humanity experienced a Malthusian trap. This means that economic progress led to population growth but not to higher living standards for the population at large (cf., Clark 2007; Galor 2011).

The escape from the Malthusian trap—and thus, from the ordonomic point of view, the entry into modernity—was brought about by innovation. It was the "invention of invention", to use a term coined by Lippmann (1929, 2009; p. 235), which made, and continues to make, the traditional factors of production—land, labor, capital—more and more productive. In this sense, the modern society is a knowledge society: its innovation process rests on the continuous generation and improvement of knowledge.

It is misleading to call this fundamental transformation from pre-modern to modern society "industrial revolution". On the one hand, the whole society is transformed, not just the business sector. On the other hand, it was not the invention of the steam engine or some other machines which revolutionized the economy. Rather, it was the other way around: the modern state and its rule of law, modern science and its processes of creative criticism, the modern business firm and its indefinite time horizon all played an important role in the invention of invention. The early Schumpeter (1911, 2006; p. 479, translated by I.P.) got it astonishingly right: "It is wrong to think that inventions created capitalism; rather, capitalism created the inventions necessary for its existence".

(2) This engine of modernity, the invention of invention, has set up a dynamic transformation process that historically started in Europe and by now has reached all continents. Judged from the European experience during the last two hundred years, this transformation process changes, in the course of time, nearly every characteristic of a pre-modern society. The constitutionalized state has become secularized, democratized, and pacified. It engages primarily in public education, social security, and public infrastructure. Nobility privileges have been removed. Non-discrimination is the rule. Citizens enjoy freedom of speech as well as freedom of contract. Modern society offers both organized pluralism and a pluralism of organizations. Due to free markets, citizens have access to goods and services, including credit and insurance. People decide in mutual consent whether they want to live with each other. They are free to choose their residence and vocation as well as their lifestyles. The social pressure to conform with traditions has been considerably reduced, while at the same time a private sphere has been created, which offers ample room for individual choice. Formerly rigid family structures have changed, and so have the social relations between old and young as well as between men and women. Last but not least, people live longer and healthier lives.

In contrast to this institutional revolution, most normative terms and concepts are rather old. With the notable exception of "sustainability", normative ideas like "liberty", "equality", or "justice" were already familiar two thousand years ago. They originate in pre-modern social structures. That is why many traditional concepts of morality stress the control (and even sacrifice) of one's aspirations. In a society without growth, many conflicts cannot be solved by unleashing win-win activities. Instead, they can only be solved by taming win-lose activities, which explains why traditional ethics lays such a strong emphasis on exercising moral restraint. However, ancient ideas about the good life in a good society do not conform well with—and indeed may be partially inadequate for—the radically new options of productive social cooperation that are available (only) in modern growth societies. Perhaps this is why the loss of tradition led to a loss of orientation that made—and still makes—many people feel estranged from modern society. And it explains why already Hegel—who developed the first philosophy of modern society—aimed at contributing to reconciliation (Hardimon 1994).

Summing up, modern society is a growth society and as such is characterized by a systematic mismatch between institutions and ideas. Therefore, the research perspective of ordonomics is focused on a specific governance problem: it addresses the diverse learning processes in which the mismatch between institutions and ideas is overcome via mutual adaptation, i.e., via institutional change that mirrors the evolution of normative ideas or by re-conceptualizing normative ideas to better fit the evolution of institutional realities. The gradual improvement, during the twentieth century, in the legal status of women is an example of the former, while the attempts by Rawls (1971, 1993, 2001) to re-think "justice" are an example of the latter.

2.2 Rational-Choice Analysis of Social Dilemma Situations

In philosophical discourse, the term "moral dilemma" is often used to describe a decision situation that confronts an individual (singular!) with difficult tradeoffs, e.g., with a tragic choice between self-sacrifice or ruining other people's lives or a tragic choice between two groups, a small one and a large one, when only one of them can be saved from certain death. In contrast, a "social dilemma" denotes a situation in which several actors (plural!) inter-act and the outcome is rational inefficiency (cf., Petrick and Pies 2007; Buttkereit and Pies 2008). The prisoners' dilemma, familiar from mathematical game theory, is a case in point (Bowles 2004; pp. 23–55).

If people find themselves in a social dilemma, they are confronted with disincentives which hinder them from pursuing a common goal. Therefore, they reach a result which they themselves find disagreeable—in technical parlance, they reach a Pareto-inferior Nash equilibrium. Due to the rules of the game they play, i.e., the specific institutional framework, each player has an incentive to behave in exactly the way he fears from others. The result is collective self-damage.

The situational logic of a social dilemma has several characteristics: (a) Players try to reach their own goals. In order to do so, they choose their individual moves in the game. (b) Players act in a social process, the outcome of which cannot be chosen. In fact, the outcome results from the interplay between different actors: it results from *inter*-action. (c) The outcome of the game is the *un*-intended consequence of an interplay of individual actions and their underlying individual intentions. (d) The moves in the game are canalized by the rules of the game, i.e., by the institutional framework that sets the *incentives* for individual actions. (e) In a social dilemma, the rules of the game exert pressure on each individual actor to behave in a way that is detrimental to the players' common interest. Thus, they end up with a result they collectively regret.

Modeling situations along these lines improves our understanding of phenomena such as mass unemployment, environmental pollution, the degradation of common pool resources, the pervasiveness of corruption, or the general underprovision of public goods. In such social dilemmas, it is not bad intentions but bad institutions which cause a systemic malfunctioning that gives rise to moral concerns.

The following example may help to illustrate the specific situational logic of a social dilemma as well as its ethical importance. Assume that for centuries people who settle along a lakefront have made their living by fishing. Due to recently improved fishing techniques, their increased productivity has decreased the available fish population. People start to realize that they run the danger of overfishing. However, this is a problem no single fisher can solve on his own. If he exhibits self-restraint, other fishers are likely to catch more. Taken as a group, the fishers find themselves in a situation where it is individually costly to behave in a way that conforms with their collective interest in preserving a natural resource. To escape from this social trap, they need an institutional reform: a collective rule-arrangement that realigns individual incentives, e.g., by introducing quotas, or by regulating the time input appropriate for fishing, or by allocation rules that specify where individual fishers are allowed to harvest (Ostrom 2012; p. 80). Taken as a group, the fishers need a collective arrangement that helps the fish population to recover.

2.3 Normative Orientation via Orthogonal Positions

Confronted with a systemic malfunctioning, moral discourse often perceives the problem as a tradeoff between the self-interest of certain actors on the one hand and the public interest on the other hand (Fig. 1a). The underlying mind-set is characterized by a tradeoff: Taking the status quo S as a starting point, the typical perception is that the pursuit of private self-interest (arrow 1) leads to a move along the tradeoff line (arrow 2) which is detrimental to public interest (arrow 3). This diagnosis naturally entails as therapy a demand—often articulated as a moral postulate—to respect public interest (arrow 4), even if this means to move along the tradeoff line in the other direction (arrow 5), which means to sacrifice private self-interest (arrow 6).

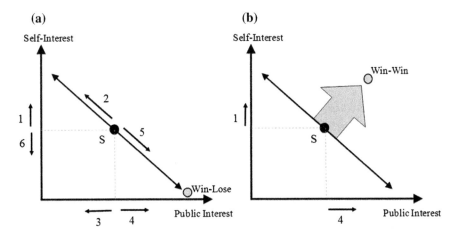

Fig. 1 Orthogonal position: a paradigm shift from win-lose to win-win

It is important to understand that this win-lose paradigm, which is so dominant in moral discourse, ultimately stems from perceiving the situation at hand as a zero-sum game. Therefore, in many cases one can shift paradigm from a win-lose perception to a win-win perception if it is possible to reconstruct the underlying situation as a social dilemma, i.e., as a non-zero-sum game (Fig. 1b). Such a paradigm change is called "orthogonal position" (Pies 2000; p. 34) because it changes the perspective by 90°. It literally changes the direction of thought and transcends the tradeoff line by drawing attention to the possibility of bringing, via institutional reform, private self-interest (arrow 1) into harmony with public interest (arrow 4). Put differently, in so far as the point denoted "win-lose" in Fig. 1a represents the "negation" of self-interest, the orthogonal position with its focus on a "win-win" solution in Fig. 1b marks a "negation of this negation". It reconciles self-interest and public interest.

In order to illustrate the crucial point, it may be helpful to return to the example discussed in the last sub-section. Assume the following situation. Before a quota is introduced—or before a functional equivalent is established, i.e., a collectively binding rule that aligns individual incentives—a single fisher is asked why he contributes to overfishing. He would probably answer that he cannot afford to catch less fish. For an outside observer this might indeed look like a clash of interest between profit-seeking and the common good, as represented by arrows 1, 2, and 3 in Fig. 1a. However, the problem is not as simple as that, and for sure it cannot be solved by a moral appeal, directed at the individual fisher, to change his behavior, as represented by arrows 4, 5, and 6 in Fig. 1a. In fact, the fisher is in a situation, together with all other fishers, where they collectively damage themselves and where at the same time an individual attempt to solve the collective problem is both costly and of no avail. However, if the fishermen succeed in establishing an institutional order that redirects their activities in such a way that the fish population can recover, their self-restraint from overfishing can be perceived as an investment and can meet their consensus. The orthogonal position in Fig. 1b reflects that it is in the long-run self-interest of fishermen to observe the public interest in a sustainable fish population.

2.4 The Interplay of Three Social Arenas: Business, Politics, and Public Discourse

Figure 2 helps to distinguish three social arenas. For expositional purposes, one can call them business, politics, and public discourse, although one should keep in mind that this ordonomic distinction of three arenas is not an ontological but a methodological scheme—a "relatively absolute absolute" (Buchanan 1989)—and hence can be applied to many cases, e.g., to learning processes within organizations.

The crucial point is that level one constitutes a basic game, while level two constitutes the according meta game, which defines the rules that channel behavior in the basic game. Level three marks the discussion about possible problems in the basic game and possible solutions to these problems that can be found in the meta game. In this sense, it is to be understood as the meta-meta game.

The following example helps to illustrate the scheme. Assume a shortage in the housing market, i.e., the basic game. As prices are high, people have difficulty in finding apartments they can afford. Assume further that in the meta-meta game of public discourse most citizens believe—or are made believe by media reports—that the source of the problem is a conflict of interest (=tradeoff) between tenants and landlords and that therefore social protection of the former requires to curb profit-seeking by the latter. Under these conditions, it might be possible that politicians in the meta game cannot help introducing price ceilings even if they know better.

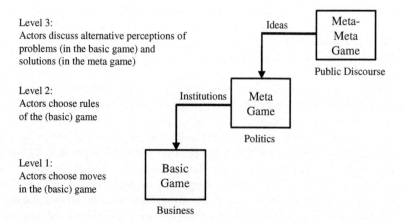

Fig. 2 The ordonomic three-level scheme to distinguish different social arenas

This, of course, has negative effects on the basic game. Since the administrative price is set to a low level, demand goes up while supply goes down. In particular, landlords lack the incentive to build new houses. Therefore, the market gets even tighter. Scarcity grows. As a consequence, more and more people have difficulty in finding an apartment. Especially people with small budgets, young children or domestic animals feel disadvantaged. Furthermore, many of them—desperate for accommodation—would be willing to pay a higher price than allowed by law, thus giving rise to all sorts of illegal behavior in order to circumvent regulation.

It is easy to imagine how these daily experiences of housing market failure might set in motion a vicious circle of political interference: strict laws prohibiting discrimination, high penalties for illegal lease agreements, public housing for the poor, etc. Such a spiral of market intervention—causing market failure, which entails more intervention that in fact aggravates the problems—explains the housing market history in many countries during the twentieth century.

It is very difficult to escape this vicious circle unless an orthogonal position in the meta-meta game makes clear that the root of the problem is the misguided perception of a tradeoff. The public interest in a functioning housing market that provides affordable accommodation is poorly served by command and control policies which partly expropriate landlords. The proper task of politics is not to tame but to institutionally (re-)direct the landlords' self-interest such that their competitive profit-seeking *serves* the public interest. This requires that politicians in the meta game resist the temptation of administering prices, thus distorting incentives. Where necessary, poor people should be given additional income so they can afford market prices that truly inform about real scarcity. In order to avoid collective self-damage, it is of crucial importance that public discourse learns and communicates the lesson that politics should improve—and not impair—the institutional working conditions of markets.

3 Ordonomics at Work: Several Illustrations

In order to show how these analytical elements fit together, this section discusses several illustrations. It starts with a historical reconstruction of an event that paved the way towards modernity. Here, the basic game is not a market failure but a religious conflict, thus providing insight in the general applicability of the ordonomic three-level scheme to distinguish social arenas.

3.1 A Conceptual Reconstruction of the Peace of Westphalia Which Ended the Thirty Years' Religious War (1618–1648)

(1) After the reformation, Protestants and Catholics found themselves in a situation akin to the prisoners' dilemma: neither side wanted to give into the other side's attempt to dominate. The result was a series of religious conflicts, culminating in the extremely bloody Thirty Years' War on the European continent, starting in 1618.

Despite enormous damages to life and limb on both sides, political negotiations to overcome the military conflict continuously failed. For thirty years, it was impossible to find a solution in the meta game that would put an end to the basic game of religious war.

Seen from the ordonomic perspective, the final reason for this failure can be located in the meta-meta game. The root of the problem was the religious mind-set which dominated both public discourse and private reasoning. As long as the central question of the dispute was to ask who has the right religion, no side was able to compromise, since this would have meant to sin and thus sacrifice one's eternal life. Therefore, people were trapped in this tradeoff thinking, the result of which was that the social dilemma in the basic game was duplicated by a social dilemma in the meta game. Peace negotiations failed, and the religious war went on.

(2) It was the invention of the idea of tolerance that finally allowed a solution to the problem (Zagorin 2003). People learned to ask the new question how they can live together peacefully and productively even if they have different confessions. The idea of religious tolerance paved the way for realizing that Catholics and Protestants—although in military conflict with each other—still had some interests in common.

This orthogonal position in the meta-meta game brought about a change in the meta game, too. With the help of conditional strategies—one's willingness to end war was tied to the counterparty's willingness to end war—the meta game was transformed from a social dilemma to a coordination game in which the joint interest in peaceful coexistence became dominant.

Once the peace treaty was negotiated, the basic game could change from religious war to mutual acceptance: conflict was substituted by cooperation.

(3) Summing up this ordonomic sketch of conceptual history, a paradigm shift in ideas led to an institutional reform, which then changed behavior. This learning process took decades, but finally it was successful because in order to end war, both parties had to agree to end war. However, as long as people had perceived that such an agreement required a compromise on behalf of one's true belief, the meta game was blocked. In order to overcome this blockade, it was necessary to transcend the tradeoff in the meta-meta game and to open one's eyes with the help of an orthogonal position.

3.2 Growth Policy and the Ordonomics of Climate Change

Faced with the prospect of climate change, countries around the world are searching for solutions to the problem of providing a truly global public good. During the last twenty years, several steps were taken—including the UN Framework Convention on Climate Change as well as the Kyoto Protocol. However, one cannot ignore the fact that in recent years the whole process of constructing a post-Kyoto process has not been exceedingly successful. The ordonomic approach can point to some conceptual mistakes that help explain—and hopefully even overcome—some of the recent difficulties.

Figure 3a interprets carbon dioxide emissions—an important greenhouse gas that is a by-product of fossil-fuel based energy consumption—as a factor of production. Take point S as the status quo. Moving to the right along the "growth path" represented by arrow 1 increases gross domestic product and at the same time exacerbates the problem of global warming. Therefore it might seem that to protect ourselves against the potential hazards of climate change requires a movement in the opposite direction along arrow 2, even if this involves reductions in GDP.

In contrast to this popular perception, Fig. 3b represents quite a different mind-set which offers an orthogonal position to the tradeoff thinking inherent in Fig. 3a. Instead of moving along a given production function PF_1, the orthogonal position emphasizes the possibility to set in motion innovative processes that effectively change the production function from PF_1 to PF_2. This is a fundamentally different understanding of "growth": generating new knowledge means that it is possible to produce the same output with less input (horizontal arrow 3), or alternatively to use the same input to produce more output (vertical arrow 4). Another possibility offered by innovative-driven growth is marked by arrow 5, which represents the so-called "rebound" effect: although innovation makes it possible to

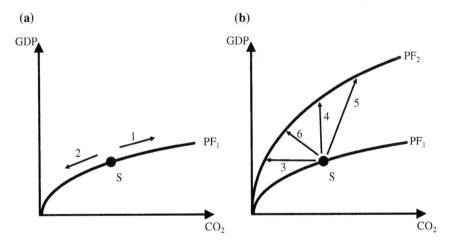

Fig. 3 Two alternative paradigms: limits to growth versus growth of limits

produce the same output with less input, output increases so much that in fact more input is needed. However, whether this rebound effect materializes is a matter of price. In the case at hand, it is politicians who finally decide on the price of carbon dioxide and therefore can make sure that the future development will be characterized by arrow 6, which represents a growth path that combines effective climate protection with further increases in GDP.

To illustrate, Germany provides a very interesting example. In recent years, a huge amount of money has been spent for carbon dioxide mitigation along arrow 2 in Fig. 3a, e.g., by subsidizing solar panels on German house roofs. Such measures are extremely expensive and at the same time very inefficient. Therefore, it is only a question of time that such policies reveal their true cost to the public and hence become increasingly unpopular. What is required here is a learning process, as a result of which the democratic public grasps the superior alternative. This consists of political measures which encourage carbon dioxide mitigation along arrow 6 in Fig. 3b, e.g., by subsidizing research and development.

3.3 Further Ordonomic Insights

(1) The above list of ordonomic applications is of course not exhaustive. For a critical examination of the semantics of responsibility and sustainability, respectively, cf., Beckmann and Pies (2008a, b); for an ordonomic analysis of moral criticisms of agricultural speculation—and a criticism of such criticisms on moral grounds—cf., Pies et al. (2013b, c); for an ordonomic approach to Business Ethics cf., Pies et al. (2009, 2010, 2011, 2013a); for an ordonomic approach to sustainability management cf., Beckmann et al. (2012a, b). Further publications on applications of the ordonomic approach comprise Pies and Schott (2001) and Pies and Hielscher (2009a, b) as well as Hielscher et al. (2012).

(2) However, instead of adding further examples, the following insights help to evaluate the heuristic power of the ordonomic approach in guiding fruitful (re-)conceptualizations of institutions and ideas:

- From an ordonomic point of view, it is a fundamental misunderstanding to perceive "market" and "state" as opposites because in fact they are complements.
- Free exchange across borders transforms international relations. Countries that were used to perceiving each other as rivals learn to regard each other as partners engaged in mutually beneficial cooperation.
- Furthermore, coercion and liberty need not contradict each other. The state power to coerce can be used in a way that does not diminish but enlarge individual freedom. This is quite generally the case if coercion is employed to sanction rules that overcome social dilemmas, e.g., by protecting property rights. In this sense, democratic consensus rests on "mutual coercion, mutually agreed upon" (Hardin 1968).

- A social market economy is not social because of its social policy but because it makes use of competition as an instrument for fostering social cooperation. It is social because it institutionally directs self-interest to serve public interest.
- Judged by its consequences—as opposed to its motivational structure—behavior in functioning markets can be understood as a form of institutionalized solidarity. In cases of emergency, market prices direct the forces of supply and demand such that people in effect help each other, even if they do not explicitly intend to do so. In fact, it is an important property of markets—often overlooked by opponents and proponents of markets alike—that they allow to extend solidarity beyond face-to-face interactions in small groups: markets facilitate solidarity among strangers.
- Many social policy arrangements are ill understood if perceived as redistribution. What at first sight seems to be a coercive win-lose activity by the social state—harming the rich, benefiting the poor—can often be reconstructed as a win-win activity that overcomes the malfunctioning of credit or insurance markets, e.g., in financing human capital investment or in covering fundamental risks of life.
- The much celebrated equity-efficiency tradeoff is often misleading because a functional social policy addresses inefficiencies and enhances the productivity of markets.
- Another dualism that is highly misleading is that between "economy" and "ecology". While it is true that markets lead to environmental pollution as long as natural resources lack property rights, it is also true that via institutional reforms markets can be re-directed to foster environmental protection.
- Pricing natural resources—and thus transforming what formerly was a free good into a private good—is very often the best way to overcome a social dilemma. There are two reasons for this. On the one hand, pricing frees market actors from the illusion that they use a costless resource. It thus sets an incentive for environmental-friendly behavior. On the other hand, this static effect is supplemented by an extremely important dynamic effect. Since pricing natural resources makes it costly to use what was once a costless factor of production, this sets in motion a knowledge-generating process in which economic actors compete for innovation. This search for new solutions is incentivized by market prices that allow successful inventors to reap pioneer profits.
- Therefore, it is generally wrong to criticize the practice of pricing natural resources as introducing indulgence for environmental sins. Such moral criticisms can be criticized on moral grounds because they neglect the static as well as dynamic effects of pricing on the behavior of both individuals and organizations. Hence they neglect that these behavioral changes brought about by markets forces are very often the most effective way to protect the environment.

(3) Fig. 4 provides a more systematic way of illustrating the ordonomic research strategy and its heuristic power (Pies and Hielscher 2012). Moral arguments may speak in favor of or against a certain behavioral pattern, while at the same time this pattern may be encouraged or discouraged by incentives. In cell I, moral behavior is rewarded. In cell III, immoral behavior is punished. These two quadrants mark a sphere of operation where Individual Ethics has an important role to play: by reflecting and communicating arguments pro virtue (cell I) as well as arguments contra vice (cell III), thus helping individuals to develop a moral character.

From an ordonomic point of view, cells II and IV are even more interesting. The defining characteristic is a clash between moral arguments and institutional incentives. It is important to note that Order Ethics can pursue two rather different strategies for solving the relevant problems.

- On the one hand, Order Ethics can contribute to an institutional reform that aligns incentives to arguments. Graphically, the direction of impact is vertical, as represented by arrows 1 and 2. For example, if environmental-friendly behavior is prohibitively costly in the status quo, the introduction of property rights might help to move a morally desired behavior from cell II to cell I (arrow 1). In likewise fashion, anti-cartel laws are instrumental in fighting collusive behavior, i.e., a form of cooperation that is morally undesired, thus moving it from cell IV to cell III (arrow 2).
- On the other hand, Order Ethics can contribute to a moral revaluation that aligns ideas to institutions. Graphically, the direction of impact is horizontal, as represented by arrows 3 and 4. For example, after prohibiting by law the age-old practice of duelling, the underlying idea of "honor" needed a fundamentally new interpretation in order to stop aristocrats from killing each other. They had to learn that what was perceived as a virtue in pre-modern society had turned into a vice in modern society (arrow 3). In likewise fashion, today many people have to learn that a whistle-blower must not be perceived as a traitor and that in a

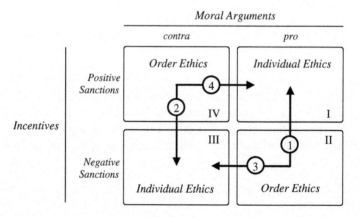

Fig. 4 The ordonomic division of labor between individual ethics and order ethics

loyalty conflict one's loyalty towards a colleague or other person might not be as important (and morally justified) as one's loyalty towards the organization, especially if these persons are involved in corruption and if whistle-blowing helps to (re-)establish the organization's moral integrity (arrow 4).

From an ordonomic point of view, Individual Ethics and Order Ethics do not contradict each other. Properly understood, they are complementary and thus can work hand in hand. Order Ethics contributes to fulfilling the social preconditions required by Individual Ethics, namely the situational fit between moral arguments and incentives.

(4) Summing up, the ordonomic approach is interested in—and tries to contribute to—societal learning processes that consist in a mutual adaption of institutions and ideas: the formal and informal rules which guide our behavior, and the language concepts which guide our thinking. That institutions and ideas do not necessarily fit together is a *signum* of modernity. Sometimes, our normative terms and concepts are not well suited for understanding the modern world. In this case, conceptual clarification may help to avoid the danger that public discourse overlooks and thereby misses the opportunity of employing institutionalized market arrangements for reaching moral goals. Sometimes, however, our modern world does not meet our normative standards. In this case, moral idea(l)s can stimulate institutional reforms which may help to correct systemic malfunctions.

Ordonomics addresses both cases: it analyzes social dilemmas, scrutinizes orthogonal positions and employs a three-level scheme to systematically distinguish the social arenas which have to be brought together in order to facilitate the mutual adaptation of institutions and ideas, which has been—and continues to be—the central characteristic of those learning processes that propel modern growth society.

References

Beckmann, Markus, and Ingo Pies. 2008a. Ordo-responsibility—conceptual reflections towards a semantic innovation. Corporate Citizenship. In *Contractarianism and ethical theory*. eds. Jesús Conill, Christoph Luetge, and Tatjana Schönwälder-Kuntze, 87–115. Farnham, Burlington: Ashgate.

Beckmann, Markus, and Ingo Pies. 2008b. Sustainability by corporate citizenship. The moral dimension of sustainability. *The Journal of Corporate Citizenship* (31), autumn 2008, 45–57.

Beckmann, Markus, Stefan Hielscher, and Ingo Pies. 2012a. Commitment strategies for sustainability: How business firms can transform trade-offs into win-win outcomes. *Business Strategy and the Environment*. doi:10.1002/bse.1758.

Beckmann, Markus, Ingo Pies, and Alexandra von Winning. 2012b. Passion and compassion as strategy drivers for sustainable value creation: An ordonomic perspective on social and ecological entrepreneurship. *Economic and Environmental Studies* 12(3), 191–221.

Bowles, Samuel. 2004. Microeconomics. In *Behavior, institutions, and evolution*. Princeton, Oxford: Princeton University Press.

Buchanan, James M. 1989. The relatively absolute absolutes. In *Essays on the political economy*. eds. James M. Buchanan, 32–46. Honolulu: University of Hawaii Press.

Buttkereit, Sören, and Ingo Pies. 2008. Social dilemmas and the social contract. In *Corporate citizenship, contractarianism and ethical theory*. eds. Jesús Conill, Christoph Luetge, and Tatjana Schönwälder-Kuntze, 135–147. Farnham, Burlington: Ashgate.

Clark, Gregory. 2007. *A farewell to alms. A brief economic history of the world*. Princeton, Oxford.

Galor, Oded. 2011. *Unified growth theory*. Princeton, Oxford.

Hardimon, Michael O. 1994. Hegel's social philosophy. The project of reconciliation. Cambridge, New York, Melbourne: Cambridge University Press.

Hardin, Garrett. 1968. The tragedy of the commons. *Science, New Series* 162(3859): 1243–1248.

Hielscher, Stefan, Ingo Pies, and Vladislav Valentinov. 2012. How to foster social progress: An ordonomic perspective on progressive institutional change. *Journal of Economic Issues (JEI)* XLVI(3):779–797.

Lippmann, Walter. 1929, 2009. *A preface to morals*, 6th ed. New Brunswick, London: Transaction Publishers.

Ostrom, Elinor. 2012. The future of the commons: Beyond market failure and government regulation. London: Institute of Economic Affairs.

Petrick, Martin, and Ingo Pies. 2007. In search for rules that secure gains from cooperation: The heuristic value of social dilemmas for normative institutional economics. *European Journal of Law and Economics* 23(3): 251–271.

Pies, Ingo. 2000. *Ordnungspolitik in der Demokratie. Ein ökonomischer Ansatz diskursiver Politikberatung*. Tübingen: Mohr-Siebeck.

Pies, Ingo, and Claudia Schott. 2001. Heroin: The case for prescription. In *High time for reform: drug policy for the 21st century*. eds. Selina Chen, and Edward Skidelsky, 113–126. London: Social Market Foundation.

Pies, Ingo, and Stefan Hielscher. 2009a. The international provision of pharmaceuticals: A comparison of two alternative argumentative strategies for global ethics. *Journal of Global Ethics* 7(1): 73–89.

Pies, Ingo, and Stefan Hielscher. 2009b. The role of corporate citizens in fighting poverty: An ordonomic approach to global justice. In *Absolute poverty and global justice*. eds. Elke Mack, Michael Schramm, Stephan Klasen, and Thomas Pogge, 233–247. Aldershot, London: Ashgate.

Pies, Ingo, Stefan Hielscher, and Markus Beckmann. 2009. Moral commitments and the societal role of business: An ordonomic approach to corporate citizenship. *Business Ethics Quarterly* 19(3):375–401.

Pies, Ingo, Markus Beckmann, and Stefan Hielscher. 2010. Value creation, management competencies, and global corporate citizenship: An ordonomic approach to business ethics in the age of globalization. *Journal of Business Ethics* 94: 265–278.

Pies, Ingo, Markus Beckmann, and Stefan Hielscher. 2011. Competitive markets, corporate firms, and new governance—an ordonomic conceptualization. *Corporate citizenship and new governance—the political role of corporations*. eds. Ingo Pies, and Peter Koslowski, 171–188. Dordrecht u.a.O.: Springer.

Pies, Ingo, and Stefan Hielscher. 2012. Gründe versus Anreize? Ein ordonomischer Werkstattbericht in sechs Thesen. In *Welt der Gründe, Deutsches Jahrbuch für Philosophie*. eds. Nida-Rümelin Julian, and Elif Özmen, Band 4, 215–230 (XXII. Deutscher Kongress für Philosophie, 11–15. September 2011 an der Ludwig-Maximilians-Universität München, Kolloquienbeiträge), Hamburg.

Pies, Ingo, Markus Beckmann, and Stefan Hielscher. 2013a. The political role of the business firm: An ordonomic concept of corporate citizenship developed in comparison with the aristotelian idea of individual citizenship. *Business & Society* 0007650313483484, first published on April 17, 2013 as doi:10.1177/0007650313483484.

Pies, Ingo, Matthias Georg Will, Thomas Glauben, and Sören Prehn. 2013b. Hungermakers?—Why futures market activities by index funds are promoting the common good, Diskussionspapier Nr. 2013-19 des Lehrstuhls für Wirtschaftsethik an der Martin-Luther-Universität Halle-Wittenberg, Halle.

Pies, Ingo, Matthias Georg Will, Thomas Glauben, and Sören Prehn. 2013c. *The ethics of financial speculation in futures markets*. Diskussionspapier Nr. 2013–21 des Lehrstuhls für Wirtschaftsethik an der Martin-Luther-Universität Halle-Wittenberg, Halle.
Rawls, John. 1971. *A theory of justice*. Oxford etc.: Oxford University Press.
Rawls, John. 1993. *Political liberalism*, (Columbia University Press), New York.
Rawls, John. 2001. *Justice as fairness. A restatement*. ed. Erin Kelly. Cambridge, MA, London: The Belknap Press of Harvard University Press.
Schumpeter, Joseph A. 1911, 2006. Theorie der wirtschaftlichen Entwicklung. Nachdruck der ersten Auflage von 1912 [eigentlich 1911, I.P.], herausgegeben und ergänzt um eine Einleitung von Jochen Röpke und Olaf Stiller, Berlin.
Zagorin, Perez. 2003 How the idea of religious toleration came to the west. Princeton, Oxford: Princeton University Press.

Theory Strategies of Business Ethics

Karl Homann

1 Introduction

In view of the enormous pressure to solve problems that exists today in the current international situation, more than a few people expect a contribution to be made by business ethics. Despite such high expectations, business ethics has been slow to develop in an academic setting, at least in Germany.[1] In my estimation, this is primarily the result of two reasons. First of all, business ethics continues to provide a model that is highly heterogeneous. By the same token, it lacks acceptance among philosophy and economics. These two reasons are closely related (indeed, the latter is at least partly due to the former) and, to my mind, may be ascribed to a general dearth of methodological reflection. This deficit, in turn, has resulted in the development of numerous misunderstandings, reciprocal assumptions, and deep and misguided antagonisms. In the meantime, quite a few scholars find that discussions about fundamental principles and methods of business ethics are unproductive and turn instead to specific practical questions. In the end, however, they are forced to grope in the dark when it comes to the various problems of such an interdisciplinary undertaking as business ethics, which, in the long run, makes the prospect of a constructive collaboration with philosophy and economics virtually impossible.

In this paper, I want to return once again to the question of how to arrive at a theory strategy in business ethics.[2] My intention here is not to indoctrinate certain

---

[1]Despite two new endowed chairs at the TU München (Prof. Dr. Christoph Luetge, since fall 2010) and at the Universität Halle-Wittenberg (Prof. Dr. Philipp Schreck, since spring 2015), my chair at the LMU München has since adopted a different focus (Prof. Dr. Julian Nida-Rümelin, philosophy and political theory).
[2]Previous works include, for instance, Homann (1994a, 1997), both reprinted in Homann (2002), pp. 45–66 and 107–135.

K. Homann (✉)
LMU, Munich, Germany
e-mail: karl.homann@wcge.org

normative concepts, or even to defend my own perspective, even though I will have a natural tendency to favor it and make arguments within its particular framework. Instead, my aim is much more to elucidate the possible paradigmatic theoretical options, analyze their respective strengths and weaknesses, and, thereby, to formulate the questions that business ethics needs to ask as a subject that strives to be equally compatible with the world experienced in everyday life ("Lebenswelt") and its fellow academic disciplines.

To begin this undertaking, it is useful to choose a point of departure that is more or less shared by all economic ethicists. This may be formulated in the following, deliberately colloquial, way: Business ethics is concerned with arriving at a qualitative "surplus" over and above the conventional understanding of capitalism and neoclassical economics concerning commercial gain, return of investment, and efficiency optimization. As I see it, there is at least consensus here among all business ethicists who want to offer normative advice and recommendations.

That said, when it comes to the theoretical framework in which this "surplus" should be explicated, there is a difference of opinion. The question is highly relevant, because the theoretical framework predetermines to a considerable degree the formulation of the problem and its proposed solutions. It is for this reason that this contribution will provide a kind of appraisal of the implications of the various theories.

In my view, business ethics has two fundamental, paradigmatic theoretical options, which can be provisionally characterized in the following manner. The first strategy uses a narrow concept of the economy and the study of economics, and must therefore claim that morality and ethics are "external economic" factors that are **opposed** to the economy and the study of economics. This conception is characterized by a "dualism" between economy and morality (or likewise the study of economics and ethics). The second strategy attempts to reconcile morality and ethics **with** the economy and the study of economics. In order to do so, however, it must substantively broaden the understanding of economics and settle on a specific understanding of morality and ethics and a specific methodology. I refer to this conception as the economic reconstruction of ethics.

I will make my observations within the framework of the second strategy, which I have pursued in my research for over 25 years.

Of course, the selection of a theoretical strategy is not arbitrary. I will therefore begin by indicating five criteria for selecting a theory in business ethics that I hold to be largely capable of consensus. A business ethics theory must be able to accommodate (1) basic moral intuitions, (2) moral problems, and (3) and empirical findings. It must further be able to (4) develop solutions to everyday problems and (5) have a plausible answer to the question of why many people adhere to moral norms, whereas many others often do not.[3]

---

[3]The question of why people often do not adhere to moral norms has hardly been systematically analyzed in the Western tradition of ethics; typically, reference is made to evil or weak wills.

In the first two sections of this paper, I will analyze the two fundamental theoretical options for a normative business ethics and make an initial evaluation according to the above-mentioned five criteria. In the third section, I will then reflect on the strengths and weaknesses of both strategies in a somewhat broader context. To conclude, I will offer an outlook on areas of future research.

2 Theoretical Strategy (I): Ethics Versus Economics

I begin my remarks here by again pointing out a commonality between both theoretical strategies. This consists in the experience that many people have, especially business managers, who are faced with contradictory—specifically, ethical and economic—demands when making decisions.

The first theoretical strategy portrays this lifeworld conflict as a one-to-one relationship and assumes the existence of two independent demands or values—neither of which, however, has the same root or can be attributed to the other. It is hypothesized that a decision is required here about which side should have priority or what the mediation of both sides should look like.

The view predominates that the primacy of ethics should be normatively enforced. A "disruption"[4] of economic logic is thus demanded, it is said that market forces need to be "subdued,"[5] and the invocation of "practical constraints" is accused of being ideological. Moderation, solidarity, and altruism are deemed to be moral values or virtues that need to be set against unrestrained self-interest. The alternate possibility—the primacy of the economy and the study of economics—does not receive serious consideration. Criticisms here include "economicism," "economic reductionism," and a failure to recognize the "moral point of view." The weaker variant of this "dualistic" conception of business ethics recognizes the (equal) standing of economic demands and calls for the "mediation" of both points of view, without however providing anything that resembles a general weighting function.

As a rule, dualistic approaches in business ethics are based on analogous approaches in philosophical ethics, where there are basically two variants.

The variant with the most ambitious claim derives the norms in a transcendental-philosophical manner from reason[6] or in a transcendental-pragmatic

---

[4]Ulrich (1996) p. 156; similarly Ulrich (1997/2008) p.398.

[5]Scherer (2003) p. 95; this could be understood as forceful containment, in German "Bändigung"; similarly Scherer et al. (2014).

[6]Classically, in the mainstream interpretation, the foundational writings of Immanuel Kant; Kant (1785/1786/2011, 1788/1996); in the Berlin Academy edition vols. IV, p. 385–463, and V, p. 1–164.

manner from the structures of language or discourse.[7] Here, reason or language/discourse contain normative implications that a human being cannot avoid, but must recognize and adhere to in his or her own actions. Obviously, the aim of this variant is to arrive at an independent foundation under pluralistic circumstances (which have continued to proliferate since the beginning of the modern era) for a universally valid morality that is free of ideological preconditions and whose essential core today is equated with human rights. To arrive at such a justification—or what Apel calls the "ultimate justification"—morality in this variant is practiced with considerable theoretical effort. In my view, this is due to the fact that an effective, convincing justification is required to determine the will or the actor's motives so that the corresponding moral action can be manifested with little difficulty. Critical here is the expectation or the requirement of a transfer—which is supposedly demanded by reason—between the initial realization and the will or the motive to act.[8]

The second variant of the dualistic conception largely does away with transcendental-philosophical and transcendental-pragmatic considerations and argues instead along anthropological lines. For some authors, a human being is a de facto moral being. To others, a human being is able to draw on a broad spectrum of motivations that extends from altruism to opportunism. In business ethics, the concern is with reinforcing the "good" motives through education, role models, poignant literature, etc. so that they become behaviorally effective and prevail over the "bad" motives or the weak will. This variant has recently been supported by research that takes recourse to insights from evolutionary biology,[9] developmental psychology,[10] and experimental economic research.[11]

Both variants demonstrate a series of shared assumptions. For example, they are both to be classified as dualistic, and they both criticize the famous (or infamous) trope of the *homo economicus* with a two-pronged—albeit differently weighted—argument. In short, they agree that the *homo economicus* is not what a human being is, nor what he should become. In both variants, the will and motivation play a central role.

Regarding the issue of the implementation of moral norms—the fourth criterion —this dualistic approach has far-reaching consequences. It is appropriate to make

---

[7] As, for instance, in the discourse ethics of the Frankfurt School; see e.g. Apel (1973/1980), Habermas (1981/1984/1987, 1983/1990, 1991/1994). P. Ulrich and his followers draw on this version of discourse ethics. H. Steinmann and his followers draw on the Erlanger variant of a discourse ethics, whose founder is P. Lorenzen; see Lorenzen (1989/1991). Steinmann and Löhr (1992/1994). In recent years, there seem to have been efforts to merge the two discourse ethics concepts, such as when Steinmann's proponent A.G. Scherer increasingly takes recourse to Habermas; see Palazzo and Scherer (2006, 2007).

[8] The assessment of psychology in the work of J. Rawls is quite compelling in this context. He developed a "moral psychology: philosophical and not psychological," and describes its role as follows: "We have to formulate an ideal of constitutional government to see whether it has force for us and can be put into practice successfully in the history of society." Rawls (1993) p. 87.

[9] See, for example, Tomasello (2009); Nowak and Highfield (2011).

[10] See Kohlberg (1981) and the extensive discussion of the Piaget-Kohlberg approach.

[11] See Ockenfels (1999), Dohmen et al. (2009), Fehr and Fischbacher (2003).

an appeal to the will or to good motives, to postulate moral behavior or, in the case of noncompliance, to assign guilt. Since a will, a motive, or guilt can only be ascribed to natural persons, only individuals come into question as the intended audience of such appeals, resulting in the strong tendency running through all the approaches toward a personal or individual ethics. Morally desirable conditions are attributed to the good will of the actors in question, and morally undesirable conditions—for instance, the deplorable news that 27,000 children die every day due to starvation and malnourishment[12]—would consequently have to be ascribed to an evil or weak will of actual individuals. Proponents of this conception live in a world tracing results back to motives,[13] a world in other words that is systematically created from the actors' respective motives. In this conception, economic ethical discourse practices are a kind of moral rearmament.

Since the proponents of this strategy realize that the appeals can nevertheless only be credited with limited success, they will often reinforce their rearmament. They thus frequently resort to (in objective order, but decreasing frequency) moralism,[14] paternalism, militancy, fundamentalism, and, more or less as a theoretical refuge, an appeal for "well-intentioned, well-informed tyrants inspired by the correct insights." This observation is not meant to discredit an important scholar like H. Jonas as the devotee of a dictatorship, even if he did attribute to Marxism the "great advantage of a pronounced "moralism."[15] Instead, the intent is to simply highlight the fact that one is hard-pressed to make cogent arguments within the scope of a dualistic conception of ethics or business ethics when seriously addressing the issue of implementation.

We have now arrived at a point where we can make an initial evaluation of this approach. It appears to meet the first three criteria mentioned at the outset: It is compatible prima facie with moral intuitions, empirical findings, and moral problems. Nonetheless, the approach appears to systematically disregard the fourth and fifth criterion.

On the fourth criterion: In the modern world, a theoretical strategy systematically excludes the conditions for the implementation of morality which does not accept into its paradigm the logic of competition or, more generally, the prisoner's dilemma,[16] summed up by the notion of preventative counter-defection. Inasmuch

---

[12]The number is taken from Singer (2009), p. 4.

[13]This translation is to be regarded as an equivalent of the German "Motivwelt", picked up from Nassehi (2010) p. 156.

[14]A critical statement in this regard: "A morality that believes itself able to dispense with the technical knowledge of economic laws is not morality but moralism, the opposite of morality." Ratzinger (1985/2010) p. 84.

[15]Jonas (1979/1984) pp. 262, 263; here "moralism" has a positive connotation. In English translation: "a well-intentioned, well-informed tyranny possessed of the right insights" Jonas (1979/1984/1985) p. 147; "a great asset of Marxism is here the emphatic 'moralism,'" Jonas (1979/1984/1985) p. 147.

[16]Competition on the same side of the market can be interpreted as a prisoner's dilemma; see Homann and Suchanek (2000/2005) p. 209ff., or Homann and Luetge (2004/2013), p 30ff.

as the Catholic Church was not in a position to respond to Galileo's scientific work, moral appeals and ethics are equally out of place today when arguing against the logic of the modern world's functional systems—here the basic functional imperative of the economy and economics. If the attempt is made in any event, this can have a variety of potentially equally disastrous consequences for the aim to realize a "surplus" above and beyond a narrow conception of the economy and economics. Three such strategies may be cited here: (1) The increasing trend toward militancy, which moreover shows its first signs in the realm of politics, has already been mentioned; (2) insofar as individuals cannot implement morality under the conditions of functional systems and competition (= dilemma structures), some people become resigned and find morality in the economy obsolete; (3) others decide to limit their behavior to, and content themselves with, what they can do as individuals. They feel their position is justified[17]—as regards their conscience, God, society, etc.—and simply let moral problems sort out themselves. This again shows the strong individualistic character of this conception of business ethics.

On the fifth criterion: The question of why human beings often do not adhere to moral norms is answered by making reference to an evil or weak will (the pursuit of profit, egoism, greed). In a motive world, it is necessary to identify the respective participants' individual motives as the cause of all cumulative, morally undesirable outcomes—which, in turn, is an individual-theoretical line of argument. Moreover, this contradicts a central stipulation of the methodology of economics, according to which the great moral issues of the world, like hunger, poverty, child mortality, climate change, unemployment, etc. are the unintended consequences of intentional, self-interested behavior. The prisoner's dilemma presents problem structures as the underlying structure of all interactions in which results systematically come to bear on a cumulative level that none of the participants had either intended or desired. These problems are therefore not attributable to the aims of individual actors. The moral problem in the structures is not the (good, evil, or weak) will of individuals—the problem is rather the other or the others. Yet this problem can only be solved by means of sanctions prescribed by informal or formal institutions. Explaining moral failure by identifying the presence of a "weak will" systematically overlooks those problem structures[18] that are central to our world's moral problems.

---

[17]D. Gauthier and R. Pippin attribute this to the fact that, in the Christian Middle Ages, the question of the justification of the individual soul before God was central; see Gauthier (1998) p. 131; Pippin (2005) p. 65. This is even the case with Calvin, whose theology has been regarded since M. Weber as the driving force behind the capitalist economy: An individual's wealth is interpreted as a sign that his soul has been chosen by God.

[18]The few representatives of an autonomous ethics of philosophy who even seriously discuss the prisoner's dilemma consistently try to overcome it by means of individual morality, dispositions, or virtues: Mackie (1977); Gauthier (1986). [Instead of the referenced "Willensschwäche," which might be translated into English as "a lack of moral feeling or concern, or a lack of some other particular interest or attitude." Gauthier (1986) p.103?] In P. Ulrich's "Integrative Wirtschaftsethik," the prisoner's dilemma is only mentioned once on less than half a page and is also to be overcome by means of individual morality; see Ulrich (1996) p. 84 and Ulrich (1997/2008) p. 68.

Indeed, it is worth pointing out here a counterargument which runs as follows: Empirical evidence shows beyond a doubt that the vast majority of people are moral actors in their day-to-day lives. This suggests, therefore, that the *homo economicus* is a paradigm that is either false or, at best, has only limited validity.

While the empirical basis of this argument seems beyond dispute, the inference remains open to question. When it comes to a scientific theory that aims to inquire into reasons and explanations, pure facticity should not be viewed as self-evident. Facticity is not to be classified as the explanation of the phenomenon—the explanans—but rather as the phenomenon that needs to be explained—the explanandum. Of course, this is so especially when there is a significant amount of counter-evidence in the form of moral failures, as in the case here. When one refers solely to pure facticity or to the "phenomena," it is not possible to get past a typology of characters and conditions pertaining to how different people behave in different situations. In the social sciences, one encounters and cultivates a variety of contradictory partial theories, and, at present, there is no reason to expect that this approach will lead to a unified theoretical core that permits methodologically controlled variation with different variables. As intriguing as such findings may be, even for my own work, an effort to arrive at a unified theory is missing. C.F. von Weizsäcker would say that this approach is "too empirical."[19] The hope held out by certain protagonists who have become disheartened with the debate over first principles and intensified their efforts concerning empirical questions is misleading. They will continue to be repeatedly confronted by the omissions of putatively successful theoretical strategies, such as when they impose a moratorium on discussion, saying, in essence, "that's just how it is"; or when they adopt the position of meta-ethical realism which, analogous to the natural sciences, now also asserts moral "facts"; and/or when they stubbornly stick to assertions of "ought," to mere appeals and ascriptions of guilt.[20]

The upshot of this first theoretical strategy is that it makes sense to seek out an alternative.

3 Theoretical Strategy (II): Ethics with Economic Methods

The idea behind this theoretical strategy is that the "surplus" in relation to the pursuit of profits, efficiency optimization, and return on investment should be realized with economic logic. This cannot be achieved, however, with either the conventional understanding of economics as the science of economics or with any of the types of ethics. It requires, first of all, the understanding of economics to be

---

[19]von Weizsäcker (1964) p. 104 (with reference to the physics of Aristotle).
[20]The formulation is based on Hegel. I have shown in Homann (2004) that Hegel himself uses such an ought, as well as in what context.

expanded. At the same time, it should be noted here that this expansion is not required, for instance, for economic-ethical aims, but has rather been developed by economists to solve economic problems, ostensibly ensuring its compatibility to economics. Secondly, it must be defined on the basis of a certain—specifically, teleological or eudemonistic—type of ethics, which while certainly not uncontroversial, can still be seriously represented. It must also be rooted in a certain—specifically, (limited) constructivistic—methodology that continues to prove its validity in the scholarship and scientific theory. This should finally assure its compatibility with the philosophy of ethics.

The conventional understanding of economics as the science of economics is expanded with respect to three dimensions.

The objective dimension: Here, a flexible concept of advantage is recognized in the tradition of G.S. Becker.[21] "Advantage" refers to anything that human beings themselves view as beneficial. Thus, besides income and wealth, this would range from health, time, and leisure to classically philosophical eudemonism, understood today as the opportunity for all people to pursue a satisfying existence. Such an understanding of economics makes it possible to economically reconstruct all of philosophy's normative ideals and principles.

The temporal dimension: Modern economics is undergoing an unprecedented shift from temporary and selective calculations to long-term advantage/disadvantage calculations. This was already implied before when it came to topics like investment and growth. Today, however, this trend has been reinforced by research on "sustainability" and order-, institutional, and constitutional economics.

The personal dimension: The expansion of this dimension is manifested in a change of emphasis from action to interaction with the aim of accounting for the interdependency of all human activity. The prisoner's dilemma[22] provides a basic model which simultaneously brings to bear shared and conflicting interests or opportunities and problems concerning "a cooperative venture for mutual advantage."[23] It further allows for these problems to be processed and, as consequence, for the problems of ethics to be analyzed in terms of economics and game theory.

This strategy, however, also demands a certain type of ethics and is by no means compatible with all types of ethics. I will now illustrate the key points of an ethics that is amenable to this strategy.[24]

---

[21] See, for example, Becker (1976, 1996).

[22] The model may be assumed to be known. On its importance for ethics, see the extensive discussion in Homann (2014); on its importance for evolutionary biology, see again Nowak and Highfield (2011); on the fact that inputs strengthen incentives for defecting, see Garapin et al. (2011).

[23] Rawls (1971) pp. 84, 126.

[24] Not compatible with this type of ethics are a deontological ethics, a cognitivist ethics and all types that rely on "metaphysical" conditions. Utilitarianism is not compatible either, in all its variants, since it cannot avoid aggregating individual utility.

Under conditions of pluralism, ethics must (1) do away with strong ideological or "metaphysical" preconditions.[25] It must instead (2) be oriented teleologically, or more precisely eudemonistically, in its modern conception. It can in fact (3) only be developed in a contract-theoretical paradigm[26] in the broadest sense according to the principle that human beings themselves and collectively[27] determine how they want to interact with each other. Ethics must (4) be able to conform to the structures of modern societies. It must, accordingly, (5) be capable of taking effect in the functional logic of subsystems, which, with regard to the economy and the study of economics, means that it must be fundamentally compatible with incentives (consistent with David Hume's observation that "in each instance [= the effect of selfishness] can only be restrained by the individual himself"[28]). (6) The passed-down personal ethics or individual ethics needs to be grounded in an order ethics, whereby it obtains a different, indeed less comprehensive, but nevertheless indispensable role. Finally, and closely tied to the latter, in establishing ethics, it is (7) necessary to already take account of its implementability under the conditions of a modern society (specifically, in accordance with the principle Hegel formulates in his "Philosophy of Right," which also holds true for ethics: The idea of morality contains the concept of ethics and its realization.[29]).

As R. Pippin emphasizes in reference to Hegel,[30] such an ethics does not demand the subduing or disruption of "nature", or, in other words—of its empirical regularity. It demands, rather, its human form. Morality can only be realized with and through the lawful order of the empirical world, not in opposition to it.

Lest an economic reconstruction of ethics might not fall prey to the criticism of reductionism and and/or economic imperialism, a commitment is also necessary to a limited constructivistic methodology. Accordingly, the economic perspective on morality is only one of many. That is to say, it also allows for the contribution of other perspectives such as those from philosophy or even psychology. A constructivistic view of science does not permit theories to directly comment on "reality," but always only within the context of a certain formulation of a problem—and only under the abstraction, not rejection, of other equally valid problem formulations in other contexts. Nonetheless, the economic understanding of the

---

[25]Following Rawls (1993).

[26]See the classic works from Rawls (1971) and Buchanan (1975), along with Brennan and Buchanan (1985).

[27]Similarly, Kant: Man is "subject only to his own and yet universal legislation"; Kant (1785/1786/2011) p. 93; emphasis omitted.

[28]Hume (1739–1740/2000) p. 316. ["There is no passion, therefore, capable of controuling the interested affection [= the love of gain], but the very affection itself, by an alteration of its direction."].

[29]The famous § 1 of Hegel's Philosophy of Right reads as follows: "The subject-matter of the philosophical science of right is the Idea of right—the concept of right and its actualization." Hegel (1821/1991) S. 25; emphasis omitted.].

[30]See Pippin (2005) pp. 59–70 (Hegel und das Problem der Freiheit).

problem is an important and indispensable perspective,[31] because a morality without empirical implementability—no matter how well-founded it may be—is ultimately meaningless.[32] The age-old principle is thus apposite: "ultra posse nemo obligatur" (no one is obligated beyond what he is able to do).[33] A business ethics developed in line with this theoretical strategy is not fundamentally concerned with the problem "should and would"—this was and remains the central problem of the autonomous philosophy of ethics, especially after Kant.[34] Instead, it is much more concerned

---

[31]Sedlácek (2009/2011) shows quite convincingly in the first part of his book that a strong economic dimension is inherent to all considerations of ethics, from the Gilgamesh epic and the Old and New Testament to Thomas Aquinas.

[32]This idea lies behind Hegel's much-criticized notion of "world history as the world's court of judgment [Weltgericht]," Hegel (1821/1986) p. 503 (§ 340). The sentence to which Hegel refers here comes originally from F. Schiller's poem "Resignation": "Die Weltgeschichte ist das Weltgericht." Schiller (1786) p. 68.

[33]This principle has not been explicitly questioned by any ethical conception. But in dualistic conceptions of ethics and business ethics, it finds only a weak echo, namely in the concept of "reasonableness": Obviously not everything that is morally required is also "reasonable," whereby this restriction is never systematically explicated, but always remains ad hoc. See, for example, Ulrich (1996) p. 448f and Ulrich (1997/2008) p. 429 ["the question whether the corporation itself can be reasonably expected to recognize the claims made on it."; emphasis in the original]; without using the concept of "reasonableness," P. Singer makes completely ad hoc deductions about what, in his opinion, is morally necessary; see Singer (2009) p. 151 ff., esp. 160ff. As to the ad-hoc nature of this concept, the following passage in J. Habermas is particularly revealing. It makes an especially strong claim in reference to the "validity," i.e. here: invalidity, of moral commandments, only to then subsequently weaken it by taking recourse to "reasonableness": "The validity of moral commandments is subject to the condition that they be generally followed as the basis of a general practice. Only if this condition of reasonableness is satisfied, are they able to give expression to that which everyone might want. "Habermas (1991) p. 136, emphasis in the original [Engl .: "autonomy can be reasonably expected (zumutbar) only in social contexts that are already themselves rational in the sense that they ensure that action motivated by good reasons will not of necessity conflict with one's own interests. The validity of moral commands is subject to the condition that they are **universally** adhered to as the basis for a general practice. Only when this condition is satisfied do they express what all could will." Habermas (1991/1994) p. 34; emphasis in the original)]. How are we to understand, for example, the "validity" of the ban on corruption in the countries of the world where corruption is common practice?

[34]In the mainstream interpretation of Kant traced back to the famous first sentence of the first section of "Groundwork of the Metaphysics of Morals" from 1785: "Es ist überall nichts in der Welt, ja überhaupt auch außer derselben zu denken möglich, was ohne Einschränkung für gut könnte gehalten werden, als allein ein guter Wille." Kant (1902 ff.) Vol. IV, p. 393; emphasis omitted. [Engl .: "It is impossible to think of anything at all in the world, or indeed even beyond it, that could be taken to be good without limitation, except a good will." Kant (1785/1786/2011) p. 15; emphasis omitted]. The "mainstream interpretation" refers to Kant's remarks in the "Groundwork " and in the "Critique of Practical Reason" to the concrete actions of people; many of the examples provided by Kant himself suggest this reference. Recent research shows that these writings were not specifically concerned with behavior, but "metaphysics," that is, the principles of behavior. Principles, however, only apply "in principle," not in every specific case. Here, Kant is much more flexible, for he also takes empirical conditions into consideration. Instructive for the business ethics here is Kant's discussion of competition or, more precisely, "Wetteifer" (rivalry); see Schönwälder-Kuntze (2013).

with the problem "should and could."[35] It centers on the question of implementation and the stability of morality under the conditions of modern society—under conditions, in other words, which were not conceded any systematic priority in the first strategy.

I would now like to turn to a fundamental cause of a great deal of misunderstanding: the proper understanding of the *homo economicus*.[36] Viewed from a constructivistic standpoint, this concept is not a philosophical or empirical conception of man, but a theoretical construct that makes it possible to evaluate the cumulative results of interactions in dilemma structures. With the *homo economicus*, the connection to reality is not established through the *homo*. It is rather borne out by the situation in which interactions take place and where the prisoner's dilemma structure is always inherent—even if it is not always manifest, but frequently remains latent. Here, if an individual wants to protect himself from exploitation, he has no choice but to act like a *homo economicus*, specifically, by adopting a strategy of preventative counter-defection. Experimental economic research falls prey to a methodological (self-) misunderstanding when it adopts the *homo economicus* as an economic concept of man and classifies inconsistent findings as counter-evidence or a falsification. What it in fact empirically observes is not a *homo economicus*, but rather human beings whose behavior is always simultaneously determined by two classes of stimuli: on the one hand, by the incentives of the problem structure of the prisoner's dilemma, from which the construct of the *homo economicus* is derived; and, on the other hand, by additional physiological, psychological, and, above all, also institutional stimuli. These stimuli, in other words, are partly innate, but also partly socially given or formed, and their function often lies in compensating or overcompensating for the incentive structures of the prisoner's dilemma and the *homo economicus*, or, alternately, in bringing them to bear in the case of competition. With lasting dilemma problem structures, the morally inclined human being will not allow himself to be continually and systematically exploited. Put another way: just as little as the law of gravity alone is able to explain any single individual falling motion, the prisoner's dilemma is similarly unable to explain any single empirical interaction.

It is precisely when actors frequently, but by no means always, adhere to moral norms that theory is well advised to assume the existence of an interaction structure on both sides. The conditions can then be reconstructed—first when going in one direction and then in the other—that characterize this identical structure. Initially, it is necessary to "imagine away" these conditions, for only then is it possible to obtain information about which determining factors give rise to the preferred—here morally desired—behavior in question. Morally desired behavior thus becomes an explanandum. In other words, the reference to the facticity of moral behavior explains nothing whatever precisely in cases of moral failure.

---

[35]Hence the title of Homann (2014).

[36]Fundamental for my viewpoint, Homann (1994b), reprinted in Homann (2002) p. 69–93.

The most productive approach, which is able to explain conformity and nonconformity alike, is the approach that addresses both shared and conflicting interests: the prisoner's dilemma.[37] The conceptual point of departure for the theoretically least desirable case, non-cooperation (classically: the natural state of man) sheds light on the factors that also in fact make cooperation (i.e. morality) possible.[38] It is the study of these factors that finally concerns business ethics.

Such a strategy has consequences for understanding important elements of the rational choice approach, a standard theory in economics. Several of these which are especially relevant for business ethics may be briefly summarized here. (1) The *homo economicus* is not a concept of man, but a theoretical construct for evaluating the cumulative results in interactions. (2) The—preventative—pursuit of individual advantage is not to be understood as an underlying motivation (of action), but as the systemic imperative of market economies.[39] Of course, there are "acquisitive" human beings, but the preventative pursuit of advantage serves in the vast majority of cases the purpose of defense (in Hobbes: *defensio*[40]) against exploitation by others in competition or, more generally, in prisoner's dilemma situations. The widespread criticism of egoism in the capitalistic economy and neoclassical economics becomes null and void and the attribution of moral failure to "a weak will" fails to address the problem structure. (3) The pervasive nonconformity to moral values and norms with respect to all of the world's existing moral problems is not attributable to an evil or weak will, but rather to a lack of regulation or order (whereby even informal regulations could certainly be effective, even if they are extremely fragile in the anonymous contexts of global society). (4) The problem concerning the implementation of morality is largely resolved: Over the long run

---

[37] The prisoner's dilemma is used exclusively to outline the problem, not to describe reality, and certainly not to make a recommendation for (economic) action.

[38] See Luhmann (1984): "The methodological recipe for this is to seek theories that can succeed in explaining the normal as improbable." Luhmann (1984) p. 114. Luhmann is opposed to the "banality" of just referring the problem "back to the world experienced in everyday life, to historical facticity"; Luhmann (1984) p. 115.

[39] See Alchian (1950). Besides the fact that "motives" can only be attributed to natural persons and the attribution of self-interested striving to companies must be taken as an indication that a "motive" is not at issue, it should further be noted here that vast numbers of people strongly dislike "selfishness" and "greed," even though they must also defend their legitimate interests against exploitation in competition. Such a "motive" is best understood as an imposed motive. These remarks are in line with the notion of a "system imperative."

[40] In the English version of the "Leviathan" from 1651, Hobbes specifies the following three causes of the struggle of all against all in the state of nature: competition, diffidence, glory: "So that in the nature of man, we find three principall causes of quarrel. First, competition; secondly, diffidence; thirdly, glory. The first, maketh men invade for gain; the second, for safety; and the third, for reputation. (...) the second, to defend them." Hobbes (1651/1996) p. 88. In the Latin version, which Hobbes published 17 years later, diffidence is not so much translated as it is replaced by "defensio"; [Lat .: "Itaque in natura humana simultatum inveniuntur tres praecipuae causae, Competitio, Defensio, Gloria" Hobbes (1668/1676) S.64] Defensio already appears in "De Cive" from 1648; it is not necessary to provide supporting evidence here.

and on balance, moral behavior must—though not in every individual case—guarantee advantages to individuals if it is to be routinely practiced or to remain stable under conditions of competition (i.e. prisoner's dilemma structures).[41]

With regard to the five criteria formulated at the outset that a business ethics must satisfy, it is possible to observe the following: Criteria four and five—pertaining respectively to implementability and the explanation of moral failure—are much better met by this strategy than the first strategy. Furthermore, if the comprehension of the problem takes as its basis the expansions of the conventional understanding of economics described above, as well as the teleological conception of ethics and a constructivistic methodology, then criteria two and three—pertaining to be adequate conceptualization of moral problems and empirical findings—are also fulfilled.

There are, however, problems with the compatibility to our moral intuitions acquired through culture and socialization, in particular with regard to the role of the will, moral motivation, autonomy, and responsibility. On the theoretical level, this strategy involves a weakening of the individual-ethical paradigm, which has extended throughout occidental-Christian ethics and was taken to the extreme by Kant and his followers. This does not mean that such an ethics no longer plays a key role for the individual, his will, and his moral motivation—it simply means that the conditions underlying the individual's behavior must be systematically accounted for and that individual ethics needs to be embedded in an order ethics. In other words, recognized or accepted moral principles—ideals, values, norms, etc.—are not able to directly influence an individual's actions because of the prisoner's dilemma structures. The hiatus, that is to say, needs to be bridged by institutions.

4 Summary: Strengths and Weaknesses of Both Theoretical Strategies

In concluding, the strengths and weaknesses of both theoretical strategies will be discussed in a somewhat broader context.

The advantage to the first strategy—concerning the dualism of the economy and morality, economics and ethics—is that it preserves continuity with the tradition of philosophical and theological ethics. This understanding of morality and ethics is also familiar to scholars through their culture and socialization. This is especially helpful for a person's orientation in his day-to-day activity, for here one only requires concise, manageable, easily graspable, and generally well-rehearsed rules. The compatibility with passed-down, culturally ingrained moral practice avoids the costs of switching to another theoretical strategy, costs which—make no mistake—could be significant, for instance, in the form of uncertainty. The process of

---

[41]In a constructivist method, theory formation is determined by the leading question. In this approach, the recognized leading question is the question about the stability of morality in society under conditions of competition or dilemma structures; see Homann (2010, 2014).

changing over to a different theoretical strategy that does not replace the first, but is rather embraced along with it without being viewed as contradictory (argued for here with preference for the second strategy) could very well take up to three generations. I would imagine the final state to resemble the situation when we are able to speak of a "sunrise" in everyday speech and prose, knowing all the while that such talk is incorrect both physically and astronomically. That said, moral intuitions have a strong emotional basis, which gives rise to the question—following Hegel—of whether it is even possible to come to terms with the complexity of the modern world by means of feelings.[42]

There are, however, three substantive reasons which speak against the first strategy. On the one hand, it disregards the structures of modern societies and thus loses its orientational efficacy for human beings. Indeed, it runs the risk of forfeiting it all together, for it does not have a satisfying answer for how to implement morality in the modern world. Today, we no longer primarily live in a world tracing results back to motives. On the other hand, "metaphysical" variables like reason or values, which many authors argue are supposed to compensate for these weaknesses, create new obstacles, especially when it comes to encounters with other cultures and different moral ideas. This strategy will not be able to influence the process of globalization in the sense of being a "surplus"—the primary concern of business ethics—because it is viewed by others, unsurprisingly, as "cultural imperialism." Finally, this strategy is not able to make constructive use of scholarly insights into morality, since it dismisses them as reductionism and economicism, as well as a violation of the "moral point of view."

To some extent, the strengths and weaknesses of the second strategy may be developed inversely. First of all, it has a plausible answer to the problem of the implementation of morality under the conditions of the modern world, namely the expectation of individual advantages, thus avoiding the pervasive moralizing and appealing, as well as the respective assignations of guilt to individual actors. In dilemma structures, no one is "guilty" of a sub-optimal result—neither the one actor nor the other, nor the actors jointly—which might otherwise require that they change their attitudes. Instead, what is called for is to recast the situation by means of collective (self-) commitment. The spotlight of self-interestedness would then illuminate the Pareto-superior solutions in such a way that the respective moral behavior of every other actor could be counted on. Second, it is precisely in the encounter with other cultures in the globalization process that the advantage/disadvantage grammar developed above offers the best basis for achieving consensus about how to understand the rules of mutual coexistence. Following J. Rawls, it is necessary to dispense with strong "metaphysical" preconditions.

---

[42] See Hegel (1821/1991) p. 16f. (Preface): "That right and ethics, and the actual world of right and the ethical, are grasped by means of *thoughts* and give themselves the form of rationality—namely universality and determinacy—by means of thoughts, is what constitutes the law; and is this which is justifiably regarded as the main enemy by that feeling which reserves the right to do as it pleases, by that conscience which identifies right with subjective conviction." Hegel (1821/1991) p. 17; emphasis in original.

Third, only this theoretical strategy is able to constructively utilize important findings from the respective sciences about morality for a humane configuration of the social world.

The principal weakness of this theoretical strategy lies in the fact that it is not compatible with the moral consciousness of most people (in our cultural environment? in Germany?) and does injury the self-understanding of many people, some of whom have invested a great deal in their images of themselves over the course of their lives. What is more, it is also not compatible with the dominant conceptions of philosophical and theological ethics. Indeed, it is actively opposed by the latter, which is due not least to the circumstance that it is not developed or understood in terms of the same complexity that has allowed for its emergence. The most important task of this theoretical strategy is thus to further build on its main features, to make them compatible with the moral intuitions of human beings and the central ideas of tradition,[43] and to show that the "surplus," the primary concern of business ethics, is better incorporated by such a conception under the conditions of the modern world than by the first, dualistic, approach.

5 Conclusion

The focus of this paper was on paradigmatic theoretical decision-making for business ethics. This made a narrow kind of stylization necessary, which may only be justified for this purpose. The goal was and is to present outlines of a paradigm that make it possible to methodically discuss in a single coherent theoretical framework economic-ethical problems that range from the foundation of the theory to specific case studies.

A crucial role is played by constructivist methodology, where different theoretical approaches refer to different issues, not directly to reality. It keeps business ethics from simply bringing together the different approaches—ethical, economic, evolutionary biological, psychological, cultural scientific, etc.—without reflecting upon the dependence of the results and the different categories on the various issues. "Integration" in the most rigorous sense cannot succeed in this way.

The theoretical strategy developed here argues for discussing ethics and economics in a close and continuous relationship to each other. It is to be assumed that sometimes ethics and sometimes economics will have more productive elaborations to offer.[44] With regard to models of leading a succeeding life, for instance, ethics (along with literature, art, religion, and historical models) has come up with much more sophisticated observations than economics, which itself has hardly anything to contribute except the requirement of incentive compatibility. The reverse, however,

---

[43]In reference, for instance, to most important and influential moral philosopher of modern times, I. Kant; see footnote 34 above.

[44]See Homann (2014), Chapters 5 and 7; for a provisional outline, see Homann (2010).

is rather true with regard to reinforcing morality by means of detailed institutional arrangements. Furthermore, it can be expected that in the process of the (further) social development of morality, ethics, and economics will alternate their leading roles over time, so that the one will have to play catch up to other in each instance.[45]

The emphasis of future research should be placed on how the relationship between order ethics and individual ethics is to be readjusted:[46] Both are essential, but so far we know little about their precise interaction under these new conditions.

References

Alchian, Armen A. 1950. Uncertainty, evolution and economic theory. *Journal of Political Economy* 58: 211–222.
Apel, Karl-Otto. 1973/1980. *Towards a Transformation of Philosophy*, tr. Glyn Adey, David Fisby, London.
Becker, Gary S. 1976. *The Economic Approach to Human Behavior*, Chicago.
Becker, Gary S. 1996. *Familie, Gesellschaft und Politik: die ökonomische Perspektive*, tr. Monika Streissler, ed. Ingo Pies, Tübingen.
Brennan, Geoffrey, Buchanan, James M. 1985. *The Reason of Rules*, Cambridge.
Buchanan, James M. 1975. *The Limits of Liberty*, Chicago.
Dohmen, Thomas, Armin Falk, David Huffman, and Uwe Sunde. 2009. Homo reciprocans: Survey evidence on behavioral outcomes. *Economic Journal* 2009(119): 592–612.
Fehr, Ernst, and Urs Fischbacher. 2003. The nature of human altruism. *Nature* 425: 785–791.
Garapin, Alexis, Daniel Llerena, and Michel Hollard. 2011. When a precedent of donation favors defection in the prisoner's dilemma. *German Economic Review* 12: 409–421.
Gauthier, David. 1986. *Morals by Agreement*, Oxford.
Gauthier, David. 1998. Mutual Advantage and Impartiality. In *Impartiality, Neutrality and Justice*, ed. Paul Kelly, 120–136. Re-reading Brian Barry's "Justice as Impartiality", Edinburgh.
Habermas, Jürgen. 1981/1984/1987. *The Theory of Communicative Action*, Vol. 2, tr. Thomas McCarthy, Boston.
Habermas, Jürgen. 1983/1990. *Moral Consciousness and Communicative Action*, tr. Christian Lenhardt, Shierry Weber Nicholsen, Cambridge.
Habermas, Jürgen. 1991/1994. *Justification and Application: Remarks on Discourse Ethics*, tr. Ciaran P. Cronin, Boston.
Hegel, Georg Wilhelm Friedrich. 1821/1991. *Elements of the Philosophy of Right*, tr. H.B. Nisbet, ed. Allen W. Wood, Cambridge.
Hobbes, Thomas. 1651/1996. *Leviathan*, ed. Richard Tuck, Cambridge.
Hobbes, Thomas. 1668/1676. *Leviathan, Sive de Materia, Forma & Potestate Civitatis Ecclesiasticae et Civilis*, London.
Homann, Karl. 1994a. Ethik und Ökonomik. Zur Theoriestrategie der Wirtschaftsethik. In *Wirtschaftsethische Perspektiven I: Theorie*, ed. Karl Homann, Berlin, 9–30.
Homann, Karl 1994b. Homo oeconomicus und Dilemmastrukturen. In *Wirtschaftspolitik in offenen Volkswirtschaften*, ed. Hermann Sautter, Göttingen, 387–411.

---

[45]This idea has been developed in greater detail—and analogously to Böhm-Bawerk's famous essay "Macht oder ökonomisches Gesetz?"—in Homann (2009).

[46]See also Pies (2011).

Homann, Karl. 1997. Sinn und Grenze der ökonomischen Methode in der Wirtschaftsethik. In *Wirtschaftsethik und Moralökonomik*, eds. Detlef Aufderheide, Martin Dabrowski, Berlin, 11–42.
Homann, Karl. 2002. *Vorteile und Anreize. Zur Grundlegung einer Ethik der Zukunft*, ed. Christoph Luetge, Tübingen.
Homann, Karl. 2004. Das Problem des Sollens. In *Joachim Ritter zum Gedenken*, ed. Ulrich Dierse. Stuttgart, 67–87.
Homann, Karl. 2009. Moral oder ökonomisches Gesetz? In *Markt, Mensch und Freiheit*, ed. Markus Breuer, Philippe Mastronardi, and Bernhard Waxenberger, Bern, Stuttgart, 35–54.
Homann, Karl. 2010. Was bringt die Wirtschaftsethik für die Ethik?. In *Ethik und Gewinn! Ethische Perspektiven in den Wirtschaftswissenschaften*, eds. Anton Burger, Heinrich Kuhn, Oliver Kohmann. Eichstätt-Ingolstadt, 69–88.
Homann, Karl. 2014. *Sollen und Können: Grenzen und Bedingungen der Individualmoral*, Vienna.
Homann, Karl, Luetge, Christoph. 2004/2013. *Einführung in die Wirtschaftsethik*, 3rd ed., Münster.
Homann, Karl, Suchanek, Andreas. 2000/2005. *Ökonomik. Eine Einführung*, 2nd revised ed., Tübingen.
Hume, David. 1739–1740/2000. *A Treatise of Human Nature*, ed. David Fate Norton, Mary J. Norton, Oxford.
Jonas, Hans. 1979/1984/1985. The Imperative of Responsibility. In *Search of an Ethics for the Technological Age*, tr. Hans Jonas with Coll. David Herr, Chicago.
Kant, Immanuel. 1785/1786/2011. *Groundwork of the Metaphysics of Morals*, tr. Mary Gregor. ed. Jens Timmermann, Cambridge.
Kant, Immanuel. 1788/1996. *Critique of Practical Reason*, tr. Mary J. Gregor. In Immanuel Kant, Practical Philosophy, Cambridge.
Kant, Immanuel. 1902 ff. *Kants gesammelte Schriften*, ed. Königliche Preußische [later, Deutsche] Akademie der Wissenschaften, Berlin.
Kohlberg, Lawrence. 1981. *Essays on Moral Development, Volume I: The Philosophy of Moral Development. Moral Stages and the Idea of Justice*, San Francisco et al.
Lorenzen, Paul. 1989/1991. Philosophische Fundierungsprobleme einer Wirtschafts- und Unternehmensethik. In *Unternehmensethik*, eds. Horst Steinmann, Albert Löhr. 2nd ed., Stuttgart, 35–67.
Luhmann, Niklas. 1984/1995. *Social Systems*, tr. by John Bednarz, Jr., with Dirk Baecker, Stanford.
Mackie, John Leslie. 1977. *Ethics. Inventing Right and Wrong*. Harmondsworth.
Nassehi, Armin. 2010. *Mit dem Taxi durch die Gesellschaft*, Hamburg.
Nowak, Martin, and Roger Highfield. 2011. *Super-Cooperators: Altruism, Evolution and Why We Need Each Other to Succeed*. New York.
Ockenfels, Axel. 1999. *Fairneß. Ökonomische Theorie und experimentelle Evidenz: Reziprozität und Eigennutz*, Tübingen.
Palazzo, Guido, and Andreas Georg Scherer. 2006. Corporate legitimacy as deliberation: A communicative framework. *Journal of Business Ethics* 66: 71–88.
Pies, Ingo. 2011. *Die zwei Pathologien der Moderne – Eine ordonomische Argumentationsskizze*, Diskussionspapier Nr. 2011 – 14 des Lehrstuhls für Wirtschaftsethik an der Martin-Luther-Universität Halle-Wittenberg, Halle.
Pippin, Robert. 2005. *Die Verwirklichung der Freiheit. Der Idealismus als Diskurs der Moderne*, mit einem Vorwort von Axel Honneth und Hans Joas, Frankfurt/New York.
Ratzinger, Joseph Kardinal. 1986. Marktwirtschaft und Ethik. In *Stimmen der Kirche zur Wirtschaft*, ed. Lothar Roos, 2nd ed., Köln, 5–58.
Rawls, John. 1971. *A Theory of Justice*, Cambridge.
Rawls, John. 1993. *Political Liberalism*, New York.
Scherer, Andreas Georg. 2003. *Multinationale Unternehmen und Globalisierung: Zur Neuorientierung der Theorie der Multinationalen Unternehmung*, Heidelberg.

Scherer, Andreas Georg, and Guido Palazzo. 2007. Toward a political conception of corporate responsibility: Business and society seen from a habermasian perspective. *Academy of Management Review* 32: 1096–1120.

Scherer, Andreas Georg, Guido Palazzo, and Dirk Matten. 2014. The business firm as a political actor: A new theory of the firm for a globalized world. *Business and Society* 53(2): 143–156.

Schiller, Friedrich. 1786. Resignation, in *Thalia—Erster Band*, 64–69. Heft 2.

Schönwälder-Kuntze, Tatjana. 2013. The Figure of 'Rivalry' and its Function in Kant's Ethics. In Luetge 2013, Vol. 1, 355–384.

Sedláček, Tomáš. 2009/2011. *Economics of good and evil. The Quest for Economic Meaning from Gilgamesh to Wall Street*, Oxford.

Singer, Peter. 2009. *The Life You Can Save: How to do Your Part to End World Poverty*, New York.

Steinmann, Horst, Löhr, Albert. 1992/1994. *Grundlagen der Unternehmensethik*, 2nd revised and expanded ed., Stuttgart.

Tomasello, Michael. 2009. *Why We Cooperate*, Cambridge.

Ulrich, Peter. 1996. *Integrative Wirtschaftsethik: Grundlagen einer lebensdienlichen Ökonomie*, Bern, Stuttgart, Vienna.

Ulrich, Peter. 1997/2008. *Integrative Business Ethics: Foundations of a Civilized Market Economy*, Cambridge.

von Weizsäcker, Carl Friedrich. 1964. *The Relevance of Science*. London: Creation and Cosmogony.

Part II
Theoretical Foundations of Order Ethics—The Economic and Social Background

A Critique of Welfare Economics

Martin Leschke

Welfare Economics:

1 Old and New Welfare Economics

"Welfare Economics" is a branch of economics that evaluates well-being. It focuses on the allocation of resources and goods and how this affects individual and social welfare. Because different states (equilibria) may exist in an economy in terms of the allocation of resources and goods, welfare economics seeks the state that will create the highest overall level of social welfare.[1] Welfare economics uses the techniques of microeconomic theory, but also macroeconomic conclusions can be drawn.

The early Neoclassical approach of Welfare Economics, which was developed by Edgeworth, Sidgwick, Marshall, Pigou and others, assumes that the individual's utility can be "scale-measured" by observation. Or, in short words: Utility is cardinal, and the utility functions of the individuals can be aggregated. The aggregation of the individual utility is the so-called social welfare.

If we think of a very simple economy, where two goods (commodity x and commodity y) are produced, the efficient production possibility frontier or transformation line (MN-line) can be shown together with a social indifference curve (SI-curve), see Diagram 1.

The "Optimum" is point Z; here social welfare reaches its maximum. In mathematic terms the marginal rate of social welfare equals the marginal rate of

---

[1]For an overview see for example Boadway/Niel (1984) or Feldman/Serrano (2005).

M. Leschke (✉)
Department of Economics, Faculty of Law and Economics,
University of Bayreuth, 95440 Bayreuth, Germany
e-mail: martin.leschke@uni-bayreuth.de

© Springer International Publishing Switzerland 2016
C. Luetge and N. Mukerji (eds.), *Order Ethics: An Ethical Framework for the Social Market Economy*, DOI 10.1007/978-3-319-33151-5_4

Diagram 1 Social optimum

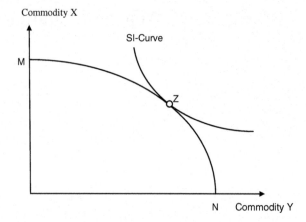

production (first differentiation of both curves). Social welfare above or to the right of our SI-curve is higher but there is no possibility to match it with the production line (MN-curve). This idea of constructing aggregate welfare functions and creating models in order to figure out the maximum welfare stems from Bergson (1938) and Samuelson (1947). The formula $W(U_1(x),...,U_n(x))$ is often considered a "Bergson-Samuelson social welfare function" with welfare "W", utility "U", and commodity "x".

The old welfare economics made interpersonal comparisons of utility and summarized individual utility, which was measured by a cardinal scale. This method was inspired by the philosopher Jeremy Bentham. In the fourth chapter of his book "An Introduction to the Principles of Morals and Legislation" (1789) Bentham introduces the method of calculating the values of pleasures and pains, a method, which is now known as the utility calculus. Bentham believed that the moral rightness or wrongness of an action is a function of the amount of pleasure or pain—the utility—which it produces. Bentham's principle of utility (called "maximum-happiness principle") regards "good" as something that produces the greatest amount of pleasure and the minimum amount of pain (the biggest difference between pleasure and pain). Thus it is the greatest happiness of the greatest number that is the measure of right and wrong.

New welfare economists (e.g., Wilfredo Pareto, John Hicks, Niclas Kaldor) distanced themselves from the idea of making social welfare judgements on the basis of interpersonal comparisons and aggregations of utility. They assume that individuals are different; so they have different scales of utility, they even may have different methods of calculating their own utility.

Political decisions based on the maximum-happiness principle may have a positive impact on the utility of several citizens on the one hand but may influence the utility of other individuals negatively on the other hand. Because of the impossibility to compare the utility of individuals it is hard to find an answer to the question "What should be done?", when individuals are affected by politics in a totally different way.

A Critique of Welfare Economics

In order to avoid such problems the Italian economist Pareto (1909, pp. 354, 617) formulated another criterion, nowadays known as the "Pareto criterion": Political action is socially desirable, if, and only if, everyone can be made better off, or at least some are made better off, while no one is made worse off. So it is each individual's perception of his or her own welfare function that counts. This principle is now a widely used principle to judge results and outcomes of economic modeling.

Given the Pareto criterion economists wondered whether the market system would lead to Pareto optimal outcomes. Mathematical oriented economists, such as Maurice Allais, Kenneth Arrow and Gérard Debreu, gave an answer by showing that any equilibrium of an ideal competitive market economy is Pareto efficient. This is the first fundamental theorem of welfare economics. In addition, it was shown that each Pareto efficient market equilibrium can be attained by appropriate initial redistributions. This is the second fundamental market theorem of welfare economics. Thus, a free ideal market economy will lead to

- efficient allocation of resources, and efficient production,
- efficient allocation of commodities and services, and efficient consumption.

This result can only be true if certain conditions are true:

- Rational actors are able to calculate and decide in a way that opportunity costs are minimized.
- Markets are ideal markets, and this means: There is no "market failure"!

Another result of welfare economics concerning not the whole market system, but a single market is that the sum of consumer surplus and producer surplus reaches it's maximum in the equilibrium point (see Diagram 2).

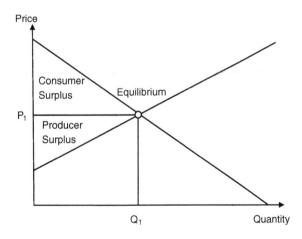

Diagram 2 Consumer and producer surplus

The consumer surplus is the difference between the amount that a consumer is willing to pay for a good or service and the amount that he is actually charged (the market price). The producer surplus is the difference between the amount that a firm is at least willing to supply a good for and the amount it is actually sold for. The total surplus is the highest in the equilibrium point. So again the ideal market guarantees an equilibrium, which is Pareto efficient.

2 Welfare Economics and Market Failure

From the viewpoint of economic welfare theory perfect markets lead to Pareto efficient results (perfect allocation of resources, goods and services). But in reality markets may not be perfect. As a result Pareto efficiency won't be reached. The economic welfare theory has identified certain market failures, such as[2]

- Externalities (Social costs or benefits, which arise outside the market and outside the contracts because property rights and regulations are not adequately specified—initial protagonist: Pigou 1920; Coase 1960);
- Merit and Demerit Goods (Merit demerit goods are commodities which are underestimated by the individuals, e.g. safety belts; whereas demerit goods are commodities which are overestimated, e.g. drugs. Reasons are incomplete information, inconsistent rate of time preference, irrational behavior—initial protagonist: Musgrave 1959);
- Public Goods (A public good is a good where individuals cannot be effectively excluded from use. As a result there is a free rider problem, so that no individual has an incentive to invest in such goods—initial protagonist: Samuelson 1954);
- Natural Monopoly (a natural monopoly is an industry where multiform production is more costly than production by one monopoly. The reason for that are high fixed cost which are sunk cost at the same time. Most of the network industries are natural monopolies, such as energy, railway—initial protagonist: John Stuart Mill 1848);
- Asymmetric Information (In contrast to neo-classical market economics, where all individuals are well-informed, there may be situations where one party has better information than the other. As a consequence this creates imbalanced power in transactions and my prevent individuals from finding agreements. Examples are principal agent problems in organizations or problems of adverse selection and moral hazard—initial protagonist: Stigler 1961);
- Economic Crises (The private sector consumption and investment may fall due to pessimistic expectation. As a result the economy may trickle down to a macro-economic equilibrium with high unemployment—initial protagonist: Keynes 1936);

---

[2]See for an overview Cowen (1988).

- Bounded Rationality (Especially followers of Behavioral Economics deny that individuals should be modeled as rational actors. Different kinds of irrationality or bounded rationality are proofed in many experiences. Such deviations from homo oeconomicus, may lead to decisions that are not Pareto efficient—initial protagonist: Simon 1947).

Welfare economics gives a diagnosis why Pareto optimality can't be reached in the market. This leads to a fundamental function of the state. Any time a market failure exists, there is a reason for possible government intervention into markets to improve the outcome. This means: Government is esteemed as a benevolent actor that is willing and able to find instruments (e.g. taxes, transfers, regulations) in order to repair market failure. If the Government is successful, the individuals will be better off. A Pareto superior situation will emerge. Basis of such governmental intervention is the following construction of thought. Given rational actors who know all opportunities and opportunity costs of all involved parties what kind of perfect contract would the parties conclude in order to eliminate market failure? Because the individuals are not able to conclude such perfect contracts the state as a "superior player" has to find solutions. These solutions can be regarded as a substitute for the "perfect contract".

3 Problems with the Pareto Criterion and Alternatives

Although Pareto was the first economist to find out an objective test of social welfare maximum on an individual basis, the criterion has been criticized: Firstly the Pareto criterion is a value judgement, of course, it is not a value free criterion, as one may think. Second there might be an infinite number of Paretian Optima. Which one should be chosen? Third nearly all policy proposals in reality cannot be judged with the help of this criterion, because there is at least one individual who is harmed by certain policy actions. If we took the Pareto criterion seriously for political action in reality, the status quo would remain forever (no matter how many people are disadvantaged).

In order to find a more realistic criterion for political action Nicholas Kaldor (1939) and John Hicks (1939) created a compensation criterion, now known as the Kaldor-Hicks Criterion. Using Kaldor-Hicks efficiency, an outcome (e.g. caused by political action) is more efficient if those individuals that are made better off could —in theory—compensate those individuals that are made worse off. So under the Kaldor-Hicks Criterion Pareto efficiency can be reached in theory but may not be reached in practice.

The Kaldor-Hicks criterion is widely applied in welfare economics. It builds the basis for cost-benefit analyses, and modern law and economics is almost entirely based on this criterion. Judges such as Richard Posner advocate using this standard to decide cases. In these fields all utility and all opportunity costs are rated in money, so that here Kaldor-Hicks efficiency is equal to what Posner calls "wealth maximization".

Although the Kaldor-Hicks criterion is widely accepted (similar to the Pareto criterion) it is confronted with several problems. First it neglects the problems of distribution completely. Why should those individuals who could be compensated in theory but are not in practice support policy action driven by Kaldor-Hicks efficiency? Second, the economist Tibor Scitovsky (1941) pointed out that this criterion is paradoxical and not consistent, because movement from social status A to social status B might be in tune with the Kaldor-Hicks criterion as well as movements back from B to A. This problem has led to the explicit "ruling out of the reversal possibility", known as the Scitovsky criterion.

Another problem with the Pareto as well as with the Kaldor-Hicks criterion is that political action is forward looking. So it is not based on reliable facts but on expected values, and expected values are associated with uncertainty (Knight, 1921). And under uncertainty it might be wise to be guided by a rule which avoids the worst cases. Such a rule is the Maxi-Min strategy. This strategy says that one should follow the policy which gives the best result of all the bad results possible, this is the maximum of the minima. Another strategy of risk avoidance is incorporated in the difference principle of the philosopher John Rawls (1971). He says that social and economic inequalities caused by policy action should lead to the greatest benefit of the least advantaged members of society. But this position has been criticized, too. Harsanyi (1975), for instance, argues that it is always rational to maximize expected utility when making a decision under uncertainty. But this, of course, cannot be rational for individuals who are risk averse. Thus, at least, it is more an empirical question than a question of logic whether one should choose according to the maxi-min rule or according to the maximum of the expected utility.

4 A Fundamental Critique of Welfare Economics

Another more fundamental critical point is that welfare theory assumes that a benevolent social planer introduces certain political action according to the Pareto criterion or any other criterion. Public Choice theory—the theory of public decision making—clearly shows in many models that politicians seek their own interest. So a benevolent social planner who has the only objective to maximize social welfare unfortunately does not exist in the real world.

As a solution one might think that for all policy action people should vote by majority rule. But even this democratic principle might cause problems. The economist Kenneth Arrow (1950) shows the impossibility of having an ideal voting structure that is reflective of specific fairness criteria, such as Pareto efficiency. This point should be emphasized by a simple example. Think of three groups A, B, C (with equal persons) which can choose between three different kinds of policies X,

Y, Z. The table below shows the preference ranking with 1 highest preference and 3 worst choice.

		Policy Alternatives		
		X	Y	Z
Groups	A	1	2	3
	B	2	3	1
	C	3	1	2

Given the choice between X and Y, the A group would vote for X, the B group would also vote for X and the C group would vote for Y. So policy plan X would win two-thirds of the votes and we could say that X is socially preferred to Y: X > Y. In a choice between policy action Y and policy action Z the A group would vote for Y, the B group would vote for Z and the C group would vote for Y. So Y is preferred to Z: Y > Z. Given these results we would expect that this would imply that X would be preferred to Z. But this does not hold. Consider a social choice by majority voting between X and Z. The A group would vote for X, the B group would vote for Z and the C group would vote for Z. So policy plan Z is socially preferred to plan X: Z > X. As a overall result we have: Z > X > Y > Z, so the social preferences are not transitive and not consistent.

Arrow (1950) proved mathematically that there is no method for constructing consistent social preferences from arbitrary individual preferences. There is no rule, majority voting or others, for establishing social preferences from arbitrary individual preferences. It is obvious that in great societies there are arbitrary individual preferences for sure. As a consequence political action must discriminate some individuals while the preferences of others are satisfied.

Given these findings traditional welfare economics faces at least four major problems: (1) The first can be named the technical problem of constructing a consistent non-discriminating social welfare function. (2) The second can be called the problem of ideal solutions, which means that welfare economics gives the unrealistic impression that all individuals are always perfectly rational and that markets work perfectly (in the absence of market failure) and that governments are able to cure market failures perfectly. (3) The third is the public choice problem, which means that welfare economics is based on the unrealistic assumption that politicians have the dominant preference to seek public interest. (4) And the fourth problem is that the neoclassical world of welfare economics is a world without morale—justice and fairness do not play a role in traditional welfare economics, but for decisions in reality they do.

These four problems cannot be solved within the tight corset of neoclassical welfare economics. Our thesis is that solutions can only come to the fore, if we change the perspective to a wider approach of institutional economics and institutional ethics.

5 A Change of Perspective

In the real world the political and economic system are working with different mechanisms of discrimination. The market price that emerges from supply and demand discriminates all individuals who do not have enough money (income) to buy the good or service. Election processes (based on a kind of majority rule) give only some politicians, parties, groups the power to govern; others are excluded and do have only the right to criticize.

And in many areas, in which individuals decide and act, those decisions are far away from being perfect. As a result of common ignorance and asymmetric information further discrimination and even situations of self harm may occur. Both the political systems and the market system do not work perfectly in reality.

But what are the advantages of the market system if an optimal allocation is not available in reality? The Austrian economist Friedrich August von Hayek has made the crucial point in his paper "The Use of Knowledge in Society" (1945, p. 519):

> "The peculiar character of the problem of a rational economic order is determined precisely by the fact that the knowledge of the circumstances of which we must make use never exists in concentrated or integrated form but solely as the dispersed bits of incomplete and frequently contradictory knowledge which all the separate individuals possess. The economic problem of society is thus not merely a problem of how to allocate 'given' resources —if 'given' is taken to mean given to a single mind which deliberately solves the problem set by this 'data'. It is rather a problem of how to secure the best use of resources known to any of the members of society, for ends whose relative importance only these individuals know. Or, to put it briefly, it is a problem of the utilization of knowledge which is not given to anyone in its totality."

From this point of view freedom and competition are fundamental pre-conditions, which force the entrepreneurs to search for better production procedures and for better goods and services permanently. So the market order is a form that gives the individuals strong incentives to be creative or, at least, to imitate improvements. The whole market system works as a discovery process. The technical and organizational progress improves the chances of the individuals to achieve their different goals.

But the market system can only fulfill this fundamental task if it is grounded on an adequate system of rules. The "rules of the game" determine whether the market process leads to patterns of results which are widely accepted or not. Accordingly, the question arises: What provides legitimacy to the institutional framework within which markets operate? Hayek (1960) emphasizes that "laws" should work as universal rules of just conduct (called "nomos") and should fulfill the following criteria (see also Daumann 2007):

- indifference (no discrimination) between individuals,
- temporal concretization (no limitation in time),
- local indifference (no dependence on local attributes).

Hayek notes that only such laws can be regarded as fair and can be widely agreed upon by the individuals. And the constitutional economist James Buchanan

(1977) stresses that the normative criterion for the market processes is a "voluntary agreement" upon the institutional framework of the market.

But such a criterion can only be hypothetical because in great societies it is not possible to achieve consensus upon the rules of the market game. But, if it is not possible to reach a voluntary agreement on the institutional framework of the market, what is a suitable criterion? Buchanan (1975) suggests that we should look at the process of choices of rules. If this (democratic) process is judged as fair by the individuals, the rules should be accepted. And when the rules are accepted, the market processes and results should be acceptable, too. This is the perspective of procedural justice. The results of the market cannot be evaluated and judged without the inclusion of the institutional framework.[3]

This side step away from welfare economics should give a hint that it is nearly impossible to provide normative statements for reality without taking into account the institutions of the market and of the political process. To ignore this is a blind spot of welfare economics.

6 Conclusion

Welfare economics tries to create efficiency-criteria for policy action and gives arguments that perfect markets work like perfect allocation machines and manage scarcity perfectly. In addition, welfare economics gives arguments that under certain circumstances markets will lead to sub-optimal results: these are the criteria of market failure. Some of these insights are essential for good policy (good governance), but they are not sufficient, because the crucial role of institutions is ignored. In reality the institutions determine the working properties of markets as well as those of politics. The institutions determine whether processes and outcomes are considered to be effective and fair, or not. If one shares this insight, one has to accept the conclusion, that welfare economics has to integrate the findings of institutional economics. This would entail a further advantage: It would open this research area for ethical questions.

References

Arrow, Kenneth. 1950. A difficulty in the concept of social welfare. *Journal of Political Economy* 58: 328–346.
Bentham, Jeremy. 1789. *An introduction to the principles of morals and legislation*. Oxford.
Bergson, Abram. 1938. A reformulation of certain aspects of welfare economics. *Quarterly Journal of Economics* 52: 310–334.
Broadway, Robin W./Bruce Niel. 1984. *Welfare economics*. Oxford.

---

[3]This fundamental finding is in tune with the results of John Rawls „Theory of Justice".

Buchanan, James M. 1975. *The limits of liberty: Between anarchy and leviathan*. Chicago.
Buchanan, James M. 1977. *Freedom in constitutional contract*. College Station.
Cowen, Tyler. 1988. *The theory of market failure: A critical examination*. Fairfax.
Daumann, Frank. 2007. Evolution and the rule of law. Hayek's concept of liberal order reconcidered. *Journal of Libertarian Studies* 21: 123–150.
Feldman, Allan M./Roberto Serrano. 2005. *Welfare economics and social choice theory*. Berlin.
Harsanyi, John C. 1975. Can the maximin principle serve as a basis for morality? A critique of John Rawls's theory. *American Political Science Review* 69: 594–606.
Hayek, Friedrich A. 1945. "The use of knowledge in society". *American Economic Review* XXXV: 519–530.
Hayek, Friedrich A. 1960. *The constitution of liberty*. Chicago.
Hicks, John. 1939. The foundations of welfare economics. *Economic Journal* 49: 696–712.
Kaldor, Nicholas. 1939. Welfare propositions in economics and interpersonal comparisons of utility. *Economic Journal* 49: 549–552.
Keynes, John Maynard. 1936. *The general theory of employment*. London: Interest and Money.
Knight, Frank. 1921. *Uncertainty, and profit*. Mifflin-Boston-New York.
Mill, John Stuart. 1848. *Principles of political economy*. London.
Musgrave, Richard A. 1959. *The theory of public finance: A study in public economy*. New York.
Pareto, Vilfredo. 1909. *Manuel d'Economie Politique*. Paris.
Pigou, Athur Cecil. 1912. *Wealth and welfare*. London.
Pigou, Athur Cecil. 1920. *The economics of welfare*. London.
Rawls, John. 1971. *A theory of justice*. Cambridge.
Samuelson, Paul. 1947. *Foundations of economic analysis*. Cambridge.
Samuelson, Paul A. 1954. The pure theory of public expenditure. *Review of Economics and Statistics* 36: 387–389.
Scitovsky, Tibor. 1941. A note on welfare propositions in economics. *Review of Economic Studies* 9: 77–88.
Simon, Herbert A. 1947. *Administrative behavior: A study of decision-making processes in administrative organization*. New York.
Stigler, George. 1961. The economics of information. *Journal of Political Economy* 69: 213–225.

Order Ethics—An Experimental Perspective

Hannes Rusch and Matthias Uhl

Abstract In this chapter, we present supporting arguments for the claim that Order Ethics is a school of thought within ethics which is especially open to empirical evidence. With its focus on order frameworks, i.e., incentive structures, Order Ethical advice automatically raises questions on implementability, efficacy, and efficiency of such recommended institutions, all of which are empirical questions to a good extent. We illustrate our arguments by presenting a small selection of experiments from economics that we consider highly informative for Order Ethics. These experiments vary in their details but share one common theme: individual decision-making and its aggregate results are tested against the background of incentive structures. In particular, these studies provide first insights on how unregulated markets influence moral behaviour over time, how trial-and-error experiences convince subjects to migrate to more efficient institutions, and how default rules can influence fundamental choices of people. We argue that Order Ethics, for which implementability of any moral claim is an essential requirement, can largely benefit from the use of such experimental methods. Finally, we suggest the provision of self-commitment devices as one example of smart policy design that avoids paternalistic intrusions into individual liberty.

1 Introduction

Today, Order Ethics has a long standing tradition within moral philosophy (see, e.g., Luetge 2012). Its central notion is that it is not individual moral failure which leads to morally detrimental decisions and actions in modern market economies.

H. Rusch (✉)
Experimental and Applied Psychology, VU Amsterdam, Van de Boechorststraat 1, 1081 BT Amsterdam, The Netherlands
e-mail: hannes.rusch@tum.de

H. Rusch · M. Uhl
Chair of Business Ethics, TU München, Arcisstrasse 21, 80333 Munich, Germany
e-mail: m.uhl@tum.de

© Springer International Publishing Switzerland 2016
C. Luetge and N. Mukerji (eds.), *Order Ethics: An Ethical Framework for the Social Market Economy*, DOI 10.1007/978-3-319-33151-5_5

Rather, the incentive structures of modern economies that are characterized by anonymous large-scale societies force morally neutral, or even virtuous, individuals to behave in a morally disadvantageous way. Order Ethics holds that individuals in an unregulated market find themselves in a Prisoner's Dilemma situation: Morally sound individual decisions could lead to a morally efficient outcome, i.e., to a situation in which the shared moral standards of all participants are upheld. Usually, morally sound decisions simultaneously imply a competitive disadvantage. It is, e.g., in the best interest of competing firms to abstain from corruptive actions. If firms try to outbid their competitors' bribes, an arms race emerges where resources are wasted that could have been allocated to more efficient uses. Abstaining from corruptive actions unilaterally, however, results in a competitive disadvantage if everybody else engages in these actions. This, of course, is foreseen by all market participants, which in consequence leads to a morally inefficient competitive equilibrium in the market. Therefore, individual rationality forces any given firm to engage in preventive counter-defection, i.e., in corruptive actions. An individually rational decision therefore leads into a rationality trap in the aggregate.

Order Ethics states that the preferable way of solving this dilemma is not to appeal to individual decision makers to act against their interest by behaving morally. Rather, we should try to change the general incentive structure on the respective markets, i.e., we should implement regulations. Once, e.g., firms are required to implement environmental standards before being allowed to enter a market, and once the compliance with these standards is effectively enforced, no one in this market has an incentive to lower the standard.

Up to now, Order Ethics has largely argued on the basis of philosophical reflections on more general economic and sociological observations. Its arguments have been substantiated with historical and case examples. With the rising of Experimental and Behavioural Economics we are now in the fortunate position to be able to test the general ideas of Order Ethics more rigorously. In this chapter, we will review some exemplary empirical studies from economics which directly test, and support, some of the claims made by Order Ethicists. We then critically discuss the role of empirical observations in Order Ethics more generally. Finally, with respect to the current debate on restrictive measures in consumer policy, we propose that experiments in Order Ethics might yield partial solutions to the problem of having to legitimize interventions into individual freedom of choice in order to raise moral standards for all. This is a problem which Order Ethics is frequently confronted with.

2 Exemplary Experiments of Order Ethical Relevance

2.1 *Markets and Morals*

In a recent study, Falk and Szech (2013) tested one of the central assumptions of Order Ethical argumentation. They claim to have shown that the exposition of ordinary people to the market mechanism of bargaining over prices indeed lowers individual moral standards, or, at least, facilitates morally disadvantageous decisions by individuals. The basic logic of their experiment was this: In a first treatment they endowed one individual with a living mouse. They then offered money to the subject. If the subject accepted the offer, the mouse was killed and the subject was paid the respective amount. The mechanism Falk and Szech used to elicit individuals' prices for a mouse's life was incentive compatible. Thus, subjects had no incentive to state prices higher or lower than the actual amount of money for which they would be willing to accept a mouse's death as a consequence of their decision. Falk and Szech then compared the average base price for a mouse's life elicited in the first treatment to two other treatments in which offers were not made by the experimenter, but rather by other subjects. Their main finding was that when subjects bargained amongst themselves, the price of a mouse's life was significantly lower than in the first treatment.

Falk and Szech argue that this result is due to the effect of being able to share the guilt of an immoral action when decisions are not made by one individual but are the result of collective negotiations, in this case bargaining over prices. In their view, two factors might lead to this result: (i) The subject accepting the low price for a mouse's life can justify its morally poor decision by arguing that it was, at least partially, also the fault of the other subject(s) who offered such low prices; (ii) Through the price negotiations the target individual is also informed about the moral standards of its interaction partners and might adjust its own standard to the perceived lower standard of the group. In combination, Falk and Szech argue, these two factors cause an 'erosion of moral values' when decisions are made collectively through a market mechanism instead of individually. While it has been argued that this conclusion reaches way too far (e.g., Luetge and Rusch 2013; Breyer and Weimann 2015), and while we have to wait for replications of their observations in other controlled studies, Falk and Szech's experiment is certainly seminal for the study of the interaction of market mechanisms and moral standards. As things stand, their findings yield strong support for the Order Ethical idea that 'immoral' decisions can be caused by the interaction of 'moral' individuals in a market, at least if the specific ways in which Falk and Szech operationalized the concepts of 'moral decisions' and 'markets' is accepted as yielding a representative model situation.

2.2 The Competitive Advantage of Sanctioning Institutions

While the result obtained by Falk and Szech has a somewhat pessimistic appeal with respect to morality in modern market economies, experimental economists have also been able to show that individual decisions can lead to morally advantageous outcomes.

Gürerk et al. (2006) have performed an experiment which analyzes the fundamental determinants of human cooperation in an experimental setting. Individuals play a public goods game with 30 rounds in which each player is endowed with 20 monetary units. In each round, every player may contribute any amount between 0 and 20 units to the public good. Each individual benefits equally from the public good, regardless of its own contribution. Since every monetary unit that is not invested into the public good is transferred to the respective player's private account, it is always in the best interest of any given player to free ride on the contributions of the others as long as the marginal per capita return of one unit invested into the public good is smaller than one, which was the case in Gürerk et al.'s design. In this case, individual interest and collective interest are opposed, which is why the situation constitutes a social dilemma. Gürerk et al.'s innovation is to let players self-select into two institutional variants of this public goods game which differ by the order framework that they employ.

Each repetition of the game is characterized by three stages. In a preliminary stage, players choose between a sanctioning institution and a sanction-free institution. In the main stage, the actual public goods game is played, i.e., the voluntary contribution is chosen. The final stage is a sanctioning stage in which those players who have self-selected into the sanctioning institution may reward or punish other players within the same institution at a cost to themselves. At the end of each round subjects receive detailed information about all other subjects in both institutions.

The experimental results show that only one third of subjects choose the sanctioning institution in the first round of the game. Astonishingly, though, in the final round more than 90 % of all subjects select into this institution, making in the clear winner in the competition with the sanction-free institution. Gürerk et al. conclude that there exists a tendency to punish norm violators after migrating from the sanction-free institution to the sanctioning institution. The thus generated cooperative culture even attracts formerly noncooperative subjects to move to the sanctioning institution where cooperation can be stabilized at a high level (Gürerk et al. 2006, 312). Note that actual punishment is eventually hardly necessary once this stabilization is achieved. The background presence of the threat suffices. While numerous experiments have shown that sanctioning institutions are able to stabilize cooperation, it still is an open and much discussed question if they do so efficiently. Some authors argue that the welfare loss caused by the costs of punishment, i.e., the money spent by the punishers and the money lost by the punished, outweighs the benefits of stable cooperation (e.g., Dreber et al. 2008). However, other authors hold that this finding is merely an artefact of artificially short laboratory experiments which do not capture the long-term benefits of sanctioning institutions

(Gächter et al. 2008). They concede that sanctioning institutions require some time at the beginning to establish cooperation and that punishment costs are high in this first phase. In the longer run, however, they argue, these costs decrease significantly and amortize at some point after which the sanctioning institutions can play out their full advantage (e.g., Frey and Rusch 2012).

The experiment by Gürerk et al., nevertheless, demonstrates in a convincing way that the institutional design, i.e., the order framework, is essential in overcoming a social dilemma. It is particularly interesting to see that there is initially a general reluctance to enter the sanctioning institution. Subjects in the sanction-free institution can only be convinced to migrate to the sanctioning institution by experiencing the competitive success of the latter through the observation of the outcomes of its population. This finding supports another claim of Order Ethics, namely that the institutional solution to a social dilemma is sometimes counter-intuitive. Our ethical categories lag behind rapid economic developments and are therefore often ill-adapted when applied to the challenges of modern societies. The laboratory enables us to test the effectiveness of institutions rather than their mere appeal before they are implemented on a large scale. Round-based experiments simulate evolutionary processes in fast motion and thus allow for the migration between competing order frameworks and the real-time experience of their consequences.

2.3 The Power of Default Rules

Institutions sometimes work in subtle ways and incentives need not be of monetary nature. Behavioural economics has identified a multitude of deviations from the predictions of standard decision theory that are either negatively considered as biases or positively as heuristics. Institutions can systematically exploit these deviations to guide subjects' behaviour in a certain direction.

Madrian and Shea (2001) analyse the results of a natural field experiment on individual savings behaviour. The authors investigate the enrolment in a voluntary savings plan of a large U.S. corporation before and after a change of the default option. In the reference situation, before the plan change, employees had to explicitly opt in for participation. After the plan change, all employees were automatically enrolled in the savings plan and had to explicitly opt out of it. When controlling for tenure, the authors find that about 37 % of subjects were enrolled before the switch of the default rule, while about 86 % participated after the switch (Madrian and Shea 2001, 1159). Furthermore, the default contribution rate suggested by the savings plan as well as the default investment allocation that the company defined for automatic enrolment was chosen by a substantial fraction of employees who were hired after the plan change. Before the plan change hardly anybody chose these specifications (Madrian and Shea 2001). The results show that a substantial fraction of employees after the change of the default rule become passive savers that remain in the status quo that the policy makers within the company have selected for them. The authors ascribe the significant raise of participation to the inertia of the employees and to the "power of suggestion" that is exercised by defaults.

Johnson and Goldstein (2003) report similar evidence from an online experiment on organ donations. In a survey, respondents were asked whether they would be willing to donate organs under three treatment conditions. In the "opt-in" treatment, they were told to imagine that they had moved to a state in which the default was not to be an organ donor. Subjects were asked whether they would confirm or change this status. The "opt-out" treatment was identical, except for the default which was to be an organ donor. In the "neutral" treatment there was no default. The differences between the fractions of subjects who answered that they would be willing to be organ donors were substantial. While only 42 % of subjects agreed to be donors in the "opt-in" treatment, this fraction rose to 82 % in the "opt-out" treatment. The "neutral" treatment induced a fraction of 79 %. This last result shows that the majority of US-Americans has a general preference for organ donation. Apparently, inertia keeps many of these subjects from voting for donation if the no-action default is not being a donor.

It is surprising that decisions as important as old-age provision or the self-determination over one's own body are prone to default rules that can be changed with negligible effort. It is yet unclear what behavioural mechanisms cause subjects' stickiness to default rules (for potential theoretical causes see, e.g., Smith et al. 2013). In any case, the reported evidence is highly relevant for Order Ethics. It suggests that choices which are morally strongly loaded and for which we would have presumed that people have clear and pretty strict preferences may be altered by the "power of suggestion".

3 The Methodological Function of Experiments in Order Ethics

If ethicists state a moral obligation of subjects to behave in a certain morally responsible manner, they often seem to forget that "ought implies can" (Kant 1794/ 2004). It is easy to appeal to virtues and it usually harvests the applause of the audience. Order Ethics, however, insists on the implementability of moral postulates. Taking the implementability into account is seen as an ethical enterprise itself. Given the structurally different problems of modern societies that differ substantially from the moral problems of our ancestors from whom we inherited our moral intuitions, Order Ethics reminds us that a noble conscience can never compensate for a well-designed institution. Experimental evidence reminds us of this fact. Few defectors are sufficient for the collapse of cooperation and the repetition of many rounds in anonymous experimental settings often leads to the erosion of individual virtues and to the convergence to a selfish Nash equilibrium. But this is not the end of the story. As the experiments quoted above have demonstrated, order frameworks which can essentially be characterized as incentive schemes, have substantial effects on human behaviour. Lacking or ill-adjusted order frameworks may aggravate or even create problems, while adequately designed ones can help to overcome social dilemmas. Experimental economics provides the necessary toolbox to study human behaviour under different incentive schemes and to understand which ones work and which ones do not. The reservations against some institutions may be so strong, that these institutions are not accepted, even though they achieve, for instance, Pareto-efficient outcomes. Round-based experiments allow us to understand whether these reservations are robust to experience. Framing experiments, i.e., such experiments that vary the wording of a situation without changing its payoff structure, allow us to understand whether the reservations against some institutions are merely caused by semantics. As the discussion on deviations from the predictions of standard decision theory, particularly on inertia, has shown, there is more that matters than monetary incentives alone when one considers the order of an economy. In this respect, the findings of behavioural experiments can inform Order Ethics.

The method of experimental economics is different from the method of experimental psychology (Hertwig and Ortmann 2001). Although experimental psychology certainly provides relevant and inspiring findings, we argue that experimental economics is particularly fruitful for Order Ethics. As opposed to experimental psychologists, experimental economists systematically incentivize subjects by monetary payoffs that depend on their choices and on the choices of their interaction partners. Incentivization is usually seen as a key characteristic of experimental economics (see, e.g., Bardsley et al. 2008). One reason for this is to make subjects really think about what they do. If faulty decisions are punished by lower payoffs, more cognitive effort is invested. Furthermore, through incentivization, subjects are forced "to put their money where their mouth is". A subject is not asked to imagine that she had a monetary endowment and to state which fraction she would give to an anonymous stranger. She is actually provided with a monetary endowment and asked to state the allocation between herself and an anonymous stranger. Since the implementability of moral claims is at the core of Order Ethics, the use of incentive structures that resemble the conditions under which the claim would have to unfold becomes crucial. A second key characteristic of experimental economics is that subjects are not deceived. Apart from the moral requirement of truth telling, this is the only way to assure that subjects are not trying to spot the "true" purpose of the experiment. A set of rules should be transparent and common knowledge. Only through the absence of deception and through the sustainable credibility of the experimenter it can be guaranteed that subjects are actually reacting to the incentive structures that the experimenter is imposing on them.

Just like Order Ethics, experimental economics is dealing with issues of implementation. Its findings constantly remind us that institutions play a huge role for human behaviour. It also offers us a scientific playground to test the key characteristics of order frameworks and to close the barn before the horse has escaped. In economic settings that are dominated by the unintended consequences of intentional actions, experiments are of tremendous value. Oullier (2013) outlines the usefulness of controlled experiments for policy makers and praises the British government as leading the way by having installed a Behavioural Insights Team (BIT) to systematically engage in such research. He emphasizes that one would not accept the launch of a new drug on the market before severe clinical testing is performed. Failed policies that have wasted huge amounts of tax money demonstrate that there is a lack of experimental testing in policy making. Order Ethics should therefore systematically use the experimental method.

4 The Problem Solving Potential of Experimental (Order) Ethics

While the above mentioned study by Falk and Szech (2013) has shown that experiments can help us to identify detrimental effects of economic institutions on morally relevant decision making, the other experimental studies also demonstrate that Experimental Ethics offers a constructive alternative to mere moral appraisals. Once we have understood the moral consequences of the institutions in question, we can use laboratory and field experiments to test for at least three things: (i) Implementability: Which of the institutional alternatives is accepted (best) by individuals? (ii) Efficacy and incentive compatibility: Do institutions actually foster the behaviour which ethicists hope they will? (iii) Efficiency: Which of the available variants of an institutional design brings about the targeted effects at the lowest cost?

In our view, the most noticeable benefit of being able to experiment with different institutional designs, however, is that paternalistic intrusions into individual freedom of choice can be avoided by smart institutional designs. There has been a lively debate on how to justify such measures, particularly in consumer and health policy, recently. The tax on fat which Denmark introduced in 2011 can serve as an example. The international debate on how to motivate more people to organ donation is another one. Frequently, political deciders justify their measures simply as being 'for the good of us all'. The increasing reluctance of citizens to accept many of such imposed measures and their frequent failure, however, shows that changes to order frameworks need to be made with greater cautiousness. We hold particularly the experiment conducted by Gürerk et al. (2006) to be seminal in this respect, because these colleagues were able to show that, given a free choice, individuals actually do self-select into the morally beneficial institutions, once they have experienced the disadvantages of the alternatives. This way of introducing new institutional designs completely solves the problem of having to justify limitations to individual freedom brought about by certain institutions: Once individuals are given the opportunity to freely decide which institution they would like to be subjected to, i.e., to self-commit to certain behaviours, there is no need to justify the implementation of these institutions anymore, simply because they are offered to, and not forced upon, free people.

Thus, we think that Experimental Ethics offers a chance to explore the conditions under which subjects are ready to self-select into morally (more) beneficial order frameworks. We are aware, however, that there certainly are problems which cannot be solved by letting people choose freely between institutional alternatives. You cannot, e.g., let people freely decide whether they would like to pay a certain tax or not. In these cases, however, the ethicist's laboratory is of great value, too. Take Denmark's fat tax as an example: A number of studies have shown that imposing higher prices for fat food has little effect on fat calorie intake (see, e.g., Ellison et al. 2013). Better consumer information through labels on products and menus seems to have stronger effects while simultaneously leaving free choice to consumers. One interesting next step would be offering individuals a binding mechanism through which they can self-commit to a healthy diet. One might think of a field experiment like the following. Take a cafeteria in which you pay by chip card. Offer two different cards to the guests, a regular one and a 'green' one. The green card offers a self-commitment device to guests, e.g., by making fat and sweet food more expensive when bought using the green card or even by disabling green card users from buying such food. It would be very interesting to see how this simple measure affects eating behaviour in that cafeteria. At the same time, such a mechanism, if successful, would sidestep the problem of intervening in the guests' freedom of choice.

Several experiments in such diverse contexts as overspending (Ashraf et al. 2006), procrastination of writing course works (Ariely and Wertenbroch 2002), or postponing to get up (Uhl 2011) have shown that a substantial fraction of subjects uses saliently available self-commitment devices to defeat their self-considered weaknesses. From the perspective of a liberal policy maker this sophistication should be acknowledged before subjects are forced through paternalistic policies to behave in their supposedly own best interest. The provision of salient self-commitment devices would be a smarter tool of policy design.

While the 'green card' study outlined above, of course, is just a rough sketch of an Order Ethical experiment, it suffices to highlight the benefits of experimenting in ethics, again. (i) Implementability: The experiment would show if, and which, guests accept the offered self-commitment device. (ii) Efficacy: It would be easily possible to monitor eating behaviour before and after the introduction of the second chip card, yielding quantitative data on the effectiveness of the measure. Additionally, unforeseen biases, e.g., short-time shifts in preferences, could be discovered in such an experiment, allowing ethicists to readjust the characteristics of the mechanisms tested. (iii) Efficiency: Different variants of the mechanism could be tested in parallel in order to find out which one achieves best results at lowest cost.

It is certainly true that experimenting in ethics, just like everywhere else, is tedious and time-consuming and cannot yield infallible results. It is also true that experimental results alone offer no solutions to philosophical questions, e.g., on the nature of 'values' (Sneddon 2009) or 'good reasons' (Stein 1996) or the like. Nevertheless, there is a systematic place for experimenting in ethics, we think. As already mentioned above, even the lowest moral standard can only be upheld if it does not require people to do the impossible, i.e., to act beyond their possibilities. As it is, at least to a good deal, an empirical question where the limits of these possibilities exactly lie, particularly because individual behaviour can lead to quite unexpected results in the aggregate (Schelling 2006), and as exploring the realm of the these possibilities necessarily requires testing, there is much room for elaborate experimental work in ethics (see, e.g., Luetge et al. 2014). As of today, this claim is the subject of a lively and arduous debate (e.g., Knobe and Nichols 2008). However, a comparison of the current situation in ethics with historic developments in other disciplines, particularly psychology and economics, we think, offers reasons for being optimistic that the reluctance of ethicists to experimental methods will cease over time (see Rusch 2014). Even psychology, a discipline which started out employing a purely introspective arm chair methodology, has become an empirical science to a large extent now. While we are very reluctant to advocate a turn to exclusively empirical methods in ethics, we do think that experimenting will become one important tool, among various others, for ethicists. For Order Ethicists in particular.

5 Conclusions and Outlook

There are schools of thought within ethics which are especially open to empirical evidence, and there are others which are not. It has been argued elsewhere that evolutionary ethics is one of the former schools (Rusch et al. 2014). In this chapter, we hope to have presented supporting arguments for the claim that Order Ethics is another one of these. With its focus on order frameworks, i.e., incentive structures, Order Ethical advice automatically also raises questions on implementability, efficacy, and efficiency of such recommended institutions. All of these questions are open to experimental testing. One might be even tempted to state that putting them to the test in the laboratory before trying them out on whole societies is indispensable and morally imperative, as doing so allows us to spot unthought-of weaknesses in institutional designs at low cost.

In this chapter, we have presented only a small selection of experiments that we consider as highly informative for Order Ethics. These experiments vary in their details but share one common theme: They study individual decision-making and its aggregate results on the background of incentive structures. In particular, these studies help us to understand how unregulated markets influence moral behaviour over time, how trial-and-error experiences convince subjects to migrate to more efficient institutions, and how default rules can influence fundamental choices of people. We have argued that Order Ethics, for which implementability of any moral claim is an essential requirement, can largely benefit from the use of experimental methods. Controlled experimental testing prevents policy makers at the macro and meso level of an economy from costly errors caused by the premature introduction of problematic institutions. This is particularly important in a world where the collective consequences of individual actions, economic as well as moral ones, are often counter-intuitive. Experimental economics with its emphasis on incentives and transparency is particularly fruitful in this regard. We have presented the provision of self-commitment devices as one example of smart policy design that avoids paternalistic intrusions into individual liberty.

In his social philosophy Popper (1945/1966) advised careful and cautious step-by-step policy making. He saw one of the strongest benefits of democratic states in the revocability of all policy changes, should they turn out to be detrimental. We think that his ideal of piecemeal social engineering can, and should, be fruitfully complemented by ethical experimenting, today.

To frame it metaphorically: Sometimes it takes an experiment to find out that airplanes with holes in their wings won't fly; and sometimes it takes an experiment to find out that institutions with the wrong incentives won't fly either.

References

Ashraf, Nava, Dean Karlan, and Wesley Yin. 2006. *The Quarterly Journal of Economics* 121: 635–672. doi:10.1162/qjec.2006.121.2.635.

Ariely, Dan, and Klaus Wertenbroch. 2002. Procrastination, deadlines, and performance: self-control by precommitment. *Psychological Science* 13: 219–224.

Bardsley, Nicholas, Robin Cubitt, Peter Moffatt, Graham Loomes, Chris Starmer, and Robert Sugden. 2008. Princeton, NJ: Princeton University Press.

Breyer, Friedrich, and Joachim Weimann. 2015. Of morals, markets and mice: Be careful drawing policy conclusions from experimental findings! *European Journal of Political Economy*. Available online at http://www.sciencedirect.com/science/journal/aip/01762680.

Dreber, Anna, David G. Rand, Drew Fudenberg, and Martin A. Nowak. 2008. Winners don't punish. *Nature* 452: 348–351. doi:10.1038/nature06723.

Ellison, Brenna, Jayson L. Lusk, and David Davis. 2013. Looking at the label and beyond: the effects of calorie labels, health consciousness, and demographics on caloric intake in restaurants. *International Journal of Behavioral Nutrition and Physical Activity* 10: 21. doi:10.1186/1479-5868-10-21.

Falk, Armin, and Nora Szech. 2013. Morals and Markets. *Science* 340: 707–711. doi:10.1126/science.1231566.

Frey, Ulrich J., and Hannes Rusch. 2012. An evolutionary perspective on the long-term efficiency of costly punishment. *Biology and Philosophy* 27: 811–831. doi:10.1007/s10539-012-9327-1.

Gächter, Simon, Elke Renner, and Martin Sefton. 2008. The long-run benefits of punishment. *Science* 322: 1510. doi:10.1126/science.1164744.

Gürerk, Özgür, Bernd Irlenbusch, and Bettina Rockenbach. 2006. The competitive advantage of sanctioning institutions. *Science* 312: 108–111. doi:10.1126/science.1123633.

Hertwig, Ralph, and Andreas Ortmann. 2001. Experimental practices in economics: A methodological challenge for psychologists? *Behavioral and Brain Sciences* 24: 383–451.

Johnson, Eric J., and Daniel Goldstein. 2003. Do defaults save lives? *Science* 302: 1338–1339.

Kant, Immanuel. 2004. *Die religion innerhalb der Grenzen der bloßen Vernunft*. Hamburg: Meiner.

Knobe, Joshua, and Shaun Nichols (eds.). 2008. *Experimental philosophy*. Oxford: Oxford University Press.

Luetge, Christoph. 2012. Fundamentals of Order Ethics: Law, business ethics and the financial crisis. *Archiv für Rechts- und Sozialphilosophie Beihefte* 130: 11–21.

Luetge, Christoph, and Hannes Rusch. 2013. The systematic place of morals in markets. *Science* 341: 714. doi:10.1126/science.341.6147.714-a.

Luetge, Christoph, Hannes Rusch, and Matthias Uhl (eds.). 2014. *Experimental ethics*. Basingstoke: Palgrave Macmillan.

Madrian, Brigitte C., and Dennis F. Shea. 2001. The power of suggestion: Inertia in 401(k) participation and savings behavior. *The Quarterly Journal of Economics* 116: 1149–1187.

Oullier, Olivier. 2013. Behavioural insights are vital to policy-making. *Nature* 501: 462–463.

Popper, Karl R. 1966. The open society and its enemies. *The spell of Plato*, 5th edn, vol. 1. Princeton, NJ: Princeton University Press.

Rusch, Hannes. 2014. Philosophy as the behaviorist views it? In *Experimental ethics*, ed. Christoph Luetge, Hannes Rusch, and Matthias Uhl. Basingstoke: Palgrave Macmillan.

Rusch, Hannes, Christoph Luetge, and Eckart Voland. 2014. Experimentelle und Evolutionäre Ethik: Eine neue Synthese in der Moralphilosophie? In *Bereichsethiken im interdisziplinären Dialog*, ed. Matthias Maring, 163–179. Karlsruhe, Baden: KIT Scientific Publishing.

Schelling, Thomas C. 2006. *Micromotives and macrobehaviour*. New York: W.W Norton & Co.

Smith, N.Craig, Daniel G. Goldstein, and Eric J. Johnson. 2013. Choice without awareness: Ethical and policy implications of defaults. *Journal of Public Policy and Marketing* 32(2): 159–172.

Sneddon, Andrew. 2009. Normative ethics and the prospects of an empirical contribution to assessment of moral disagreement and moral realism. *The Journal of Value Inquiry* 43: 447–455. doi:10.1007/s10790-009-9164-x.

Stein, Edward. 1996. Without good reason. *The rationality debate in philosophy and cognitive science*. Oxford, New York: Oxford University Press.

Uhl, Matthias. 2011. Do self-committers mind other-imposed commitment? An experiment on weak paternalism. *Rationality, Markets, and Morals* 2: 13–34.

Order Ethics and Situationist Psychology

Michael von Grundherr

1 Introduction

We tend to belief that people lie because they are dishonest or that they give money to the poor because they are generous. So-called situationists hold that these explanations are unjustified and rely on a "fundamental attribution error" (Harman 1999; Ross 1977). Based on a series of experiments, they argue that counter to intuitions situations are important determinants of human behaviour, while individual traits are less influential.

At first glance, order ethics looks like the normative cousin of situationism. It argues that moral demands must be backed by institutions, which ensure that moral rule-followers are not exploited by free riders. In other words: moral behaviour can only be demanded in certain types of (institutionally shaped) situations. Social psychology can indeed provide empirical backup for order ethics, or so I will argue.

In the course of this argument it will turn out that social psychology can also help to dispel a common misconception about order ethics. Order ethics needs not see anticipation of punishment by *external* institutions as the psychological motive for moral action. Instead, it can regard the term "institution" as a proxy for a complex interplay between internal self-regulation, social institutions and internalised moral motives. I will give a rough sketch of these mechanisms and argue that understanding them is vital for applied order ethics and institutional design.

M. von Grundherr (✉)
Research Center for Neurophilosophy and Ethics of Neuroscience,
LMU Munich, Munich, Germany
e-mail: mvg@lrz.uni-muenchen.de

2 The Need for Institutions: Normative and Psychological Arguments

A classical argument for order ethics starts with a contractarian consideration. Moral rules and corresponding sanctions are legitimate only if every member of a society would assent to them. (Luetge 2013; von Grundherr 2007, 43 ff.) If moral rules impose unacceptably high burdens on some individuals, these people would not consent and consequently the rules are not legitimate. (cf. Gaus 2011, 161–162, 315ff.) A moral rule and the corresponding sanctions imply unacceptably high burdens if they are not compatible with the rational pursuit of one's non-moral preferences in the long run.[1]

Contractarianism provides a hypothetical procedure to test the acceptability of moral rules and sanctions. It assumes a morality free state of nature and asks to which scheme of moral rules and rule enforcement someone who rationally pursues his or her non-moral preferences would assent. In this state of nature, people face a central problem: cooperation does not get off the ground. Imagine we agree to help each other build our houses. We do this because you are a skilled carpenter and I am a good bricklayer. We both fare better if I lay all the bricks for both houses and you carpenter both roof structures. But if I fulfil my part of the contract, you fare even better if you defect and build only your roof structure, leaving me with a roofless house. And if I defect and do not come to your building site to lay the bricks, you'd better not help me anyway. We both reason this way and we will both defect, although originally we had a strong interest in cooperation.

This type of cooperation dilemma is pervasive. Contracts, division of labour or cooperation that requires specific investments all imply mutual dependence and share the same structure. If all moral preferences are screened out, such cases have the same structure as the house-building case above. Refusing to cooperate is the rational strategy for all participants. In terms of game theory, all these situations are one-shot prisoners' dilemmas.

At this point, the contractarian thought experiment introduces a new option. The people in the state of nature can switch on moral rules and corresponding institutions—but only if they come to a unanimous decision. Rational agents would not assent to an institutionally sanctioned rule that forces themselves to cooperate, but leaves some others the choice to defect. They would give their assent to a rule that only binds others—but this cannot lead to general agreement. So it is rational for them to accept a rule if they can be sure that everyone else reliably follows it. This implies the central normative thesis of order ethics. One can only justifiably demand moral rule following if there are institutions, i.e. a social order, that changes the situation so that general compliance with the rules can be reliably expected by everyone in the long run.

---

[1]These preferences do neither have to be monetary nor even selfish, but moral preferences must be excluded lest the argument become circular. (von Grundherr 2007, 50f.).

This test procedure is a purely normative argument, which checks if moral demands are fair and reasonable. It stipulates fully informed and fully rational agents without moral preferences. These rational test dummies are not psychological agents and a descriptive psychological theory is plainly irrelevant for the argument so far.

Psychological situationism comes into play at the next stage. In order to make the central normative thesis applicable to real world questions, order ethics must flesh out the concept of institutions. For the normative argument, moral institutions are everything that changes the expected payoffs for rational agents with fixed non-moral preferences. The prototype of a real world institution is an organization that punishes rule breakers. Informal social pressure, e.g. exclusion from future cooperation, can also play this role. But there is no reason why moral institutions should not also be implemented psychologically via internalized sanctions and self-regulation mechanisms that are developed by all members of society and become part of a common culture. The normative argument excludes moral preferences only hypothetically in its test procedure.

The crux of the matter, then, is whether such a system of psychologically implemented institutions can be effective without an external social order. I assume that standard order ethics tends to claim that individual psychological regulation is not sufficient to guide moral behaviour. This is essentially an empirical hypothesis. Formal game theory cannot decide whether there are widely shared psychological mechanisms that fulfil the role of institutions. At this point, situationist psychology steps in and shows that a reliable system of internal institutions is practically impossible without at least some external backup.

3 Determinants of Moral Behaviour

Situationism claims that there are not any stable and broad dispositions for moral behaviour and that it is pragmatically impossible for normal moral agents to acquire an individual disposition to follow moral rules reliably. Situationists support their claim with psychological experiments showing that intrapersonal behaviour is not consistently moral over time and varies between situations that morally require the same behaviour.

3.1 Situationist Experiments

In a recent handbook article, the social psychologist John A. Bargh summarizes that "many of the classic findings in the field—such as Milgram's obedience research, Asch's conformity studies, and Zimbardo's mock-prison experiment—seemed to indicate that the external forces swamped the internal forces when the chips were down" (Bargh 2007, 555). The "classic findings" can be grouped as follows:

- **Influence of authority and institutional expectations:** Milgram showed in a now classic study that subjects are willing to administer severe electric shocks to another (supposed) subject if instructed by an experimenter to do so (Milgram 1963), while subjects who may choose the strength of the shock themselves, only give very low doses of shock. In their so called Samaritan study, Darley and Batson (Darley and Batson 1973) sent participants of a theological seminary to another building to give a talk. On their way, the subjects met a person who sat motionless and slumped in a doorway, coughed and groaned. 63 % of the subjects who were told by the experimenters that they had plenty of time inquired about the well-being of the person and were willing to help. Subjects who believed to be in moderate or great hurry helped only in 45 or 10 % of cases.
- **Influence of social roles:** In a basement of Stanford University, Zimbardo and colleagues let their subjects takes roles in prison simulation. A randomly selected group played guard, while the other took the role of prisoners (Haney, Banks, and Zimbardo 1973). Zimbardo had to cancel the experiment after a few days: after a short time the "guards" began to torment the "prisoners" mentally and to humiliate them (physical violence was explicitly forbidden).
- **Influence of moods and emotions:** Isen and Levin (1972) showed that people who have found a small coin are significantly more likely to help a passing stranger to pick up lost documents, compared to people who have not found a coin.
- **Influence of the number of bystanders:** In an experiment by Darley and Latané (Darley and Latané 1968), subjects overheard a (simulated) seizure of another (supposed) subject on an intercom system. 85 % of those subjects who believed that they were the only potential helpers informed the experimenter, but only 31 % of the subjects who believed that four other people had also heard the attack did so.

These experiments were reproduced repeatedly, and global effects, though with differences, were confirmed.[2]

---

[2]Haslam and Reicher (2012) repeated the prison experiment and found—in contrast to Zimbardo —that the guards used their power only hesitantly. They argue that people do not automatically take roles, but only if they accept them as a result of social identification with the group (see also Haslam (2006)). Lüttke (2004) summarizes Milgram's experiments and replications from 1960 to 1985, a recent (partial) replication can be found in Burger (2009), for a virtual reality replication see Slater et al. (2006). Carlson et al. (1988) summarize results on mood effects and analyze various functional explanations. Fischer et al. (2011) provide a meta-analysis of studies on bystander behaviour, where they also report studies that find an increase of helping behaviour.

3.2 Situationism, Dispositionalism and Interactionism

These experiments show that situations have a considerable influence on moral behaviour. But not even the most ardent situationist should claim that situations are the *only causes* of behaviour. Situations govern individual behaviour only because individuals have dispositions to react to situations in a certain way. Agents are therefore always "structuring causes" (Dretske 1993) of their actions. Consequently, it is trivially true that both situation and internal disposition are causally necessary for a certain type of behaviour to happen. If either of these factors had been different or missing, the person would have behaved differently.

According to the standard conditional analysis, a person has a disposition to show behaviour of type B in situations of type S if and only if this person would (be likely to) show B-behaviour if an S-situation were the case. I will call S the type of eliciting situations and B the type of reactive behaviour. The relation between S and B can be statistical. There need not be a strictly deterministic relation between interesting *types* of situations and *types* of behavioural responses. Situations of the same type can vary in causally important details, so that it is only likely, but not necessary that a certain type of reaction is triggered. This applies to almost all interesting psychological dispositions: Berta is generous if she often, but not always, gives money to the poor and Anton deserves to be called dishonest, even if he does not always lie.

For ethics, interesting types of eliciting situations are situations that are normatively equivalent, e.g. situations that call for helpful behaviour. It is extremely unlikely that we get anything but statistical dispositions then. Moral norms cut the world rather artificially from a psychological point of view, i.e. situations that call for helpful behaviour may vary extremely in other respects.

Individual dispositions shape actions more effectively if they are broad in the following sense. A person with a broad disposition reacts to a wide range of circumstances with similar behaviour (S is large and B is comparatively narrow). Broad dispositions minimize the effect of situations. It is usually plausible to attribute actions to broad dispositions. John's being on time can be attributed to his punctuality if he is on time for meetings, for dates, for cinema etc. Broad and narrow are relative terms, however: if one observes people only in similar situations (e.g. only at work), a disposition may marginalize the effect of almost all observed situations and the person may show highly consistent behaviour. The very same disposition may be narrow if one observes the person in a wider range of circumstances, e.g. at work and at home.

Situations shape actions more effectively if they override dispositional differences, i.e. if people with different dispositions react similarly to a change in the situation. This does not mean that they all do the same thing, but that their behaviour changes in a systematic way. One way to override dispositional differences is to appeal to widespread, strong dispositions that many people share, e.g. their motivation to survive, to eat, or even more radically, the physical dispositions of their bodies such as inertia.

There is a third type of effect: a situation may lead to a larger interpersonal spread in the behaviour than another situation, even if people do not behave differently on average. Such a situation amplifies interpersonal dispositional differences. Good competence tests or exams are examples of this interaction effect. They construe a situation that provides the opportunity to display different dispositions or abilities. Such a situation can be called weak. A strong situation, on the other hand, blocks the interaction effect. It may, for instance, trigger various parallel dispositions (offer monetary and non-monetary incentives, for instance).

This philosophical analysis can be operationalized in terms of statistics (cf. Krueger 2009): if dispositions are broad, interpersonal behavioural differences will be rather stable across situations. For instance, if the disposition of helpfulness is broad, people who are more helpful than others in situation A will also be more helpful than others in situation B. In this case, behaviour of a person in one situation varies systematically with her behaviour in other situations. Correlations of behaviour within subjects over situations are therefore indicators for broad dispositions or person effects.

Situation effects can be measured independently of person effects. For example, even if those people who help more in situation A also help more in situation B, it may still be the case that everyone helps less in situation B. Such differences in the mean behaviour of subjects are the statistical signature of situation effects. ANOVA (analysis of variance) is the standard statistical tool to identify and measure these effects.

If individual dispositions and situations interact, the spread or variance in behaviour is different in different situations. This, again, may happen independently of the other two effects. If interaction effects occur, situations make behaviour more heterogeneous and thus amplify the effect of dispositions. Strong situations lead to little variance in the behavioural data, weak situations lead to more variance in behavioural data.

3.3 Situationist Experiments Show Both Situation and Interaction Effects

The prototypical situationist experiments show that the average behaviour shifts between situations. This is an indicator for situation effects. In Milgram's experiment, the mean dose of shock administered by all subjects increased significantly in the experimental condition.

In addition, however, many situationist experiments show that the variance of the behaviour, too, increases in the experimental condition (Krueger 2009, 130). This indicates interaction effects. When the subjects in Milgram's experiment could choose the strength of the shocks themselves, 95 % of subjects stopped increasing the shocks as soon as the victim expressed pain. (Lüttke 2004, 437) This means that the vast majority of subjects uniformly abstained from obviously hurting other people and thus did not vary significantly from a moral point of view. When the experimenter asked subjects to administer stronger shocks in the experimental condition, the behaviour of the subjects was much more diverse from a moral point of view. In one of the early experiments, 26 out of 40 subjects obeyed completely and gave the maximum shock of 450 V (Milgram 1963). In this experiment, the victim responded for the first time after the 300 V shock and pounded at the wall. The victim protested again at 315 V and afterwards did not reply at all. A total of 9 subjects stopped at 300 and 315 V, another 5 subjects stopped at the next 4 levels. Thus a quarter of the subjects reacted immediately to the victim's protest, and about 10 % did so with some delay, which means that there was much more morally relevant variance in the experimental condition.

Clear situation effects usually depend on widespread and strong dispositions that do not vary strongly between individuals. There is certainly a widespread disposition to obey to authorities, which explains much of the situation effect in Milgram's experiment. Interaction effects tend to appear when situations trigger not only one, but different similarly strong dispositions. Milgram himself concluded in his 1963-article: "At a more general level, the conflict stems form the opposition of two deeply ingrained behavior dispositions: first, the disposition not to harm other people, and second, the tendency to obey those whom we perceive to be legitimate authorities." (Milgram 1963, 378) Individuals must weigh these values and as they make inconsistent requirements, they must decide for one side. This is far from the simple situationist story: individuals are not slaves of situations, but react consistently to conflicting incentives. Their behaviour mirrors rational trade-offs within their individual value system. (Krueger and Massey 2009)

Thus even clearly observable situation effects do not reduce disposition effects. Higher external pressure regularly leads to interaction effects that make differences in individual dispositions visible. This is relevant for order ethics. Institutions should avoid provoking value conflicts. Resulting interaction effects may increase variance in behaviour and make it less reliable.

3.4 Difficult Situations and Competences

So far I have assumed that paradigmatic individual dispositions are preferences or motives of individuals. But this is oversimplified. Abilities or competencies are equally important dispositional factors and situations may also trigger behaviour via this route. They can make it difficult to apply competences if they are a-typical, ambiguous, distracting or highly complex.

Anecdotal evidence from civil courage cases suggests that moral sensitivity, judgment competence and general action competence are important predictors of actual moral behaviour. If people clearly see that a victim needs help, that intervention is morally required and that there is a feasible and rather riskless way to help, they are much more likely to intervene. Civil courage trainings focus on building these types of competences.

In the moral context, the main difficulties for moral agents lie in (a) detecting morally relevant situations, (b) judging them correctly and (c) finding a feasible action or intervention plan. In a classic study, Clark and Word (1974) could show that people are very likely to provide help to a worker who had an accident if the situation is obvious. Helping decreased rapidly if it was less clear that the worker needed help. This, again, is not a pure situation effect: the mean number of helpers dropped, but, in addition, the increased variance in behaviour reveals an interaction effect. While 100 % offered help in the clear situation, there was a 36/64 %—split in the moderately ambiguous situation and still about 20 % offered help in the very unclear situation.

The Milgram experiment, too, confronted the subjects with a situation that was difficult to judge. Normal judgment heuristics fail in such a context: in a new situation it is normally a good rule of thumb to follow the advice or instructions by someone who is highly competent and experienced. Milgram's mock-experimenter represented a highly reliable institution (Yale University) and seemed to conduct experiments professionally. When this person advised the subjects to harm someone else, normal subjects probably experienced cognitive dissonance, which was hard to dissolve: was the experimenter right and the inflicted harm was not that bad? Was the standard belief that universities can be trusted wrong? Was this person mad although he looked completely sane? Furthermore, the subjects were alone and under time pressure, so that they could not calibrate their judgment in a considerate exchange with other people.

Even if people make a correct moral judgment about a situation, they still do not know what exactly they should do. If you see that someone is threatened by a gang on the street and you correctly judge that you have a prima facie duty to help, you must still decide how to intervene. Mostly the least risky and most successful strategy is to talk to the victim and try to escape with him or her without confronting the attacker at all. Many people do not know this and do not know how to implement it practically.

An interesting result from recent psychological field studies supports this hypothesis. Bullying at schools is a rather well studied case of systematic immoral behaviour. Defending a bully victim is risky, because opposition to bullies may result in the loss of status in the peer group, which is highly important for students. Thus many students do not intervene and take an outsider role. In a recent study, Thornberg and Jungert (2013) found that defenders and outsiders differ in the degree of their (perceived) self-efficacy. If you think that you can intervene efficiently and without detrimental effects to your social position and popularity, you are much more likely to act according to your moral judgment.

There is a more indirect effect of difficult situations, too. Situations may amplify differences in moral motivation and the effects of external incentives due to a variety of effects. Ambiguity makes excuses easier and immoral behaviour can be rationalized more easily. If someone really wants to take the immoral option in an unclear situation, he will find a way to justify it to himself. The blocking of self-regulation (moral disengagement), which is known to correlate consistently with immoral action (Bandura et al. 1996), becomes easy. If someone is not motivated to behave immorally, he will be more receptive to moral reasons.

Moreover, high moral motivation paired with only few concurring non-moral motives may lead to more epistemic investment (take a second look, go back, ask whether someone needs help). Consequently, people with high moral motivation are more likely than people with low motivation to recognize the moral relevance of an ambiguous situation at all.

The classical Samaritan study (see Sect. 3.1) is a good example of these effects. The stimulus situation is rather ambiguous:

„When the subject passed through the alley, the victim was sitting slumped in a doorway, head down, eyes closed, not moving. As the subject went by, the victim coughed twice and groaned, keeping his head down."(Darley and Batson 1973, 104)

Even if there is no value conflict (hurry /be on time vs. helping), a large proportion (37 %) of the subjects does not offer help. Remember that when Clark and Word (1974) tried to make a helping situation clear, this rate was 0 %. When there is an additional conflicting motivation, this rate drops quickly. You can easily imagine typical excuses, subjects may have invented: Maybe he's just drunk. He does not look that sick. He does not need immediate help and other will pass who have more time.

These considerations provide a good framework for many cases in applied business ethics. Take the example of corruption. Bribing officials may become an implicit standard in a company, even if it is denied in official communication. There may even be quasi-formal processes and best-practice models. Rationalizations in euphemistic language (everyone has to give a small present now and then, otherwise we leave the market to less scrupulous competitors …) may become common company lore. People who are known to participate in the practice of corruption may be successful in their careers and provide role models. Even if an employee rejects corruption and thinks that it is detrimental both to the company and to society, she faces a difficult situation. Maybe the rationale her seniors provide for corruption is not that bad? They have proven their judgment and experience in many other cases. She may also lack practical agency competence and may fail to belief in the efficiency of her upright intervention: Is whistleblowing career compatible? Who's on my side? How do I best start a conversation about corruption? Can I be a successful sales person without corruption?

4 Implications for Order Ethics

The normative argument for order ethics shows that a society needs to establish effective institutions as a prerequisite for justifiable moral demands (see Sect. 2). The argument is neutral about whether these institutions are external (social) or internal (psychological) to individuals. Can findings of social psychology arbitrate in the latter issue? This was our initial question.

4.1 Efficient Institutions Rely on Psychological Dispositions

A large body of research in social psychology shows that situations exert significant and relevant influence on moral behaviour. The current state of experimental findings speaks against the existence of reliable moral dispositions that work in the absence of an external institutional framework. Although every single study may be criticized as highly specific, the types of experiments described in Sect. 3.1 as well as numerous replications and variations do not leave much room for doubt. The analysis in the previous sections allows understanding the underlying mechanisms more systematically.

In principle, widespread moral dispositions can function as institutions. They build a psychological environment that regulates the behaviour of non-psychological rational agents. On the one hand, moral dispositions are efficient in this role: they are omnipresent, impose all cost and effort on potential offenders and are cheap for the rest of society, once they are established by education. On the other hand, they are systematically limited in their effectiveness. The critical moral rules govern situations that had been prisoners' dilemmas before morality came into play. Therefore moral dispositions lead to an internal conflict: while defecting is non-morally rational, cooperating is morally required. As I have explained in Sect. 3.2, empirical findings predict that such a conflict triggers high behavioural variance. If behavioural variance increases, correcting mechanisms must exert higher pressure on individuals to push everyone's behaviour reliably below the threshold of immorality. Without turning into an unacceptable terrorizing super-ego, self-regulation is likely to reach its limits here.

If prisoners' dilemma situations are on the agenda of the social contract negotiations, behavioural variance may make individuals unwilling to self-regulate. Assume you are not a saint but a normal human who accepts only justifiable burdens of morality. You would be willing to acquire internal controls that favour cooperative behaviour; but you must reject to cooperate in the long run if you cannot be sure that all others will also cooperate.

How do external institutions perform in comparison? An external institutional framework makes use of the situation-dependence of moral behaviour. It eliminates those situations, in which people tend to behave immorally. They can reduce or eliminate value conflicts by reducing the non-moral cost of moral behaviour. This framework needs not be formal and does not have to rely on codified rules and specialized roles. It can also be an informal reaction pattern of the social environment, e.g. informal punishment by social exclusion. External institutions are more stable and may reduce behavioural variance better than internal psychological regulation.

However, it would be precipitous to play down the importance of internal self-regulation. External institutions do work neither effectively nor efficiently without complementary moral self-regulation. External institutions always have gaps: it is practically impossible for a society to control every action of every individual. Surveillance states, which try to approximate full control, are prohibitively costly for at least some members of a society and are not likely candidates to be agreed on in the social contract. Steven Pinker (2011) provides ample anthropological evidence showing that humans could only leave the historical 'state of nature' in a civilization process that established *both* strict external institutions *and* individual cultivation.

Consequently, efficient external institutions had better not override all moral and non-moral dispositions to social behaviour with threats that appeal to more basic needs. Instead, they have most power when they back up internal self-regulation. This does not mean that people are naturally good; internal self-regulation has to be learned in a long socialization process. But once people have learned to control their behaviour according to moral rules, e.g. to be honest, external institutions can make sure that moral behaviour is in their non-moral interest. If breaking a contract is punished with a fine, it becomes both morally and non-morally unattractive. Ideally, then, external institutions reduce conflicts between internalized moral rules and non-moral preferences. This makes situations strong and reduces behavioural variance.

To summarize: good institutions create strong situations, given a certain background of individual moral dispositions.

4.2 Different Types of Institutions

So far I have mainly focused on situations that pose motivational challenges to individuals. In these cases people may see what is morally right, but they are not motivated to act accordingly. Corresponding institutions provide incentives. In Sect. 3.4 I have introduced another important type of situations, namely difficult or ambiguous cases, in which people do not see what is the right thing to do; even if they tried, they would not succeed to act morally.

Adding difficulty and ambiguity to situations can lead to the same effect as adding value conflicts: the average behaviour becomes less moral and the variance increases at the same time. Corresponding institutions make situations easier to handle for individuals. First, they can make situations less ambiguous in order to support people with a given judgment and action competence. Role models, for instance, cannot solve motivation problems, but they may be highly efficient in clarifying situations and making behavioural options visible.[3] Take the corruption case: if a successful department head consistently opposes and avoids corruption, others can see that morally correct behaviour is possible and compatible with one's career. This exemplary behaviour also makes it clear that company lore about the unavoidability and acceptability of corruption is wrong and cannot be used as an excuse. Second, institutions can provide education. This can include training of moral sensitivity or action competence. Civil courage trainings are a good example.

---

[3] I owe this idea to Karl Homann.

In these trainings, people learn to recognize critical situations in which victims need help, but they also learn how to intervene with minimal risk for themselves.

Typically, situations produce a combination of motivational and competence challenges. As explained in Sect. 3.4, the Samaritan experiment shows that morally ambiguous situation can amplify the effect of value conflicts. Ambiguity makes it easier to find excuses for rule breaking or to reinterpret the situation as morally irrelevant. Furthermore, if morally good and low-cost behavioural strategies are hard to figure out, moral behaviour has high perceived cost. In order to counterbalance these effects by incentives for moral behaviour, an institution must intervene intensively (e.g. impose harsh punishments for rule breaking). Apart from being costly, this may lead to a new value conflict for individuals. In the Samaritan experiment, such an institution could impose a large fine on not helping people in need. The subjects might then face an additional conflict between the value of punctuality and the monetary risk. If the fine is not prohibitively high, different people will make different trade-offs and in sum this will lead to undesirable behavioural variance. It is probably impossible to reduce this variance by an incentive-based institution without imposing unjustifiable burdens on individuals. More generally: it is highly inefficient and implies burdens for society to use incentive institutions in order to compensate for competence deficits or ambiguity.

On the positive side: the cost of incentive-providing institutions is lower if the situations are clear for all participants (either because they are objectively easy to interpret or because people have relatively high competences). Making the situation clearer, training moral sensitivity or increasing the belief in helper-self-efficiency might have the same effect as imposing an unjustifiably high fine (cf. Clark and Word 1974).

5 Conclusion

Social psychology is neutral about the basic normative claim of order ethics, namely that moral demands are only justifiable if they are backed up by a system of institutions that make moral behaviour reliably expectable and reduce the conflict between non-moral wellbeing and moral requirements. But social psychology can help to corroborate and specify what I've called the psychological thesis of order ethics: individual psychological dispositions are not strong enough to build working "internal institutions". Based on empirical findings, I have argued that individual self-regulation is unlikely to guarantee reliable moral rule following. A system of external institutions is indispensable, but it will not work effectively without internal moral-regulation either. Moral dispositions of individuals are usually not sufficient for a justifiable institutional framework—but they are very likely necessary.

With the help of a well-considered picture of social psychology, order ethics can also avoid a central misunderstanding, namely that it promotes external punishment instead of moral cultivation of individuals. Institutions in the sense of order ethics must functionally integrate widespread psychological dispositions such as moral motives, self-control and internalized sanctions.

For the practical application of order ethics, the interaction of different external institutions, internal self-regulation and internal judgment competences is highly important. What is the ideal balance between internal self-regulation and external social institutions? How much rule conformity can already be achieved by clarifying the situation and educating people? The lower the burdens of this coordinated interplay are for all individuals, the better are the chances to justify it.

References

Bandura, Albert, Claudio Barbaranelli, Gian Vittorio Caprara, and Concetta Pastorelli. 1996. Mechanisms of moral disengagement in the exercise of moral agency. *Journal of Personality and Social Psychology* 71: 364–374.
Bargh, John A. 2007. Social psychological approaches to consciousness. *The Cambridge handbook of consciousness*: 555–569.
Burger, J.M. 2009. Replicating milgram: Would people still obey today? *American Psychologist* 64: 1–11.
Carlson, M., V. Charlin, and N. Miller. 1988. Positive mood and helping behavior: A test of six hypotheses. *Journal of Personality and Social Psychology; Journal of Personality and Social Psychology* 55: 211–229.
Clark, Russell D., and Larry E. Word. 1974. Where is the apathetic bystander? Situational characteristics of the emergency. *Journal of Personality and Social Psychology* 29: 279–287.
Darley, J.M., and C.D. Batson. 1973. " From Jerusalem to Jericho": A study of situational and dispositional variables in helping behavior. *Journal of Personality and Social Psychology* 27: 100–108.
Darley, J.M., and Bibb Latané. 1968. Bystander intervention in emergencies: Diffusion of responsibility. *Journal of Personality and Social Psychology* 8: 377–383.
Dretske, Fred. 1993. Mental events as structuring causes of behavior. In *Mental causation*, ed. John Heil, and Alfred R. Mele, 121–136. Oxford: Clarendon Press.
Fischer, P., J.I. Krueger, T. Greitemeyer, C. Vogrincic, A. Kastenmüller, D. Frey, M. Heene, M. Wicher, and M. Kainbacher. 2011. The bystander-effect: A meta-analytic review on bystander intervention in dangerous and non-dangerous emergencies. *Psychological Bulletin* 137: 517–537.
Gaus, Gerald F. 2011. *The order of public reason; A theory of freedom and morality in a diverse and bounded world*. 1. publ. Cambridge [u.a.]: Cambridge Univ. Press.
Von Grundherr, Michael. 2007. *Moral aus Interesse: Metaethik der Vertragstheorie*. 1st ed. Berlin, New York: de Gruyter.
Haney, C., C. Banks, and P. Zimbardo. 1973. Interpersonal dynamics in a simulated prison. *International Journal Of Criminology And Penology* 1: 69–97. doi:10.1037/h0076835.
Harman, Gilbert. 1999. Moral philosophy meets social psychology: Virtue ethics and the fundamental attribution error. *Proceedings of the Aristotelian Society* 99: 315–331.
Haslam, S.Alexander. 2006. Rethinking the psychology of tyranny: The BBC prison study. *British Journal of Social Psychology* 45: 1–40.
Haslam, S.Alexander, and Stephen D. Reicher. 2012. Contesting the "Nature" Of conformity: What Milgram and Zimbardo's studies really show. *PLoS Biology* 10: e1001426. doi:10.1371/journal.pbio.1001426.
Isen, A.M., and P.F. Levin. 1972. Effect of feeling good on helping: Cookies and kindness. *Journal of Personality and Social Psychology* 21: 384–388.

Krueger, Joachim I. 2009. A componential model of situation effects, person effects, and situation-by-person interaction effects on social behavior. *Journal of Research in Personality* 43: 127–136. doi:10.1016/j.jrp.2008.12.042.

Krueger, Joachim I., and A.L. Massey. 2009. A rational reconstruction of misbehavior. *Social Cognition* 27: 786–812.

Luetge, Christoph. 2013. The Idea of a Contractarian Business Ethics. In *Handbook of the philosophical foundations of business ethics*, ed. Christoph Luetge, 647–658. Netherlands: Springer.

Lüttke, Hans B. 2004. Experimente unter dem Milgram-Paradigma. *Gruppendynamik und Organisationsberatung* 35: 431–464. doi:10.1007/s11612-004-0040-7.

Milgram, Stanley. 1963. Behavioral study of obedience. *Journal of Abnormal Psychology* 67: 371–378.

Pinker, Steven. 2011. *The better angels of our nature: The decline of violence in history and its causes*. London: Allen Lane.

Ross, Lee. 1977. The intuitive psychologist and his shortcomings: distortions in the attribution process. In *Advances in Experimental Social Psychology*, ed. Leonard Berkowitz, 10:173–221. New York: Academic Press.

Slater, Mel, Angus Antley, Adam Davison, David Swapp, Christoph Guger, Chris Barker, Nancy Pistrang, and Maria V. Sanchez-Vives. 2006. A Virtual reprise of the stanley milgram obedience experiments. *PLoS ONE* 1: e39. doi:10.1371/journal.pone.0000039.

Thornberg, Robert, and Tomas Jungert. 2013. Bystander behavior in bullying situations: Basic moral sensitivity, moral disengagement and defender self-efficacy. *Journal of Adolescence* 36: 475–483. doi:10.1016/j.adolescence.2013.02.003.

Order Ethics, Economics, and Game Theory

Nikil Mukerji and Christoph Schumacher

Abstract We offer a concise introduction to the methodology of order-ethics and highlight how it connects aspects of economic theory and, in particular, game theory with traditional ethical considerations. The discussion is conducted along the lines of five basic propositions, which are used to characterize the methodological approach of order ethics.

Keywords Economic ethics · Business ethics · Methodology · Game theory · Prisoner's dilemma · Dilemma structures · Pareto-efficiency · Kaldor-Hicks-criterion

1 Introduction

Many ethicists and economic-ethicists, in particular, believe the following two claims. Firstly, there is an irresolvable conflict between the normative requirements of ethics and economic theory. When dealing with an issue that touches upon the spheres of both of these subjects, the most reasonable thing to do is to find an appropriate balance between the requirements of both (e.g. Okun 1975). Some authors go even further. They claim that economic thinking has to be thought of as

---

This chapter reproduces some material that has previously been published in Mukerji and Schumacher (2008). We thank A B Academic Publishers for their permission to reproduce it here.

N. Mukerji (✉)
Faculty of Philosophy, Philosophy of Science, and the Study of Religion,
Ludwig-Maximilians-Universität München, Munich, Germany
e-mail: nikil.mukerji@lmu.de

C. Schumacher
School of Economics and Finance, Massey University, Auckland, New Zealand
e-mail: C.Schumacher@massey.ac.nz

© Springer International Publishing Switzerland 2016
C. Luetge and N. Mukerji (eds.), *Order Ethics: An Ethical Framework for the Social Market Economy*, DOI 10.1007/978-3-319-33151-5_7

subordinate to ethical considerations and that economic rationality has to be transformed ethically (e.g. Ulrich 1993, 2001). Secondly, the realization of an ethically desirable outcome requires sacrifices on the part of individuals. They have a choice between acting in their own self-interest and acting in the service of an ethical goal. As ethicists, we have to convince them to make the required sacrifices in order to make them do the right thing.

Order ethics differs from the mainstream in ethical theory in that it rejects both of these tenets which may be called, respectively, the *Conflict-Paradigm* and the *Self-Sacrifice-Paradigm*. Contrary to the former, they believe that there is, in fact, no conflict between economic and ethical ends. This has to do with the roles that order ethicists ascribe to philosophy and economics. They believe that the best way to make sense of philosophical ethics is to interpret it as a goal-setter, while the most reasonable way to interpret economics is to view it as a discipline which teaches us how ethical goals can be achieved. On this picture, ethical and economic goals cannot conflict, because economics—properly understood—is purely descriptive and does not have any independent goals. Contrary to the second tenet, order ethicists believe that there is no inherent contradiction between acting ethically and acting in one's own self-interest. Rather, the aim of ethical inquiry is to find institutional arrangements under which it is possible for individuals to act ethically *by* pursuing their own self-interest.

On the following pages, we introduce and discuss the order-ethical methodology. In doing that, we highlight the role that economics and, in particular, game theory play in it and how they help to supersede the Conflict-Paradigm and the Self-Sacrifice-Paradigm. The discussion revolves around five fundamental propositions, which are used to characterize the order-ethical methodology. These propositions are as follows:

(1) **Overcoming Dilemma Structures (DS) in pursuit of efficient outcomes is *the* fundamental problem of ethics.**
(2) **The problem of DS is to be solved at the institutional level through a change to a Pareto-superior rule.**
(3) **The concept of a DS is to be used as a *heuristic*. Every interaction that is subject to ethical investigation has to be modelled in terms of a DS, if possible.**
(4) **An existing institutional arrangement is ethically justified, if and only if there is no Pareto-superior alternative.**
(5) **If we do not find a Pareto-better state of affairs, we should look for a Kaldor-Hicks-superior state. If we can find one, there is a potential for a Pareto-improvement under a suitable redistributive rule.**

What we have to say about these propositions will, for the most part, be rather theoretical and abstract. In Chap. "Is the Minimum Wage EthicallyJustifiable? An Order-Ethical Answer" of this compendium, we do, however, offer a case study that illustrates how the methodology we lay out here can be applied to a practical social-political issue, viz. the problem of minimum wage legislation.

2 The Fundamental Problem of Ethics

The foundations of the order-ethical approach were mainly laid by the pioneering work of James M. Buchanan (e.g. Buchanan 1959, 1975; Buchanan and Tullock 1962; Brennan and Buchanan 1985). Subsequent authors, notably Karl Homann (e.g. Homann 2003; Homann and Suchanek 2000/2005), have adopted Buchanan's research programme and have worked on theoretical refinements, concreteness, and applicability. Central to the approach that has emerged from these authors' efforts is the familiar notion that modern society is a 'joint venture for mutual advantage' (Rawls 1999: 6). In modern society everyone's well-being relies on others. We have a *common* interest in bundling our strengths and working collectively. But, of course, we are not indifferent when it comes to the distribution of the proceeds. We prefer a greater share to a smaller one. Since there is scarcity, this conflicts with the interests of others. Thus, our joint societal effort is marked by a *shared* interest in a functioning social order that allows the maximal acquisition of mutual gains from interactions with others. But it is also marked by *conflicting* interests in the distribution of these gains (Petrick and Pies 2007). According to order-ethics, the fundamental problem of ethics lies in this co-existence of common and conflicting interests that is inherent in a modern society.

In order to analyse the fundamental problem of ethics more closely, we need to cast it in more technical terms. For this purpose, the resources of game theory are very useful. Game theory is a branch of economics that studies the interactive choices of individuals—called *players*—that are assumed to optimize their utilities or payoffs. A *game* is a situation in which two or more players can choose from a set of options—called a *strategy set*. Their choices influence both their own payoffs and the payoffs of the other players. There is a vast number of different games, each of which is interesting in its own right. In the context of order ethics, however, one type of game is particularly interesting, viz. the one in which the interacting parties have common and conflicting interests. The most well-known exemplar of this type of game is the so called Prisoner's Dilemma (PD). Table 1 depicts it in its matrix form.

Table 1 The prisoner's dilemma

		Player 2	
		C	D
Player 1	C	I (3,3)	II (1,4)
Player 1	D	III (4,1)	IV (2,2)

To explain, in the PD two players, 1 and 2, interact symmetrically and have an identical strategy set that encompasses a cooperative strategy, C, and a defective strategy, D. The players' payoffs are found in the cells I, II, III and IV and are numbered 1–4. The first number represents the payoff of player 1 and the second number represents the payoff of player 2. The numbers are supposed to be interpreted *ordinally*. That is, they merely represent a ranking. A high number indicates that the respective player has a high preference for the respective outcome, while a low number signifies a low preference. The numbers do not, however, give us any information as to the relative preference of one outcome *vis-a-vis* another. E.g., a payoff of 4 cannot be interpreted as being twice as good as a payoff of 2.

It is easy to see that the players in a PD have common and conflicting interests. Each player prefers the other player to play C, whereas the other player prefers to play D. Therein lies their conflict of interests. But players also have a common interest which becomes apparent through a swift analysis. The most likely outcome of the game is that both players choose D, since, individually speaking, D is the best strategy to play for each player regardless what the other player does. Game theorists, therefore, call it a *dominant strategy*. If both players choose their dominant strategy, D, they end up in box IV which is *Pareto-inefficient*. That means that there is an alternative outcome, viz. box I, which is better for both of them than box IV. That outcome is *Pareto-efficient*. Players 1 and 2 have a shared interest to resolve their PD in order to ensure that they achieve the Pareto-efficient outcome rather than the one that none of them wants.

To model the situation in a modern society that involves multiple players, the PD can be generalized to an *n-players PD* or *Dilemma Structure* (DS). Like in the ordinary PD, the players can choose from identical strategy sets that contain a cooperative strategy, C, and a defective strategy, D. Again each player prefers the other players playing C, while she always prefers to play D. Furthermore, the outcome in which everybody plays D is Pareto-inefficient, since everybody would prefer an outcome where all players play C.

The prototype of a DS is the well-known *Tragedy of the Commons* popularized by Hardin (1968). Hardin tells the story of a pasture that is used by a number of herdsmen to graze their animals.

> As a rational being, each herdsman seeks to maximize his gain. Explicitly or implicitly, more or less consciously, he asks, "What is the utility to me of adding one more animal to my herd?" This utility has one negative and one positive component.
>
> 1) The positive component is a function of the increment of one animal. Since the herdsman receives all the proceeds from the sale of the additional animal, the positive utility is nearly +1.
> 2) The negative component is a function of the additional overgrazing created by one more animal. Since, however, the effects of overgrazing are shared by all the herdsmen, the negative utility for any particular decision-making herdsman is only a fraction of -1. Adding together the component partial utilities, the rational herdsman concludes that the only sensible course for him to pursue is to add another animal to his herd. And another; and another. . . . But this is the conclusion reached by each and every rational herdsman sharing a commons. Therein is the tragedy. (Hardin 1968: 1244)

The structure of the interactive choice situation described by Hardin is as follows. Given that all herdsmen have put n animals on the pasture, each faces a choice between playing a cooperative strategy, C, or a defective strategy, D. D consists in putting one additional animal on the common pasture. C is to refrain from doing so. (Once the herdsmen have made their choice, they face essentially the same choice problem again.) No matter what the other herdsmen do, each individual herdsman prefers to play D, i.e. add one more animal to his herd. D is the dominant strategy. At the same time, every herdsman prefers all others to play C, i.e. to refrain from adding one more animal. Therein consists their conflict of interest. But the herdsmen also have a shared interest in overcoming the DS that lies in their interaction. They know that the outcome of the game is likely the Pareto-inefficient overuse of their common resource. A moderate use of the pasture by all would be better for all herdsmen.

Order ethicists believe that DS such as the one described by Hardin are omnipresent in human interactions.[1] Since everybody suffers damage from DS they believe that

(1) **Overcoming DS in pursuit of efficient outcomes is *the* fundamental problem of ethics**.

3 The Roles of Ethics and Game Theory

Proposition (1) gives rise to the all-important question how it is possible to overcome DS. Before we explain how order ethics answers this question, however, we would like to draw attention to a fact that might be overlooked, particularly by economists. It is the fact that, on order ethics, the idea of Pareto-efficiency assumes the role of an *ethical* goal. This may be surprising, because the notion of efficiency is mostly seen as belonging to the realm of economics and not ethics. A brief consideration of the roles of ethics and economics makes it plausible, however, that this is not the case and that efficiency is, in fact, an ethical ideal. To this end, let us first clarify the notions of ethics and economics.

Ethics asks, roughly, what is worth pursuing and what should be done. Whereas the empirical sciences are, for the most part, definable by the scientific objects that they study, the scope of ethics can be understood best through a peculiarity of its assertions. Ethical statements have a *normative* content. They say what *ought* to be the case and what *ought* to be done. In contrast, economics and, in particular, game theory deals with the analysis of human behaviour and interactions from a *descriptive* viewpoint and from such a viewpoint only (Friedman 1953). It analyses what should be done, *if one wants to achieve a certain aim*. The imperatives uttered

---

[1]Petrick and Pies (2007) summarize a few views regarding this claim.

by economists are, therefore, to use Kant's (1785) terminology, merely *hypothetical* in nature.

These considerations, order ethicists insist, make it clear that the Conflict-Paradigm (which most ethicists subscribe to) is false. On order ethics, economic and ethical aims cannot conflict, because ethics has the role of the goal-setter, while economic theory and the branch of game theory, in particular, has no independent goals. These disciplines merely teach us how our ethical goals can be achieved. In due course, we will say more about that. Before we do that, however, we should say a bit more about the ethical goal of Pareto-efficiency.

4 Pareto-Efficiency as an Ethical Goal

As we have established, the principle of Pareto-efficiency is an ethical goal. This, however, is not to say that it is a justified ethical goal. It may be interesting to ask, therefore, what order ethicists might argue to support it. In this short chapter we cannot, of course, give an encompassing discussion of the reasons in favour of and against the Pareto-efficiency criterion. What we can do, however, is to compare it with one of its rivals, viz. utilitarianism, in order to show that it is at least not implausible.

Utilitarianism faces two well-known complications. The first is methodological. It is unclear how, if any, utility can be objectively measured and interpersonally compared (Jevons 1871). The second objection is ethical. Even if utility could be compared throughout individuals, how do we justify sacrificing one person's well-being to promote another's (Rawls 1971)?[2] The idea that a person is instrumentalized for the benefit of another conflicts with the well-entrenched moral principle that everyone is to be treated *as an end in itself* and never as a means (Kant 1785).

The Pareto-efficiency criterion solves both these problems. Firstly, it does not require interpersonal comparability of utility. To apply the criterion, we merely need to assume that individuals are capable of evaluating and comparing outcomes *intra*personally. Secondly, it protects all individuals against being instrumentalized. One state of affairs is judged better than another only if *all* individuals prefer it. There are no trade-offs between the well-being of different individuals.

The Pareto-efficiency criterion might become even more palatable as attention is called to the fact that it is, indeed, nothing else but an abbreviation of the age-old ethical principle of unanimous consensus, as used in contractualist approaches to moral philosophy, such as in Hobbes (1651/1955) and Locke (1689/1952) and more recently, e.g., in Rawls (1999) and Nozick (1975).[3]

---

[2]Mukerji (2013) offers a brief and accessible overview over some of the most common criticisms of utilitarianism.

[3]This aspect of Pareto-efficiency has first been pointed out by Wicksell (1896).

Of course, the Pareto-efficiency criterion is not impervious to criticism. As Arrow (1951/1963) has famously shown, it is logically incompatible with a number of rather weak criteria for social choice. Sen (1970) has pointed out that it conflicts with a weak and appealing notion of individual rights. Further authors, such as Cohen (1995) and Mukerji (2009) have discussed objections to the Pareto-efficiency principle on grounds of justice. In the present chapter, we cannot discuss these considerations. Some of them are, however, taken up in the contribution by Heider and Mukerji in this volume (Chap. "Rawls, Order Ethics, and Rawlsian Order Ethics").

5 The Implementation Problem

As we pointed out above, proposition (1) raises the question how DS can be overcome and Pareto-efficient outcomes achieved. There are, in principle, two approaches. The first may be called the *Moralist Approach*. In keeping with what we have called the Self-Sacrifice-Paradigm of ethics, it assumes that individuals have to make sacrifices to promote the cause of ethics (e.g. Ulrich 1993, 2001; Habermas 1962/1990; Steinmann and Löhr 1992; Laffont 1975; Etzioni 1987). They should depart from their individually rational self-seeking behaviour and adopt a *moral* point of view. This is because in DS the rational pursuit of self-interest evidently leads to an outcome that is bad for all.

Let us examine more closely how the Moralist Approach would work. To this end, let us turn our attention once again to the simplest version of a DS, viz. the PD game as shown in Table 1. We said that the likely outcome of the PD is the Pareto-inefficient box IV. Proponents of the Moralist Approach argue that the problem lies in the selfishness of the players' choices. To solve this problem, we should appeal to the players and admonish them to choose from the moral point of view. To illustrate, let us briefly take a look at two well-known explications of the moral point of view, Kant's Categorical Imperative (CI) and the Golden Rule (GR).

The CI in its 'universal law formula' commands to 'Act only according to that maxim whereby you can at the same time will that it should become a universal law' (Kant 1785). It, thus, lays out a test for the moral quality of individual behaviour. We are supposed to formulate a maxim, or decision logic, that governs our behaviour. Then we are to recast this maxim on the collective of agents. Everyone is assumed to adopt it. It is then asked whether we can possibly will that the maxim is, in fact, generally adopted. Using this hypothetical generalization we are in some sense confronted with the (positive and/or negative) effects of our behaviour on others. The effects of our actions are, thus, internalized and the self-interested calculus of the individual is ethically transformed. The logic of the GR is similar. It commands us to treat others as we would want to be treated *by* others. With this principle, too, we counterfactually internalize the effects of our behaviour on others.

We can now contrast the behavioural implications from both viewpoints in regards to the DS. As stated above, the logic of self-interest recommends that both individuals play D, since this strategy optimizes the payoff to the individual. However, if we put D to the test from the moral point of view, it is not advisable anymore. This is plausible in both the Kantian and GR version. For compare C and D as candidates for universal laws. If individual payoff maximization became a universal law, every individual would choose D in a dilemma situation and we would constantly end up in the inefficient box IV.[4] In contrast, if everyone adopted the maxim to choose the strategy that maximizes the payoff to the other person, we would all cooperate and end up in the ethically desired quadrant I. (Following a slightly different reasoning, we get the same normative implication from the GR.) In principle, an ethical transformation of self-interested individual choice behaviour can hence promote the ethical end of efficiency in a DS.

Logically speaking, then, the Moralist Approach checks out. If both players obey the moral norms, they do, in fact, end up in box I which is better for both of them. Order ethicists have rejected this solution, however, since they believe that it is not realistic. They take it to be unlikely that players 1 and 2 will, in fact, consistently behave in accordance with the moral rules. Here is why. Player 1 knows that player 2 strictly prefers to play D. There is, hence, no assurance that 2 will, in fact, play C. And even if she does, playing D is always better for player 1 and, hence, very tempting. So the Moralist Approach seems to founder on what order ethicists call the "implementation problem" of ethics. It is the problem how it can be ensured that individuals do, in fact, obey the moral norms.

To overcome the implementation problem, order ethicists favour the *Incentive Approach* that is rooted in economic theory (Buchanan 1990; Homann 2003). Economic theory teaches that individuals follow incentives. To ensure that they play by the rules of ethics it must, hence, be ensured that they have an incentive to do so. It must be ensured, in other words, that the ethically preferable strategy C yields a higher payoff to the individual than the ethically dispreferred strategy D (Homann 2001). Put in more technical terms, the idea is to alter the payoff structure of a DS so as to create a new game in which strategy C becomes more attractive *vis-a-vis* D. An example of such a game is shown in Table 2 (Mukerji and Schumacher 2008).

In the Reversed PD, C, C is the best possible outcome for all. At the same time, C is the dominant strategy for both players. By turning a PD into a Reversed PD, it is possible, then, to perfectly align the ethical goal of an efficient outcome with the respective self-interest of the players. In practice, this is accomplished by adding a new Pareto-efficient rule to the *institutional* arrangement that generates the payoff structure. Such a rule either punishes individuals who play D or rewards individuals who play C (or does both). The effect is that both players get an incentive to play C, such that the outcome of the interaction is Pareto-efficient.

---

[4]In Kant's terminology, playing C would be an "imperfect duty", rather than a "perfect duty". For the distinction between the two see, e.g., Johnson (2012).

Table 2 Reversed prisoner's dilemma

		Player 2	
		C	D
Player 1	C	I (3,3)	II (1,2)
	D	III (2,1)	IV (0,0)

To illustrate, consider the aforementioned Tragedy of the Commons described by Hardin (1968). Under the current institutional system every herdsman is allowed to put as many animals on the pasture as he likes. The result is resource overuse. The Incentive Approach would, hence, recommend introducing a rule which rewards those who keep the number of animals within reasonable bounds and/or punishes those who do not. This would create a private incentive for *each* herder to do what is best for all.

The second basic tenet of the order-ethical methodology can be condensed, then, into the following proposition.

(2) **The problem of DS is to be solved at the institutional level through a change to a Pareto-superior rule**.

6 Clarifications and Refinements I—the Heuristic Use of Dilemma Structures

So far, we have introduced two propositions. Proposition (1) tells us that overcoming DS is the fundamental problem of ethics. Proposition (2) proposes that DS are to be solved at the institutional level by way of rule changes that alter the structure of interactions. Taken together, these two ideas take us a long way towards a comprehensive methodology for solving ethical problems. But a few clarifications and refinements are still in order.

We should add, firstly, that neither proposition specifies how we can detect moral problems in the first place. Proposition (1) merely says what ethical problems consist in, according to order ethics. Proposition (2) merely tells us how we can solve moral problems once we have identified them. So how do order ethicists identify moral problems?

Many ethicists would favour an *Intuitive Approach*. They would contend that we merely need to *look* at the world we live in in order to detect moral problems. Initially, this idea seems to be rather promising. It apparently works in a wide variety of cases. Phenomenons like mass poverty, environmental pollution, and global warming are genuine moral problems and our intuitions pick up on them. Though order ethicists acknowledge this, they nevertheless reject the Intuitive Approach. Their reason for doing so is that it may produce two types of errors. It may, firstly, yield false positives. That is, it may lead us to believe that a given situation is a moral problem, though in fact it is not. E.g., many of us perceive the market economy as a morally problematic institution. It is, after all, based on the idea of competition between market participants. Superficially, this is the opposite of solidarity. Order ethicists believe, however, that there is a good ethical justification for the market economy, since it produces efficient results (Homann and Luetge 2004/2005). The second problem about the Intuitive Approach is that it may yield false negatives. That is, it may fail to pick up on genuine moral problems. The second problem is due to the fact that moral problems are often hard to detect by way of intuition, since the losses that society suffers from inefficient institutional arrangements are not always easy to spot. A case in point is the phenomenon of corruption. All members of society have an interest in a public sector that works effectively and does so at the lowest possible costs. Corruption increases these costs to society at large, thus harming everybody. However, when corrupt dealings are well concealed the losses to society may not even become known.

Due to the problems of the Intuitive Approach, order ethicists advocate what may be called the *Heuristic Approach*. It is expressed in the following proposition.

(3) **The concept of a DS is to be used as a *heuristic*. That means that every interaction that is subject to ethical investigation has to be modelled in terms of a DS, if possible**.

The reasoning that takes us to Proposition (3) is very simple. The idea is that, if we construe all interactions in society as possible DS, we will avoid both types of error. We will, firstly, avoid false positives. We will recognize, e.g., that a functioning market order is Pareto-efficient and thus morally justified, even though it initially looks problematic. We will, secondly, avoid false negatives. If we find that it is, in fact, possible to construe a given situation as a DS, we may identify a moral problem that our intuitions might not have been capable of detecting.

7 Clarifications and Refinements II: The Moral Ambivalence of Dilemma Structures

At this point, it is important to prevent a likely misunderstanding. It may seem that, on order ethics, it is always desirable to resolve a DS. But this is not so. As Petrick and Pies (2007) explain, the heuristic of DS has to be applied in a sufficiently differentiated way. We cannot simply focus on atomic interactions. Rather, we always have to keep the big picture in mind. Sometimes DS are nested into one another and it may turn out that stabilizing a particular DS is for the sake of solving a higher order DS. To see this, consider once again the case of market competition. Even though competitors in a particular market would find it desirable to collude, they have a higher-order interest in institutionalized competition in all markets. They are at the same time customers in other markets and benefit from competition in these markets, since it guarantees cheep and high-quality products. Stabilizing competition rather than collusion is in their own higher-level interest, since they can be expected to incur a net benefit from competition as a generalized norm. We should not assume, therefore, that order ethics demands all DS to be resolved. Some DS should not be resolved when this helps to overcome a higher-order DS.

8 Clarifications and Refinements III: Policy Assessment

Social and economic ethicists are often interested in evaluating public policies. It should be mentioned, therefore, that order ethics provides a helpful guide to policy assessment, which is implicit of Propositions (1) and (2). In the interest of clarity, we state it explicitly:

(4) **An existing institutional arrangement is ethically justified, if and only if there is no Pareto-superior alternative**.

We apply this principle as follows. When we consider the ethical justification of a given institutional arrangement we first take stock of the alternative institutional arrangements. Then, we examine whether at least one of them can make everyone in society better off. If not, we accept it as ethically justified. If there is a better institutional structure, we reject the current arrangement as ethically unjustified.

9 Clarifications and Refinements IV: The Heuristic Use of the Kaldor-Hicks Criterion

Before we conclude we should clarify one more point. As we said above, the Pareto principle, which is the normative foundation of order ethics, appears to be a rather weak and appealing criterion for the ethical evaluation of a social arrangement. Some ethicists may feel, however, that it is indeed too weak. They want to make ethical judgements that go beyond the narrow confines of the Pareto principle. To illustrate, suppose, e.g., that we have to evaluate two distributions of, say, dollar amounts, A and B, between individual 1 and individual 2, where A = (100, 100) and B = (99, 1000). Both of these distributions are efficient according to the Pareto criterion, since it is not possible to move from A to B or vice versa without making either 1 or 2 worse off. *Pace* egalitarians, many people may find B more attractive than A, however. After all, if we move from A to B, 1 loses much less than 2 gains.

How can this intuition be explained? The cognoscenti of economic theory realizes, of course, that distribution B is superior to A according to the Kaldor-Hicks-efficiency criterion (Kaldor 1939; Hicks 1939). According to that criterion, B is better than A because, under B, 2 could in theory compensate 1 for her loss *vis-a-vis* A and still be better off than under A. Perhaps this principle can offer a better fit with our considered moral verdicts than the Pareto principle? Perhaps we should change our notion of efficiency and accept the Kaldor-Hicks criterion instead of the Pareto principle?

Order ethicists would reject this. They would argue, firstly, that there is, in fact, no valid basis for an interpersonal judgement that does not violate the requirement of ethical neutrality between 1 and 2. Secondly, they would remind us that the Pareto criterion is not just an ethical requirement. It is also a pragmatic requirement. It is hard to see how a Kaldor-Hicks-superior outcome can be achieved, if it makes some individuals worse off, since these individuals will presumably oppose and work against the implementation of that outcome (Mukerji 2009, 78–83).

Nevertheless, we believe that the Kaldor-Hicks-criterion has a role to play in the order-ethical methodology. Though, according to order ethics, it is not suitable as an ethical ideal, it can be used as a *heuristic*. When a Kaldor-Hicks-superior outcome is possible in principle, there is a potential for a Pareto-improvement, too (Mukerji and Schumacher 2008). For this reason, a further proposition should be added to the order-ethical methodology.

(5) **If we do not find a Pareto-better state of affairs, we should look for a Kaldor-Hicks-superior state. If we can find one, there is a potential for a Pareto-improvement under a suitable redistributive rule**.

Let us illustrate what Proposition (5) purports by going back to the above example. Let us assume that the current distribution A is (100, 100) and that it would be possible to put in place a policy, P, which would lead to a new distribution B, i.e. (99, 1000). In this situation, order ethics does not allow us to introduce P. B is Kaldor-Hicks-superior to A, but it is not Pareto-superior. In implementing it, we would harm 1. However, as Proposition (5) suggests, the fact that a Kaldor-Hicks-superior outcome, viz. B, is possible in principle indicates that there is a potential for an outcome, C, that is Pareto-better than A. As Proposition (5) indicates, engineering such an outcome would involve a redistributive rule. As policy makers we may suggest, e.g., that 2 pay 1, say, 100 units of money in compensation, if 1 consents to policy P being implemented. This would create a new alternative, C (199, 900), under which everyone is better off than in A.

It may seem as though Proposition (5) makes an almost trivial point. But it is an important point nevertheless, since it holds two important lessons. Firstly, resourcefulness is a virtue when it comes to policy making. One example for this can be found in our discussion of the minimum wage that we offer in Chap. "Is the Minimum Wage EthicallyJustifiable? An Order-Ethical Answer". When a minimum wage policy is in place, it likely leads to a deadweight loss. That means that there are potential economic benefits that cannot be realized due to the existence of the minimum wage. Abolishing it would unlock them. They would, however, only accrue to firms. Workers, on the other hand, would be harmed. This situation calls for an intricate scheme of measures that offers benefits to both firms and to workers, such that they can all agree that these measures should be implemented. Within that scheme—and that is the second lesson we learn from Proposition (5)—redistributive measures are not to be shunned. Libertarians and neo-liberals often condemn redistributive policy measures. On order-ethics, however, they are perfectly justified as long as they are used to bring about an institutional change that benefits all.

10 Conclusion

Let us sum up. In this chapter, we offered a brief statement of the order-ethical methodology, emphasizing in particular the roles that economics and game theory play in it. We proposed to characterize it using five basic propositions. In explaining these fundamental tenets, we pointed out how order ethics opposes traditional views in ethics. These pertain, most importantly, to the relationship of ethics and economics and the (in)compatibility of morality and self-interest. The first proposition says that overcoming Dilemma Structures (DS) in pursuit of efficient outcomes is *the* fundamental problem of ethics. It contradicts the received notion that ethical and economic ends inherently conflict—a view which we referred to as the *Conflict Paradigm*. The second proposition says that the problem of DS is to be solved at the institutional level through a change to a Pareto-superior rule. The idea is to reshape the institutional framework that regulates the interactions of individuals in society in order to bring moral behaviour into alignment with self-interested behaviour. This idea opposes what we called the Self-Sacrifice Paradigm of ethics which holds that morality and self-interest are incompatible. The remaining three propositions that we discussed can be seen as clarifications of the first two. The first two propositions help us to understand what the goal of ethics is and how this goal can be achieved. The third instructs us how we can identify ethical problems. It says that the concept of a DS is to be used as a *heuristic*. The suggestion is that every interaction in society should be construed as a DS. If this is possible, we face an ethical problem. If not, all is well. The forth proposition instructs us as public policy makers and helps us to evaluate existing institutional arrangements. It says that they are ethically justified, if and only if there is no Pareto-superior alternative. The fifth and final proposition tells us how order ethical policy makers should proceed when a Pareto-superior policy is hard to find. In this case, it suggests, we should look for a Kaldor-Hicks-superior state. If we find one, there may be a potential for a Pareto-improvement under a suitable distributive rule. As we said in the introduction, our remarks may have been rather abstract. In Chap. "Is the Minimum Wage EthicallyJustifiable? An Order-Ethical Answer", we offer a case study in public policy where we use the order-ethical methodology to study the ethical justification of minimum wage laws.

References

Arrow, Kenneth. 1951/1963. *Social Choice and Individual Values*. New York; London; Sydney: John Wiley & Sons.
Brennan, G., and J.M. Buchanan. 1985. *The reason of rules—constitutional political economy*. Cambridge: Cambridge University Press.
Buchanan, J.M. 1959. Positive economics, welfare economics, and political economy. *Journal of Law and Economics* 2: 124–138.
Buchanan, J.M. 1975. *The limits of liberty—between anarchy and leviathan*. Chicago: University of Chicago Press.
Buchanan, J.M. 1990. The domain of constitutional economics. *Constitutional Political Economy* 1: 1–18.
Buchanan, J.M., and G. Tullock. 1962. *The calculus of consent: Logical foundations of constitutional democracy*. Ann Arbor: University of Michigan Press.
Cohen, G.A. 1995. The pareto argument for inequality. *Social Philosophy and Policy* 12(1): 160–185.
Etzioni, A. 1987. Toward a Kantian socio-economics. *Review of Social Economy* 45(1): 37–47.
Friedman, M. 1953. *Essays in positive economics*. Chicago: University of Chicago Press.
Habermas, J. 1962/1990. *Strukturwandel der Öffentlichkeit. Untersuchungen zu einer Kategorie der bürgerlichen Gesellschaft* (2nd Ed.). Frankfurt am Main: Suhrkamp.
Hardin, G. 1968. The tragedy of the commons. *Science* 162: 1243–1244.
Hicks, J.R. 1939. The foundations of welfare economics. *The Economic Journal* 49(196): 696–712.
Hobbes, T. 1651/1955. *Leviathan*. Oxford: Blackwell.
Homann, K. 2001. Ökonomik: Fortsetzung der Ethik mit anderen Mitteln. In *Vorteile und Anreize*, ed. Christoph Luetge, 243–266. Mohr Siebeck: Tübingen.
Homann, K. 2003. *Anreize und Moral: Gesellschaftstheorie – Ethik – Anwendungen*, ed. Christoph Luetge. Münster: LIT-Verlag.
Homann, K., and C. Luetge. 2004/2005. *Einführung in die Wirtschaftsethik* (2nd Ed.). Münster: LIT-Verlag.
Homann, K., and A. Suchanek. 2000/2005. *Ökonomik: Eine Einführung* (2nd Ed.). Tübingen: Mohr Siebeck.
Jevons, W.S. 1871. *The theory of political economy 1*. London: Macmillan.
Johnson, R. 2012. Kant's Moral Philosophy. In *The stanford encyclopedia of philosophy* (Summer 2012 Ed.), ed. Edward N. Zalta. http://plato.stanford.edu/archives/sum2012/entries/kant-moral.
Kaldor, N. 1939. Welfare propositions of economics and interpersonal comparisons of utility. *The Economic Journal* 49: 549–552.
Kant, I. 1785/1993. *Grounding for the Metaphysics of Morals* (trans: James W. Ellington). Indianapolis: Hackett Publishing Company.
Laffont, J.J. 1975. Macroeconomic constraints, economic efficiency and ethics: An introduction to Kantian economics. *Economica* 42(168): 430–437.
Locke, J. 1689/1952. *The second treatise of government*. Indianapolis: Bobbs-Merrill.
Mukerji, N. 2009. *Das Differenzprinzip von John Rawls und seine Realisierungsbedingungen*. Münster: LIT-Verlag.
Mukerji, N. 2013. Utilitarianism. In *Handbook of the philosophical foundations of business ethics*, vol. 1, ed. Christoph Luetge, 297–312. Dordrecht: Springer.
Mukerji, N., and C. Schumacher. 2008. How to have your cake and eat it too: Resolving the efficiency-equity trade-off in minimum wage legislation. *The Journal of Interdisciplinary Economics* 19(4): 315–340.
Nozick, R. 1975. *Anarchy, State, and Utopia*. Oxford: Blackwell.
Okun, A. 1975. *Equality and efficiency—the big tradeoff*. Washington, D.C.: The Brookings Institution.

Petrick, M., and I. Pies. 2007. In search for rules that secure gains from cooperation: the heuristic value of social dilemmas for normative institutional economics. *European Journal of Law and Economics* 23(3): 251–271.
Rawls, J. 1971/1999. *A theory of justice* (Rev. Ed.). Harvard University Press: Cambridge, Mass.
Sen, A. 1970. The impossibility of a paretian liberal. *Journal of Political Economy* 78(1): 152–157.
Steinmann, H., and A. Löhr. 1992. *Grundlagen der Unternehmensethik.* Stuttgart: Poeschel.
Ulrich, P. 1993. *Transformation der ökonomischen Vernunft,* 3rd ed. Bern: Haupt.
Ulrich, P. 2001. *Integrative Wirtschaftsethik – Grundlagen einer lebensdienlichen Ökonomie,* 3rd ed. Bern: Haupt.
Wicksell, K. 1896. *Finanztheoretische Untersuchungen.* Jena: Fischer.

Biblical Economics and Order Ethics: Constitutional Economic and Institutional Economic Roots of the Old Testament

Sigmund Wagner-Tsukamoto

> *You will feed on the wealth of nations,*
> *And in their riches you will boast.*
> (Isaiah 61: 6)

Abstract Order ethics emerged in the first half of the 20th century in the German-speaking world. It shares many conceptual parallels with constitutional and institutional economics, as pioneered by Buchanan, North, Ostrom or Williamson in the second half of 20th-century USA. The article draws on such conceptual parallels to set out how concepts of order ethics, through the identification of institutional and constitutional economic principles, can be utilized and reconstructed within the Old Testament text. The chapter demonstrates that a high level of success has been attained. Conceptual ideas like dilemma structure, the homo economicus, interactions over capital exchange, institutional rule structures, and mutual gains as interaction outcome, as they delineate constitutional and institutional economics, can be identified in the Old Testament. I focus on the Torah, specifically the Paradise story, the Jacob stories, the Joseph stories, the stories of the exodus events, and the stories of the settlement phase, when the Israelites were led by Joshua, Saul, David and Solomon. These stories belong to the oldest and best-known parts of the Old Testament.

Keywords Order ethics · Institutional/constitutional economics · Old testament text · Dilemma structure · Homo economicus · Incentive structures · Mutual gains

1 Introduction

Historically, in the German speaking world, order ethics and order economics are closely associated with the Freiburg School and Walter Eucken. In the first half of the 20th century Eucken set out a liberal research program; focused on organizing a

S. Wagner-Tsukamoto (✉)
School of Management, University of Leicester, University Road, Leicester Le1 7RH, UK
e-mail: s.wagner-tsukamoto@le.ac.uk; sawt444@aol.com; saw14@le.ac.uk

market economy and state activity in a market economy, and disassociating himself from laissez faire economics. The purpose of this review is not to develop and distinguish conceptual overlaps and connections between order ethics/order economics and institutional/constitutional economics. This has been done elsewhere, both by those who support the research program of order ethics and institutional/constitutional economics (Homann 1994, 1997, 1999; Pies 1996, 2011; Lütge 2002), and by those who criticize it (Bernhardt 2009; Gerlach 2002). Both groups, regardless of how contrasting their views on economics and ethics may be, generally subsume order ethics under institutional and constitutional economics (e.g. Bernhardt 2009, p. 4; Gerlach 2002, p. 211).[1]

Order ethics and institutional/constitutional economics analyze rule structures that govern national and international economic systems; business organizations and non-profit organizations; as well as individual behavior *in the context* of institutional rule structures. This research program is methodologically grounded in the model of the homo economicus (the idea of rational self-interested choice) and a dilemmatic model of interest conflicts, such as the prisoner's dilemma. On this basis it is examined in order to ascertain how—even in the presence of merely self-interested agents and conflicting interests among agents—institutional rule structures can effectively and efficiently govern capital exchange. In normative institutional perspective, the transformation of zero-sum interactions into non-zero-sum, win-win interactions (i.e. mutual advantages of interacting agents) is frequently but not necessarily always the desired goal. Order ethics and institutional/constitutional economics analyses, however, do not stop at the interaction level of individual agents: As noted, such interaction analysis is projected to larger societal, systemic questions of wealth, economic growth and welfare standards in society, of the guarantee and regulation of contractual freedom and of private property rights, of the upholding and regulation of competition in a market economy, and so forth.

Order ethics challenges the widely claimed dualism in ethics research which puts economics in opposition to ethics. Such opposition has been diagnosed, for instance, in business ethics research, through behaviorally approached conceptions of a 'business ethics oxymoron' (e.g. Collins 1994, p. 7; Duska 2000, pp. 119–120, 124; Nash 2000, pp. 278–279, 281, 283), or a 'stakeholder management paradox' (e.g. Goodpaster 1991, 2000, pp. 191, 196–198), or claims towards the necessity of behaviorally driven interdisciplinary integration programs between ethics and economics (e.g. Gerlach 2002; Sen 1990; Simon 1993; Werhane 2000; Windsor 2006; critically on this project Wagner-Tsukamoto 2013d). However, order ethics neither views economics as opposed to ethics, nor uses it as a substitute to ethics, but stresses the 'unity of both' (Lütge 2002, p. 227). In this understanding, economics is the continuation of ethics—but with different means, as compared to traditional,

---

[1] Indeed, the Walter Eucken Institute of the University of Freiburg translates its German name of its discussion papers series 'Diskussionspapiere zur Ordnungsökonomik'—which literally could be translated into English as 'discussion papers on order economics'—indeed as 'Discussion Papers on Constitutional Economics'.

behavioral ethics. It avoids behavioral intervention with individual behavior as such (Homann 1994, 1999; Suchanek 1994; Lütge 2002).

Analysis is methodically grounded in a gains/loss calculus (homo economicus) and a dilemmatic model of interaction conflict (such as the prisoner's dilemma). These concepts are mere methods to investigate institutional design. An ethics with economic *means* is the goal, reflecting intervention with constitutional and institutional rule structures. This analysis is directed at the intervention with norms—but norms understood in situational terms as constitutional and institutional rules. Norms are to be designed in a manner so that rule-following is induced on the grounds of self-interested choice. Analytical strategies and the normative-practical advice that they drive set out this program then; they are rather different when compared with the ones of traditional, behavioral ethics or the ones of behavioral economics, economic sociology, etc.

In the following, my review sets out that theses and conceptual principles of order ethics can be coherently reconstructed for the Old Testament text.

1. Methods of institutional and constitutional economics, such as the homo economicus and the dilemma structure, are traced in the Old Testament text and their methodical role in instructing storytelling in the Old Testament is investigated. Most typical here is the Paradise story.
2. Concepts of interaction analysis, which concern capital exchange and the governance of capital exchange through institutional and constitutional economic structures, are searched for in Old Testament stories, exemplarily so for the Paradise story, the Jacob stories, the Joseph stories, the exodus stories, or the stories of the settlement phase.
3. Old Testament stories are analyzed for mutual gains as interaction outcome, generated through successful constitutional and institutional intervention. Conversely, mutual loss is looked for that was caused by unsuccessful or lacking strategies to align self-interests of interacting agents through institutional (re-)design.

On a methodological note, regarding how I textually analyze the Old Testament, I want to stress that my research is grounded in the narrative, text-critical approach to Old Testament research which treats the text as prose fiction and storytelling (Arnal 2010; Brett 2000a, 2000b; Clines and Exum 1993; Wagner-Tsukamoto 2009a, pp. 12–18; Wagner-Tsukamoto 2009b, pp. 149–152; Wagner-Tsukamoto 2014a). The implication from this is that all agents who appear in the text (including God), are treated as fictional characters. Therefore I disassociate from questions which ponder the possibilities of attributing factual, historiographical or archaeological significance to the characters and events described in the text. My textual research strategy leaves room to reconnect my analysis to many research programs, to theology, to secular and non-secular studies of religion, and to 'scientific' research programs such as economics.

In other (especially normative) respects, I find much of interest in the 'real-world' nature and significance of the Old Testament text, especially when thinking about the societal, historic contexts from which these stories emerged as early as some 4000 years ago. It is difficult to believe that these stories did not come with some normative purpose regarding the governance of society—institutional and constitutional economic purposes, so my argument states. Many point here towards elitist purposes that these stories hold regarding leadership advice in governance contexts of antiquity (Snyman 2012, pp. 674–675; also Toorn 2007, pp. 1–6, 263).

Through identifying and reconstructing the aforementioned ideas for the Old Testament text, the research programs of order ethics and institutional/constitutional economics gain additional support and credibility. Here, fundamental questions arise regarding how to maintain, as far as an inquiry into ethics and economics is concerned, a differentiation of modernity from antiquity, and to sustain claims to a dichotomy or dualism between ethics and economics in general, and ancient ethics and modern economics in particular.

Significantly, it has to be examined how far the aspiration of order ethics to reconcile economics and ethics can be projected back to antiquity. Moreover, the reconstruction of institutional and constitutional economic concepts for the Old Testament text raises questions regarding a theory of religion that substantively connects to economics. Can Smith's economics, as this has been continued by order ethics, be staged on the Old Testament text? Can we see the emergence of an economic theory of rational religion? In the concluding parts, the chapter returns to these questions.

2 Methodical Roots of Order Ethics in the Old Testament Text: Dilemma Structure and Homo Economicus

Can we find ideas on the homo economicus and the dilemma structure in the Old Testament, and if so, is a methodical application of these ideas apparent? The Paradise story is illustrative already. Ultimately, Adam and Eve give into what Buchanan (1975, p. 27) might call 'private incentives', violating God's property rights and the initial start-up distribution of property rights inside paradise. Their theft of fruit from the divine tree clearly marks them out as self-interested—and potentially as worse, in what Buchanan (1975) and Williamson (1975, 1985) describe as predatory and opportunistic behavior.

Are we observing here a character failure and a trait of human nature, which could be condemned as sinful and overtly greedy behavior, as has been done by mainstream biblical research (e.g. Armstrong 1996; von Rad 1963; Westermann 1984)? Indeed, this diagnosis of character failure may imply that biblical research suggested a dark, selfish image of human nature when it sets out its research program and analyzes the Old Testament. Nevertheless, I advocate caution in this respect, pointing at the *methodical* necessity of invoking the homo economicus, or worse models, such as Hobbes's bellicose human being at the outset of storytelling in the Old Testament (Wagner-Tsukamoto 2009a, 2009b, 2010, 2012b, 2012c, 2013a, 2014a). I argue that such a model of human nature is necessary for both economic reading strategies of the Paradise story and for other analyses, including theological ones, albeit operationally different in structure. Consequently, methodical clarifications appear to be necessary; (a) regarding reasons as to why a self-interested model of human nature is visible in the Paradise story, and (b) regarding purposes as to how this model instructs subsequent storytelling in the Old Testament after the paradise events.

Methodical reasons that explain why the homo economicus shows up in the Paradise story cannot be understood without looking at capital contribution-capital distribution conflicts that loomed in paradise almost from the beginning. Here, the homo economicus does not appear in isolation. Rather, it is embedded in a dilemmatic model of interest conflicts that involved Adam and Eve on the one side, and God on the other, and how the two parties interact. Capital contribution conflicts arose in relation to the amount of work Adam and Eve had to perform inside paradise to keep paradise cultivated (labor capital), and how this curtailed free time (time capital). Considerable distribution conflicts arose in relation to the most precious goods in paradise, the divine trees, which exclusively belonged to God. God was an uncooperative trader, unwilling to share even the smallest amount of fruit from these trees with Adam and Eve (Wagner-Tsukamoto 2009a, 2009b, 2012c, 2014a). In Buchanan's (1975) terms, an imperfect status quo can be diagnosed (see also Vanberg 2004). In the Paradise story, this reflected a start-up distribution of rights that had been solely created by God, with God exclusively owning fruit from the divine trees. In Buchanan's (1975, p. 23) terminology, these fruit are likely to classify as 'x-goods':

> All 'goods' save one, which we shall call x, are available to each person (A and B) in superabundance. But good x is 'scarce'. No production is required for its enjoyment, however, and quantities of this good simply 'fall down' in fixed proportions onto each of the two persons ... . There are no property rights, no law, in this economy.

At the outset of the Paradise story, all fruit from the divine trees 'fell down' on God alone. Buchanan's constitutional economics argues that such states are unstable and will escalate, with theft and raiding happening regarding x-goods. In the Paradise story, such an escalation process can be observed when the divine fruit are stolen. As Buchanan (1975, p. 24) suggests, contest over x-goods leads into the natural distribution state or Hobbesian state of nature; and only from here, subsequently constitutional and institutional economic ordering and contracting for rule structures can set in.

However, initially when entering the natural state, even a prisoner's dilemma outcome is feasible, with mutual loss resulting on both sides, (Wagner-Tsukamoto 2012c, 2014a; see also Wagner-Tsukamoto 2009b). When Adam and Eve took the divine fruit, on God's side loss appeared to be unavoidable anyway; on Adam and Eve's side, the diagnosis of a loss *or* gain outcome is ambivalent: It depends on Adam and Eve's valuation of losing access to paradise as compared to what they gained from leaving paradise. Mathematical-logical conditions can be enunciated which clarify this ambivalence (Wagner-Tsukamoto 2012c). These clarifications help to reconcile conflicting interpretations of Adam and Eve's theft in biblical research, either as positive, as a fall into knowledge and liberation, or as negative, as a fall into original sin and tragedy (Wagner-Tsukamoto 2009b, 2014a).

The homo economicus is instrumentally useful and necessary for setting up such dilemma analysis for the Paradise story. Storytelling, of course, does not come to an end in the Old Testament with Adam and Eve's expulsion from paradise, rather it begins. The scene is set for stories about new and potentially fairer, more mutually advantageous social contracting between humans and God, through the covenants, and among humans. A variety of institutional and constitutional schemes of social contracting emerge (property rights regimes; taxation systems; hierarchical, bureaucratic structures, etc.; see below). From here we can understand the purpose and the heuristic necessity of applying a dilemmatic model of interest conflicts and of the homo economicus: These models heuristically instruct subsequent interaction analysis in the context of institutional ordering. This also implies that we should be able to re-identify homo economicus, tamed or untamed, and dilemma structure, resolved or unresolved, in later Old Testament stories, depending on whether institutional economic structures, as found in a certain story, did or did not resolve the problems of the natural state or Hobbesian war (Wagner-Tsukamoto 2010, 2014a, 2015a, 2015b).

Institutionally untamed appearances of the homo economicus, coupled with escalating dilemma interactions, can be found in the early Jacob stories, the stories surrounding the exodus events, and many stories of the settlement phase, especially under Joshua's and Saul's leadership, and in the stories of Rehoboam. Then the natural state or 'war of all' is quite literally fought out driven by rather self-interested agents on all sides that escalate interactions. The Jacob stories here already spin intricate nets of tit-for-tat interactions in which agents steal, suffer revenge, steal again, and suffer revenge again, and so forth (Wagner-Tsukamoto 2009a, 2010, 2013a). Here, the patriarchal figure of Jacob, which in the conclusion of the Jacob stories is elevated to become the founding father of Israel, has puzzled and frustrated mainstream biblical interpretation, being identified as 'defrauding', 'deceiving' and engaging in 'monstrous crimes' (von Rad 1963, pp. 273, 276, 304; for further references, see Wagner-Tsukamoto 2013a, pp. 85–86). Also, dilemmatic, loss-loss situations characterize most interaction outcomes in the Jacob stories. Only in the conclusion of these stories this changes, through institutional economic intervention, so my argument contends (see below). Therefore, a heuristic and ultimately normative purpose can be attributed to dilemma analysis (including the application of the homo economicus model) that instructs the generation of successful, win-win outcomes when the Jacob stories came to an end.

There are discomforting stories in the Old Testament in which previously well-ordered, mutual gains-societies disintegrated into warfare with mutual loss being the apparent consequence. The couplet Joseph stories–exodus stories is one such example. In the exodus stories, mutual loss results because of the pharaoh's one-sided institutional intervention with population management policies and industrial management strategies as well as Moses's tit-for-tat response strategies

(Wagner-Tsukamoto 2008, 2009a, 2010). The figures of the pharaoh, Moses, and the God of the Moses stories here mirror models of rather self-interested, even selfish agency.

Of course, the exodus stories are preceded by the Joseph stories of Genesis, and there are explicit conceptual connections between both stories (Exodus 1: 8–10). In the Joseph stories, we can diagnose a resolved dilemma, engineered through the clever institutional economic policies of Joseph (Wagner-Tsukamoto 2001, 2009a, 2010, 2015b). Then, mutual gains resulted for both Egypt and Israel as interaction parties. However, in the exodus stories, Joseph's policies were given up, as noted above: Exodus (1: 8) laconically forewarns of this by stating that 'A new king, who did not know about Joseph, came to power in Egypt.' The outcome was mutually disastrous; we meet a dilemma scenario and (self-)destructive homo economicus behavior is played out.

The other couplet of stories which lends itself to a similar interpretation is the one of the Solomon stories (including the David stories) and the stories of Rehoboam (Wagner-Tsukamoto 2013b). Under Rehoboam, interactions escalate and a mutual loss-dilemma results. The previously integrated, economically high-performing Israelite state of Solomon breaks up. Reasons as to why this happened can be attributed to the interest-disequilibrating institutional strategies of Rehoboam (especially his changes to taxation system and labor force management).

The general thesis here is, from the point of view of institutional economic reconstruction, that the Torah is heuristically informed by an economic dilemma scenario and by the model of the homo economicus—from its very outset, as this was visible for the Paradise story. There are, to some degree or other, exceptions to this, especially the stories involving the early patriarchs Noah, Abraham, and Isaac (I return to them in the conclusion of this chapter).

3 Concepts of Constitutional and Institutional Governance Over Capital Interactions in the Old Testament

The search is on for incentive structures, broadly understood in constitutional and institutional economic terms, in the Old Testament text. Incentive structures signal gains and losses in relation to how agents make contributions to and receive distributions from an interaction. They reflect how initial contribution standards and distribution standards had been decided on. The question is whether they align self-interested choice behavior in such a manner that cooperation and the generation of mutual gains succeeds.

In the initial state of nature, no such arrangements can be reasoned to exist, as Buchanan (1975) stresses. Only over time can agents negotiate and establish incentive structures to escape from the natural state (in which mutual gains from cooperation are forsaken). When agents are caught up in the natural state, constant attack and defense activities arise regarding what is claimed as own property and how others' property is contested—and this is very costly for all involved. Through establishing constitutional and institutional structures by means of economic ordering, property claims can be safeguarded and all agents can better their situation by saving on attack/defense costs, so Buchanan argues. In the next section, I trace in the Old Testament text the *outcome* of mutual gains that were achieved through constitutional and institutional ordering. In this section, I look at ordering and incentive structures as such, how they were established and could resolve interaction conflict.

The Paradise story does not start with the natural distribution state which we understand to be a state of constant warfare among parties. Initially, it reflects a comparatively undemocratic, unilaterally ordered and imposed status quo, where contribution standards and distribution standards for Adam and Eve had been set by God alone. Citizen sovereignty, as Vanberg (2004, p. 154, 156, 2006, p. 11, 2014, pp. 18–20) approaches this idea appears to be absent (also Buchanan 1999b, p. 288). Rules regarding contributions and distributions had been set up by God alone. Certain work contributions were expected of Adam and Eve, and distributions to them excluded any share in the fruit from the divine trees. The latter apparently reflected the most precious assets in paradise, since they defined divinity. Adam and Eve's subsequent theft from the tree of knowledge can be explained with respect to the way gains and losses were staked by initially existing rules regarding the allocation of x-goods, the fruit from the divine trees (Wagner-Tsukamoto 2009a, 2009b, 2012b, 2012c, 2014a): At least the *possibility* of a prisoner's dilemma existed.

As a result of the paradise interactions, cooperation between God and Adam and Eve broke down. A natural distribution state, even as prisoner's dilemma can be observed. The incentive logic of the initial paradisiacal situation points at this outcome, with interest disequilibrating rather than interest realigning structures being in place (Wagner-Tsukamoto 2012c). So, in the tradition of Luce and Raiffa (1957, p. 97), the occurrence of a prisoner's dilemma can be projected to an 'irrational logic of the situation' (i.e. to incentive structures) but not to character failure. The situation was 'incentive-incompatible' and governance contracts were 'incomplete', as Williamson (1975, 1985) may put this.

Comparable prisoner's dilemma-type processes can be found in the Jacob stories wherein Jacob exploited loopholes in incentives schemes that concerned inheritance rights, shepherding arrangements, property rights of Jacob's employer Laban, etc. Existing incentive structures, which governed capital exchange between Jacob and his interaction partners, did not resolve interest conflicts. In institutional economic terms, we can connect this to ideas of a 'contracting dilemma' and 'incomplete contracts' that existing structures reflected (Williamson 1985, pp. 29–35, 62–63; Wagner-Tsukamoto 2003, pp. 100–106; Lütge 2005, pp. 113–114). In the Jacob stories, then dilemmatic tit-for-tat, revenge interactions got under way, which saw Jacob lose out time and again too (Wagner-Tsukamoto 2009a, 2010, 2013a).

Ultimately, the Jacob stories end with the economic resolution of such interaction conflicts, by setting out new institutional arrangements that resolved conflict in economic terms, through schemes of compensation payments or through new property regimes regarding land usage. So, in the tradition of Buchanan we can argue that the Old Testament's discussion of initially escalating tit-for-tat interactions (i.e. interactions that lead into the natural state) came with a *normative* purpose: an analysis of intervention with institutional economic arrangements is begun and such analysis culminated in outlining strategies to prevent conflict, even when self-interested behavior is a possibility. Jacob's uniqueness here lay with his resemblance (unlike the other earlier patriarchs) to the model of the homo economicus (see Sect. 2).

The Joseph stories and the Solomon stories portray a rich array of constitutional and institutional structures (taxation systems; property rights regimes; bureaucratic hierarchy, etc.) which actually resolved interaction conflict in a mutually advantageous way (Wagner-Tsukamoto 2001, 2009a, 2010, 2013b, 2015b). Both the 'protective state' and the 'productive state', to draw on Buchanan's (1975) distinction of types of constitutional ordering, were successfully established. Yet, a prisoner's dilemma here was only resolved for the time being; at an underlying level, it remained present. This is highlighted by what happened when the well-functioning incentive structures of the Joseph and Solomon stories were undermined in subsequent stories. In the exodus stories, the pharaoh changed population management policies and industrial management routines. Contribution-distribution standards were altered, and this happened in a way which saw Israel significantly disadvantaged in its interactions with Egypt. A similar observation applies for the stories of Rehoboam, which follow the Solomon stories: Taxation regimes and industrial management practices were intervened with in a way which disadvantaged a large number of members of the Israelite society. This altered the status quo, social unrest resulted amongst the Israelites, and Israel as an integrated state broke up.

4 Mutual Gains as Interaction Outcome

In order to resolve interaction conflict and leave the natural distribution state behind, normative constitutional and institutional economics suggests intervening with and (re-)designing incentive structures in such a manner that conflicting interests are realigned ('equilibrated'; Williamson 1985, pp. 29, 33–34, 76). The 'irrational logic of the situation' is to be changed, as Luce and Raiffa (1957, p. 97) put this. Mutual gains are the desired interaction outcome (Buchanan 1975, 1999a; Pies 1996; Lütge 2005; Vanberg 2006, p. 3). The 'wealth of nations' or 'public good' is the ultimate goal of economic intervention, as Smith and Mandeville noted early on. Can we observe mutually advantageous interaction outcomes in the stories of the Old Testament, with mutual gains resulting from situational, systemic intervention with incentive structures?

Already in the Jacob stories a mutual gains program emerged through intervention with incentive structures. Incentive structures were changed to economically appease interaction partners of Jacob, whom he had disadvantaged in earlier exchanges. Institutional changes included changes to property rights regimes, for instance in land ownership (Genesis 32: 36: 6–8) and the introduction of schemes for compensation payments, for instance through the giving of livestock (e.g. Genesis 32: 13–21).This supported in economic terms exit from the natural state and the kind of tit-for-tat interactions Jacob, Laban and Esau had been caught up in from Genesis (31) onwards (Wagner-Tsukamoto 2009a, 2010, 2013a).

In the Joseph stories, Joseph introduced institutional changes to property rights regimes for farming, and a new taxation policy was set up that developed anti-cyclical fiscal policy (Genesis 41: 34, 47: 13–19, 24). These changes increased wealth for the Egyptian society then depicted in Genesis, Egypt being better buffered against economic downturns; changes to property rights regimes increased the efficiency and productivity of farming (Wagner-Tsukamoto 2015b).

The generation of mutual gains was also facilitated by Egypt's tall, de-personified hierarchies for governing society. Here, we can project North and Weingast's (1989) argument to the Old Testament that successful wealth creation in a society must be accompanied by credible institutional constraints to rulership at the top of a society. Hierarchical organization has such credibility and commitment generating effects on institutional governance: Hierarchy creates a corporate, bureaucratic persona; it de-personifies governance. In this respect, we can expand on some of Williamson's (1975, 1985) arguments regarding transaction cost savings of hierarchies, projecting them to the 'credibility' and 'commitment' generating effects of governmental hierarchy. Such effects facilitate market exchange and wealth creation in a market economy since they help to credibly constrain a ruler from arbitrary, ad hoc confiscation of property of subjects (Wagner-Tsukamoto 2009a, 2010, 2015b). We find at the end of Genesis a depiction of a generally wealthy society, with manifold international trade relationships established, and a host of immigrants working in Egypt, including Joseph and the Israelites. They shared in the wealth created in this society, and such economic success helps explain to a very considerable degree why at the end of Genesis, Joseph received the longest and most favorable blessing of Jacob (Genesis 49: 22–26).

The Solomon stories mirror what happened in the Joseph stories. Through institutional governance, drawing on work specialization, taxation policy, and the hierarchical stratification of society, wealth generating policies were facilitated and safeguarded (Wagner-Tsukamoto 2012a, 2013b, 2015b). A pluralistic, polytheistic society is depicted in which '… the king made silver as common in Jerusalem as stones' (1 Kings 10: 27). Clearly, the people's 'happiness' was maintained, the people being as '… numerous as the sand on the seashore; they ate, they drank and they were happy' (1 Kings 4: 20). Also importantly, regarding the diagnosis of democratic institutional governance, the people remained the legitimating source of a social contract: The Solomon stories are very clear on this when the 'people' and the 'assembly' are referred to as the final source of governance (1 Kings 8: 1–5, 14, 22; see also 1 Kings 12: 6). The stories portray a comparatively democratic, pseudo-modern constitutional monarchy.

We also find the agonizing opposite to mutual gains as interaction outcome in the Old Testament. An exemplary case is the very first story, the Paradise story (Wagner-Tsukamoto 2012c; see also Wagner-Tsukamoto 2009a, 2009b, 2010, 2012b, 2014a). Indeed, this story can be regarded as the meta-heuristic which instructs all further story-telling in the Old Testament. It sets up a dilemma scenario where mutual loss could result, depending on how Adam and Eve valued gains from defection in relation to the losses they suffered. This also sets up an analytical strategy that is guided by the principle that the '... "irrational" (interaction outcome of the prisoner's dilemma) is inherent in the situation' (Luce and Raiffa 1957, p. 97; see also von Neumann and Morgenstern 1947, p. 13). This typifies the conceptual and normative approach of constitutional and institutional economics, targeting the situation to try and prevent mutual loss-outcomes. As noted, the Jacob stories illustrate this situational approach to resolving an underlying dilemma scenario; the Joseph stories and the Solomon stories are explicit: A potential dilemma was then resolved through clever, mutual gains-generating policies.

This diagnosis is further underlined by what happened in the immediate aftermath of the Joseph stories and the Solomon stories: We can observe escalating, dilemmatic interactions which in their final outcomes left all parties worse off and led to re-entry into the natural state (Wagner-Tsukamoto 2008, 2009a, 2013b, 2015b). Constitutional and institutional economics reconstructs such irrational, mutual loss-outcomes in terms of interest disequilibrating institutional interventions of the key antagonists. They destabilized the status quo in the exodus stories and in the Rehoboam stories, leading to the collapse of previously stable, high-performing and well-ordered societies. In the exodus stories, we have the pharaoh, who manipulated population management policies and industrial management strategies exclusively in Egypt's favor; his opposition being Moses and the God of the Israelites, who retaliated by appropriating and destroying various types of capital of the Egyptian society. Mutual gains generating strategies for social ordering were given up. The stories that followed the Solomon stories tell a similar tale. Rehoboam changed tax policies and labor management practices (1 Kings 12: 14, 16). As a result, the people revolted against him and the state split (1 Kings 12: 18). This return to anarchy and the institutional economic reasons that can be put forward in this connection compare well to the break-down of cooperation in the exodus stories. Therefore these stories, by counter-thesis, strongly and dramatically emphasize the program and approach of constitutional and institutional economics regarding the analysis and prevention/resolution of mutual loss, prisoner's dilemma-type situations.

5 Conclusions

Constitutional and institutional economic reconstruction of the Old Testament reveals that concepts of dilemma structures, the homo economicus, interactions over capital exchange, incentive structures as governance mechanism and mutual gains (or mutual loss) as interaction outcome, as they set out modern constitutional and institutional economics, permeate this ancient text. This gives rise to some fundamental questions and theses.

Why would the Old Testament seek constitutional and institutional economic strategies for thinking about social conflict? Specifically, why would the Old Testament, and especially the Torah, turn away from behavioral modes of governance and social contract, as they can be found in the stories of the early patriarchs Noah, Abraham and Isaac? These three patriarchs were God-fearing and highly religious figures, being faithful and obedient to God. They closed covenants in a religious, behavioral tradition, as mainstream theology and mainstream biblical research might expect of them.

For analyzing why behavioral religious social contracting can be observed in the early patriarchal stories, but more economized social contracting appears in other stories as traced in this review. Economic reasons can be given regarding the effectiveness and efficiency of both approaches: Indeed both can be suggested to optimize on savings/attack costs and transaction costs (and other costs too, if applicable) and affect economic growth/performance of a society. But the two different approaches can work equally well. An important intervening variable is context. Changes in context can be reasoned to differently affect costs of religious, behavioral contracting in comparison to costs of institutional/constitutional economic contracting.

For the Old Testament text, shifts in context can be projected to the shifts in approaches to social contract as storytelling unfolds. The contexts described in the Old Testament changed (a); with regard to the degree and nature of urbanization that can be observed in the Old Testament text, from pre-modern urbanization to modern urbanization as the textual history of the Old Testament unfolds, and (b); with regard to the rise of pluralism and polytheism as interaction conditions as storytelling advances. With such changes setting in, we can conceptualize in economic terms shifts from religious, behavioral contracting in the early patriarchal stories to the economized governance strategies in later stories (Wagner-Tsukamoto 2009a, 2013c). For the Old Testament text, changes in urban contexts and the rise of pluralism as an interaction condition can explain, because of their effects on attack/defense costs and transaction costs and growth/performance of these societies, why we see in stories like the Joseph stories and the Solomon stories comparatively modern constitutional and institutional economic governance emerge and succeed, with high performing, mutual gains societies coming into full bloom.

Such conceptual strategies to analyzing context shed light on reasons as to why Buchanan comparatively favored a very one-sided view of constitutional economic governance, which he perceived as modern. Nevertheless, some critical comments apply regarding how Buchanan differentiated his constitutional economics from pre-modernity and ancient ethics.

Buchanan (1975, p. 117) disassociated himself from a supposedly pre-modern moral precepts approach, brandishing it as non-enlightened because of its reliance on the 'shivering human being' before God (Buchanan 1975, pp. 130–131; discussed in more detail by Wagner-Tsukamoto 2010, 2014a, 2015b). This reflects

Buchanan's moral, normative stance regarding what type of institutional, constitutional governance is preferable, and he clearly wanted to place himself in this regard in the tradition of the North American, European and particularly the Scottish Enlightenment.

Buchanan (1975, p. 117) admitted that a moral precepts approach to societal governance can be effective and supposedly efficient too. It can show ways out of the natural distribution state, as we find this state arise in the Old Testament in the outcomes of the Paradise story, when interactions had dramatically broken down. Yet, Buchanan more generally rejected a religious approach because he equated it with the moral precepts approach, merely behaviorally read by him and being equated by him as non-enlightened and non-economic.

As noted, in Old Testament stories, we find religious, behavioral, faith-based moral precepts approaches to social contract especially in the Noah, Isaac or Abraham stories. This mirrors Buchanan's behavioral reading of the moral precepts approach or the religious approach. But this is not the full picture. Other stories like the Paradise story, the Jacob stories, the Joseph stories, the exodus stories and the stories of the settlement lend themselves to a considerable degree to a different approach to social contract. Constitutional and institutional economic reconstruction is highly successful here. From here we can critically comment on Buchanan (Wagner-Tsukamoto 2009a, 2010, 2014a, 2015b). The diagnosis of pseudo-modern strategies to constitutional and institutional economic governance in Old Testament stories implies various things: First, on the one hand we have the often and widely historically claimed dualism and dichotomy between economics in the classical and neoclassical tradition of Smith, Friedman, Buchanan, or Becker, (to name but a few), and on the other hand traditional ethics (in our case: religious/biblical ethics), cannot be inevitably upheld. The conceptual economic fabric of order ethics and constitutional/institutional economics, which vividly shines through in very many stories of the Old Testament, underlines this thesis. Such claims to dualism may implicitly or more explicitly underlie much research on order ethics too, as such research emerged out of the studies of Eucken; as it can be identified in Buchanan's studies.

Surprisingly, as noted above, Buchanan aimed to uphold this dualism (Wagner-Tsukamoto 2009a, 2010, 2014a, 2015b)—as did indeed Smith (1776/ 1976, pp. 789–793) when proposing a concept of 'rational religion' that he aimed to dualistically split from Bible and biblical religion (Minowitz 1993, pp.154–156, 166). I contest this dualistic split for Buchanan as for Smith (as for many others; Wagner-Tsukamoto 2014a, 2014b): A concept of rational religion, as Smith had already aimed to set out, can be proposed through economics that approaches and re-conceptualizes biblical religion in economic terms; in a sense through Smith's very own economics. Then, a different conceptual 'layer' of religion becomes visible, which reflects the blurring of disciplinary boundaries between religious theory and economics.

Indeed, we can suggest that this economic layer of religion has contributed to the pervasiveness of religion over time, as North (1991, p. 111) and Williamson (2000, p. 596) raised this question of the pervasiveness of religion. This thesis deserves careful scrutiny for societies that began establishing market economies since antiquity.

In consequence, economic reconstruction of the Old Testament allows us to contest the differentiation of modernity (and the Age of Enlightenment) from supposedly pre-modern antiquity and ancient times. On grounds of economic reconstruction of ancient religious text, the equating of the outgoing Middle Age with the beginning of modernity and the Enlightenment, and the equating of antiquity and ancient times with pre-modernity and traditionalist ethics needs considerable philosophical and ethical adjustments. This conceptual contest is negotiated through setting out a rational economic approach to religion that grounds itself in biblical religion and in the Old Testament.

References

Armstrong, K. 1996. *In the beginning. A new reading of the book of Genesis*. London: Harper-Collins.
Arnal, W. 2010. What branches grow out of this stone rubbish? Christian origins and the study of religion. *Studies in Religion* 39(4): 549–572.
Bernhardt, W. 2009. Wirtschaftsethik auf Abwegen. *Freiburg Discussion Papers on Constitutional Economics* 09/8, Walter Eucken Institut, Albert-Ludwigs Universität Freiburg, 27 pp.
Brett, M.G. 2000a. Reading the Bible in the context of methodological pluralism: the undermining of ethnic exclusivism in Genesis. In Carroll MDR (ed) *Rethinking contexts, rereading texts: contributions from the social sciences to biblical interpretation*, Sheffield: Sheffield Academic Press (JSOT Supplement 299), pp. 48–78.
Brett, M.G. 2000b. Canonical criticism and Old Testament theology. In *Text in context*, ed. A.D.H. Mayes, 63–85. Oxford: Oxford University Press.
Buchanan, J.M. 1975. *The limits of liberty. Between anarchy and leviathan*. Chicago: University of Chicago Press.
Buchanan, J. M. 1999a. What should economists do? In *The Collected Works of James M. Buchanan*, Vol. 1, Indianapolis: Liberty Fund, pp. 28–42.
Buchanan, J. M. 1999b. The foundations of normative individualism. In J. M. Buchanan (ed.), *The Logical Foundations of Constitutional Liberty*, Vol. 1, The Collected Works of James M. Buchanan, Indianapolis: Liberty Fund, pp. 281–291.
Clines, D.J.A., and Exum, J. C. 1993. The New Literary Criticism. In Exum J. C. and Clines D. J. A. (eds.), *The new literary criticism and the hebrew bible*, Sheffield: JSOT Press (JSOT Supplement 143), pp. 11–25.
Collins, J.W. 1994. Is business ethics an oxymoron? *Business Horizons* 37(5): 1–8.
Duska, R. 2000. Business ethics: oxymoron or good business? *Business Ethics Quarterly* 10(1): 111–129.
Homann, K. 1994. Ethik und Ökonomik. Zur Theoriesstrategie der Wirtschaftsethik. In *Wirtschaftsethische Perspektiven I*, ed. K. Homann, 9–30. Berlin: Duncker & Humblot.
Homann, K. 1997. Sinn und Grenze der ökonomischenMethode in ther Wirtschaftsethik. In Aufderheide, D. and Dabrowski, M. (eds.), *Wirtschaftsethik und Moralökonomik. Normen, soziale Ordnung under der Beitrag der Wirtschaftsethik*, Berlin: Duncker & Humblot, pp. 11–42.

Homann, K. 1999. Die Relevanz der Ökonomik für die Implementation ethischer Zielsetzungen. In Korff W. et al. (eds.), *Handbuch der Wirtschaftethik*, 4 Volumes, Gütersloh: Gütersloher Verlagshaus, Vol. 1, pp. 322–343.

Gerlach, J. 2002. Theologische Wirtschaftsethik als interdisziplinäre Aufgabe. *Zeitschrift für Wirtschafts- und Unternehmensethik* 3(2): 205–225.

Goodpaster, K.E. 1991. Business ethics and stakeholder analysis. *Business Ethics Quarterly* 1: 53–72.

Goodpaster, K.E. 2000. Conscience and its counterfeits in organizational life: a new interpretation of the naturalistic fallacy. *Business Ethics Quarterly* 10(1): 189–201.

Luce, R. D., and Raiffa, H. 1957. *Games and Decisions. Introduction and Critical Survey*, New York: J. Wiley.

Lütge, C. 2002. Über Sinn und Methode einer Ordnungsethik. *Zeitschrift für Wirtschafts- und Unternehmensethik* 3(2): 226–229.

Lütge, C. 2005. Economic ethics, business ethics and the idea of mutual advantages. *Business Ethics. A European Review* 14(2): 108–118.

Minowitz, P. 1993. *Profits, Priests and Princes. Adam Smith's Emancipation of Economics From Politics and Religion*, Stanford: Stanford University Press.

Nash, L. 2000. Intensive care for everyone's least favorite oxymoron: narrative in business ethics. *Business Ethics Quarterly* 10(1): 277–290.

Neumann, von, J., and Morgenstern, O. 1947. *Theory of Games and Economic Behavior*, Princeton, NJ: Princeton University Press.

North, D.C. 1991. Institutions. *Journal of Economic Perspectives* 5(1): 97–112.

North, D.C., and B.R. Weingast. 1989. Constitutions and commitment: the evolution of institutions governing public choice in seventeenth-century England. *The Journal of Economic History* 49: 803–832.

Pies, I. 1996. Public choice versus constitutional economics: a methodological interpretation of the Buchanan research program. *Constitutional Political Economy* 7(1): 21–34.

Pies, I. 2011. Walter Eucken als Klassiker der Ordnungsethik—Eine ordonomische Rekonstruktion. *Journal for Business, Economics & Ethics* 12(2): 222–249.

Rad, von, G. 1963. *Genesis. A Commentary*, London: SCM Press.

Sen, A. 1990. Rational fools: a critique of the behavioral foundations of economic theory. In *Beyond self-interest*, ed. J.J. Mansbridge, 25–43. Chicago: The University of Chicago Press.

Simon, H.A. 1993. Altruism and economics. *American Economic Review. Papers and Proceedings* 83(2): 156–161.

Smith, A. 1776/1976. *An Inquiry into the Nature and Causes of the Wealth of Nations*, 2 Volumes, Oxford: Clarendon.

Snyman, G. 2012. The African and Western hermeneutics debate: mimesis, the Book of Esther, and textuality. *Old Testament Essays* 25(3): 657–684.

Suchanek, A. 1994. *Ökonomischer Ansatz und theoretische Integration*. Tübingen: Mohr Siebeck.

Toorn, van der, K. 2007. *Scribal culture and the making of the Hebrew Bible*, Cambridge, MA: Harvard University Press.

Vanberg, V.J. 2004. The *Status Quo* in contractarian-constitutionalist perspective. *Constitutional Political Economy* 15: 153–170.

Vanberg, V. J. 2006. Democracy, citizen sovereignty, and constitutional economics. *Freiburg Discussion Papers on Constitutional Economics* No. 06/2, Walter Eucken Institut, Albert-Ludwigs University of Freiburg, 20 pages.

Vanberg, V. J. 2014. James M. Buchanan's contractarianism and modern liberalism. *Constitutional Political Economy* 25, pp. 18–38.

Wagner-Tsukamoto, S.A. 2001. Economics of Genesis. On the institutional economic deciphering and reconstruction of the legends of Genesis. *Journal of Interdisciplinary Economics* 12: 249–287.

Wagner-Tsukamoto, S.A. 2003. *Human nature and organization theory*. Cheltenham: Edward Elgar.

Wagner-Tsukamoto, S.A. 2008. An economic reading of the exodus: on the institutional economic reconstruction of biblical cooperation failures. *Scandinavian Journal of the Old Testament* 22 (1): 114–134.

Wagner-Tsukamoto, S.A. 2009a. *Is God an Economist?. An Institutional Economic Reconstruction of the Old Testament*, Basingstoke: Palgrave Macmillan.

Wagner-Tsukamoto, S.A. 2009b. The Paradise story: a constitutional economic reconstruction. *Journal for the Study of the Old Testament* 34(2): 147–170.

Wagner-Tsukamoto, S.A. 2010. Out of a slave contract: the analysis of pre-hobbesian anarchists in the Old Testament. *Constitutional Political Economy* 21: 288–307.

Wagner-Tsukamoto, S.A. 2012a. Questioning the Weber thesis: capitalist ethics and the Hebrew Bible? *Sociology Mind* 2(1): 1–11.

Wagner-Tsukamoto, S.A. 2012b. The tree of life: banned or not banned? a rational choice interpretation. *Scandinavian Journal of the Old Testament* 26(1): 102–122.

Wagner-Tsukamoto, S.A. 2012c. After the theft: natural distribution states and prisoner's dilemmas in the Paradise story. *Old Testament Essays* 25(3): 705–736.

Wagner-Tsukamoto, S.A. 2013a. Homo economicus and the stories of Jacob: on the methodological relevance of rational choice theory for studying the Hebrew Bible. *Method and Theory in the Study of Religion* 25: 78–100.

Wagner-Tsukamoto, S.A. 2013b. State formation in the Hebrew Bible: An Institutional Economic Perspective. *Journal for the Study of the Old Testament* 37(4): 391–422.

Wagner-Tsukamoto, S. A. 2013c. The city metaphor and pluralism in Genesis: institutional economics between pre-modern and modern urbanism. *Working Paper, School of Management, University of Leicester*, in the Leicester Research Archive (LRA): http://hdl.handle.net/2381/27894.

Wagner-Tsukamoto, S.A. 2013d. The Adam Smith problem revisited: a methodological resolution. *Journal des Economistes et des Etudes Humaines* 19: 63–99.

Wagner-Tsukamoto, S. A. 2014a. *The Economics of Paradise. On the Onset of Modernity in Antiquity*. Basingstoke, UK: Palgrave Macmillan.

Wagner-Tsukamoto, S. A. 2014b. Rational religion: economic paterns in biblical thought. *Working and Research Paper, School of Management, University of Leicester*, Leicester Research Archive: http://hdl.handle.net/2381/29200.

Wagner-Tsukamoto, S. A. 2015a. Ethical principles of Old Testament economics: implications for the teaching of business ethics. *Journal of Religion and Business Ethics* 3, Article 16.

Wagner-Tsukamoto, S.A. 2015b. The genesis of cooperation in the stories of Joseph: a constitutional and institutional economic reconstruction. *Scandinavian Journal of the Old Testament* 29: 33–54.

Werhane, P.H. 2000. Business ethics and the origins of contemporary capitalism: economics and ethics in the work of Adam Smith and Herbert Spencer. *Journal of Business Ethics* 24(3): 185–198.

Westermann, C. 1984. *Genesis 1–11. A commentary*. London: SPCK.

Williamson, O.E. 1975. *Markets and Hierarchies*. New York: Free Press.

Williamson, O.E. 1985. *The economic institutions of capitalism*. New York: Free Press.

Williamson, O.E. 2000. The New Institutional economics: taking stock, looking ahead. *Journal of Economic Literature* 38: 595–613.

Windsor, D. 2006. Corporate social responsibility: three key approaches. *Journal of Management Studies* 43: 93–114.

Part III
Theoretical Foundations of Order Ethics—The Philosophical Background of Order Ethics

Order Ethics and the Problem of Social Glue

Christoph Luetge

1 The Problem Setting

It is an old question of philosophy—from Plato and Aristotle to Hobbes, Hume, Kant, and Hegel—to ask what holds human societies together. However, during the last century, and especially since the dawn of globalization, this question has gained much importance as societies face a previously unknown degree of cultural, social, and economic pluralism.[1] It is not clear how or even whether age-old answers to this problem can have bearing on modern social problems. To give an example of how modern problems differ from pre-modern ones, consider how collective structures and social arrangements in modern societies are far more vulnerable to the actions of individuals or small groups than in earlier days, which has been known in theory long before, and has been made clear by events like September 11, 2001 or the revelations of Edward Snowdon.

In view of this situation, many contemporary positions in social and political philosophy (some of which will be discussed here) have been asking the following question: Granted that actors in modern societies strive for advantages and benefits, do we still need some kind of a *social glue* beyond this mere quest for advantages and benefits? I would like to call this kind of social glue a *moral surplus*.[2] A moral surplus is a moral capacity or capability which the citizens of a modern society have

---

This chapter reproduces revised material that has previously been published in C. Luetge, 2016. "Order Ethics and the Problem of Social Glue", *University of St. Thomas Law Journal* 12, 2: 339–359. We thank the publisher for their permission to reproduce it here.

[1] For accounts of the phenomenon of globalisation, cf., e.g., Stiglitz (2002) and Bhagwati (2004).
[2] For this term, cf. Luetge (2015).

C. Luetge (✉)
Chair of Business Ethics, Technical University of Munich, Munich, Germany
e-mail: luetge@tum.de

to adopt in order to keep their society stable. This moral surplus, according to these positions, is necessary in addition to rules and incentive structures. It may, however, differ in degree and strength.

In this paper, I will discuss some contemporary philosophical positions, which (except for the last one—K. Binmore) argue that modern societies do indeed require a moral surplus to prevent human societies from destabilizing. The positions analyzed in the following sections are the discourse ethics of J. Habermas, J. Rawls' political liberalism, D. Gauthier's contractarian moral theory, and finally, K. Binmore's game theory-based contractarianism. As I can dedicate only a short part of this article to each of these positions, I will restrict myself to the following question: Can the moral surplus in question remain stable in the face of opposing incentives?

This question can be explicated in the following, rather simple, way: The prime situational model for interactions that concern drastically disadvantageous incentives to all actors is the prisoners' dilemma (PD).[3] In PD situations, actors behaving cooperatively are permanently faced with the possibility of being "exploited" by others, therefore they pre-emptively stop cooperating. This leads to a situation where rational, self-interested actors end up with a result that leaves everyone worse off, and no one better off.[4] Two of the four approaches discussed here (Gauthier and Binmore) regard the PD as their conceptual starting point.

I will argue that the question whether the moral surplus can remain stable must be answered negatively in each of the cases discussed, with the exception of Binmore. None of the first three surpluses can remain stable against opposing incentives in PD situations. I will start with Habermas' discourse ethics.

2 Habermas: Rational Motivation

In arguing for the importance of discourses as grounds for normative theory, Habermas makes a fundamental assumption—the participants of a discourse must allow their behavior, at least partially, to be motivated by a *rational motivation*.[5] With the help of this concept, Habermas explicates the difference between his two opposing types of actions: strategic and communicative. This difference represents a central antagonism in Habermas' theory. While strategic action (*strategisches Handeln*) is affected by incentives and sanctions, communicative action

---

[3]For conceptualizations of the prisoners' dilemma, cf. Axelrod (1984).—Sometimes this situation is also called the *prisoner's* dilemma. I deliberately use the plural because it is an *interaction* problem for *both* actors, not just a unilateral decision problem for a single actor.

[4]*Iterating* PD situations means introducing sanctions, i.e. incentives. If this is done by way of institutions, then this is in agreement with my approach (cf. Sect. 6). If not, then it is unclear what could be meant by iterating a PD situation 'in real life', *without* relying on institutions for stability.

[5]Cf. Habermas (1981/1984/1987), vol. 1, pp. 26 and 29; Habermas (1983/1990), pp. 58 and 109; Habermas (1992/1996), p. 5.

(*kommunikatives Handeln*) is led by rational motivation.[6] But what, then, *is* rational motivation and where does it come from?

It is difficult to find an answer to this question in Habermas' writings. In *Theory of Communicative Action,* he simply postulates: "If arguments are valid, then insight into the internal conditions of their validity can have a rationally motivating force."[7] Yet a few pages earlier, there is a footnote in which Habermas admits that the concept of a rational motivation has not yet been analyzed satisfactorily.[8]

In later works, the situation does not get much better. In *"Diskursethik: Notizen zu einem Begründungsprogramm,"* the necessity of a rational motivation is stressed several times,[9] but only in one instance is a justification given. Here, Habermas relies on the illocutionary effects of a speech act.[10] He assumes that speech acts can force actors to perform certain actions and refrain from others. The core of this assumption is the idea of a performative contradiction.[11] According to Habermas, a rationally motivated actor is led by the desire to avoid a performative contradiction.

It is doubtful whether a speech act has such a binding force. It seems as if Habermas recognizes this problem himself, as he invents a dialogue with a fictitious skeptic who doubts exactly this binding force of speech acts.[12] However, Habermas responds that the skeptic may well stick to his position but then has to "be silent." He cannot escape the *Lebenswelt*, which, according to Habermas, is formed by cultural tradition and socialization, which in turn work through rational motivation. If he tried to escape, he would end in "schizophrenia and suicide."[13]

In the 1990s, Habermas' thought developed in new directions. He faced the problem of the skeptic again in "Remarks on Discourse Ethics." Here, Habermas first seems to weaken the power of rational motivation by attributing to moral norms only "the weak motivating force of good reasons."[14] He goes as far as stating that "the validity of moral commands is subject to the condition that they are *universally* adhered to as the basis for a general practice,"[15] thus implying that individuals might be allowed to behave "immorally" when faced with possible by others. This would be the case in prisoners' dilemma situations.[16] However, in the rest of his article, Habermas does not consider this a problem of ethics. Rather, he

---

[6]Cf. Habermas (1983/1990), p. 58.
[7]Habermas (1981/1984/1987), vol. 1, p. 29; cf. also Habermas (1981/1984/1987), vol. 1, p. 42.
[8]Habermas (1981/1984/1987), vol. 1, p. 26, fn. 28 (p. 411).
[9]Cf. Habermas (1983/1990), pp. 58, 72, 109.
[10]Habermas (1983/1990), p. 58.
[11]For further explication, cf. Habermas (1983/1990), pp. 80f.
[12]In Habermas (1983/1990).
[13]Habermas (1983/1990), p. 102.
[14]Habermas (1991/1993), p. 33.
[15]Habermas (1991/1993), p. 34.
[16]Binmore (1994, 1998) and Homann (2002) both assign the PD a central role in their ethical or ethically relevant approaches.

writes, it can only be argued within the discourse of *law* that some norms might be valid yet not reasonable (*zumutbar*) because of their lack of general acceptance.

Consequently, this leads Habermas to include institutions in his conception, which were rather neglected in his earlier work. He recognizes that the problem of compliance to norms cannot be solved by postulates of rational motivation or by citing developmental psychology.[17] In B*etween Facts and Norms*, he explicitly develops an account of law and institutions. However, even here it is clear that he does not rely on sanctions and incentives alone as a means for governing modern societies. Rather, the citizens must still have certain characteristics—they have to accept not only the legal rules, but also normative claims resulting in turn from the idealized discourse assumptions.[18] Habermas still assumes a "coordination of plans of actions"[19] by language— and thus still the existence of rational motivation working via speech acts. Consequently, Habermas' main claims are still intact in his second, institutional, phase.

Now the question mentioned above becomes relevant: Can rational motivation remain stable in view of opposing incentives? One problem in Habermas' argument concerning speech acts is his reconstruction of the *Lebenswelt*.[20] In my view, there are alternative and less harmonious reconstructions of the *Lebenswelt* possible, in which the binding force of speech acts is much weaker. One major example is the game-theoretic approach that reconstructs all human interactions as "riddled" with dilemma situations like the prisoners' dilemma.[21] These situations can be either manifest (as in open market interactions with competition being obvious) or hidden. Hidden PD situations that have been overcome are exemplified prominently in all the institutions like police and jurisdiction that come into effect as a consequence of the social contract which enables the actors to escape from the natural state (i.e., a PD situation). Sanctioning institutions are often solutions to prisoner's dilemma situations.

In a phenomenalistic perspective that does not look beyond the surface, it appears the individuals who act according to these institutions have been moved by a rational motivation. However, in another perspective, the "deeper" structures behind become visible, and it becomes clear that it is not just rational motivation, but rather incentives and possible sanctions (in this case, informal) that hold this social practice in place. This casts doubt on Habermas' claim to have found the only reconstruction of everyday practices.

Moreover, while Habermas introduces institutions into his conception in later works, thus allowing for sanctioning by legal rules, he still relies on his original idea of rationally motivated individuals. Institutions are assigned only a secondary place, while the original moral surplus survives intact. Therefore, Habermas' conceptions can be regarded as a chief example of a moral surplus theory.

---

[17] In some (earlier) works (cf. Habermas 1983/1990), he makes extensive use of L. Kohlberg's developmental psychology.

[18] Cf. Habermas (1992/1996), pp. 17f. and 459ff.

[19] Habermas (1992/1996), p. 34.

[20] Habermas (1992/1996).

[21] Like Binmore (1994, 1998).

3 Rawls: The Sense of Justice

Rawls' conception of justice as fairness (JF)[22] is known so well, I can limit myself to some very general remarks. I will focus here on the conception as it is presented in *Political Liberalism*.[23] Its main starting point is the idea that JF is political, not a metaphysical conception. For Rawls, this is the only conception of justice suitable for modern, pluralistic societies, where pluralism of values and norms must be regarded as a permanent condition.[24] The constitution of a modern state cannot be built on any comprehensive (e.g., philosophical or religious) doctrine, but only on an idea which avoids conflicts between these doctrines—a political conception. It can be characterized by the following four points:

(1) The conception must be freestanding. It must be possible to present this conception without reference to comprehensive doctrines. It should, however, be possible to find arguments for this conception from the point of view of different doctrines.[25] Rawls hopes that JF will eventually be supported by an overlapping consensus of reasonable doctrines.[26]
(2) The conception will judge only the basic structure of a society, that is, only the basic institutions—like freedom of speech, property rules, etc.—which have extraordinary importance for the citizens.[27]
(3) The main content of this conception are the two famous principles of justice. First, all people have equal claims "to a fully adequate scheme of equal basic rights and liberties, which scheme is compatible with the same scheme for all."[28] Second, social and economic inequalities are justified only insofar as they are "attached to positions and offices open to all under conditions of fair equality of opportunity" and they must be to the greatest advantage of the least advantaged.[29]
(4) The acceptance of these two principles can be reconstructed as a choice of rational actors in an original position.[30] While the construction of this original position is less relevant here and has been discussed elsewhere,[31] it is important to note that it is only a means of presentation, a think tool not to be understood in an ontological sense.[32]

---

[22]Cf. Rawls (1971, 1993).
[23] There are some interesting differences between the "Theory of Justice" and "Political Liberalism", but I cannot go into detail here.
[24]First in Rawls (1985).
[25]Cf. Rawls (1993), pp. 10f.
[26]Cf. Rawls (1993), pp. 58ff.
[27]Cf. Rawls (1993), pp. 11f.
[28]Here again, I use the wording employed in Rawls (1993), p. 5.
[29]Rawls (1993), 6.
[30]Cf. Rawls (1993), pp. 22ff.
[31]Cf. already Dworkin (1975).
[32]Cf. Rawls (1995), p. 203.

While the conception of justice described so far is generally known, it is only part of the story. Just like Habermas, Rawls regards a moral surplus as indispensable for the stability of modern societies. According to Rawls, the citizens of a modern state must have two "moral" capabilities. First, they must have personal conception of the good, and second, be motivated by a sense of justice.[33] While the first is rather unproblematic and will not be discussed here, the second is quite interesting and poses a number of problems.

Rawls characterizes the sense of justice[34] as an integral part of a well-ordered society[35] and defines it as "the capacity to understand, to apply, and normally to be moved by an effective desire to act from (and not merely in accordance with) the principles of justice."[36] The central passage "to act from" is important—Rawls explicitly does not want to say that individuals comply with rules because of expected benefits. Rather (in my reading of this passage), the principles of justice must be complied with even if no personal benefits can be made out.

This becomes clear again in a second, more general definition of the sense of justice, which is defined here as the capability "to honor fair terms of cooperation."[37] The phrase "to honor" is important—fair rules can be honored by all actors regardless of the incentives in effect. Rawls does not talk about governance by incentives in this context. The rules of a fair society are characterized as fair, but he does not say if they are to be sanctioned. In particular, he does not say how counterproductive consequences—in PD situations, for example—might be avoided. If my reading of Rawls is correct, he would have to call for compliance with norms or rules even if there were PD-like incentives running against it.[38]

This is one of the main themes in JF, which becomes visible in several opposing concepts that Rawls constructs: the reasonable versus the rational, the *modus vivendi* versus the overlapping consensus, and the constitutional consensus versus the overlapping consensus.[39] In all three cases, Rawls' moral surplus, the sense of justice, plays a decisive role. First, the individuals who are just rational, but not reasonable, lack the sense of justice. Second, an overlapping consensus can only be formed by individuals acting from the sense of justice. I will focus here on the second point.[40]

---

[33] Rawls (1993), 35.

[34] The sense of justice appears first in "The Sense of Justice" (Rawls 1963).

[35] A society is well-ordered according to Rawls if (a) the two principles of justice are generally accepted, (b) the basic structure conform with these principles, and (c) the citizens possess a sense of justice (cf. Rawls 1993, pp. 35ff.).

[36] I use the more elaborated wording in Rawls (1993), p. 302 (my italics) rather than the shorter version on p. 19.

[37] Rawls (1993), p. 302, my italics.

[38] Cf. also Rawls (1993), p. 35, where he writes that the "citizens have a normally effective sense of justice *and so* they generally comply with society's basic institutions" (my italics).

[39] For the following, cf. Luetge (2015), ch. 3.4.2.

[40] The difference between the rational and the reasonable has been widely analysed, cf., e.g., Davion and Wolf (2000) and Kukathas and Pettit (1990).

Rawls emphasizes that JF has to be supported by an overlapping consensus of reasonable comprehensive doctrines and not just by a "mere" *modus vivendi*. He defines the *modus vivendi* as a contract between two parties with opposing goals. Both parties are interested in keeping the contract.[41] However, they would break it if the situational conditions changed and their own interest could be better pursued at the others' expense. According to Rawls, this situation cannot serve as a basis for social stability. A consensus founded only "on self- or group interests," being only the result of "political bargaining,"[42] must be regarded as inherently unstable—if the conditions changed, so would the *modus vivendi*, with the result of social stability eroding.[43] Rawls also assumes that a society collapses if its conception of justice and its democratic order are not "supported by at least a substantial majority of its politically active citizens."[44]

In view of this, Rawls wants to build social stability on a stronger basis—on an overlapping consensus of reasonable comprehensive doctrines. This consensus comprises Rawls' idea that the individuals must be able to agree on a political conception of justice like JF, not only from self-interest—and thus not only from an interest in general compliance to the rules of the contract—but on the basis of their personal comprehensive doctrines. While these doctrines certainly differ in many regards, the overlapping consensus is considered possible for two reasons.[45] First, the political values of all members of a society are very important, as they determine the basic structure of social life. Second, Rawls insists that reasonable comprehensive doctrines have always left room for interpretation, as the development both of Christian and Islamic thought show. Theologians and philosophers have continuously been able to demonstrate how religious and philosophical values are compatible with political values. This is possible, according to Rawls, because a political conception does not say anything about the truth of comprehensive doctrines. These doctrines must only accept the existence of other reasonable comprehensive doctrines.

For the problem at hand, it is relevant that an overlapping consensus differs from a *modus vivendi* in the following three respects:

(1) The overlapping consensus does not depend on changing circumstances and is therefore more stable.[46]
(2) The overlapping consensus comprises conceptions of the person and the society and also principles of justice. It is thus much "deeper" than a *modus vivendi*, as it extends into the moral domain. Moral reasons, which are

---

[41] A *modus vivendi* is thus not comparable to a 'cease fire' as opposed to a peace treaty, but is rather a 'simple' (exchange) contract. .
[42] Rawls (1993), p. 147.
[43] Id.
[44] Rawls (1993), p. 38.
[45] Cf. Rawls (1993), pp. 133ff.
[46] Cf. Rawls (1993), p. 148.

developed on the basis of reasonable comprehensive doctrines, determine the acceptance of the conception of justice.[47]

(3) Rawls defines the overlapping consensus not as a point of convergence, where conflicting interests converge and where people agree "on accepting certain authorities, or on complying with certain institutional arrangements."[48] Mere adherence to the rules is thus not enough for the citizens. Rather, what Rawls demands is adherence for the right reasons. According to him, this demand for the use of reason is a functional one, as it is in the interest of social stability.[49] If, as I will argue, stability could be achieved without an overlapping consensus, then Rawls' argument would be undermined.

For Rawls, the *modus vivendi* will thus not yield sufficient stability. We might be inclined to take this for granted, as the *modus vivendi* seems indeed rather weak. However, Rawls goes on to argue against an intermediate concept that lies between the *modus vivendi* and the overlapping consensus—the constitutional consensus. The latter might evolve from the *modus vivendi* and implies agreement on at least part of the values of political liberalism, in particular about the political procedures and some basic rights and liberties.[50] As a result, the constitutional consensus should give a society at least a little more stability than the *modus vivendi*, even if the sense of justice is not yet in effect.

But Rawls regards the constitutional consensus as still too narrow. It should only be a first basis for a discussion between different political groups with political doctrines of their own.[51] In order to dispute peacefully in public, the groups have to develop political conceptions of justice. They have to learn how to argue and how to convince other groups. This would lead to a more differentiated discussion of questions of justice, in the course of which an overlapping consensus might arise, by agreeing, among other things, on basic rights and liberties.[52]

Rawls concedes, however, that the "different social and economic interests" might impede this development.[53] Under the following two conditions, the conflicts might turn out to be insurmountable: if the different conceptions of justice are "supported by and encourage deeply conflicting political and economic interests,"[54] and if the conflicts of interests cannot be overcome by a constitution, then "a full overlapping consensus cannot, it seems, be achieved."[55] This seems to imply that such conflicts can only be balanced by constitutional rules, not by any moral

---

[47]Id.
[48]Rawls (1993), p. 147.
[49]Id.
[50]Cf. Rawls (1993), pp. 158f.
[51]Rawls (1993), pp. 164ff.
[52]Id.
[53]Rawls (1993), p. 167.
[54]Rawls (1993), p. 168.
[55]Rawls (1993), p. 168.

surpluses. But if that is the case, where is the higher dignity of the overlapping consensus vis-à-vis the constitutional consensus and the *modus vivendi*, which likewise require both the balancing of interests? Is the overlapping consensus nothing but a long-entrenched constitutional consensus?

It is clear that Rawls has more than that in mind. Overcoming conflicts of interests is apparently a necessary, but not a sufficient, condition for an overlapping consensus. The overlapping consensus offers more stability than the two lower levels, but it can only come into effect if the citizens develop a moral surplus, that is, the sense of justice.[56] However, there still remains a problem when trying to separate the different forms of consensus. Rawls goes on to argue that an overlapping consensus is necessary in a functional way to avoid conflicts.[57] But remember that certain types of conflicts can impede the overlapping consensus. So is this a vicious circle? Could it be that the very conflicts that are to be avoided by an overlapping consensus might impede it? To put it differently, could it be that the overlapping consensus does not really solve these conflicts, but only seemingly?

Rawls does not make it clear how strong a conflict must be in order to impede an overlapping consensus. Does it have to be a very deep constitutional conflict, like that of abolishing slavery in the United States, or would smaller conflicts (e.g. over the construction of new highways) suffice? Rawls would probably respond that this is not a question for philosophical theory, but only for practical application. Nevertheless, in order to make claims about the stability of different levels of consensus, I think a theory of conflicts would be a desideratum. This theory would have to explain which types of conflicts an overlapping consensus could avoid and which types might impede it.

In sum, Rawls regards the sense of justice as an indispensable element in the development of an overlapping consensus which in turn could generate sufficient social stability. There is, however, a certain tension in his argument—between the claim that the sense of justice must not be based on interests, on the one hand, and the claim that the overlapping consensus fulfils a social function in avoiding conflicts (which should be in the interests of all), on the other hand.

4 Gauthier: Dispositions

In his 1986 book, *Morals by Agreement*, D. Gauthier tried to develop an account of morals as based purely on self-interest, thus starting with assumptions fundamentally different from those of the previous two approaches. Gauthier starts by stating

---

[56]For a critical account of this, cf. Mills (2000).

[57]He writes that a "constitutional consensus will prove too narrow", as a democratic people will have to be "sufficiently unified and cohesive" in order to cover, among others, basic matters of justice. Otherwise, "conflict will arise about these" (Rawls 1993, p. 166).

that moral problems arise due to PD situations.[58] In a PD situation, the participants recognize that the result of their (rational) actions is quite unwanted by all parties. The solution proposed by Gauthier is that all actors should commit themselves to a certain principle of justice—the principle of "minimax relative concession" (MRC).[59] In MRC, each individual accepts a rule that minimizes her highest possible relative concessions to others.[60] Gauthier argues that MRC is to be adopted in a two-step procedure. First, the actors choose MRC from self-interest. Afterwards, however, MRC is to constrain the actors' self-interest.[61]

Gauthier tries to show that MRC would be chosen by rational, utility-maximizing actors for the sake of greater benefits in the long run. However, he recognizes that this is not enough and that the problem of compliance to MRC is not solved easily by pointing to its rationality. Gauthier reminds us of "Hobbes' Foole." In the *Leviathan*,[62] the Foole is introduced to show that an actor's acceptance of a contract is not a sufficient condition to be motivated to comply with the contract. The Foole sees the remaining PD and argues that it would be best for him if all others complied, but he himself could break the contract.

Now, it is important to note that Gauthier does not want to enforce compliance by sanctions and incentives. This would be "a political, not a moral, solution,"[63] which would neglect a central difference between morals and interests—"Were duty no more than interest, morals would be superfluous."[64] Morals would be more efficient in solving interaction problems, because, according to Gauthier, the cost of supervision and enforcement of norms would be reduced to zero.[65] A voluntary keeping of moral agreements would make at least some institutions unnecessary. Gauthier is thus not against political solutions per se, but hopes to substitute them by "cheaper" means.

Gauthier's alternative proposal is that all actors should internalize MRC by adopting a disposition to constrain their actions. He distinguishes between two types of actors: straightforward maximizers (SMs) and constrained maximizers (CMs).[66] While both types maximize their utility, CMs do so under condition of other actors' utility. CMs adopt a disposition to cooperate, which Gauthier also calls the "idea of mutual benefit."[67] A CM complies with mutually agreed norms if she thinks that her expected utility would be positive in the case of general compliance, thereby tolerating at least some degree of free-riding. She will *not* punish defection

---

[58]Cf. Gauthier (1986), pp. 12, 82, 103f.
[59]Gauthier (1986), p. 157.
[60]Cf. also Gauthier (1997).
[61]For the following, cf. Luetge (2015), ch. 3.5.
[62]Hobbes (1651/1991), ch. 15.
[63]Gauthier (1986), p. 163.
[64]Gauthier (1986), p. 1.
[65]Gauthier (1986), pp. 164ff.
[66]Gauthier (1986), 15f.
[67]Gauthier (1986), p. 157.

by defecting herself. An SM, by contrast, will always try to directly maximize his utility without being inhibited by any internalized constraints.

Gauthier shows that in some evolutionary settings, CMs have an advantage over SMs. If CMs can expect to frequently meet other CMs, they can stabilize cooperation within their group and thereby realize large gains from group-internal cooperation. If this leaves the CMs better off than the SMs, the disposition to cooperate could well spread fast within a society.[68] Gauthier admits, however, that if all other actors within a society are SMs, then the remaining CMs must also behave like SMs.[69] In this situation, morality would have no chance. Moreover, Gauthier states explicitly that a CM is not "just" a very sophisticated SM that cooperates because she expects greater benefits in the long run.[70] Rather, she cooperates even if she does not expect positive retribution.[71] She cooperates because her disposition makes her a moral actor. Here, it becomes clear that, contrary to his original intention, Gauthier disconnects morals from advantages and benefits.

CMs and SMs are conceptualized as having different natures. Specifically, CMs are fundamentally different from the *homo oeconomicus*, which implies a "*radically contractarian* view of human relationships."[72] This, according to Gauthier, would commit us to treating other people only as means for (even if mutual) benefits. The *homo oeconomicus* would only have "asocial motivations"[73] in that he would not be motivated by the intrinsic value of human relations. This makes him not only asocial, but also irrational, because Gauthier thinks it rational to comply with intrinsic values.

A question that remains is how the internalization of dispositions might take place in practice, with the explicit purpose of maintaining a stable society.[74] The problem of social stability is not, as I have already mentioned, to be solved by institutions and sanctions, because these are regarded as "unproductive transfer [s]."[75] In the long run, at least, the individuals would not accept that resources be wasted on unproductive transfers, which could be used in more efficient ways if all complied with the principle MRC. Eventually, Gauthier thinks, all actors must understand that it would be best to stick to MRC.[76]

However, PD situations remain a problem. Even for Gauthier, the central element "in a contractarian theory is not the introduction of the idea of morality, but

---

[68] Gauthier (1986), ch. VIII.
[69] Gauthier (1986), p. 181.
[70] Gauthier (1986), p. 169.
[71] Cf. Gauthier (1986), pp. 169f. esp. fn. 19.
[72] Gauthier (1986), p. 319, italics in original.
[73] Gauthier (1986), p. 319.
[74] Cf. Gauthier (1986), p. 179.
[75] Gauthier (1986), p. 197.
[76] Gauthier (1986), ch. VII.

the step from hypothetical agreement to actual moral constraint."[77] What can help actors out of PD situations which persist even after people internalize the necessary dispositions? How can dispositions be an actual moral constraint if some individuals pretend to be CMs but do not actually cooperate with others? If some such covert SMs must be reckoned with, it is quite doubtful whether the CMs can uphold their dispositions. While Gauthier admits that a CM must act like an SM in a population consisting entirely of SMs, he seems to be confident that a sufficiently large number of CMs is enough to make cooperation among them fruitful.[78] But how many are necessary? While Gauthier cannot be expected to give a figure, he does not even mention the relevant central idea of the PD, whereby one (even one *potential*) defector is enough to destabilize a social arrangement or a moral norm. So if Gauthier took PD situations seriously, he would be forced to abandon this theory and thereby his moral surplus.

However, in the last chapter of *Morals by Agreement*, Gauthier seems to introduce an additional concept—education. This is a rather casual remark, but I think of great importance to his approach:[79] "... an essentially just society must be strengthened through the development of the affections and interests of the young."[80] This seems to be the moral, not political, solution that Gauthier has in mind. But it seems to me that it is not an alternative to sanctioning norms. After all, education cannot go without sanctions. Or does Gauthier rely on some concept of anti-authoritarian education? In that case, the PD would remain—how can norms (or dispositions) be enforced if there is no sanctioning mechanism to bring SMs to cooperate?

It becomes clear that Gauthier recognizes the problem of implementation, but ultimately underestimates it.[81] The introduction of dispositions as a moral surplus can only be a makeshift, not a systematic solution.[82]

5 Binmore: Empathetic Preferences

In his seminal "Game Theory and the Social Contract," K. Binmore has proposed a contractarian approach which he calls "naturalistic," as it relies heavily both on game-theoretic and on sociobiological concepts. A central demand of Binmore's

---

[77] Gauthier (1986), p. 9.

[78] Cf. Gauthier (1986), pp. 182ff.

[79] Cf. also Gauthier (1997), which stresses, too, the importance of education (esp. p. 148).

[80] Gauthier (1986), p. 351.

[81] To some extent, this has been recognized by Buchanan (1988/1991, p. 195) and Harman 1988, who doubts whether rational actors would accept a distribution as a result of a hypothetical contract. However, in my view, it is not the hypothetical character of the contract that poses a major problem, but rather the kind of social structures in effect (PD situations).

[82] According to Binmore (1994, pp. 26f. and 80), Gauthier invents a non-existent enforcement mechanism.

Order Ethics and the Problem of Social Glue

naturalism throughout his books is 'No commitments!' I will discuss this demand first, and then elaborate on Binmore's concept of "empathetic preferences," which are supposed to be necessary for social stability in modern societies. However, as I will show, these empathetic preferences are fundamentally different from the moral surpluses discussed so far.

Binmore emphasizes that a naturalistic approach must abandon all authorities legitimated by metaphysics. According to him, the vast majority of contemporary approaches in political philosophy—among them, Rawls, Harsanyi, Gauthier, and Nozick—give metaphysical justifications for rules and institutions.[83] The common idea of these approaches is that actors can make commitments. Binmore defines a commitment as an "action in the present that binds the person who makes it irrevocably in the future."[84] A commitment is thus a "binding unilateral promise,"[85] (i.e., a promise that ultimately cannot be revoked and therefore—this is my interpretation—is not and does not have to be enforced by sanctions, but can obviously be secured in some alternative way). A commitment is not equivalent to a rule which an actor observes because she expects it to be beneficial to her (at least in the long run).

The major problem in assuming the possibility of commitments is the construction of a plausible mechanism of enforcement.[86] It is difficult to commit oneself as well as convincing others that one has committed oneself. One possible solution is to provide (financial) "hostages." For example, a company that has made a commitment to environmental protection may sign a contract in which they commit themselves to paying a fixed amount of money if the commitment is broken. And there are other more subtle mechanisms of securing commitments via reputation mechanisms. These are, however, commitments that are enforced via sanctions, and not the kind of commitments that political philosophers like those mentioned above have in mind.

Binmore proposes a different concept—empathetic preferences.[87] The intuitive idea behind this is that even a *homo oeconomicus* actor can adapt his actions better to that of other actors if he can predict their behavior. Moreover, Binmore distinguishes sharply between a sympathetic and an empathetic preference as follows: Actor A reveals a *sympathetic preference* if it can be deduced from his behavior that he puts himself into actor B's position *and* adopts B's preferences.[88] By contrast, actor A reveals an *empathetic preference* if it can be deduced from his behavior that

---

[83] Binmore (1994), p. 161.
[84] Id.
[85] Id.
[86] Cf. Binmore (1994), p. 162.
[87] This goes back to Harsanyi's "extended sympathy preferences", cf. Harsanyi (1977). By employing the concept of 'empathetic preferences', Binmore wants to highlight the difference between the classic concept of sympathy in D. Hume's works and his modern one. Cf. Binmore (1994), pp. 28, 58ff., ch. 4.3.1 and Binmore (1998), ch. 2.5.4.
[88] Cf. Binmore (1994), p. 286.

he puts himself into actor B's position *without* taking on B's preferences. In this case, A sticks to his own preferences. He can still compare his preferences to B's and evaluate or criticize the latter. To cite Binmore's comparative preferences example, "I would rather be Eve eating an apple than Adam wearing a fig leaf."[89]

Binmore argues that the ability to empathize,[90] and not the ability to sympathize[91] with others, is what makes a human being. He speculates about the evolutionary history of this ability, which may have been advantageous for coordinating behavior in hunter-gatherer societies.[92] And he distinguishes between three time horizons in which empathetic preferences play a role: short, medium, and long run.[93]

In the *short run*, the personal preferences of an actor, as well as her empathetic preferences, are fixed.[94] That is, the actor empathizes in exactly the way her empathetic preferences prescribe and deliberates "morally" in this way. Here, moral norms are conventions, which work as short cuts for long economic calculations. While morals do not play a role on the level of the social contract framework, they do influence the individuals' actions within this framework. Morals are functional in the short run.[95]

In the long run, all preferences, personal and empathetic, are subject to change, as the actor adapts to new situations and new rules.[96] Here, new social contracts are negotiated and existing ones modified. The personal and empathetic preferences adapt to these new situations. It is interesting to see that in the long run, all moral content erodes out of the preferences. Over longer periods of time, the actors arrive—via "moral" empathy—at the same result as if they had been bargaining straightaway all the time. Binmore makes it clear that, in the long run, morals serve long-run interests, and more importantly, no moral norms can remain stable that are systematically opposed to incentives.[97]

Finally, in the medium run, the personal preferences remain fixed while the empathetic ones may change.[98] According to Binmore, evolution will bring the

---

[89] Binmore (1994), p. 290.

[90] I prefer to use the term '*ability* to empathize', as it is a more general concept than the empathetic preferences. The latter are preferences that a particular actor reveals in a concrete case with regard to one or several other actors. These may change from one actor to another and from case to case.

[91] But according to Elster (1989), 'love and duty', i.e., sympathy in Binmore's terms, are the "cement of society". Binmore (1994, p. 24) responds that modern societies do not need cement, rather they are like a dry-stone wall in which each stone is kept in place only by the other stones, i.e., by reciprocity. To maintain reciprocity, however, greed and fear suffice.

[92] Cf. Binmore (1994), pp. 57 and 288ff.

[93] Binmore (1994), ch. 1.3.

[94] Id.

[95] Cf. Binmore (1998), ch. 4.6.8.

[96] Cf. Binmore (1994), p. 90.

[97] Cf. Binmore (1994), ch. 1.3.

[98] Id.

latter into "empathy equilibrium."[99] in which all actors have equal empathetic preferences. It is already in this situation, as in the long run, that all moral content erodes from the social contract framework. The actors end up with a result identical to a Nash bargaining equilibrium.[100] However, this is at variance with the actors' own impression. Due to the semantics employed, they still think that they are guided by moral deliberation in the traditional sense. Binmore consequently regards the ability to empathize as—at least partially—genetically "hard-wired."[101]

The difference between the long and medium run is that in the medium run, evolution has not had enough time to shape personal preferences and adapt them to new environments and situations. By distinguishing between the three time horizons, Binmore defines the role of empathetic preferences in society—they are used for coordination, or more precisely, for reforming existing social contracts and consenting to new ones. They are used as a heuristic tool for finding directions in which new social contracts may develop. In this sense, Binmore regards the empathetic preferences as an important part of morality.[102]

The question is now is whether empathetic preferences can be regarded as a moral surplus in the sense of Habermas' rational motivation or Rawls' sense of justice? I think not, for the following reasons. Upon closer inspection, it becomes clear that empathetic preferences have fewer consequences for their bearers than the other moral surpluses discussed here. In Rawls' and Habermas' works, one gets the impression that both authors already have in mind a rather precise idea how the citizens should act, or at least which rules they should adopt. In addition, both works show—to different degrees, but nevertheless—clear traces of an opposition to economic approaches or more general to those that rely on self-interest for their implementation.[103]

This impression does not arise when reading Binmore. First, the empathetic preferences exhibit a peculiar quality—assuming their existence does not preclude anything for the detailed design of rules and institutions.[104] If A can put herself in B's position, she will in some way try to assess B. On the one hand, if A regards B as rather unreliable or as only interested in short-run gains, she will anticipate B's defection, adapt her own behavior, and tend to "counter-defect pre-emptively" herself.[105] If, on the other hand, A regards B as reliable *and* if there are no contrary

---

[99]Binmore (1994), p. 65. Cf. also ibid., ch. 1.2.7, 1.3, and pp. 290ff.

[100]Cf. Binmore (1994), p. 88. For the Nash equilibrium, see Nash 1950, 1951.

[101]Binmore (1994), p. 133, (1998), p. 182. He does not rely entirely on genetic concepts, however, but uses Dawkins' (1976) concept of the "meme". Cf. Binmore (1994), pp. 65f.

[102]Binmore (1994), p. 241.

[103] Cf. Rawls' strict separation between the *modus vivendi*, the constitutional consensus and the overlapping consensus (see Sect. 3).

[104]However, this can also be seen as a shortcoming of Binmore's work: He does rely exclusively on evolutionary game theory, as Dore (1997, pp. 236f.) emphasizes, too. While this is certainly relevant to modern societies, we cannot however go without other branches of economics and other social sciences for the detailed design of institutions.

[105]Cf. Homann (2002), p. 98; Homann and Luetge (2013), p. 35.

incentives for A to defect, A will tend to cooperate. But this is an open-ended process, the result of which cannot be precluded by the philosopher.

Second, and more important in my mind, the ability to emphasize cannot, unlike the moral surpluses reconstructed here, *be exploited* by other actors. Consider this: If A constrains her behavior in a PD situation (e.g., by subscribing to a rational motivation or a sense of justice), she risks being exploited by B. This can only be avoided if B constrains his behavior in the same way as A (i.e., by way of sanctions or the like). But if A can just empathize with B in a PD situation (i.e., rely on empathetic preferences), she does not necessarily risk exploitation, especially not in a situation where B acts in ways different from A. For example, suppose that one of the two prisoners in the classic PD situation (X) is motivated by a sense of justice. If the other (Y) knows this but is not motivated in this way himself, he can exploit X without any problem by confessing (i.e. defecting). But if X "only" has empathetic preferences, this does not necessarily lead to exploitation. It would only mean that X might anticipate the reaction of Y to his own "moral" behavior. X could, for example, use this knowledge to try to turn the tables and exploit Y. In any case, Y cannot gain any unilateral advantage from knowing that X has adopted empathetic preferences, as Y would have to count on the fact that X would anticipate this—by empathizing with Y.

Therefore, I suggest not putting the ability to empathize in the same basket as the moral surpluses discussed above. It does not preclude any particular action, and it cannot be exploited.

6 Order Ethics as an Alternative View: Stability from Advantages and Incentives

The idea behind the approach which I would like to sketch here is to develop an account of norms as functional for social stability while weakening the assumptions on the actors' part (i.e., minimizing the necessary moral surplus). This alternative view is a conception of ethics that proceeds systematically not from the problem of justification, but from the problem of implementation of norms.[106]

Some philosophers, both in the analytic as well as in the continental tradition, believe that the justification of norms has always been the key problem of ethics. However, an informed view of economic and social history[107] tells us that the questions of norm implementation *and* justification have generally been posed together, but this was not made explicit in former centuries. The implementation of norms that had already been justified was not regarded as particularly difficult for

---

[106]For the order ethics approach, see Luetge (2014, 2015), Homann (2002), Luetge et al. (2016), Homann and Luetge (2013), Luetge (2005). The corresponding idea in Binmore's approach is the requirement to *first* regard only the relevant equilibria and *then* pick one of them as the desirable.

[107]For such a view on Ancient Greece, see Meier 1998.

two reasons. First, the modern pluralism of values and life styles had not yet developed, and second, social relations were not yet as anonymous as in modern times. In particular, commonly accepted norms could be enforced much more easily through face-to-face sanctions.[108]

Since the beginning of modern times, however, this situation has changed dramatically. As N. Luhmann has described, modern societies consist of functionally differentiated sub-systems.[109] The actors in modern societies must act in social subsystems under many completely different governance mechanisms. With regard to ethics, this often leads to laments about loss of values. The question how norms can be enforced therefore becomes much more pressing under modern conditions and must be put at the beginning of a conception of ethics for modern societies. I would like to call such a conception an *order ethics*, or in a different regard, an *ethics of advantages and incentives*. We must count on the fact that all actors look for their advantage (whereby the term "advantage," of course, covers not only material advantages), and we have to set the right incentives in order to deal with this quest for advantages.

Order ethics can be set in a contractarian framework and derived from a thought experiment. For this argument I refer to B. Ackerman, who has renewed the classic social contract argument with the aid of a science-fiction thought experiment:[110] A group of spacemen lands on a newly discovered planet and tries to build a society there. The spacemen have to deliberate about the rules of this society in much the same way as the rational actors in the social contract setting of an original position. Ackerman, however, explicitly uses the science-fiction scenario in a very peculiar way, namely to get rid of the question how rules that have been agreed on can be effectively enforced.[111] He assumes that in his fictitious scenario, violations of rules can be sanctioned automatically by means of a superior technology (laser cannons).

I do not think this approach leads us very far. Therefore, I have changed Ackerman's setting, because the perfect enforcement of rules via technology simply is not available, even in a futuristic world. If one drops the assumption that there are laser cannons guaranteeing compliance, Ackerman's thought experiment can be sensibly taken further. Also, I add the idea that the people aboard the ship already have very different values and backgrounds. The result is a situation in which rules have to be designed for a new situation in a society with great pluralism.

From this revised thought experiment, the main thesis of an order ethics can be developed in four steps. First, the problem must be clear for which an order ethics might be a solution. This problem is the *problem of social order*.[112] Second, the problem cannot be solved by way of an *individual ethics*. An individual ethics (ideally) assumes that morally problematic states are caused by actors' immoral

---

[108]Cf. Luetge (2015), ch. 2.
[109]Cf., e.g., Luhmann (1997).
[110]Cf. Ackermann (1980).
[111]Ackermann (1980), p. 34.
[112]Cf. also Hayek (1973), ch. 2.

motives or preferences. Consequently, this position calls for a change of motives, or a change of consciousness. The main mechanism of governance is (moral) appeals, and may be supported by education.

However, in those structures typical of modern societies (i.e., PD situations)[113] an ethics remains fruitless that addresses primarily the individual. So in a third step, an order ethics assumes that morally problematic states are not caused by immoral preferences or motives, but by specific structures of interaction. Therefore, moral claims should aim at revising the conditions which apply to all actors (i.e., the rules of the game). The main governance mechanism is the design of *incentive* structures. Moral norms cannot be brought into opposition to the logic of advantages and incentives.

Fourth and finally, some refinements have to be made to the social contract framework. I limit myself to the following two: Contrary to what some critics of this approach believe, rational actors can invest in the future. They can invest in better rules, but they can also invest in moral behavior. There is still room for moral behavior in a social-contract-based order ethics approach, but this behavior can be explained with the help of the concept of incomplete or open contracts. As many contracts in modern societies are systematically incomplete,[114] the actors must fill in the gaps in contracts with their own "moral" behavior—in their own interest.

The arguments in the preceding sections make it clear that it is not systematically fruitful to base normativity on anthropological capabilities or characteristics, the moral surpluses. But if these moral surpluses are not sustainable, what are the alternatives? The alternative social governance mechanism that an order ethics would argue for is not based on anthropological findings, characteristics or surpluses, but on situations. A modern society that wants to profit from deep specialization and competition has to switch to a system of governance by rules. With the use of pre-modern governance mechanisms, the benefits of modern societies cannot be appropriated.

Which rules and which governance mechanisms are necessary for an interaction depends only on the situational conditions. For example, there might be situations where informal governance by moral norms still works, and where the partners can count on at least approximately equal normative backgrounds. In such situations, governance by moral norms may still be an option. However, these cases are not very frequent in modern societies under conditions of globalization. The number of interactions between individuals with vastly different cultural, social, and normative backgrounds is continually and rapidly growing. These individuals cannot rely on common moral surpluses; they can only rely on common mutually accepted rules—or they might devise new rules adapted to their situation.

The question is whether even for these cases of rule governance some—maybe weak and not anthropological, but rather situational—capability is necessary. Of the concepts discussed here, only the ability to empathize would be a candidate.

---

[113] As in Gauthier and Binmore, PD situations occupy a pivotal place in this approach.
[114] Cf. Hart (1987), Hart and Holmström (1987) and Luetge (2005).

Notwithstanding this, I argue that if we abandon any moral surpluses, there are three minimal—and very general—assumptions that must be given to guarantee functional governance by rules and social stability: sociality, ability to communicate and ability to invest.

The first two are rather trivial. That is, there must be some social group and some mode of communication in effect within this group. But the third is more interesting and important. Individuals that always maximize utility in the *short* run cannot form a stable society. This is nothing spectacular and is not peculiar to social stability or morals. Every company must be able to invest in the future. In fact, any form of action and cooperation requires thinking and planning, which in turn requires investing (i.e., saving some resources now for greater benefits in the longer run).

Together, these three assumptions might be taken as a minimal basis for modern globalized societies which cannot rely on moral surpluses. The actors must only be able to communicate and invest. An order ethics can then go on to only require these actors to one, comply with the rules, and two, engage from their own interest in the further development of these rules in mutually beneficial ways. Such further development can only come into effect if the individuals affected agree to it. In view of PD situations, it is systematically not enforceable against the wishes of these individuals.

However, there is a role for what I would like to call *heuristics*. These heuristics are values and ideas from philosophical, religious, scientific, literary, artistic, or other traditions. They can point the actors in new directions where new gains of cooperation may be found. But they are conceived here in a very different way than the moral surpluses. Most important, they are not conceptualized against the logic of advantages and incentives. They do not erode in PD situations. By contrast, the moral surpluses that Habermas, Rawls, and Gauthier argue for are all conceptualized in opposition to interests, advantages, or incentives.

To sum up, an order ethics starts in much the same way as Gauthier and Binmore suggest. All three approaches regard moral norms in a functional way—as a possible means for governing societies. All three stress the importance of interactions, and all three see no fundamental contradiction between morals and self-interest. However, the order ethics approach aims at solving the problem of implementation primarily by means of rules or institutions, not (unlike Gauthier) by dispositions, and not (unlike Binmore) solely by the ability to empathize. Maybe Binmore would agree with my approach, as he is not at all opposed to employing institutions for implementing norms. They are not, however, what he focuses on. I would therefore think that order ethics and Binmore's evolutionary approach are two complementary conceptions.

The theoretical advantage of both the ability to empathize and the ability to invest lies in the fact that they do not require the individuals to act against the logic of advantages and incentives, especially in PD situations. A practical application might be that a "morally driven" semantics used in the political sphere, which constructs sharp contradictions between values and interests, between rational motivation and incentives, between acting from principles of justice and acting "merely" in accordance with them, leads us to dead ends and theoretical blockades.

If, however, a revised semantics rather employs concepts like "investing," "mutual self-interest," "mutual gains," or "win-win-situations," then even the moral surpluses might be made productive. They might be seen as part of a heuristics which asks for, suggests and pleads for, *investing* in the individuals' own self-interest. Eventually, this could turn out to be the heuristics not only of occidental, but of many traditions of ethics. To show this in detail is, however, a task for the future.

References

Ackerman, B. A. 1980. *Social justice in the liberal state*. New Haven: Yale University Press.
Axelrod, R. 1984. *The evolution of cooperation*. New York: Basic Books.
Bhagwati, J. 2004. *In defense of globalization*. Oxford: Oxford University Press.
Binmore, K. 1994. *Game theory and the social contract: Vol. 1: Playing fair*. Cambridge, Mass., London: MIT Press.
Binmore, K. 1998. *Game theory and the social contract: Vol. 2: Just playing*. Cambridge, Mass., London: MIT Press.
Buchanan, J. M. 1988/1991. The Gauthier enterprise. In Paul (1988), 75–94, reprinted in *The Economics and the Ethics of Constitutional Order*. Ann Arbor: University of Michigan Press 1991, 195-213.
Davion, V., and C. Wolf (eds.). 2000. *The idea of a political liberalism: essays on Rawls*. Lanham et al.: Rowman & Littlefield.
Dawkins, R. 1976. *The selfish gene*. Oxford: Oxford University Press.
Dore, M. 1997. On playing fair: Professor Binmore on game theory and the social contract. *Theory and Decision* 43: 219–239.
Dworkin, R. 1975. The original position. In *Reading Rawls*, ed. N. Daniels. Oxford: Blackwell.
Elster, J. 1989. *The cement of society: a study of social order*. Cambridge: Cambridge University Press.
Gauthier, D. 1986. *Morals by agreement*. Oxford: Clarendon.
Gauthier, D. 1997. Political contractarianism. *Journal of Political Philosophy* 5(2): 132–148.
Habermas, J. 1981/1984/1987. *The theory of communicative action*, 2 vol., Boston: Beacon Press.
Habermas, J. 1983/1990. *Moral consciousness and communicative action*, Cambridge, Mass: MIT Press.
Habermas, J. 1991/1993. *Justification and application: remarks on discourse ethics*, Cambridge, Mass: MIT Press.
Habermas, J. 1992/1996. *Between facts and norms: contributions to a discourse theory of law and democracy*, Cambridge, Mass: MIT Press.
Harman, G. 1988. Rationality in Agreement: A Commentary on Gauthier's Morals by Agreement, in: Paul (1988), 1–16.
Harsanyi, J. C. 1977. *Rational behavior and bargaining equilibrium in games and social situations*. Cambridge: Cambridge University Press.
Hart, O.D. 1987. Incomplete contracts. In J. Eatwell et al. (Eds.), *The New Palgrave: A Dictionary of Economics*. Vol. 2: 752–759. London, Basingstoke: Macmillan.
Hart, O.D., and B.R. Holmström. (1987). The theory of contracts. In T. F. Bewley (Ed.), *Advances in Economic Theory*: Ch. 3. Cambridge: Cambridge University Press.
Hayek, F. A. v. 1973. *Law, Legislation, and Liberty. Vol. 1: Rules and Order*, Chicago: University of Chicago Press.
Hobbes, T. 1651/1991. *Leviathan*, ed. by R. Tuck, Cambridge: Cambridge University Press.
Homann, K. 2002. *Vorteile und Anreize: Zur Grundlegung einer Ethik der Zukunft*. Ed. by C. Luetge. Tübingen: Mohr Siebeck.

Homann, K., and C. Kirchner. 1995. Ordnungsethik. *Jahrbuch für Neue Politische Ökonomie* 14: 189–211.

Homann, K., and C. Luetge. 2013. *Einführung in die Wirtschaftsethik*, 3rd ed. Münster: LIT.

Kukathas, C., and P. Pettit. 1990. *Rawls: a theory of justice and its critics*. Cambridge: Polity Press.

Luetge, C. 2005. Economic ethics. *Business ethics, and the idea of mutual advantages, Business Ethics: a European Review* 14(2): 108–118.

Luetge, C. 2014. *Ethik des Wettbewerbs: Über Konkurrenz und Moral*. München: Beck.

Luetge, C. 2015. *Order ethics or moral surplus: what holds a society together?*. Lanham, Md.: Lexington.

Luetge, C., Armbrüster, T., and Müller, J. 2016. Order ethics: bridging the gap between contractarianism and Business Ethics. *Journal of Business Ethics*, forthcoming

Luetge, C., and H. Rusch. 2013. The Systematic Place of Morals in Markets: Comment on Armin Falk & Nora Szech "Morals and Markets", *Science* 341 (6147), 16th August 2013, p. 714.

Luhmann, N. 1997. *Die Gesellschaft der Gesellschaft*, 2 vols., Frankfurt/M..

Meier, C. 1998. *Athens: A portrait of the city in its golden age*. New York: Metropolitan.

Mills, C. 2000. Not a mere Modus Vivendi: The Bases for Allegiance to the Just State. In Davion und Wolf (2000), 190–203.

Nash, J. 1950. Equilibrium Points in N-Person Games. *Proceedings of the National Academy of Sciences* 36: 48–49.

Nash, J. 1951. The Bargaining Problem. *Econometrica* 18: 155–162.

Paul, E. F. (ed.). 1988. Gauthier's new social contract. *Social Philosophy and Policy* 5, No. 2, Social Philosophy and Policy Center.

Rawls, J. 1963. The sense of justice. *Philosophical Review* 72(3): 281–305.

Rawls, J. 1971. *A theory of justice*. Cambridge: Mass.

Rawls, J. 1985. Justice as fairness: political not metaphysical. *Philosophy & Public Affairs* 14: 223–251.

Rawls, J. 1993. *Political liberalism*. New York: Columbia University Press.

Rawls, J. 1995. Reply to Habermas. *Journal of Philosophy* 92(3): 132–180.

Stiglitz, J. E. 2002. *Globalization and its discontents*. New York: Norton.

Rawls, Order Ethics, and Rawlsian Order Ethics

Ludwig Heider and Nikil Mukerji

Abstract This chapter discusses how order ethics relates to the theory of justice. We focus on John Rawls's influential conception "Justice as Fairness" (JF) and compare its components with relevant aspects of the order-ethical approach. The two theories, we argue, are surprisingly compatible in various respects. We also analyse how far order ethicists disagree with Rawls and why. The main source of disagreement that we identify lies in a thesis that is central to the order ethical system, viz. the requirement of incentive-compatible implementability. It purports that an ethical norm can be normatively valid only if individuals have a self-interested motive to support it. This idea conflicts with the Rawlsian view because there are cases where it is not clear, from the standpoint of self-interest, why everybody should support its moral demands. If the thesis of incentive-compatible implementability is, in fact, correct, a proponent of JF would have to reform her views. We suggest how she could do that while salvaging the heart of her normative system as a "regulative idea". The conception that would result from this reformation may be seen as a new variant of order ethics, which we propose to call "Rawlsian Order Ethics."

Keywords Difference principle · Distributive justice · Equality of opportunity · Freedom · Income redistribution · Justice · Liberty · Order ethics · Pareto · Rawls · Rawlsian order ethics · Rights

1 Introduction

John Rawls's theory of justice has become *the* focal point of the modern debate in moral and political philosophy. As Robert Nozick has commented, "[p]olitical philosophers now must either work within Rawls' theory or explain why not."

L. Heider · N. Mukerji (✉)
Faculty of Philosophy, Philosophy of Science, and the Study of Religion,
Ludwig-Maximilians-Universität München, Munich, Germany
e-mail: nikil.mukerji@lmu.de

(Nozick 1974, 183) If Nozick is right, then this holds, in particular, for the proponents of order ethics, which is a rising paradigm in the business ethics debate. Order ethicists must clarify how far they agree with Rawls' views and explain why and to which extent they depart from them. In this paper, we take on this task. We examine the commonalities between Rawls' conception of justice "Justice as Fairness" (JF) and order ethics and analyse how order ethicists justify their departures from the Rawlsian view.[1]

Our main conclusions are as follows. First, order ethicists agree with many of Rawls' ideas. Second, there are certain aspects of Rawls' theory that seem irreconcilable with order ethics. As we explain, the main reason for this is that order ethicists hold specific views about the implementability of ethical norms. This leads them to normative conclusions that are different from Rawls'. Third, if order ethicists are indeed right about the conditions under which ethical norms are implementable, proponents of the Rawlsian view would have to reform their views. This, however, does not mean that they would have to become full-blown order ethicists. Rawlsians could salvage the heart of their normative system—viz. the idea that the least well off in society should be made as well off as possible—as a "regulative idea" that guides the search for implementable norms. This would give rise to a new variant of order ethics, which has hitherto escaped the attention of moral philosophers. We propose to call it "Rawlsian Order Ethics".

Here is how we shall proceed. First, we will focus on the commonalities between Rawls' conception JF and order ethics. Then, we will analyse the differences between the two theoretical approaches and examine their justification from the order-ethical viewpoint. Finally, we will examine Rawlsian Order Ethics, which is a synthesis between Rawls' conception and orthodox order ethics.

2 Social Institutions as the Primary Subject

Theories of justice differ in regards to their primary subject matter. According to Plato, justice is a virtue of the human soul, which makes it a property of human beings. It may also be ascribed to the acts of a person or the statements that she makes. Rawls, however, uses the term differently. To him, justice is the "first virtue of social institutions" (TJ, 3). His conception of justice, JF, is the attempt to formulate normative rules for the institutional order of society—its "basic structure", as Rawls calls it. More precisely, Rawls wants to devise rules for "the way in which the major social institutions distribute fundamental rights and duties and determine the division of advantages from social cooperation." (TJ, 6)

---

[1] We do not wish to go into the various criticisms of Rawls's theory, however. For a critique from the perspective of Amartya Sen's theory, see the contribution by Mike Festl (Chap. "Boost up and Merge with. Order Ethicsin the Light of Recent Developmentsin Justice Theory", this volume).

Order ethics also focuses on the institutional structure of society. Its theoretical starting point lies in the observation that modern-day ethical problems are the result of failed interactions between individuals. Order ethicists believe that interactions fail due to dilemma structures (DS). DS are interactions in which the rational pursuit of self-interest leads to a situation that is dispreferred by all. The simplest case of a DS is the so called Prisoners' Dilemma (PD) in game theory, as shown in Table 1.

In a PD two individuals, 1 and 2, interact. Both can choose between two acts, C and D. (C stands for Cooperation, D for Defection.) Quadrant I represents a situation in which 1 and 2 both choose C. Quadrant II represents a situation in which 1 chooses C and 2 chooses D and so on. The numbers that are attached to the quadrants represent the order of preferences or payoffs that 1 and 2, respectively, associate with them. 1 prefers III over I, I over IV and IV over II. 2 prefers II over I, I over IV and IV over III. Note that the structure of the interaction in a prisoners' dilemma is such that, whatever 2 does, 1 prefers to choose D. Since the situation is symmetric, 2 also prefers to choose D no matter what 1 does. If both act rationally, they will end up in a situation, viz. IV, which both 1 and 2 disprefer to another possible outcome, viz. I. Therein lies their dilemma.

In modern society, DS like this arise manifold. When they do, order ethicists propose to change the rules of the interaction between 1 and 2 in order to help them get from quadrant IV to the preferred quadrant I.[2] They follow an Incentive Approach that is rooted in economic theory (Buchanan 1990; Homann 2003). Individuals are given incentives to choose C rather than D. This is ensured by altering the payoff structure of the PD so as to create a new game in which strategy C becomes more attractive *vis-a-vis* D. An example of such a game is shown in Table 2 (Mukerji and Schumacher 2008).

In the Reversed PD, both individuals choosing C is the best possible outcome for all. But it is also the act most preferred by the individuals. By turning a PD into a Reversed PD, it is possible, then, to align the shared interest in getting from quadrant IV to quadrant I with the self-interest of the individuals. In practice, order ethicists propose to achieve this by modifying the social institutions that shape the structure of the interaction between 1 and 2 (Luetge 2005). Order ethicists, hence, agree with Rawls in that they view the institutional structure of society as the primary subject of interest in moral-philosophical inquiry. Homann and Blome-Drees (1992) refer to it as "the systematic locus of morality".[3]

---

[2]This is a simplified statement of the order-ethical view. Order ethicists do not hold the view that all DS should be resolved. For further elaboration on this point, see the contribution by Nikil Mukerji and Christoph Schumacher on order-ethical methodology (Chap. "Order Ethics, Economics, and GameTheory", this volume).

[3]The German verbiage is "der systematische Ort der Moral".

Table 1 Prisoners' dilemma

		Individual 2	
		C	D
Individual 1	C	I (3,3)	II (1,4)
Individual 1	D	III (4,1)	IV (2,2)

Table 2 Reversed prisoner's dilemma

		Individual 2	
		C	D
Individual 1	C	I (3,3)	II (1,2)
Individual 1	D	III (2,1)	IV (0,0)

3 Procedural Justice

A further point that is noteworthy about Rawls' conception of justice is its emphasis on due process. According to JF, the question whether a given societal outcome is just can only be answered by looking at the institutional process from which it results. The rules and regulations required by JF are such that "the outcome is just whatever it happens to be" (TJ, 74). Rawls refers to this idea as "pure procedural justice" (PPJ).

Order ethicists can accept PPJ. On order ethics, there is no mention of just or ethical *results*. As we explained in the previous section, the role of an order ethicist is to suggest institutional amendments which help individuals to achieve an outcome that all prefer. Once these required rules are in place, individuals are free to act and interact within them as they wish. The theory does not require them to achieve a particular end-state or to work towards a particular distribution of social goods. It is thus in line with PPJ.

4 Rights and Liberties

At this point, we have to delve deeper into JF and examine its basic principles. Let us ask, then, what, according to Rawls, makes a society just?

On Rawls' view, a society is just to the extent that it distributes the relevant social values according to the following "principle of equality":

> All social values – liberty and opportunity, income and wealth, and the social bases of self-respect – are to be distributed equally unless an unequal distribution of any, or all, these values is to everyone's advantage. (TJ, 54)

A few points are in order to clarify this principle. Firstly, the relevant values to which it applies are so called *primary* goods. These are goods "that every rational man is presumed to want" (TJ, 54), no matter his personal conception of the good and life plan. Secondly, they are *social* goods. That means they are created by social institutions. The list of values does not include natural goods (e.g. health, vigour, intelligence and the like) since these goods cannot be shared out by society.[4] Thirdly, the principle has quite a drastic egalitarian tendency. All goods are to be distributed equally. Exceptions are allowed only if an unequal distribution is to everyone's advantage.

At this point, we are not interested in Rawls' reasons for adopting the principle of equality. Instead, we want to focus on its normative implications on the principled level. To analyse them, it is instructive to first divide the primary social goods into five categories—viz. rights, liberties, opportunities, income and wealth—and to apply the above principle to it.

Let us consider the first two categories. It is easy to see that Rawls' principle demands the equal distribution of rights and liberties. The reason for this is that any unequal distribution of these goods only makes people worse off and nobody better off. To illustrate, consider the following example. Assume Ludwig and Nikil both enjoy a particular right, e.g. the right not to be physically harmed. If we were to take some of that right away from Nikil, this would not benefit Ludwig. His rights endowment would stay the same. But it would obviously harm Nikil. If anything, an unequal distribution of the right not to be harmed would, hence, make things worse overall. The only permissible distribution of that right consists, therefore, in the maximal and equal endowment of both Ludwig and Nikil. The example makes clear why Rawls concludes that

---

[4]Conceivably though, natural goods may at some stage turn into social goods since it may become possible to affect the distribution of these goods through modern technologies that are currently discussed under the label human enhancement. For a discussion, see Mukerji and Nida-Rümelin (2014).

each person is to have an equal right to the most extensive scheme of equal basic liberties compatible with a similar scheme of liberties for others. (TJ, 53)

This idea is known as Rawls' "first principle" of justice.[5] At this point, we cannot examine the precise extent to which order ethicists can endorse it. But we can make a few points that make it at least plausible to assume that they can do this to a rather large extent. To qualify this thesis, we should, however, start with a distinction between two ways in which one may endorse a moral principle. This distinction concerns the motivation behind the endorsement. This motivation can be *intrinsic* or *extrinsic*. In the former case, we subscribe to the principle in question because we believe that it should be obeyed for its own sake. In the latter case, we do not believe that the principle should be obeyed for its own sake. Rather, we believe that obeying it is a means to achieving a given end. To be sure, then, Rawls' motivation for endorsing his first principle is intrinsic. He believes that society must ensure the acknowledgement of equal basic liberties for its own sake. Order ethicists are committed to denying this idea. Their theory is not about rights at all. To an order ethicist, they are intrinsically unimportant because the central and single goal of their theory is to find out how the institutional order of society can be reformed in order to make everybody better off. But this may allow order ethicists to endorse rights and liberties in the extrinsic sense. To this end, they would have to argue that giving individuals equal basic liberties would, in fact, make everybody better off. Whether that is true is largely an empirical question. But it is a priori not implausible. Hobbes (1651/1996) has a well-known argument to this effect that order ethicists often cite. Hobbes suggested that in a "state of nature" where everybody was free to do whatever they liked, life would be "solitary, poor, nasty, brutish and short." (p. 84) In such a situation, everybody could be made better off by recognizing and enshrining into law certain fundamental rights, e.g. the right not to be physically harmed. It may be questioned, of course, whether this line of reasoning would ultimately lead order ethicists to endorse the full range of basic liberties that Rawls has in mind. It should be pointed out, however, that at least some order ethicists have suggested that their theory is compatible with a rather far-reaching and inclusive scheme of equal basic liberties (see, in particular, Homann 2003, Chap. 5).

---

[5]As it stands, this formulation is rather imprecise because it does not tell us which liberties Rawls regards as "basic". He clarifies this by giving us the following list:

political liberty (the right to vote and to hold public office) and freedom of speech and assembly; liberty of conscience and freedom of thought; freedom of the person, which includes freedom from psychological oppression and physical assault and dismemberment (integrity of the per- son); the right to hold personal property and freedom from arbitrary arrest and seizure as defined by the concept of the rule of law. (TJ, 53).

5 Equality of Opportunity

Rawls' "second principle" applies to the allocation of opportunities, income and wealth. It demands that

> social and economic inequalities are to be arranged so that they are both (a) reasonably expected to be to everyone's advantage, and (b) attached to positions and offices open to all. (TJ, 53)

Let us consider clause (b) first. This part of the second principle is known as the principle of fair equality of opportunity (FEO). The reasoning that takes us from Rawls' principle of equality to FEO is straightforward. Desirable positions and offices in society are limited. By giving one person a greater chance to achieve them, we ipso facto give another person less of a chance.[6] For this reason, there must be an equal distribution of opportunities, as FEO demands.

Can order ethicists endorse FEO? Again, that depends. Since the aim of order ethics consists solely in institutional reform for mutual advantage, its proponents cannot, of course, endorse fair equality of opportunity as an end in itself. Perhaps, then, they can endorse it as a means to an end? This depends, of course, on the way we interpret the concept of equal opportunity.[7] But it also depends largely on the answer to a host of empirical questions. While it is rather clear what the legal acknowledgement of equal basic liberties demands in practice, it is not at all clear what the principle of equal opportunity requires. It is hard to judge, e.g., whether the introduction of an affirmative action program or a female quota would increase or reduce the degree to which the ideal of equal opportunity is fulfilled. Since we do not know the precise demands of the principle of fair equality of opportunity, it is hard to tell whether order ethicists would be able to accept them. We suspect, however, that the ethical implications of order ethics will largely concur with FEO. Here is (the sketch of) an argument to that effect.

Rawls distinguishes between formal equality of opportunity and fair equality of opportunity. The former idea requires merely that nobody is legally (or otherwise) prohibited from occupying desirable positions while the latter demands that

> those who are at the same level of talent and ability, and have the same willingness to use them, should have the same prospects of success regardless of their initial place in the social system. (TJ, 63)

But, of course, the fulfilment of formal equality of opportunity is a precondition for fair equality of opportunity. Therefore, FEO will probably share all the demands of the principle of formal equality of opportunity. Now, if order ethicists were at least able to endorse the demands of the latter principle, they would be able to endorse at least some demands of FEO. But that seems likely. Order ethicists have commonly argued for a free market system, which plainly satisfies the requirements

---

[6]Opportunities, in other words, are "positional goods" (Hirsch 1977), as economists call them.
[7]There are various notions of equal opportunity. For an overview, see Arneson (2008).

of formally equal opportunities (e.g. Homann and Luetge 2004/2005, 55–60). In practice, their demands will, therefore, at least partly concur with FEO. As Homann and Luetge 2004/2005, 60–66) argue, however, order ethicists should go even farther than that. Order ethics does not only demand a market economy. It also calls for certain social policies to be put in place to the extent that they make everyone in society—rich and poor—better off.[8] It is reasonable to suppose that these social policy measures will tend to have an empowering effect on the less fortunate in society and will, at least to a certain degree, enable them to compete for desirable positions in society. It is not clear whether this is sufficient to fulfil Rawls' FEO. But it seems that order ethicists are quite likely to endorse at least some of the implications of that principle.

6 Self-Interest and Moral Motivation

Part (a) of Rawls' second principle is commonly known as the "difference principle". It applies to the primary goods of income and wealth and allows inequalities regarding these goods on the condition that they are "reasonably expected to be to everyone's advantage". In fact, as the cognoscenti of the Rawlsian theory has already realized, this is not the final version of the principle. We shall state the final version below. Before that, however, we want to draw attention to the fact that Rawls does, in principle, allow inequalities of income and wealth. Since he does not allow inegalitarian distributions of rights, liberties and opportunities, we should obviously ask why.

The answer to this question is that income and wealth are essentially different from rights, liberties and opportunities. We cannot increase everybody's share of the latter goods by giving to some people more of them than to others. But we can make everybody better off monetarily if we allow an inegalitarian distribution of income and wealth. The reason for this is that monetary inequalities can motivate people to increase their efforts. This holds, in particular, for the more talented members of society. As Rawls explains, "[t]heir better prospects act as incentives so that the economic process is more efficient, innovation proceeds at a faster pace, and so on."[9]

This said, we want to expose a further commonality between Rawls' views and the ideas of order ethicists. As we have already explained, the latter also emphasize the importance of incentives in institutional design. They start from the observation that DS are omnipresent in modern society. To the extent that they cause damage,

---

[8]Order ethicists commonly draw on the argument proposed by Sinn (1986). He argues that the social welfare state can be seen as an insurance which enables individuals to take risks. Some of the risk takers are actually successful and the wealth they create for everyone in society outweighs the costs of the social insurance.

[9]Cohen (1991) refers to this reasoning as the „incentive argument" for inequality. A reconstruction of it can be found in Mukerji (2009, 31–33).

order ethicists propose to solve them at the institutional level. When such DS are detected, they propose to introduce a new rule that sanctions the actions of the interacting parties. Their DS is resolved because they get an incentive—either a prospective reward or a prospective punishment—to behave in a socially preferable fashion. We can conclude, then, that when it comes to the role of incentives in institutional design order ethicists largely agree with Rawls' ideas. Like Rawls, they believe that incentives are a helpful tool that we can use in order to address ethical problems.

But it would be a mistake to conclude that when it comes to the role of incentives order ethicists agree with Rawls *tout court*. They do not. In Rawls' system, incentives are only part of the story. Rawls does not assume that all ethical problems should (or could) be solved by offering individuals incentives. In securing the cooperation of all members of society, he believes, we should not only appeal to people's self-interest. We should also nurture their moral capacity, which he calls a "sense of justice". "A sense of justice", Rawls explains, "is an effective desire to apply and to act from the principles of justice and so from the point of view of justice." (TJ, 497) He makes it very clear that such a sense of justice is incompatible with a purely selfish disposition to act. "We cannot preserve a sense of justice and all that this implies", Rawls says, "while at the same time holding ourselves ready to act unjustly should doing so promise some personal advantage." (TJ, 498) In contrast, at least some order ethicists have argued that we can solve all ethical problems without supposing that individuals possess any moral motivation whatsoever. Luetge (2007a, b), in particular, has argued that moral norms can be implemented in a society as long as individuals are able to communicate and to invest.

7 Efficiency as a Normative Requirement

At this point, we have to examine the Rawlsian difference principle more closely. In the previous section, we mentioned that the version of the principle that we introduced is not the formulation that is usually cited and discussed. Rawls is widely known for his view that the justice of a society depends only on the welfare of its least fortunate members. In fact, a few pages after the first formulation of the second principle, which we quoted above, Rawls suggests a second version. It demands that

> "[s]ocial and economic inequalities are to be arranged so that they are.. to the greatest expected benefit of the least advantage". (TJ, 72)

Why does Rawls introduce two seemingly contrary versions of the difference principle within a few pages? To be sure, the first version (DP1) that we considered in the previous section is not an imprecise (or even wrong) formulation of the actual difference principle. Rather, the second version (DP2a), which calls for the maximization of the material endowment of the least advantaged, is an interpretation of the first. How so?

Fig. 1 The OP-curve

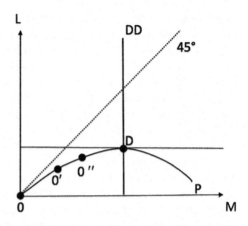

Let us reconsider the first version of the difference principle, DP1, that we discussed above. It says that "social and economic inequalities are to be arranged so that they are.. reasonably expected to be to everyone's advantage". As Rawls notes elsewhere, the idea of mutual advantage that is employed here has to be specified against the background of "a suitable benchmark of comparison." (PL, 16) The term "suitable" obviously requires an explanation. So Rawls goes on to clarify that it means suitable to the idea of *free and equal persons*. According to Rawls, this idea suggests a benchmark of equality. That is, the relevant standard of comparison of mutual advantage is a distribution of income and wealth that allots to everybody an equal share. Now, if we combine this benchmark of equality with DP1 we get the interpretation of DP1 which demands that social and economic inequalities be arranged so that they are to the greatest expected benefit of the least advantaged. In other words,

$$DP2a = DP1 + \text{benchmark of equality}$$

Since this is certainly not obvious, here is a sketch of the graphical argument which employs the so called "OP-curve".

For simplicity, let us assume that there are only two social groups, M and L. M-individuals, it shall be supposed, are more advantaged than L-individuals insofar as they have dispositions that make them more efficient workers. Under any economic regime that conditions their distributive shares on their productivity M-individuals would receive a greater material endowment than L-individuals. Now suppose that the economic institutions of society did not allow any incentive payments, such that everybody gets the same income and wealth. In other words, we start at the benchmark of equality that Rawls demands. Figure 1 depicts it as 0.

0 is at the origin of the coordinate system spanned by the axes, M and L. M and L represent the material endowments of the M-individuals and the L-individuals, respectively. To be sure, the origin does not suggest that everybody has zero material endowments. What it does suggest is that M-individuals and L-individuals

both have the same material endowments. (We do not know, of course, how much income and wealth they have. But as it turns out, that is, in fact, irrelevant.) Now, if Rawls is right about the motivating role of incentives, we can assume that both M-individuals and L-individuals would benefit if system 0 was transformed into system 0', which offers mild incentive payments. These will presumably motivate individuals to increase their efforts, which will, in turn, increase overall output. And if the incentive payments to M-individuals are smaller than the overall growth in income and wealth, it will be possible to make everyone in society better off than under system 0. Moving from 0 to 0' would, hence, be sanctioned by the first formulation of the difference principle, DP1. 0' lies northeast of 0, but south of the 45° line, which is the geometric locus of all equal distributions in M-L space. Presumably, once we have transformed 0 into 0', we can still increase incentive payments and make everyone better off. In other words, we can move from 0' to a new regime 0" which lies northeast of 0'. There will be a continuum of possibilities along the OP-curve south of the 45° line. That curve is meant to represent the set of arrangements where the material endowment of L is maximal, given the endowment of M.[10] That means that it can, at the same time, be seen as a *possibility frontier*. The economically feasible arrangements lie on the OP-curve or below. Any move along the curve is sanctioned by DP1 until we get to point D, where the slope of the OP-curve becomes zero. D is the arrangement where the introduction of any further incentive payments would actually make L-individuals worse off. Obviously, then, DP1 calls for the realization of D. Now, note that D is the maximum of the OP-curve. That is, it represents the arrangement where the material endowment of the least advantaged, L, is maximized. This shows that when we select an equal distribution as a benchmark for mutual advantage and input it into DP1, we get DP2a.

Now that we have shown how the Rawlsian interpretation of the difference principle, DP2a, can be derived from DP1, we would like to draw attention to an important characteristic of it. As Rawls emphasizes, "the difference principle is compatible with the principle of efficiency." (TJ, 69) To explain, the principle of efficiency is fulfilled if and only if the distributive arrangement in a society is such that it is impossible to make anybody better off without making anybody else worse off. DP2a is evidently consistent with this principle. It demands that arrangement D be put in place. As Rawls explains, at D, "it is indeed impossible to make any one representative man better off without making another worse off". (TJ, 69) We cannot increase the endowment of L-individuals since D is *per definitionem* the point in M-L space where their endowment is maximized. We could increase the endowment of M, but only at the cost of making L worse off. So the demands of DP2a are, as Rawls rightly claims, consistent with the principle of efficiency.

This is worth pointing out because the principle of efficiency also plays a great role in order ethics. As we have stressed above, the idea behind order ethics is to find DS in social interactions and to resolve them in order to make everyone better

---

[10] As Rawls says, the arrangements that the OP-curve represents are in that sense *efficient*.

off. Order ethicists will not rest before the potential for mutually beneficial institutional reforms has been exhausted. Once that vision has been realized, the distributive arrangement in society will be efficient. Like Rawls, order ethicists subscribe to the requirement of efficiency.

8 The Redistribution of Income and Wealth

At this point, we can move on to another important topic in moral and political philosophy, viz. the issue whether it is permissible for the state to redistribute income and wealth. It is obvious that the demands of the Rawlsian difference principle call for a certain degree of redistribution. To be sure, this is no logical consequence of DP2a. It may be that in certain societies a pure free market system might, by itself, lead to the egalitarian distribution that the principle calls for. But this is rather improbable. In all likelihood, we will only be able to fulfil the demands of the Rawlsian difference principle if we are willing to allow a substantial redistribution of income and wealth to take place.

This fact has prompted many conservative and, in particular, libertarian writers to utter serious criticisms of the Rawlsian view.[11] Nozick, e.g., has famously said that the taxation necessary to fulfil the demands of the difference principle were "on a par with forced labor" (1974, 169). But order ethicists, it seems, should have no beef with Rawls when it comes to redistributive measures. In fact, they should advocate such measures whenever they are the best means to making everybody better off. Mukerji and Schumacher (2008) discuss the issue of the minimum wage from an order-ethical perspective. They conclude that, under normal market conditions, order ethicists should favour a tax-funded wage subsidy instead of a wage floor. In other words, they suggest that order ethicists should endorse a certain degree of redistribution. Other writers have uttered similar views in regards to further policy questions. As we have said above, Homann and Luetge (2004/2005) give an order-ethical justification of the social welfare state.

Of course, when it comes to the issue of *how much* redistribution is called for, the degree to which the implications of Rawls' position coincide with the practical requirements of order ethics remains an open question. But there is no disagreement as to the question whether redistribution is morally permissible *in principle*.

---

[11]For an overview of the exchange on income redistribution between conservatives, libertarians, and egalitarians, see Barry (2011).

Fig. 2 The OP-curve (with comparatively equal status quo)

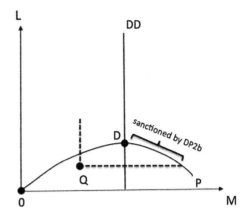

9 Economic Inequality

The commonalities between the demands of Rawls' difference principle, DP2a, and the requirements of order ethics that we have been able to uncover so far can, in fact, be explained rather easily. As it turns out, the guiding normative principle behind order ethics can be construed as an alternative interpretation of the difference principle, DP2b. On that interpretation, the normative foundation of order ethics can actually be seen as a close cousin of Rawls' difference principle (Mukerji 2009). As we explained above, Rawls' DP2a is derived from DP1 in conjunction with a benchmark of equality. DP2b can also be derived from DP1 when the benchmark of equality is replaced by the status quo.[12]

$$DP2b = DP1 + \text{status quo}$$

With this clarification in mind, we can start examining a fundamental difference between Rawls' conception of justice and order ethics. In the following, we are interested to find out when the implications of DP2a and DP2b are compatible with one another and when they conflict.

Since DP2a and DP2b are both based on DP1 and differ merely in their benchmark for mutual advantage, the extent to which the implications of DP2a and DP2b are compatible should, it seems, depend on the difference between the benchmarks. In fact, it turns out that this is roughly correct. Let us distinguish two cases.

Case 1: The distribution in the status quo is comparatively equal

Figure 2 illustrates Case 1, where the status quo, Q, is located in the area west of the line DD that passes through D. In Case 1, the implications of the order ethical

---

[12]Order ethicists follow the economist James M. Buchanan in his pragmatic observation that "[a]ny proposal for change involves the status quo as the necessary starting point." (Buchanan 1975/2000, 101)

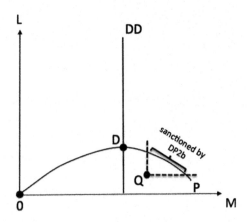

Fig. 3 The OP-curve (with comparatively unequal status quo)

principle DP2b are compatible with the implications of the Rawlsian DP2a. DP2a demands that we move to D under all circumstances. DP2b also sanctions such a move. However, the requirements of DP2b are less stringent. In fact, it also sanctions any move to any point on the OP-curve that lies east of D and in the orthogonal space northeast of Q. These points are less egalitarian than D. There is, hence, a certain tension between the implications of DP2a and DP2b.

Case 2: The distribution in the status quo is comparatively unequal

Figure 3 illustrates Case 2, where the status quo, Q, is located in the area east of DD. Here, the implications of DP2a and DP2b conflict. DP2a still demands a move to D while DP2b demands a move to some point on the OP-curve that lies in the orthogonal space to the northeast of Q. In Case 2, there is then no room for agreement between DP2a and DP2b, i.e. between the Rawlsian conception of justice and order ethics.

10 The Problem of Implementation

Why do order ethicists disagree with Rawls in Case 2? Why do they not adopt D as their ethical goal? Some order ethicists would certainly object to D on normative grounds. But their main beef with it is pragmatic. As Homann (2001) explains, order ethicists believe in the following claim, which is one of the most fundamental tenets of their view.

Incentive-Compatible Implementability (ICI)
The incentive-compatible implementability of an ethical norm is a necessary condition for its normative validity.

Order ethicists take ICI to be a constraint on ethical requirements, which limits the normative demands that can justifiably be made. It may be seen as the logical product of three separate claims that order ethicist subscribe to in conjunction.

Realism (R)
The implementability of an ethical norm is a necessary condition for its normative validity.
Cooperation (C)
The implementation of an ethical norm requires the cooperation of the members of society.
Weak Incentivism (WI)
Members of society will cooperate in the implementation of an ethical norm if and only if it is not in their rational self-interest not to support it.[13]

R seems rather unobjectionable as a normative view and Rawls, it seems, would agree to it.[14] Whether C is true is an empirical issue. It certainly depends on its precise interpretation. Maybe certain rules can be implemented against the will of certain minorities, such that universal cooperation is not always necessary for implementability. But after the advent of terrorism, we know that even small groups in society can have a great impact on society as a whole.[15] Therefore, it is reasonable to assume that a rather high degree of cooperation will be necessary to implement ethical norms in society. When it comes to the issue of implementation, the only point of contention between order ethicists and Rawlsians is the status of WI. Order ethicists accept it while Rawlsians reject it. The latter think that individuals act not only from self-interest. As we explained above, they believe that moral agents can be instilled a sense of justice. Order ethicists do not deny that individuals act from a variety of motives, including moral ones. They doubt, however, that individuals will follow their sense of justice in the long term if this means that they are thereby made worse off. In other words, they will not cooperate in the implementation of policy proposals that contravene their long-term self-interest. This explains why they do not adopt D as an ethical goal in Case 2. Under D, M-individuals would be worse off than under the current arrangement Q. M-individuals, order ethicists would argue, will thus oppose the implementation of D. And their opposition will make it impossible to implement D. Rawls, of course, would say that D is realisable if M-individuals possess a strong enough sense of justice. Here lies, then, a further point of contention between the system of order ethicists and the Rawlsian view.

---

[13]Perhaps some order ethicists would also accept a stronger version of incentivism:
Strong Incentivism (SI)
Members of society will cooperate in the implementation of an ethical norm if and only if it is in their rational self-interest to support it.

[14]Rawls devotes a lot of attention to the "problem of stability" and seeks to show that his conception of justice could, in fact, be implemented and stabilized in a well-ordered society. See, in particular, TJ (Book III) and JF (Chap. 5).

[15]We owe this point to Karl Homann.

11 Rawlsian Order Ethics

At this point, we do not wish to discuss whether order ethicists or Rawlsians are right about the empirical warrant of WI. For argument's sake, however, let us assume that WI corresponds, at least roughly, to the empirical facts. If so, do Rawlsians have to abandon DP2a and adopt DP2b in its stead? This would certainly be an ugly toad for them to swallow. As we have seen above, proponents of the Rawlsian view favour quite egalitarian social arrangements. By adopting DP2b, they would commit themselves to the view that under certain conditions very inegalitarian distributional outcomes are ethically acceptable. But Rawlsians would not have to go that far. As Mukerji (2009) argues, they can stay true to their core contention, viz. that the least advantaged members of society should be made as well off as possible, even under non-ideal social conditions. Should it turn out that, given the contingent constraints of human psychology, realizing DP2a is impossible, they can still use this principle as a "regulative idea". If we are faced with Case 2 and the only realizable social arrangements lie in the space east of D, then Rawlsians should propose to implement that arrangement which is geometrically closest to D. The conception of justice that results from this modification, synthesises the spirit behind the Rawlsian view with ICI, which is perhaps the most important aspect of the order ethical system. Hence, it deserves the name "Rawlsian Order Ethics". Up to this point, this possibility has not attracted much attention. However, should the debate about the implementability of ethical norms converge on the order ethical view, then Rawlsians Order Ethics is the obvious point in logical space that Rawlsians should retreat to. In that case, the conception may conceivably become quite important.

12 Conclusion

In summary of the above, we may conclude that order ethics is surprisingly compatible with the Rawlsian conception of justice. Both take social institutions as their primary subject and both accord the idea of procedural justice an important role. Furthermore, many of the moral implications of order ethics seem to converge with the Rawlsian positions. Like Rawlsians, order ethicists seem to endorse a rather encompassing scheme of individual rights and liberties. And it is rather plausible to suggest that they will, at least to a large extent, go along with the Rawlsian views about fair equality of opportunity. In addition, order ethicists and Rawlsians have a lot of common ground when it comes to the role of incentives in policy making, efficiency as a normative requirement and the in-principle legitimacy of income redistribution. Comparatively minor differences aside, then, the only substantial point of contention between order ethicists and Rawlsians lies in the fact that the latter always advocate a rather egalitarian scheme of distribution while the former tolerate rather inegalitarian distributive arrangements. If order ethicists are right about the conditions under which ethical norms can be implemented in society, then Rawlsians will have to give up their relentless call for a perfect distributive scheme in which the least well off members of society are made as well off as they conceivably can be. Rawlsians will have to settle for less. This does not mean, however, that they have to swallow order ethics hook, line, and sinker. As we have suggested towards the end, Rawlsians can accept the order ethical idea that the principle of incentive-compatible implementability constrains moral demands, while allowing the Rawlsian difference principle to play the role of a "regulative idea". We proposed to call this combination of views "Rawlsian Order Ethics". Time will tell whether it holds any promise.

References

Arneson, Richard. 2008. *Equality of opportunity*. The Stanford Encyclopedia of Philosophy (Fall 2008 Edition), ed. Edward N. Zalta. http://plato.stanford.edu/archives/fall2008/entries/equal-opportunity.
Barry, Christian. 2011. Redistribution. The Stanford Encyclopedia of Philosophy (Fall 2011 Edition), ed. Edward N. Zalta. http://plato.stanford.edu/archives/fall2011/entries/redistribution.
Buchanan, James M. 1975/2000. *The limits of liberty: Between anarchy and leviathan*. Indianapolis, Indiana: Liberty Fund.
Buchanan, James M. 1990. The domain of constitutional economics. *Constitutional Political Economy* 1: 1–18.
Cohen, Gerald A. 1991. Incentives, inequality, and community. In *The tanner lectures on human values 13*, ed. Grethe B. Peterson, 1992, 262–329. Utah: University of Utah Press.
Hirsch, Fred. 1977. *The social limits to growth*. London: Routledge & Kegan Paul.
Hobbes, Thomas. 1651/1996. *Leviathan*, ed. John Gaskin. Oxford: Oxford University Press.
Homann, Karl. 2001. "Ökonomik: Fortsetzung der Ethik mit anderen Mitteln", in: Homann (2002), 243–266.
Homann, Karl. 2002. *Vorteile und Anreize*, ed. Christoph Luetge. Tübingen: Mohr Siebeck.
Homann, Karl, and Franz Blome-Drees. 1992. *Wirtschafts- und Unternehmensethik*. Göttingen: Vandenhoeck & Ruprecht.
Homann, Karl and Christoph Luetge. 2004/2005. *Einführung in die Wirtschaftsethik*. Münster: LIT-Verlag.
Luetge, Christoph. 2005. Economic ethics, business ethics and the idea of mutual advantages. *Business Ethics: A European Review* 14(2): 108–118.
Luetge, Christoph. 2007a. Social glue under conditions of globalisation: Philosophers on essential normative resources. In *Globalisation and business ethics*, ed. Karl Homann, Peter Koslowski, and Christoph Luetge, 191–201. Hampshire: Ashgate Publishing Company.
Luetge, Christoph. 2007b. *Was halt eine Gesellschaft zusammen?*. Tübingen: Mohr Siebeck.
Mukerji, Nikil. 2009. *Das Differenzprinzip von John Rawls und seine Realisierungsbedingungen*. Münster: LIT-Verlag.
Mukerji, Nikil and Julian Nida-Rümelin. 2014. Towards a moderate stance on human enhancement. *Humana.ment—Journal of Philosophical Studies* 26:17–33.
Mukerji, Nikil, and Christoph Schumacher. 2008. How to have your cake and eat it too: Resolving the efficiency-equity trade-off in minimum wage legislation. *The Journal of Interdisciplinary Economics* 19(4): 315–340.
Nozick, Robert. 1974. *Anarchy, state, and utopia*. New York: Basic Books.
Rawls, John. 1971/1999. *A theory of justice (Revised Edition)*. Cambridge: Harvard University Press (cited as *TJ*).

Rawls, John. 1993/1996. Political liberalism. *Political liberalism – expanded edition*. New York: Columbia University Press Books (cited as *PL*).
Rawls, John. 1999/2003. Justice as fairness. In *A restatement (third edition)*. ed. Erin Kelly. Cambridge: Harvard University Press (cited as *JF*).
Sinn, Hans-Werner. 1986. Risiko als Produktivitätsfaktor. *Jahrbücher für Nationalökonomie und Statistik* 201: 557–571.

Boost up and Merge with. Order Ethics in the Light of Recent Developments in Justice Theory

Michael G. Festl

Something is going on in the state of justice theory. Slowly but surely, a novel paradigm emerges. When elaborated further, this paradigm—elsewhere I call it the pragmatist paradigm (Festl 2015)—could, before long, challenge the approaches to justice that are derived from the epochal work of Rawls (1971/1999). Despite a severe challenge by Neo-Aristotelian approaches to justice, these Rawlsian approaches remain dominant in the field.[1] Rawlsian approaches ('RSA' for 'Rawlsian standard approach' in the following), as I understand them, start with a procedure for deducing the set of principles a perfectly just society would adhere to. Their most famous procedure is the thought experiment of contract theory, which asks which principles of justice a state would adopt if it were formed anew by rational individuals. In a second step, these approaches deductively apply the principles thus derived to decide real-world problems with a bearing on justice. In proceeding this way, the RSA strictly separates the justification of norms, yielded by the thought experiment, from the implementation of norms, yielded by the deductive application of the justified norms to problems.

The pragmatist paradigm, as the currently emerging one, rejects this separation and thereby undermines the very bedrock of the RSA. Instead, the pragmatist approach—I have Amartya Sen, Axel Honneth and my own approach in mind[2]—starts with the identification of existing injustices and, in what could be called a hands-on approach, intends to decide such problems by relying, as far as possible, on norms that are already implemented in existing practices. The paper at hand investigates how this new approach to justice is connected with the order ethical

---

[1] For an extensive elaboration on both of these approaches to justice theory, see Festl (2015, 43–159).
[2] I will reference all three in the following.

M.G. Festl (✉)
School of Humanities and Social Sciences/Philosophy, University of St. Gall,
St. Gall, Switzerland
e-mail: michael.festl@unisg.ch

approach in business ethics, as elaborated primarily by Karl Homann and Christoph Luetge.

The first section sheds light on the pragmatist approach by contrasting Sen's theory with the RSA. The second section demonstrates that Sen's theory bears an astonishing resemblance to order ethics. Building on this, the third section introduces the main point of Honneth's theory of justice and carries this point further. In so doing, I provide a first glimpse of my own approach to justice. By discussing the relation between the justification and the implementation of norms that a pragmatist approach adopts, the fourth section elaborates on my approach and explains its relation to order ethics.

1 Sen's Problem-Based Justice Theory

Amartya Sen, practical philosopher and winner of the Nobel Prize in economics, obtains the philosophical concepts his justice theory relies on by criticising existing theories, especially the theory of John Rawls, whom he regards to be the godfather of contemporary justice theory. Sen reproaches Rawls for having committed the original sin of justice theory—namely, trying to deduce once and for all, and without paying due attention to existing societies, the set of principles to which each and every society is supposed to adhere to if it is to be just. Admitting that Rawls's 'transcendental' approach is intellectually challenging and interesting, Sen criticises Rawls and the RSA for yielding a theory of justice that is incapable of contributing to the solution of real-life problems with a bearing on justice (2009, 5–8). He invokes two intertwined arguments to make his point: first, the RSA's procedure for deducing principles of justice does not deliver the agreement about what justice consists of that its supporters desire ('issue of the *feasibility*'); second, even if such an agreement could be reached, it would still not yield the surplus value with regard to increasing justice in the real world that the RSA hopes it would ('issue of the *redundancy*') (ibid., 9).

Elaborating on the first argument, Sen reminds his readers of the notorious discussions about the distribution of goods which people should subscribe to under the terms specified by Rawls's thought experiment on the negotiation of a social contract. Although, in his most influential work, Rawls claimed that a just state needs to distribute resources according to the so-called difference principle,[3] Sen points out that in his later work, Rawls was forced to concede that this is not self-evident at all (ibid., 58). Quite the opposite, Rawls's argument—and, by extension, the RSA as a whole—is characterised by arbitrariness on this decisive point; the justice principles deduced via Rawls's thought experiment only *seem*

---

[3]The difference principle states that inequalities between individuals are only legitimate if they work to the advantage of the least well-off members of society (Rawls 1971/1999, 131). For a detailed discussion of the difference principle, see the contribution of Ludwig Heider and Nikil Mukerji (in this volume).

necessary because, in a preceding step, Rawls elaborated a very specific concept of the person, which, in turn, makes the principles of justice he ultimately defends a foregone conclusion (ibid., 6). Hence, in Sen's view, the transcendental deduction of principles of justice, on which proponents of the RSA heavily rely, is a shenanigan.

To underscore this critique, Sen conceives an example of three children—Anne, Bob and Clara—who argue about the ownership of a flute (ibid., 12–15): Anne demands she should be made the owner of the flute because she is the only one among the three who is actually able to play the flute; Bob, on the other hand, postulates ownership on the grounds that, due to his family's poverty, the flute would be his first and only toy; whereas Clara claims ownership by voicing the argument that she made the flute. According to Sen, one can find at least one justice theory in support of each argument, even though these theories all share the conviction that their results are derived from a transcendental, and therefore indubitable, deduction of principles of justice. Utilitarians, so Sen argues, would give ownership to Anne because, thanks to her capacity to actually play the flute, she, and her potential listeners, would derive the highest utility if Anne possessed the flute; egalitarians, and here most advocates of the RSA belong, would invest Bob with ownership of the flute in order to increase the equality between the kids; libertarians and Marxists would bestow ownership on Clara on the grounds that she should not be deprived of the right to enjoy the full fruit of her labour. Sen thus concludes that it is characteristic of problems with a bearing on justice to garner various credible but mutually exclusive solutions (ibid., 12 and 14). As a result, the effort to discover the Holy Grail of justice, i.e., the set of principles of justice that unambiguously decides, once and for all, all normative problems, fails on the issue of feasibility.

However, Sen does not leave it at that. He claims, furthermore, that even if the RSA found a set of justice principles everyone could agree on, this set would not deliver the desired result. It would be of no avail to decide a problem with a bearing on justice in the real world. This is, according to Sen, the case because the physiognomy of the perfectly just society is not a reliable guideline for arbitrating actual problems of justice. Sen argues that facing the choice between a painting by Picasso and one by Dalí, it is superfluous to know that Leonardo's *Mona Lisa* is, from a transcendental perspective, the perfect painting (ibid., 16). The problem is that the plethora of different dimensions of ideals such as 'beautiful', 'good' and 'just' prevents ranking the different options by measuring which is in closest distance to the ideal and is therefore the preferable one. Thus, coming back to Sen's example, due to the diversity of criteria for judging paintings, it cannot be decided which of the two choices bears the closer resemblance to the *Mona Lisa* (ibid., 98). Moreover, so Sen continues, proximity to the perfect state, even if it could be ascertained, is not necessarily a useful guide when choosing between options: a 'person who prefers red wine to white may prefer either to a mixture of the two, even though the mixture is, in an obvious descriptive sense, closer to the preferred red wine than pure white wine would be' (ibid., 16). As a result, Sen determines that the knowledge of perfect beauty or, *mutatis mutandis*, of perfect justice is not sufficient to rank the choices that are *actually* faced. Hence, acquaintance with the principles the perfectly just state would adhere to is of no help when it comes to deciding problems of justice in the real world.

As a surrogate for deducing eternal principles of justice, Sen suggests justice theorists should start from actually existing problems with a bearing on justice. The discernment of such problems should be followed by identifying as well as evaluating the options that are available for dealing with the problem. Sen, thus, promotes what I call a problem-based approach: the elaborations of justice theory should start from problems of justice that really exist. According to Sen, his understanding of justice theory neatly dovetails with the fact that what moves people is 'not the realization that the world falls short of being completely just— which few of us expect—but that there are clearly remediable injustices around us which we want to eliminate' (ibid., vii).

But how can a theory of justice that does not start with principles tell whether there even is a problem of justice? After all, to determine that situation x constitutes a problem of justice, it needs to be determined that x contradicts what is deemed just in this or that respect. The answer is that Sen does not mean to start without the reliance on principles whatsoever. He emphasises, however, that every problem-based approach must be wary of relying on a fixed scheme of principles of justice. Instead, such an approach needs to flexibly rely on various normative principles which cause moral discontent if they are not realised. Whether a principle of justice is justified *in the concrete case* needs to be seen as the outcome of an investigation into the problem at hand and must not be decided in a priori fashion.[4] Still, within his call for flexibility, there is one moral concept for identifying a problem with a bearing on justice that is especially dear to Sen: capabilities. But, again, Sen does not regard the focus on capabilities to be the one and only path to epiphany. 'The capability perspective does point to the central relevance of the inequality of capabilities in the assessment of social disparities, but it does not, on its own, propose any specific formula for policy decisions' (ibid., 232f.).

Based on this focus on capabilities, Sen argues that a problem of justice is to be ascertained when there is an individual who does not have the possibility—the capability—to do what 'he or she has reason to value' (ibid., 231). An example would be, if there is a society in which it is taken for granted that every member should be able to lead an autonomous life and if to go shopping on one's own is regarded to be part of such a life, then a problem of justice exists if some individuals cannot go shopping on their own because they are, for example, physically challenged. In such an instance, the capability approach recommends the allotment of extra resources from society to the physically challenged so that they could, if they desired to do so, go shopping on their own (e.g., the pecuniary resources necessary to buy a wheelchair). Following Sen, the essence of justice theory consists of such investigations with the aim of ridding the world of existing injustices.

---

[4]Sen even invokes his plea for flexibility against Anderson and Nussbaum, who try, in different ways, to build upon his theory (2009, 232f.).

It is obvious that the application of the capability approach also rests on prior decisions with a normative bearing. Otherwise, it would be impossible to distinguish between what counts as an ethically justified demand of individuals against society and what has to be disqualified as something that might, indeed, increase the wellbeing of quite a number of individuals but that society cannot rightfully be expected to support. From this angle, Elizabeth Anderson critically asks how Sen can be sure that individuals should not be entitled to enjoy a luxury vacation in Tahiti every year (1999, 316). To address such kinds of claims, Sen invokes the importance of discourses. He thereby affirms Adam Smith's emphasis on exchanges with people from different backgrounds and cultures. Sen argues that these kinds of discourses are most fertile for normative issues because they force people to approach considerations of justice from a standpoint they do not regularly assume. And to bring these different standpoints into exchange is, according to Sen, most prone to free people from the peculiar moral blindness that each and every specific cultural standpoint entails (cf. Sen 2009, 406 for an impressive example).

2 Order Ethics and Sen

Sen's arguments about the proper procedure for justice theory constitute a major reinforcement of order ethics. As a matter of fact, Sen's suggestions are so similar to core assumptions of order ethics that it is even tempting to say that, with Sen, justice theory arrives where the order ethical approach to business ethics had been waiting all along. I will elucidate the hitherto overlooked commonalities between Sen, as a proponent of the pragmatist approach to justice, and order ethics by focussing on three aspects. This exploration makes clear, I hope, that both approaches are mutually enforcing as well as mutually fertile.

First of all, there is Sen's critique of the RSA. As we saw, Sen argues that justice theory misses its task when concerning itself with deducing the one and only set of principles of justice—the Holy Grail. In a similar vein, order ethicists criticise the majority of approaches in business ethics for relying on grand schemes about the supposed demands of justice and thereby intend to tell individuals how they should act. The majority of ethical theories, so order ethicists contend, see their primary task in preaching that individuals ought to lead a morally decent life and, consequently, in conceiving what such a life entails (Luetge 2005, 109). In their critique of this majority position, order ethicists especially target the assumption that underlies this approach, namely that the moral problems that beset society are caused by the unethical behaviour of individuals. Yet, so order ethicists argue, the conditions of modern society call for a more sophisticated explanation of the causes of moral problems than just pointing at individual shortcomings. Hence, the key concern of ethics should no longer be the conception and the justification of normative schemes that are expected to regulate individual behaviour (cf. Luetge 2012 for a succinct argumentation).

If we take a closer look at the reasoning of order ethicists, it becomes clear that their reproach resembles the 'issue of the feasibility' that Sen levels against the RSA. Order ethicists defend their critique of the majority of ethical theories by invoking the sociological observation (cf. Luhmann 1998) that, at least since the Enlightenment, Western society has been characterised by pluralism with regard to ethical values, and this pluralism, so order ethicists round out their argument, renders efforts to devise the one and only scheme of *the* ethical life obsolete (Luetge 2005, 111; Homann 2001, 2f.). Sen, as well as order ethicists, argues that the hope for full agreement in the domain of ethical values has become futile. There is no Holy Grail anymore that could be discovered.

Moreover, just as Sen with his 'issue of the redundancy', order ethicists amplify their critique by adding that even if a fully-fledged understanding of justice were possible, it would not be capable of delivering the benefits its advocates hope. As I showed, Sen's argument of the redundancy is organised around the observation that grand schemes of what justice entails are not only unattainable but even superfluous. Knowledge of a perfect state of justice is, according to Sen's argument, irrelevant when ranking the actually attainable choices for dealing with moral problems because all these choices fall short of perfect justice in one way or another. This argument is complemented by order ethicists when they point out that quite a number of ethical problems in modern-day society bear the characteristics of a prisoner's dilemma. In a prisoner's dilemma, the moral outcome is never one in which all parties could maximise their individual wellbeing (more on the prisoner's dilemma below). In this sense also, order ethicists build their theory from the assumption that, for most moral problems, there is no perfect solution. Again, in a nutshell, when order ethicists argue that ethics should not be about conceiving and justifying grand schemes for individual moral behaviour, they find a parallel in Sen's demand that justice theory should give up its effort to transcendentally deduce the one and only set of principles of justice.

The second commonality between Sen and an order ethicist is the assumption that actual problems with a bearing on justice constitute the proper starting point for normative theories. Just as is true for Sen (see above), order ethicists take a clean sweep of the RSA's effort to start by constructing *ex nihilo* the set of normative principles to which a fully just society would adhere to. Homann and Suchanek, for example, affirm that their theory starts from the '[s]tatus quo', as opposed to commencing with the creation of a 'tabula rasa' (2005, 31, fn. 9; similar Luetge 2012, 12).[5] Likewise, the turning away from delineating the physiognomy of the

---

[5]Consequently, to say that order ethics goes back to contract theories is merely a half-truth. It is true when we understand contract theories—with Buchanan and also partly with Hobbes—as modelling the idea that moral action is prone to exploitation when it is not protected by rules ensuring that the moral actor is also remunerated for her behaviour in terms of an increase of her individual utility. In that sense, one could say that the main achievement of contract theory is its awareness of what is now called the prisoner's dilemma. On the other hand, contract theory cannot be called a predecessor of order ethics if it is understood—with Rawls and Nozick, and also partly with Kant and Locke—as a thought experiment in order to deduce the principles a society in

fully just society to contributing to the solution of real problems of justice is confirmed by order ethicists when they consciously refrain from speaking of Pareto-*optimality* and instead rely on the terminology of Pareto-*superiority*. In other words, they aim at improvement, solving problems, as opposed to perfection, attaining a state without problems. Therefore, it is, in my view, legitimate to maintain that both —Sen as well as order ethics—rely on a problem-based approach.[6]

The proximity hereby established between these two approaches is confirmed by the way order ethicists determine the existence of a problem with a moral bearing. Just like Sen, they rely on a heuristic. Whereas Sen resorts to the capability approach, order ethicists rely on the prisoner's dilemma.[7] Hence, although the capability approach and the prisoner's dilemma are not compatible in every respect,[8] both serve the same function in the architecture of their respective theories. Both heuristics serve, in the words of Sen, as the theory's 'informational focus' (2009, 231); they are, among other things, needed to determine the existence of a problem of justice. Sen ascertains that there is a problem of justice if an individual lacks the capability to do something that can be taken for granted in the society she lives in. Order ethicists conclude that there is a problem worthy of a normative inquiry if there is an interaction-situation that is characterised by a prisoner's dilemma—i.e., a situation in which the action most beneficial for the individual parties concerned does not, in the aggregate, lead to the morally preferable outcome for society as a whole (cf. Homann and Luetge 2005, 17).

Such is the case, so a standard example runs, when companies renounce investing in higher environmental standards, as such investments would put them at a disadvantage compared to their competitors. To overcome such a situation, order ethics pleads for changing the rules of the game ('Spielregeln'). The aim of this change is that the individual action that yields a morally inferior result for society as a whole is rendered less attractive for the individual parties concerned than the individual action that harvests the morally superior result for society. In the words of order ethicists, the interaction needs to be rendered 'incentive-compatible' via the establishment of appropriate 'rules' (Luetge 2005, 113; also Suchanek 2001/2007, vi). In our example, it could prove effective to introduce a tax that punishes environmentally unfriendly production so as to render the refusal to implement environmental policies detrimental to the individual success of the companies involved. Hence, the aim of order ethics is to modify the incentives for individuals so that these incentives trigger individual behaviour that leads to outcomes that are

---

(Footnote 5 continued)

search of perfect justice would adopt if it could start anew (cf. for Buchanan's explicit rejection of such a use of contract theory his 1975/2000, 98 and 210).

[6]Luetge explicitly states that order ethics needs to be assessed based on its capacity to solve normative problems (2004, 118).

[7]Homann and Suchanek emphasise that they regard the prisoner's dilemma as a heuristic (2005, 383f.).

[8]As opposed to the prisoner's dilemma, the capability approach is not derived from game theory, to name just one distinction.

morally superior in the aggregate. In the terminology of Buchanan (1991), an inspirational figure for order ethics, the 'choices of rules' are supposed to yield more beneficial 'choices within rules'. In summary, when order ethicists commence with the identification of an actual problem of justice by relying on a heuristic, they find a parallel in Sen's procedure and its reliance on the capability approach.

The third commonality between Sen and order ethics pertains to how both approaches deal with the fact that the application of their respective heuristics is preceded by certain decisions with a normative bearing. That such decisions are not only entailed in the capability approach but also in the prisoner's dilemma is implied by the fact that the, on aggregate, best among the attainable choices needs to be determined. When translating a real-life situation into a prisoner's dilemma, order ethicists necessarily rely on an ethical all-things-considered perspective on what is morally most appreciable for society as a whole. Otherwise, they would be incapable of identifying the outcome they want to attain with their modification of incentives for individual action. Order ethicists are well aware that implementation lacks orientation as long as it does not rest in a normative argument about what shall be implemented.

Not unexpectedly by now, just as Sen, order ethicists also hereby point to the importance of deliberation. Considering that both theories start from the sociological premise that Western societies are characterised by strong pluralism, it is little surprise that both also share a call for deliberation. When it is futile to search for a fully fledged theory on what justice demands—the Holy Grail—it becomes sensible to strive for as much agreement as possible with regard to particular problems of justice. And deliberation is the vehicle to get society closer to these particular agreements.[9] In this vein, already Buchanan has argued for the crucial role of discourses when deciding the choices of rules, i.e., the goals behind the readjustment of incentives (1975/2000, 222). Recently, this has been taken up by Luetge when he emphasises the importance of consent (2012, 14f.) To cut a longer story short, order ethicists who point to the significance of deliberation when it comes to the normative issues that precede the application of the prisoner's dilemma find a parallel in Sen's elaboration on what precedes the application of the capability approach.[10]

---

[9]It is needless to say that this call for deliberation has little in common with the Habermasian idea that discussions free from coercion could lead to morally indubitable outcomes (for a good discussion of the advantages and disadvantages of such an idea, see Habermas 1990). It is exactly the point of Sen and order ethics that such security in the realm of ethics is unattainable.

[10]As space considerations prevent a more thorough juxtaposition of Sen and order ethics, I can merely mention that there is also an aspect in which Sen and order ethics differ, at least a little: compared to Sen, order ethics puts a heavier emphasis on the role of institutions when it comes to promoting justice. This is due to the fact that order ethics builds on Buchanan's public-choice theory (PCT), whereas Sen relies on his own work in social-choice theory (SCT) and calls PCT his more conservative rival (2009, 291). Both PCT and SCT indeed share, as the names betray, a choice-oriented approach—that is, an approach that aims at the ranking of options for action— but, in simplified terms, whereas PCT is mainly about methodically reconstructing social outcomes via the aggregation of individual choices in order to influence those choices, SCT intends to uncover

3 Honneth's Normative Reconstruction

The greatest potentials for improving Sen's approach as well as that of the order ethicists arguably lie in getting a better handle on the issue of which normative decisions precede the use of their respective heuristics. Their references to deliberation, though well-intentioned and surely to the point, often remain in the abstract. However, as I intend to demonstrate by referring to further developments in justice theory, it is possible to put more flesh on the bones of this issue. In order to elaborate on this, to the extent that the scope of this paper permits, I first refer to recent work by Axel Honneth and then develop it further. In doing so, I provide a first idea how a theory could look that fully exploits the potentials of a problem-based approach to justice. This sketch will be extended in the next section and connected to order ethics.

In line with Sen and order ethics, Honneth identifies the strict separation between the justification of norms and their implementation as the greatest weakness of the RSA (2014, 55). Also Honneth alleges that the RSA is thus doomed to become powerless in the face of the normative problems modern-day society grapples with (2012, 35). Instead of trying to construct the set of principles the perfectly just society would live by, Honneth advocates that justice theory should assume an empirically informed standpoint when dealing with problems of justice. Therefore, Honneth replaces the RSA's *ex nihilo* construction of principles by what he calls 'normative reconstruction' (2014, 6).

Based on the practical philosophy of G.W.F. Hegel, Honneth's aim is to render explicit the norms already institutionalised in society. Based on this reconstruction of actual society, Honneth searches for potentials of justice that are implied by these norms but are not yet realised in practice. The philosopher from Frankfurt regards the hereby identified gaps between the norms institutionalised in society and the principles by which society actually lives as a society's normative shortcomings with regard to its own intentions and considers the claim to close these gaps justified. Thus, Honneth extrapolates from the 'internal meaning' of a society's ambition with regard to justice what this society can be expected to live up to (ibid., 4f.). As his procedure is, from the beginning, entangled with what is going on in society, it is, so Honneth hopes, immune to the danger of being unable to contribute to the solution of actual problems with a bearing on justice—the implementation issue. Honneth calls his approach a 'theory of justice as social analysis' (ibid., 3; 'eine Theorie der Gerechtigkeit als Gesellschaftsanalyse', as the German original has it) and thereby relies on a terminology that is stunningly similar to Homann's

---

(Footnote 10 continued)

contradictions between social decisions resulting from individual choices and axioms of rationality (e.g., Condorcet's paradox). However, when the concepts of both of these economic theories are transferred to justice theory, the commonalities outweigh the differences, especially when compared to other conceptions in justice theory.

alternative slogan for order ethics, namely economic ethics as normative theory of society ('Wirtschaftsethik [als] normative Gesellschaftstheorie' 1997, 38).[11]

In his recent book *Freedom's Right*, Honneth conducts the normative reconstruction he calls for. This yields an extensive conceptual as well as empirical investigation starting with the last centuries of Western society and ending in the present decade. Honneth retraces the key normative developments in the realms of the family, the economy, and the state (2014, 123–335). However, his, undoubtedly very impressive, reconstruction is rather general in covering numerous areas and could be criticised for being too detached from actual problems of justice so that, contrary to Honneth's intentions, it is not of real informational value for dealing with current problems of justice. Therefore, I think it is best to regard this general reconstruction as providing the frame for more focussed reconstructions that revolve around concrete problems of justice—reconstructions that might then be closer to, and thus more capable of dealing with, real problems. Be that as it may, my point is that it is very productive to combine the essence of Honneth's idea of approaching the domain of justice from a standpoint informed by the norms implicit in societal practices with Sen's and order ethicists' adherence to a problem-based approach. Such a combination can be regarded as the inheritance of a pragmatist approach to justice (cf. Dewey 1927/2008, 1932/2008; Putnam 2002).[12]

Starting, like Sen and order ethics, from a concrete problem with a bearing on justice, Honneth's normative reconstruction should be invoked to attain a firm focus on the concrete problem at hand. In other words, after having discerned a concrete problem, the justice theorist starts an empirical investigation of the normative practices associated with the problem. Like Honneth, but more in the concrete, the justice theorist delves into current normative practices with a bearing on the problem, and these normative practices serve as guidance in dealing with the problem—i.e., help in identifying the proper choices of rules, in the language of order ethics. This implies, first and foremost, expounding how society typically deals with similar problems and what norms it invokes for justifying these practices. With 'society', I hereby mean all the people who are affected by the problem at hand. In this sense, each problem constitutes its own society, namely the ones it affects. The current practices of these people should hence determine the starting point for overcoming the problem.[13] And if the justice theorist, in relying on this approach, is able to identify a norm that is already embraced in the practices of the society in question—especially when the norm is invoked in similar situations—this constitutes a good argument for regarding the actualization of this norm as the pivotal challenge with regard to the problem at hand.

---

[11]The common forebear of Honneth and Homann is, obviously, to be found in the practical philosophy of Hegel, especially Hegel's *Grundlinien der Philosophie des Rechts* (1821/1986). This issue would justify a thorough investigation.

[12]For extensive elaborations see Festl (2015, 377–474).

[13]I am very explicit on this in Festl (2015, 380–402).

It is important to note that this approach is not supposed to replace discussions that aim at reaching a widespread agreement on how to deal with the problem in question. However, in my view, this approach is a necessary extension of any theory that, like Sen and order ethicists, claims to operate based on the status quo. Deliberation is hence to be complemented, not to be abolished. And if the result of a deliberation is confirmed by the kind of investigation I suggest, then this is, I suppose, as far as we can get with regard to objective conclusions concerning a normative problem.

4 Justification and Implementation in a Pragmatist Approach to Justice

A further agreement between the approaches I am here concerned with is that overcoming a truly normative problem entails ranking different norms with regard to their legitimacy in the situation. Thereby, the actualisation of all of these norms is desired in general (otherwise they could not count as norms), but the norms conflict in the specific situation, that is, the situation does not allow for a full actualisation of all the relevant norms. 'Some part of the ideal must be butchered' (James 1897/1956, 203). Religious tolerance and animal rights are, for example, norms that are supported in general but that conflict under certain conditions, e.g., in practices of slaughtering. In the event of such a conflict, the empirical investigation into the *status quo* of the people affected by the problem is supposed to help determine the norms that should have priority in the contested situation. After this has been achieved, so the approach to justice that I defend argues, the heuristic of the prisoner's dilemma is one out of a number of possible heuristics (the capability approach is another) that are consulted to identify the necessary policy measures to implement the actualisation of the norms that have priority. There is, hence, a division of labour: the normative reconstruction (Honneth) investigates what is the right thing to do in the face of a concrete problem; the heuristics (Sen and order ethics) are devoted to the implementation of the right thing.

The theoretic relation between the prisoner's dilemma and the normative reconstruction is, thus, that the decision of which norm has priority—a decision triggered by the normative reconstruction—determines the values for filling out the pay-out matrix of the prisoner's dilemma. Thus, part of my pragmatist approach to justice—I call it 'justice as historic experimentalism'—can be understood as a merger of Honneth's normative reconstruction with order ethics' approach to the implementation of norms and the latter's heavy reliance on a heuristic. Obviously, there is a plethora of issues which need to be addressed to establish this approach, let alone render it convincing, for example, when is it justified to say that somebody is affected by a problem, what is constitutive of a problem that can be regarded as similar to the one in question, how is the normative reconstruction linked with deliberation etc. Unfortunately, this goes way beyond the limits of the paper at hand.[14] But, there is one aspect to the relation between the normative reconstruction and the prisoner's dilemma I want to elaborate on in the remaining pages.

It might seem that my pragmatist approach is not so different from the RSA in that it reintroduces the traditional relation between the justification and the implementation of norms—namely: 'implementation follows justification'. After all, the normative reconstruction that revolves around the problem in question could be regarded as a surrogate to the deduction of principles of justice, whereas the use of heuristics, such as the prisoner's dilemma, substitutes the application of norms, and, even more, the former has priority over the latter. So my pragmatist account is nothing but new wine in good old Rawlsian bottles. However, this would be a misconception. The main reason is that I reject any hierarchical understanding of the relation between the two main components of my approach. Instead, the idea is that, far from simply falling in line, the second component—the heuristics—regulates the first—the normative reconstruction: if the heuristic shows that the norm that should, according to the normative reconstruction, have priority in the situation cannot be actualised in practice (or only with undesired side effects), the normative reconstruction's result is rejected. Hence, another normative reconstruction in light of this new finding is elicited, i.e., the normative reconstruction starts anew but now under the premise that the norm that has won priority in the prior investigation can, for the time being, not be implemented.

The connection between the normative reconstruction and the heuristics that is hereby implied is supported by the rule 'ought implies can'. If there is an 'ought' without a 'can', the 'ought' is no longer a pertinent 'ought'. It is not connected to the realm of problems of justice. It is an empty shell. Therefore, the search for a new 'ought' is imperative; the procedure of the pragmatist justice theory is started anew. So in my approach, implementation does not follow justification, is not inferior to it. Instead, my approach relies on a recursive process between implementation and justification. And, with regard to a specific problem, this process only comes to an end when an 'ought' is found that is pregnant with a 'can'. In such a happy instance, heuristics such as the prisoner's dilemma are supposed to serve as the 'ought's' midwife. The connection that my pragmatist theory thereby establishes between 'ought' and 'can' is very different from the RSA. It fully rejects the latter's insistence that there is a set of normative principles we need to be devoted to under all circumstances, even if most of the set's elements are, for the time being, unattainable.

The main reason why, despite the rejection of a hierarchy between the normative reconstruction and the heuristics, the pragmatist investigation of a problem of justice nevertheless always starts with the reconstruction is that this sequence guarantees that the side of the 'can' is pushed really hard. The greatest danger of a normative theory that elevates the implementation of norms to the same level as the justification of norms is that the increased emphasis on implementation leads to selling justification short. Such a justice theory is tempted to be satisfied too easily

---

[14]As already mentioned, I outline the current status of my approach in Festl (2015, 377–474).

with the excuse that, normatively, the actualisation of norm x would be much appreciated, but, realistically, it is not feasible. To nip this danger in the bud, my approach starts with the highest demands in the realm of the 'ought' so as to guarantee that the 'can-side' is forced to do its best when searching for ways to implement the 'ought', and, in order to do its best, the 'can-side' needs to rely on powerful heuristics, such as the prisoner's dilemma.

The probably most exciting aspect of the recent developments in justice theory that I tried to sketch in this paper is that more and more philosophers in the field agree that the implementation of norms needs to play a bigger role. The justification of principles of justice remains superfluous if it does not rest in a convincing conceptualisation of these principles' implementation. Slowly but surely, justice theory bids farewell to the separation between the justification of norms and their implementation. No justification without implementation! This is the new motto. Order ethicists have been gathering around this motto for quite some time. Thus, my pragmatist approach to justice profoundly agrees with order ethics. Based on this agreement, it takes, as was shown, the main idea of order ethics up and embeds it in a wider theory of justice. In this sense, order ethics is boosted up and merged with.

References

Anderson, E.S. 1999. What is the point of equality? *Ethics* 109(2): 287–337.
Buchanan, J.M. 1975/2000. The limits of liberty. Between Anarchy and Leviathan. In *The collected works of James M. Buchanan*. Vol. 7. Liberty Fund. Indianapolis.
Buchanan, J.M. 1991. *The economics and the ethics of constitutional order*. Ann Arbor: The University of Michigan Press.
Dewey, J. 1927/2008. The public and its problems. Dewey, J. In *The later works. Volume 2, 1925–1927*. ed. Jo Ann Boydston, 235-372. Carbondale: Southern Illinois University Press.
Dewey, J. 1932/2008. Ethics, Dewey, J. In *The later works. Volume 7, 1932*. ed. Jo Ann Boydston. Carbondale: Southern Illinois University Press.
Festl, M.G. 2015. *Gerechtigkeit als historischer Experimentalismus. Gerechtigkeitstheorie nach der pragmatistischen Wende der Erkenntnistheorie*. Konstanz: Konstanz University Press.
Habermas, J. 1990. *Moral consciousness and communicative action*. Cambridge: Polity.
Hegel, G.W.F. 1821/1986. Grundlinien der Philosophie des Rechts oder Naturrecht und Staatswissenschaften im Grundrisse. In *Werke in zwanzig Bänden, auf der Grundlage der Werke von 1832–1845*. eds. Moldenhauer, E., and Michel, K.M. Suhrkamp. Frankfurt/M.
Homann, K. 1997. Sinn und Grenze der ökonomischen Methode in der Wirtschaftsethik. In *Wirtschaftsethik und Moralökonomik. Normen, soziale Ordnung und der Beitrag der Ökonomik*. eds. Aufderheide, D., and Dabrowski, M., 11–42. Berlin: Duncker und Humblot.
Homann, K. 2001. Ökonomik: Fortsetzung der Ethik mit anderen Mitteln. In *Vorteile und Anreize*. ed. Luetge, C., 243–266. Mohr Siebeck: Tübingen.
Homann, K., and C. Luetge. 2005. *Einführung in die Wirtschaftsethik*. Münster: LIT.
Homann, K., and A. Suchanek. 2005. *Ökonomik: Eine Einführung*. Tübingen: Mohr Siebeck.
Honneth, A. 2012. *The i in we. Studies in the theory of recognition*. Cambridge: Polity.
Honneth, A. 2014. *Freedom's right. The social foundations of democratic life*. Cambridge: Polity.

James, W. 1897/1956. *The will to believe and other essays in popular philosophy*. New York: Dover Publications.

Luetge, C. 2004. Ordnungsethik—naturalistisch konzipiert. In *Fakten statt Normen? Zur Rolle einzelwissenschaftlicher Argumente in einer naturalistischen Ethik*. ed. Luetge, C., and Vollmer, G., 117–127. Baden-Baden: Nomos.

Luetge, C. 2005. Economic ethics, business ethics and the idea of mutual advantages. *Business Ethics: A European Review* 14(2): 108–118.

Luetge, C. 2012. Fundamentals of order ethics: Law, business ethics and the financial crisis. *Archiv für Rechts- und Sozialphilosophie*. Beihefte 130: 11–21.

Luhmann, N. 1998. *Die Gesellschaft der Gesellschaft*. Frankfurt/M: Suhrkamp.

Putnam, H. 2002. *The collapse of the fact/value dichotomy and other essays*. Cambridge MA, London: Harvard University Press.

Rawls, J. 1971/1999. *A theory of justice*. Revised edition. Cambridge, MA: Harvard University Press.

Sen, A. 2009. *The idea of justice*. London: Allen Lane.

Suchanek, A. 2001/2007. *Ökonomische Ethik*. Tübingen: Mohr Siebeck.

Deconstructive Ethics—Handling Human Plurality (Shaped) by Normative (Enabling) Conditions

Tatjana Schönwälder-Kuntze

On the following pages, I present a programmatic proposal for an ethical model that sets out by analysing *norms*—that is, it does *not* start with a certain idea of what human beings 'are' or 'must be' *in order to ground normativity*. That means to presuppose no kind of reasoning grounded in any so-called autonomous subject, nor in any other kind of prescribed determinations of, or properties belonging to, human lives. Starting with a *formal analysis of norms and with their categorization* rather than with grounding norms at first might provide an answer to severe objections against the basis of European enlightened ethics. That basis is centred in a well-defined rational subjectivity which has not only forgotten its own dependency but has also excluded and still excludes any other kind of human rationality, as well as any of those human beings who do not fit in Mayer (2007). From a historical or genealogical point of view, this basis even seems to be constructed by such exclusions—be they cultural or conceptual.

1 Norms as the Theoretical Starting Point

While stating that norms themselves constitutively work with exclusions—whatever it may be that they exclude—as e.g. Hegel or Butler point out, I will also support the claim that the Eurocentric model of ethics and its grounding are grown norms in themselves. In the following document,s to be grown shall mean not to have any universal content, which were then only to be discovered at some point in time. It shall also imply that these norms are by no means meant to be presupposed as some universal human constant. Consequently, the 'enlightened' ethical model

---

T. Schönwälder-Kuntze (✉)
Faculty of Philosophy, Philosophy of Science and the Study of Religion,
Ludwig-Maximilians-Universität München, Munich, Germany
e-mail: tatjana.schoenwaelder@lrz.uni-muenchen.de

along with its basic concepts, such as 'subjectivity', 'dignity', 'responsibility', 'autonomy', 'intentionality', 'sovereignty', or in one phrase, any well-formed 'subjective freedom' cannot serve as point of departure or basic grounding for any justification of specific kinds of normativity or universal norms.

Moreover, from an epistemological point of view, there arises another problem with the traditional grounding in the 'subject': following Nietzsche, Sartre, Levinas, Foucault, Butler, or Nancy, to name but a few, we find good reasons to assume that we never really *know* how we or other persons mentally 'function' in a strong epistemological sense. We experience others, indeed most of the time even ourselves, through visible attitudes, behaviours, and (re)actions—but there is not necessarily an 'inner subjectivity' beyond to cause that outer performance. So how could we be able to ground ethics and norms within a well-formed subjectivity, if we do not even really *know* what makes a real human being? Nevertheless, proponents of this enlightened rationality still call their basis universal, superior, and the best (see e.g. Habermas 2011), while others (!) call its universal claim paternalistic, imperialistic, exclusionary, and destructive. Although this is not the place to go deeper into these accusations and discussions, it is necessary to indicate them in order to motivate my approach.[1]

Besides these discursive reasons, there are also systematic reasons to start with an analysis of norms: It also responds to the indubitable fact that every human being is born into a (social) world which is already structured or ordered by different norms. We may take the picture of a prism to clarify what is meant: The basic thesis presented in this paper is that every human being is brought up within a plurality of different norms crossing or intersecting each other. Thus, norms produce *and*

---

[1]There are different possibilities to distinguish ethical models: One contemporary pattern is to draw a distinction between normative, descriptive, and meta-ethics, or between applied and grounding ethics. A third could be to distinguish ethics from theories concerning the social which have a strong ethical impetus, but refuse to provide an explicit ethical model, at least a model which has systematic features—let's call them ethical non-ethics or positively: deconstructive ethics. Calling them non-ethics indicates the prevailing refusal of their representatives to theorize systematically their mostly extensive ethical considerations. Thus their theoretical status is a bit strange, insofar as they describe in a critical way how ethics and norms work—this is the deconstructive side—but without stating explicitly what theoretical basis legitimates such a critique. Therefore they are subject to a lot of accusations from theorists who find themselves very well legitimated due to their last foundation in e.g. Aristotle, Kant or God, to name but a few. This is true for Habermas' discourse ethics which is based on a very strict (western) idea of reason and the ability to take part in rational negotiations. It is also true for Martha Nussbaum's enabling ethics grounded above all in Aristotle. Although the traditions that I refer to as deconstructive ethics see themselves in the tradition of European Enlightenment, they try to avoid some of the aporias introduced by the dialectics of Enlightenment: moral rationality in its modern formation and hence modern morality was not able to avert 'Auschwitz' and other genocides during the 20th century. More than that, it was neither able to avert a lot of other iniquities such as colonization or two world wars. Furthermore, there are a lot of voices which do not only wonder about its power to avert horrible developments, but ask to what extent this concept of rationality is also the ultimate *cause* of such developments. Although the following theorists argue from very different standpoints—*though they are all but one voice*—see e.g. Spivak (1988), Spivak (2004), Žižek (1994). See also Adorno and Horkheimer (1943/1996), Sartre (1983/1992), Luhmann (1990), Butler (2003/2005), etc.

provide a normatively shaped point which can be seen as the room in which beings become (socially shaped) human individuals. That does not mean that individuals are fully determined by these crossing points—rather, these crossing points describe and provide their unique spaces of possibilities. From this point of view, human plurality is explained by, or derived from, the plurality of norms to which every single person is subjected—apart from the genetic conditions, talents, or features that everyone will bring along. So, this paper also presents a third way of thinking differences—not in a realistic framework which presupposes plurality and not in an idealistic framework which derives every difference from a thinking consciousness shaping the world by drawing distinctions and making differences. Rather, this third way considers differences within a conditioning framework which makes plurality and individuality *possible*, such that the condition of the possibility of human individuality and plurality is seen to be grounded in the plurality of different social norms, which are in turn historically formed.

To start with the indubitable and ubiquitous existence of norms—in the sense in which Michel Foucault, in *The Order of Things*, points out "the fact, in short, that order exists" (Foucault 1994; Preface, xx)—might not only help to avoid some of the theoretical rejections and practical problems of which we have been made aware by many different philosophers, especially those from the so called 'post-modern/post-structuralistic' line corner. It might also help to find a systematic order for the interaction of norms, individuality, plurality, and ethics. This implies a very wide understanding of the notion of 'norm', transcending its reductive ethical meaning. Because norms are seen as something on which everybody depends, in a positive sense they shape and enable human beings lives long before enabling any cognitive understanding. Yet, as norms must likewise be recognised for their negative, destructive, and exclusionary power, we must state that norms are necessary and menacing at once, that they are ethically ambivalent. It is then mandatory to distinguish those norms which are necessary from those which are superfluous and destructive in order to find ways to make the latter less effective or aggrieving.

2 Norms, Individuals, and Societies

Aside from the two basic assumptions: that we deal with norms whenever (human) beings are concerned, and that we do not *know* what human beings 'are'—one can presuppose that (human) plurality is based on norms.[2] This leads to the question: *How are the norms connected to this plurality of singularities?* The question can be

---

[2]Kant, Sartre, Levinas, or Jean-Luc Nancy, to name but a few, presuppose plurality without giving a reason for its provenance. Hegel prominently answered this question by stating a consciousness which differentiates (and connects at once) by negating (and synthesizing). He is followed by a wide range of theorists which could be subsumed under the label: philosophers of difference. My suggestion here is not to take one of these alternatives but to claim that norms are the differentiating power.

answered by stating that we find a *constitutive* and *reciprocal* contiguity or connection between norms and single human lives, imparted by the concrete organisation of their plurality, i.e. society. We could even say that norms at once differentiate *and* connect individuals.[3] The differentiation might be seen as an effect of various intersecting norms 'creating' the individual, thereby connecting different individuals due to the fact that they share certain norms. Yet the three themselves—norms, individuals, and societies—must be seen to be, in their concrete forms, socio-cultural-historic *variable effects*, which depend on and orientate each other as concrete phenomena. Norms, individuals, and society are taken to be 'conditioned conditions' which can be defined by their reciprocal dependency. To be a 'conditioned condition' does not mean to be determined; rather, it expresses that something depends on something other as its necessary, but not sufficient, condition.[4] Thus, it means to be a *condition of the possibility* of something, according to the Kantian understanding. Hence, it has nothing to do with causality or with complete determination.

This acceptance of the reciprocal and actual interoperation between individuals, society, and norms opens different fields of research: One could examine the genealogy of the effected triple and how they are connected, as e.g. Hegel, Marx, and Sartre have done prominently and with quite different results. One could analyse the effects that (moral) norms have on single persons or how they interact, as e.g. Nietzsche and Foucault have shown with their detailed genealogical analyses. Or one could start with describing how norms work, what different kinds of objects or levels are shaped or even induced by them, or how it is possible to critique them in order to make transformations possible, as J. Butler does. It then becomes obvious that a wide range of norms exists, and that they are involved in forming nearly all that is relevant for human lives. If we then define *ethics* as a set of norms which rule and order our living together—be that in bigger or smaller contexts—and which are, thus, also necessary, we may formulate the theoretical challenge for ethics as follows: *How to handle human plurality with as few norms as possible, but as many norms as necessary, without excluding any kind of human being from the outset.*

Michel Foucault formulates this liberal ideal of minimal domination as follows: "I think this is really the point where the main ethical task and the political fight for respecting the law, the critical reflection and the ethical search for what permits grounding individual freedom intertwine." (Foucault 1984). In other words: *The task is to create an ethical model which can distinguish between necessary and unnecessary norms by respecting the evolved and evolving plurality of mankind.* That means

---

[3]The double effect of distinguishing and connecting at once refers, of course, to Hegel and also to G. Spencer Brown's *Laws of Form*. The first chapter starts with the definition: "Distinction is perfect continence". LoF:1.

[4]The difference between necessary and sufficient conditions is a very crucial point which will come up again in different contexts: a necessary condition designates what is necessary in order to make something happen; it determines the event *in no way*; a sufficient condition determines what happens in any case—therefore the difference should not be ignored.

to avoid reducing that plurality to one model of man—e.g. enlightened subjectivity—and instead to ground norms which should and could serve for really everybody.[5] To present my proposal, I will start by *describing formally* the different levels on which norms have impact, followed by a short sketch of how norms work, i.e. how they are intermediated and become effective. Thirdly, I will show how norms may be criticised *normatively*, followed by some remarks about the norms ruling the model itself. I will close with some questions that arise from this ethical model. Obviously, at this point the analysis will move away from a purely formal description and on to a normative offer. I present this model within a compendium of order ethics due to its emphasis on the difference between the *dependency* and the *conditions* of (social) life and the necessity to find rules in order to conserve, sustain, and organise these conditions last to serve human beings—and not to afflict them.

3 Normative Impact, or: Invariable and Variable Conditions of Human Lives and Their Actions

It is possible to distinguish different levels of normative impact on human lives (see Table 1): A level of *conditions* and a level of *dependency*. Every human being depends, in its being and behaviour, on different conditions: some *invariable* and *necessary*, others *variable conditions*, and all of which form and rule, albeit not entirely, its *being* and its *actions*. Therefore, there are at least three levels: The level of conditions, parted into two sublevels, and that of concrete actions and behaviour. The difference between invariable and variable conditions can be marked as follows: *invariable conditions* are those without which no (human) life has the possibility to exist—at least at the beginning (infancy) and mostly at the end (old age). Such conditions are e.g. other people, or at least one person who cares for the individual, as well as the required nutrition and shelter. In other words: attention and feeding *from others* are indispensable conditions on which everybody depends. They are imperative to sustain concrete lives, and they imply that there are already others who could care. Nobody produced or invented those conditions—but everybody depends on them, inevitably. In contrast to these absolutely indispensable invariable conditions, *variable conditions* are those which are subject to socio-historic-cultural transformations, e.g. any kind of social orders like tribes or states, any kind of constitutions, laws, or right(s); in a word: any kind of *institutionalised conditions*.

If we now ask how these conditions are connected with norms, we see that the invariable conditions are no norms in and of themselves, because of their status as actual fact. But they can of course be addressed by norms which have direct or indirect impact on single lives. We might call the norms belonging to the

---

[5]Judith Butler distinguishes "necessary and variable norms". I think this naming is misleading, because it could imply that necessary norms are not variable, which is not the case. See Butler (2002, here: 205–207).

Table 1 Different levels of normative impact on human lives

Levels of		Norms	As	In order to
Conditions	*Invariable conditions:* others, nutrition, space	*Facilitating* ns	*Commandments*	*Protect the very* **conditions** *of life*
	'Recognisability'	*Constitutional* ns	Categories of perceptions	*Include/exclude certain lives*
	Variable conditions: rights etc.	*Institutional* ns	*Prohibitions interdicting certain actions*	*Widen the range of possible lives and actions*
Dependency	*Behavior abd actions*	*Habitual norms*	*Commandments prescribing certain actions and behavior*	*Interdict more possibilities/diversity*

indispensable level of conditions *facilitating norms*, insofar as they refer to the 'natural' environment. And yet, at this basic level, there are already norms which rule on *recognisability* (see e.g. Butler 2009: p. 5, passim), which is a kind of perception category which decides whether someone is entitled to those basic conditions. Therefore they have an including or excluding effect. We might call them *constitutive norms*. Obviously, these two kinds of norms develop very differently. The first are—at least insofar as they concern our environment—subject to more or less open discussions on an international political level, e.g. in some parts of the millennium goals formulated by the UN in 2000. The latter are mostly ignored and merely implicit in human perceptions. Sometimes, they are objects of critical philosophical reflections (see e.g. Butler 2009; Menke 2009), which unmask their shaping and normalising effects.[6] Thus, we can identify two different kinds of norms which belong to the first, basic level of conditions: facilitating and constitutive norms—both are, *like any norm*, subject to transformations, *even if the level they belong to is unalterable*. Facilitating norms are *commandments to protect* the very *conditions* of life, i.e. their task is to make lives possible. Constitutive norms, on the other hand, do not *only* work in order to protect, but on the contrary work also to exclude certain human beings which do not fit them—I will return to this point later.

The second kind of conditions, the institutionalised conditions, are norms in themselves, insofar as institutions such as written constitutions, such as the law and

---

[6]The philosophical discourse which is relevant here refers to Lacan and his difference between the 'symbolic real' and 'reality'. Whereas the latter never pervades *perfectly* in the formatting normative 'symbolic real', the 'symbolic real' always refers to something *more, superfluous, excluded*, which becomes visible only with regard to the symbolic and which is therefore somehow produced, or at least defined by it. Thus 'symbolic real' would stand for the normalized which is shaped out of 'reality' and which can be thought and seen only through the symbolic. See Lacan (1955/1973).

the different powers of the state etc. can be seen to be 'curdled norms'. Therefore, we might call them *institutionalised norms*. They include prohibitions not only to make lives as such possible, but to enable human beings to live a life in freedom and peace with others. To name them, institutional norms should reminds us that their task is to provide and shape the social *conditions* of life and actions without determining them directly, even if some actions are excluded by them. But the exclusion of some actions serves to make *more action possible*—in the same sense as Kant describes the Right: "Right [...] comprehends the whole of the conditions under which the voluntary actions of any one Person can be harmonised in reality with the voluntary actions of every other Person, according to a universal Law of Freedom"(Kant 1797: 230). Therefore, the prohibition of some actions plays on another level than the actions themselves. The difference could be explained by the difference between interdictions and commandments, which also play on different logical levels: the first secure the *possibility* of any action by excluding actions which would destroy the necessary *conditions* of actions; the latter directly determine actions.[7] Thus, institutional norms are prohibitions in order to protect the conditions of free actions within societies.

Finally, we can identify a third group of norms which can be called *habitual norms* because they normatively prescribe many specific actions and behaviours— be they directed towards others or oneself. Their task is to shape, i.e. normalise behaviour, not least to evaluate others encountered in our daily life. With respect to their *content*, these four kinds of norms—the facilitating, the constitutive, the institutional, and the habitual norms—are all subject to socio-cultural-historical transformations. Nevertheless, I would insist that they are *as norms in their pure form* universal, insofar as we can find them in very different modes all over the world in every society at any time. Of course it is not possible to assign every single norm exactly to one of these groups; depending on different points of view, some of them might belong to different groups. However, a matrix like this might help to distinguish different tasks that different norms fulfil, be it intentionally or otherwise.

Furthermore, the matrix offers the possibility to distinguish between useful norms which serve to protect the very conditions of life, which thereby make lives possible and which widen the range of possible lives and actions on the one hand; and

---

[7]It is crucial to distinguish between *prohibitions* and *commandments*: While the first just describe one action which is not allowed and thus leave all the remaining possible actions untouched, the latter describe an action positively. A *prohibition* is therefore just a negative determination which *excludes* just *one concrete action* but does not determine any other action. A commandment, on the other hand, determines the action positively. It is interesting to see that the Bible offers in the Decalogue—after the first three commandments which refer directly to interactions with God— only one further commandment: the fourth, which is about honoring father and mother in order to allow you to live longer (!) on the arable soil given to you by Him (after the translation of Buber/Rosenberg). So it is a kind of conjunction between the first three and the rest. The other six only formulate prohibitions—so that the social is far away from being positively determined by the Decalogue. It is just limited insofar as some actions are excluded—to make social life possible. Of course, they refer to the very condition of life—not to be killed—and to *property*. But this is another topic.

superfluous norms, which work by excluding, shaping, and normalising human beings, their actions, and their behaviour, and thus do not help to make life liveable for every single person on the other hand. It seems as if facilitating norms and institutional norms could belong to the group of useful norms which are needed in order to sustain the possibilities of human lives and of their living together. On the other hand, constitutional and at least the majority of habitual norms could be identified to be superfluous—but this is not to be decided here, for any society, however it has been constituted, has to deliberate how much diversity it welcomes. At this point, the goal is only to offer some kind of order and to discover hidden purposes.

4 Intermediation of Norms, or: On Normative Effectiveness

Norms do not exist 'in themselves'. Instead, they exist in different modes of practices. Even though some of them are also written down in codices, some of them only continue orally, and some of them exist implicitly until they become discovered. This is because they must be *applied* in any case, in the sense that they interdict directly, permit indirectly, or orient practices, actions, or behaviour, to be an affecting norm. Thus, norms need someone, or something, to use them: i.e. a transported or used subject of the norm. Furthermore, norms need a field to act on—the object of the norm. Seen like this, all norms have a grammatically three-tiered form: subject, object, and the norm itself. Outside this relation, they do not exist, and there are no norms at all. While facilitating norms act partially on things like nutrition or space and constitutive norms decide whether a human being is allowed to live, the rest of the norms identified above act on human beings and on their actions or behaviour.

Asking how norms are intermediated, we can distinguish, again, two different ways or implementing practices: *personal* and *institutional intermediation*. To the first group belong all kinds of relation(ship)s with others which are not only ruled by norms themselves, but which also transport any kind of norms through face-to-face communication, i.e. by any kind of care or responsiveness.[8] There are different modes in which we may encounter others within face-to-face situations: with respect, with contempt, and with disregard (see e.g. Watzlawick 1999). All of these can depend on the conviction that we *know* how human beings are structured, briefly: how they *are*; or they depend on the conviction that we do not know what 'really' makes a human being. Thus, the kind of means the 'you' which will be used to intermediate norms depends on the attitude a person takes in relation to others. All of this need not to be known or to be part of reflections—rather, it will mostly work unconsciously or as an unknown. In any case, the addressed person will react constitutively and mostly adequately to the attitude it experiences—be it by disowning or adopting the norms.

---

[8]See Butler (2005, especially 65–81). In her description, she refers to Emmanuel Levinas and to psychoanalysis.

On the other hand, institutional intermediation often rests on more or less explicitly excluding functions,[9] be it that the number of allowed admissions to positions is limited by various means (certificates etc.) or that somebody is threatened with various sanctions, i.e. again, with different types of exclusions. Both situations of intermediation work by requiring some kind of reaction from the human being, i.e. from the object on which the norm acts. The subject who actively transports norms, is obviously the one who or the institution which addresses the 'object'. The practice of addressing is different whether we look at organisations or face-to-face situations. Organisations sustain their entrance codes by reproducing them over and over again, even if they are also from time to time transformed due to the tasks the organisation has to fulfil. In face-to-face situations, norms are sustained by mimesis and by oral or physical repetition that leads to a mimesis and repetition on the side of the object, too. Thus, we can identify as mediating means any kind of *habitual, ritualised* behaviour, action, or code.

In both kinds of intermediation, norms become effective because the life of their (human) object depends on them in a strict sense: someone who does not (learn to) respond to responsiveness will, most likely, be excluded from society, just as transgressing certain institutional norms means to be excluded by sanctions. Therefore, it is extremely important for human beings to learn and imitate the given rules in order to survive and to become a player within the social games. Even if there is some space for individual decisions or variation, it is no question of agreement, but rather of survival. At this point, it becomes obvious why it is so important to draw a distinction between necessary norms that enable people to live together and superfluous norms which lead to a likewise superfluous normalisation of human plurality. To determine the boundary, I would, again, follow Kant's definition of the basic Right, which limits actions only insofar as they could destroy the possibility of others to act freely. This brings us immediately to the question and the necessity of critique. Thus, we now change the mode of this undertaking: from pure description into a normative proposal and grounding.

5 Intended Social Transformation, or: How to Criticise Dominant Norms

First, we should remember that we assume norms to be subject to socio-cultural-historical changes and that they are therefore transformable—a premise not shared by many today. But even if norms might be seen to be inborn, because human beings 'are' rational beings or because we 'are' God's children, it seems to be helpful to assume that most norms developed contingently within societies and are

---

[9]I have Michel Foucault's and Niklas Luhmann's analysis in mind. Both argue that organizations, i.e. every kind of organized plurality, work through exclusionary functions. See Foucault (1972), Luhmann (2000).

not built intentionally—except when laws and rights are explicitly formulated. But even in these cases, we often deal with customary law reconstructed by hindsight. That does not mean to deem the provenance and forming changes and challenges of norms to be irrelevant. And yet it does mean that we cannot ground them within any specific type of rational subjectivity, be it divine or human, but must consider them to be a more or less contingent product of human plurality. It is of course possible to ask why certain norms are still valid, while others have disappeared; and of course, the answers could be used to legitimate further norms—but this should be a question of reflective deliberation.

Secondly, to criticise a norm implies a criterion by which to measure its appropriateness and to decide whether it should be disestablished, transformed, or sustained. Such a criterion, of course, requires another norm for legitimation. At this point we can, again, only propose one criterion, which claims to be universal, insofar as every human being should be able to agree with it: *Does the norm serve to make a free life for everybody possible and does it serve to reduce socially produced pain?* Putting it negatively broadens the point: *Does the norm stabilise conditions which exclude or destroy lives, and does it help to increase pain?*[10] To be very clear, I have to add that reducing pain does not mean to dream of a world without suffering, but instead to dream of a world as a place where people stop doing harm to others due to superfluous norms. It is to emphasise that this criterion is in itself two-tiered: the first part plays on the level of the conditions, while the second part plays on the level of singularity.[11] Hence, this model is based on another distinction: it does not distinguish between private and public as e.g. Hannah Arendt did, or between the subject and the others, as Hegel and others did. Instead, the crucial difference lies between conditions and dependency or reliance in a *non-causal* understanding.

The advantage of this proposed criterion should be to refocus ethics on conditions—while the single individual may no longer be subject of over-determination and normalisation. It is important to remember that it is a criterion to distinguish and evaluate *norms* and not certain actions, behaviours, or various types of being. It can be applied to every group of norms identified above: it is possible to ask the question referring to facilitating norms concerned with the invariable conditions of life, to constitutive norms which decide whether a being is a human being, to institutional norms as much as to habitual norms. All of them could be probed on whether they fulfil this criterion.

---

[10]This formulation is reminiscent of Kant's and Isaiah Berlin's distinction between positive and negative freedom: the latter means to be free *of* pain, determinations etc.; the former means to be free *to* live one's life as one wants to. See Kant (1795).

[11]I would suggest to interpret the Kantian *categorical imperative* as two-tiered as well: The 'subjective maxims' are the rules orienting singular actions and behaviors on the level of singularities. The test if these 'subjective maxims' can serve as an 'objective right' should be taken literally: check whether your personal rules could be formulated as a right, one might say as a *condition*, which does not limit the possibilities of others—in the sense of the basic Right.

We can find this idea of a necessary two-tier model also in Dewey (1915, 1935/1999).

6 Ethical Attitude, or: Basic Convictions

At this point, we can no longer postpone disclosing the norms that rule this paper itself. As mentioned at the beginning, it is based on so-called 'post-modern' theory building. That means above all to accept the premise that mostly normatively produced human plurality cannot *and should not* be reduced to one single model or form of rationality, thinking, or feeling. Secondly, it is to accept that every plurality develops ruling norms, be it intentionally or contingently. These should be considered to be subject to socio-cultural-historic changes, and thus they can be transformed intentionally—even if this is often possible only 'in the long run'. In short, there is no norm which could and should not be questioned and adjusted.[12] The third premise was that we do not even really *know* what makes a 'real' human being, i.e. we must assume that there is no universal substance, pattern, or structure which truly includes every single existence. Consequently, knowledge about what human beings *are* in themselves could not build a premise. Rather, we should settle on a kind of *ignoramus et ignorabimus* on what human beings *are* as a premise. Not to know from the beginning how others function implies an ethical attitude which may be called *respect*.

If we take a look at the etymological roots of 'respect', we see that it derives from the Latin 'respectare', which means 'to look at', 'to look around', 'to look for', 'to look back', 'to notice something behind oneself', 'to regard', and also 'to turn around', or 'to look *again*' etc. If we notice something, we do not necessarily see it already; maybe we just hear or sense something. Furthermore, respect implies to repeat our gaze, to look at the other again and again in order to see something which probably will be transformed again. Thus, respect has to be understood as an attitude which is based on a constitutive ignorance and which is not to be deleted. Instead, respect seems to claim the transformation of one's own standpoint in order to better see the other. Thus, it also signifies an attitude which could be described as a principal question, an offer or invitation to initiate some kind of 'interspect' with the other.

What do we gain if we try to understand ethics in this way? From my point of view, there is a pragmatic and a theoretical reason that make it worth thinking about. Considering that there are a lot of adequate rejections of traditional models which start with fixed definitions of what human beings are, this model may provide a possibility to find solutions *without laying down certain values or specific rights at the beginning*. Deliberating on facilitating norms e.g. could be done without asking for 'last groundings' and without talking about 'guilt' or 'responsibility', because it is necessary for everyone to sustain the conditions of life. The question of who is allowed to speak must be answered by the communities themselves—in any case, there is no legitimisation for us to tell others to whom they should give or withhold credit. It seems to me that one possibility to avoid the Eurocentric pitfall

---

[12]Most norms receive their legitimization ex post as well, as they only become explicit in the moment of severe social transformations, and thus in times of uncertainty and angst. See Brandom (1998).

could be to focus systematically on the *conditions of the possibility of (human) lives* instead of defining (a priori/rationally or 'naturally'/'empirically') what human beings are or should be. They are important insofar as the conditions are to be oriented in order to open possibilities and to reduce pain. They are not important as objects of normative knowledge. It then follows that the aim is not to create imperatives which rule actions and create beings, but to find rules which help to conserve and improve the *conditions of* (human) life—no matter what those lives will look like, 'be', or act like, except that they do not destroy other lives.

To conclude this programmatic paper, I will point out some questions that arise from this model. If we want to take the reduction of socially created pain as a criterion for ethics, we have to define pain and ground this criterion. This includes questions such as: What extension can be ascribed to it? It seems to be very clear that there could be no categorical imperative like: Avoid any pain wherever and whenever it may arise—simply because of situations or aims which demand pain. Moreover, 'avoid pain' needs to be derived semantically or materially from this sketched systematic order of norms. Another aspect is that I focussed—so far—only on the enabling and conditioning effect of norms. But we could add that norms also serve to stabilise societies, and ask whether this might lead to a second criterion for norms. That would imply examining what weight social stability *should* have and at what point it turns to destroy livelihood. This might lead to a new—also two-tiered —order of freedom and stability, or at least to a discussion, once more, of necessary and superfluous norms and to the question of how much transformation our societies can, want, and, above all, *must* stand. If life could be described as a permanent transformation—we may seek out theories which include constitutively transformation, instead of defending it. If we interpret the orders suggested by 'order ethics' as liquid, we may find a way to integrate transformations as a constitutive factor of ethics—and human beings.

Acknowledgments I would like to thank Hans G. Ulrich and Stephan Packard for their critical comments, helping to clear up this paper; and especially Stephan Packard for his judicious re-reading of my English. The work on this paper was possible due to a generous Heisenberg-grant sponsored by the German Research Foundation (SCHO 1077/3-1).

References

Adorno, Theodor W., Horkheimer, Max. 1943/1996. *Dialectic of enlightenment*. London: Verso.
Brandom, Robert. 1998. *Making it explicit. Reasoning, representing and discoursive commitment*. Boston: Harvard University Press.
Butler, Judith. 2002. The question of social transformation. In *Undoing gender*, ed. idem (2004), 204–231. NY/London: Routledge.
Butler, Judith. 2003/2005. *Giving an account of oneself*. NY: Fordham University Press.
Butler, Judith. 2005. *Giving an account of oneself*. NY: Fordham Univ. Press.
Butler, Judith. 2009. Introduction. In: idem (2009). *Frames of war. When is life grieveable*. London: Verso.
Dewey, John. 1915. *German philosophy and German politics*.

Dewey, John. 1935/1999. *Liberalism and social action.* Prometheus Books.
Foucault, Michel. 1972. *L'ordre du discours.* Paris: Gallimard.
Foucault, Michel. 1984. 'L'éthique de souci de soi comme pratique de la liberté' in: idem. (2001). *Dits et Ecrits. tome 2. 1976–1988*, no 356. Paris: Gallimard.
Foucault, Michel. 1994. *The order of things.* Vintage Books edition, Copyright © 1970 by Random House, Inc.
Habermas, Jürgen. 2011. "The political": The rational meaning of a questionable inheritance of political theology. In *The power of religion in the public sphere*, ed. Judith Butler, Jürgen Habermas, Charles Taylor, Cornel West, 15–34. NY: Columbia University Press.
Kant, Immanuel. 1795. *Groundwork for an Ethics*, Third Part. In *Liberty: Incorporating four essays on liberty*, ed. Isaiah Berlin (1969/2002). Oxford: OU Press.
Kant, Immanuel. 1797. *Metaphysics of morals.* AA 6:230.
Lacan, Jacques. 1955/1973. Seminar on 'The Purloined Letter' from Écrits'. *Yale French Studies* 48:39–72 (translated by Jeffrey Mehlmann).
Luhmann, Niklas. 1990. *Paradigm Lost. Über die ethische Reflexion der Moral.* Frankfurt: Suhrkamp.
Luhmann, Niklas. 2000. *Organisation und Entscheidung.* Opladen/Wiesbaden: Westdeutscher Verlag.
Mayer, Hans 1975/2007. Aussenseiter. Frankfur/Main: Suhrkamp.
Menke, Christoph. 2009. Das Nichtanerkennbare. Oder warum das modern Recht keine »Sphäre der Anerkennung« ist. In *Sozialphilosophie und Kritik*, ed. Rainer Forst et al., 87–108. Frankfurt/Main: Suhrkamp.
Sartre, Jean-Paul. 1983/1992. *Notebooks for an ethics.* Chicago: UC Press.
Spivak, Gayatri C. 1988. 'Can the subaltern speak?' In *Colonial discourse and post-colonial theory: A reader,* ed. Patrick Williams, Laura Chrisman (1994), 66–111. New York: Harvester/Wheatsheaf.
Spivak, Gayatri C. 2004. 'Righting wrongs'. *The South Atlantic Quaterly* 103:2/3.
Watzlawick, Paul. 1999/2011. *Pragmatics of human communication.* W. W. Norton & Company.
Žižek, Slavoj. 1994. 'Introduction'. In *Mapping ideology*, ed. idem (1994), 1–33. London: Verso.

Contrasting the Behavioural Business Ethics Approach and the Institutional Economic Approach to Business Ethics: Insights from the Study of Quaker Employers

Sigmund Wagner-Tsukamoto

Abstract The paper suggests that in a modern context, where value pluralism is a prevailing and possibly even ethically desirable interaction condition, institutional economics provides a more viable business ethics than behavioural business ethics, such as Kantiansim or religious spiritual ethics. The paper explains how the institutional economic approach to business ethics analyses morality with regard to an *interaction* process, and favours *non-behavioural, situational* intervention with *incentive structures* and with *capital exchange*. The paper argues that this approach may have to be prioritised over behavioural business ethics which tends to analyse morality at the level of the *individual* and which favours *behavioural* intervention with the individual's *value, norm and belief system*, e.g. through ethical pedagogy. Quaker ethics is taken as an example of behavioural ethics. The paper concludes that through the conceptual grounding of behavioural ethics in the economic approach, theoretical and practical limitations of behavioural ethics as encountered in a modern context can be relaxed. Probably only then can behavioural ethics still contribute to raising moral standards in interactions amongst the members (stakeholders) of a single firm, and equally, amongst (the stakeholders of) different firms.

Keywords Behavioural approaches to business ethics · Economics and business ethics · Pluralism · Quaker industrialists · Stakeholder theory

---

This chapter reproduces revised material that has previously been published in S. Wagner-Tsukamoto, "Contrasting the Behavioural Business Ethics Approach and the Institutional Economic Approach to Business Ethics: Insights From the Study of Quaker Employers", *Journal of Business Ethics* 82, 4: 835–850. We thank Springer Science + Business Media B.V. for their permission to reproduce it here.

S. Wagner-Tsukamoto (✉)
School of Management, University of Leicester, Leicester, UK
e-mail: s.wagner-tsukamoto@le.ac.uk

© Springer International Publishing Switzerland 2016
C. Luetge and N. Mukerji (eds.), *Order Ethics: An Ethical Framework for the Social Market Economy*, DOI 10.1007/978-3-319-33151-5_13

> [T]he language of morality is in the... state of grave disorder... What we possess, if this view is true, are the fragments of a conceptual scheme, parts which now lack those contexts from which their significance derived.... We possess indeed simulacra of morality, we continue to use many of the key expressions. But we have—very largely, if not entirely—lost our comprehension, both theoretical and practical, or morality.... [W]e are all already in a state so disastrous that there are no large remedies for it.
>
> (A. MacIntyre, *After Virtue* 1985, pp. 2, 5)

The key thesis of this paper is that an institutional business ethics that is informed by economics, especially the so-called New Institutional Economics (as explained later), is preferable to behavioural ethics for ensuring high moral standards in business interactions. This is so because, as a guide to social interaction, behavioural ethics, even an institutionally oriented one, depends upon like-mindedness of interacting agents in order for business ethics to prosper; for instance, Donaldson and Dunfee's (1999) project of institutional, behavioural ethics here conceptualizes 'social ties that bind' (similarly Osterhout et al. 2006 and their project of a contractualist business ethics). However, the modern condition is one in which like-mindedness is scarce, as reflected by interaction conditions of value pluralism, ethnic diversity, etc. One way to view this is as a problem to be overcome—by constructing and promoting like-mindedness through arguing (Donaldson and Dunfee, similarly Rawls) or otherwise talking away (Habermas) moral disagreement. Another way to view this is as a constraint on institutional design—adopting social norms less dependent for their success upon like-mindedness and abandoning norms more dependent on like-mindedness. The condition of modernity is then endorsed. The paper favours this latter approach. In this respect, the paper fundamentally differs from behavioural, institutional business ethics which at least facially may be focused on the institutional, such as social ties that bind or integrative social contracts (e.g. Donaldson and Dunfee 1999; similarly, Oosterhout et al. 2006). Where the institutional analysis of this paper departs from these theorists is in taking seriously moral disagreement. For Kantian stakeholder theorists and behavioural social contractarians within business ethics, moral disagreement is shallow and may be dissolved through institutions promoting public, social reason. In contrast, for the present study, moral disagreement and value diversity are deep and the road to improvement is to design economic institutions that facilitate social interactions while leaving moral disagreement intact. That is something the New Institutional Economics can contribute to business ethics research and practice and behavioural business ethics, even institutionally focused one, cannot.

The means by which the key thesis of the paper is established and argued for is the analysis and contrasting of how behavioural business ethics and an economic approach to business ethics differently conceptualise questions of morality—simply 'defined' questions of 'doing good in social behaviour'. And this analysis is primarily conducted through a historic case study of British Quaker employers and their failing attempts to implement a behavioural business ethics.

The mainstream in business ethics research and business ethics consultancy largely takes a behavioural approach to assessing questions of corporate morality, either an individualistic behavioural stance or an institutional, behavioural one. Theoretical research and the resulting consultancy are grounded in behavioural ethics in the tradition of Aristotelian virtue ethics, Kantian stakeholder ethics, or religious spiritual ethics. Quaker ethics is a good example of this tradition. Quaker employers like Cadbury or Rowntree in 19th- and 20th-century Britain attempted to fully implement this ethics in a business context.

Analytically and practically, behavioural ethics narrowly handles questions of morality at the level of the individual: If an ethical problem occurs, this is theoretically conceptualised as the 'human condition', e.g. deficits in virtuous character traits, a lack of acceptance of moral duties, a lacking internalisation of religious spiritual values by the individual, etc. In order to practically solve an ethical problem, the strengthening of the individual's ethical value, norm and belief system (of 'behavioural institutions') is recommended. A social, institutional dimension can show here up, too. At many business schools, behaviourally oriented business ethics seminars and courses try to teach managers and prospective managers proper behavioural ethical conduct, aiming to (re)-moralize the behaviour of the individual in order to do away with weak moral predispositions and ensure moral like-mindedness (e.g. Collins 2000; von Dran et al. 2001; Hill and Stewart 1999; Murphy 1998).

At least implicitly, already Mandeville and Adam Smith advocated an economic approach to business ethics. Regarding its very nature, they proposed and understood the economic approach as an alternative ethics to behavioural ethics. Hayek (1960, 1976), Buchanan (1975, 1987a), Friedman (1970) clearly sensed this, too, as did Homann's economic research on business ethics, interpreted as 'incentive ethics' (Homann 1997, 1999; see also Wagner-Tsukamoto 2005, 2007b). In this tradition of an economics approach to ethics, the present paper develops a critical perspective on behavioural business ethics, suggesting that the (institutional) economic approach may have to be prioritised over behavioural business ethics in order to promote business ethics.

Issues of practical intervention in particular reveal sharp differences between the institutional economic approach and a behavioural approach to ethics. Behavioural ethics, including behavioural economic research on ethics (e.g. Etzioni 1988; Frank 1988, 2003; Margolis 1982; Simon 1993) and behavioural institutional business ethics, intervenes practically with institutions that are interpreted as the internalised value, norm and belief structures of the individual ('behavioural institutions'). The targets is the human condition in order to solve social, ethical problems; its approach to practical intervention is of a therapeutic, pedagogic, communicative, habituating nature, (re)-educating, counselling, appealing, and preaching to individuals in order to make them behave 'better'; the behavioural (e.g. 'sociological', 'psychological', 'theological') effectiveness of human behaviour is to be improved (See, for instance, Argyris 1992; Fort 2000; Habermas 1988, 1990; Hill and Stewart 1999; Key 1997; Kieser 1993, pp. 113–23; Lampe 1997; Murphy 1998; Van Oosterhout et al. 2006; Schanz 1982, p. 72; Siu et al. 2000; Warner 1994, p. 1161). Moral like-mindedness among agents or stakeholders is the intervention goal. In stark contrast, institutional economics intervenes with institutions understood as incentive structures—'governance structures,' as Williamson's (1975, 1985) New Institutional Economics outlined. Thus, non-behavioural institutions or situational conditions (the 'rules of the game') are focused on in order to handle problems in social behaviour. Examples are employment contracts, salary systems, promotion systems, bonus allocation systems of the firm, etc.

Significant differences can be expected between an economic and a behavioural research program on business ethics: firstly, regarding the *theoretical conceptualisation* of morality and institutions for enacting morality in social behaviour; secondly, regarding favoured avenues for *practically intervening* with human behaviour in order to solve moral problems and the *practical success* a research program on (business) ethics enjoys; and thirdly,—which, however, is not further explored in this paper—regarding *analytical tools and methods* applied in an ethical debate.

The key thesis of this paper is that, unless subsumed under an economic approach to ethics, the success of behavioural business ethics to solve the moral problems of a firm is likely to be in doubt. MacIntyre identified practical problems for virtue ethics (as quoted above) and this is confirmed for many behavioural business ethics programs. For instance, Izzo (2000) and Seshadri et al. (1997) found that behavioural business ethics programs frequently fail. However, as much as practical failure was diagnosed and acknowledged, this disappointed and mystified Izzo (2000) and Seshadri et al. (1997). Here, the present paper moves a step ahead: It explores, through institutional economics analysis, reasons why behavioural business ethics is difficult to implement in certain—'modern'—contexts. The key thesis is that the firm (its managers and stakeholders) could only be expected to act morally in a behavioural ethical sense if this were viable in the face of value pluralism, or put in a different way, in the face of self-interested choice, as it is institutionally imposed on firms in a market economy, for instance, through business laws which protect competition among firms or which subject unprofitable firms to bankruptcy proceedings and are thus eliminated from the market place.

To develop my arguments I draw on various sources from the contemporary business ethics literature but also on one very insightful historic case study, namely the attempt of British Quaker firms like Cadbury and Rowntree to implement certain religious spiritual beliefs in business practice in the decades from 1900 to 1940. Their attempt partly succeeded but partly failed. This mystified Quaker employers. The paper here sheds new light on reasons why behavioural ethics sometimes succeeds and sometimes fails in a modern business context by reconstructing behavioural ethical intervention in economic terms.

In the following, the first section outlines key theoretical concepts of behavioural ethics and contrasts them with the concepts of the institutional economic approach to ethics. The second section explores the practical limits of behavioural ethics in relation to the condition of modernity, namely how value pluralism characterizes many social arenas of society and the institutional setting of the market economy in particular. The final section concludes the paper.

1 Theoretical Limitations of Behavioural Ethics: The Search for Individual Goodness and Social Harmony in Business Behaviour

The analysis of the fragility of morality in social behaviour is, in one form or another, the starting point of most ethical research. An institutional, social focus is apparent, at least in the background, for most moral philosophy and political economy. Hobbes' *Leviathan* (especially Chaps. "Contrasting the Behavioural Business Ethics Approach and the Institutional Economic Approach to Business Ethics: Insights from the Study of Quaker Employers", "The Constitution of Responsibility: Toward an Ordonomic Framework for Interpreting (Corporate Social) Responsibility in Different Social Settings" and "Companies as Political Actors: A Positioning Between Ordo-Responsibility and Systems Responsibility") here discussed the potential 'war of all'. Much earlier Greek philosophy and biblical thought proceeded similarly (See Wagner-Tsukamoto 2001, 2003, 2007a). As much as a behavioural approach and an economic approach to ethics are likely to share such a starting point, they differ regarding their respective understanding of what causes morality to be fragile in social behaviour, and of practical avenues for raising levels of morality in social behaviour. In the following, behavioural ethics' conceptualisation of morality is discussed, especially with regard to what makes morality fragile. Furthermore, its understanding of *institutions* is compared with the one of institutional economics. Generally speaking, the idea of the institution is understood as social structures which order social interactions and resolve problems in organisational behaviour. Institutions are '… systems of established and prevalent social rules that structure social interactions' (Hodgson 2006, p. 2; North 1990, pp. 3–5). They reflect the 'rules of the game' and have to be strictly distinguished from the 'moves of the games' made by agents and even more so from the agents themselves (Hodgson 2006, p. 9). As explained further below, the kind of social rules this study is especially interested in are *economic institutions* which could be said to be '… prevailing rule structures that provide incentives and constraints for individual action' (Hodgson 2006, p. 6).

1.1 A Behavioural Understanding of Morality and of Behavioural Institutions for Enacting Morality

In the theoretical perspective, the individual is focused on by behavioural ethics. The fragility of morality is analysed as a problem of human nature (e.g. Gosling 1973, p. 1 on virtue ethics; see also the behavioural literature quoted above). In the same way, institutions are conceptualised as *behavioural institutions*: as internalised, intrinsically enacted cognitive, affective and emotive structures of the individual, which reflect an individual's values, norms and beliefs regarding good social conduct. Such internalised structures are meant to (pre)-dispose the individual towards socially desirable behaviour. Morality is thus conceptualised by focusing on the behavioural—psychological, sociological, theological—'constitution' of the individual. Behavioural economics here targets the economic 'constitution' of the individual, including ethical pay-offs in the utility function of the individual (e.g. Margolis 1982). In the social perspective, institutional ordering comes here as the intervention with the human condition by means of influencing behavioural manifestations of values, norms and beliefs through '... purposive investment by authorities such as the state or the church [or a firm] in propaganda with the intention of creating new sets of values in the citizens' (Eggertson 1993, p. 27). This is done in order to facilitate *social* interactions. Donaldson and Dunfee (1999) similarly speak of integrative social contracts and social ties that bind interacting agents (See also Fort 2000).

For religious ethics, such as the Quaker ethics, this approach can be spelled out as:

> '[T]he Quaker precept [was] that it is the spirit in which one individual approaches the other which determines the harmony of their relationships.... Much was seen [by the Quakers] to depend on the 'goodness' of individuals; in other words on their psychology—what is in the mind.' (Child 1964, p. 305)

The generation of 'trust' is here a key issue, as the Quaker literature generally stresses (e.g. Vernon 1958; Windsor 1980). Specific principles of Quaker ethics, as identified by Child (1964), describe ethical ideals regarding good individual and social behaviour:

(1) a dislike of one person profiting at the expense of another;
(2) the promotion of the value of hard work;
(3) the advocacy of egalitarianism in social behaviour;
(4) a dislike of conflict.

Once internalised, these precepts of Quaker ethics were expected to make the individual act—on grounds of internalised 'correct personal spirit' (Child 1964, p. 296)—in a moral manner, specifically in an altruistic, egalitarian, pacifistic, compassionate manner.

Thus, through principles that promote such behavioural ethical ideals, behavioural ethics sets out what kind of values, norms and beliefs the good person should cherish and what good social behaviour should look like.[1] In the social perspective, morality is expected to result from the simple aggregation of individually good behaviour, morality being interpreted as social harmony, trust, equality or peace and being grounded in the concept of a value consensus. This approach to behavioural ethics can be related to concepts of behavioural contracting, e.g. 'social contracting'[2] or 'psychological contracting' (Schein 1980). If successful, behavioural contracting yields homogeneous values, norms, and beliefs amongst individuals—the value consensus—which behavioural ethics relies upon for effectively solving moral problems. Moral disagreement among interacting

---

[1] As discussed below, such principles of behavioural ethics can, to a considerable but not full degree be reconstructed through an economic approach to ethics.
[2] See, for example, Fort (2000) who reviewed Donaldson and Dunfee's approach.

agents is thus eliminated and like-mindedness is ensured. Ethical research in the tradition of economic sociology (e.g. Etzioni 1988, p. xii) or behavioural economics (March 1978; Sen 1990; Simon 1993, pp. 159–60, 1976, p. xxxv, pp. 102–3, 242; in certain respects, even Williamson 1998, pp. 15–17, 1985, p. 391) is similar. Equally, institutional, social contractarians (e.g. Donaldson and Dunfee 1999) may be 'institutional' in nature but their approach in large degrees draws on concepts of *behavioural* institutions ('social ties that bind') rather than the *non-behavioural*, economic institutions the present paper has in mind, as discussed in the following.

1.2 An Alternative Program: An Economic Conceptualisation of Morality and of Institutions for Enacting Morality

In contrast to the behavioural approach, the economic approach to ethics does not necessarily link the idea of morality to ideals of social harmony, equality or peace as such but interprets and qualifies them in economic terms. With regard to a single interaction, e.g. a two-person interaction, institutional economics reconstructs the behavioural ideal of social harmony through the ideal of realizing mutual benefits for the agents involved in an interaction. A positive, non-zero-sum model of social interactions is here implied: Mutuality of gains means that one person's gains do not come at the expense of another person. The idea of mutuality of gains is in this respect compatible and reconcilable with the principles of behavioural ethics, such as Quaker ethics. Only in zero-sum games, no win-win outcomes are feasible, and only then does one person's gains come at the expense of others. From this it already becomes clear that the idea of individual gain as such is not in conflict with business ethics, as explicitly or implicitly implied by many behavioural (business) ethics researchers.[3] In positive, non-zero-sum games, mutuality of gains emerges as interaction outcome 'already' on grounds of self-interested choice.[4] Individual goodness, understood as altruistic, egalitarian, or pacifist behaviour, is not required for morality, here understood as mutuality of gains, to prosper.

As much as a behavioural ideal of social harmony can be so reconstructed in economics terms, limits of an economic reconstruction of a behavioural

---

[3]Besides, behavioural researchers often interpret personal gain merely on empirical-behavioural grounds. However, the idea of self-interest, as applied in economic research, may have to be methodically interpreted in the first place (Wagner-Tsukamoto 2003).

[4]The present paper here shares Cima and Schubeck's (2001) position that self-love can constitute a sound conceptual starting point for moral philosophy. But differences exist (1) regarding the present paper's moral evaluation of pareto-inferiority or 'economic injustice', as Cima and Schubeck might call it; (2) regarding the present paper's positive evaluation of governmental intervention and the restriction of individual liberty; (3) regarding the present paper's suggestions on realigning economics with behavioural ethics through the concept of ethical capital; (4) regarding a methodological interpretation of self-interest.

Societal outcomes of firm-firm interactions / Extent of 'economic harmony' in firm-firm interactions	Ethical outcomes at societal level: 'Public good'	Unethical outcomes at societal level: 'Public loss'
Cooperation (Pareto-superiority) in firm-firm interactions	'Fair cooperation': joint ventures, mergers, strategic alliances	'Unfair cooperation': cartels, monopoly situations
Competition (Pareto-inferiority) in firm-firm interactions	'Fair competition': 'survival of the fittest', bankruptcy of 'unfit' firms	'Unfair competition': predatory competition

Fig. 1 Firm-firm interactions and morality

understanding of morality are reached for zero-sum interactions. In an economic approach to business ethics, even win-lose outcomes of so-called zero-sum interactions and loss-loss outcomes of non-zero-sum interactions are under certain circumstances morally desired and approved (See Fig. 1). That means, not only social harmony (in economic speak: pareto-superior, win-win outcomes) but also a breakdown of social harmony (pareto-inferior, win-loss or loss-loss interaction outcomes) can be judged by economics as ethical, depending whether a break-down of social harmony at the interaction level contributes to public good (economic growth; 'the wealth of nations') at a macro-level of society (ideally: the international community). Equally, social harmony (and mutuality of gains) at the level of the interaction may be judged as unethical by economics, namely when society loses as a result thereof. Figure 1 illustrates for firm–firm interactions this ethically ambivalent nature of social harmony (pareto-superiority; cooperative, win-win outcomes of firm-form interactions) and a break-down of social harmony (pareto-inferiority; competitive, win-lose outcomes of firm-firm interactions) and how this reflects on economics' understanding of morality.[5]

---

[5] For other types of stakeholder interactions, such as firm-customer interactions, cooperation (pareto-superiority) stands a better chance of comprehensively reflecting an economic understanding of morality.

For example, even for zero-sum interactions, such as competitive processes in a market economy and outcomes like bankruptcy of some firms, which may imply loss and hardship for certain stakeholders, an economic approach to business ethics would not necessarily diagnose a moral problem but underwrite such interactions *on moral grounds*—if society at large benefited from them, and if institutional rules, such as bankruptcy laws, which organized such interactions withstood ethical scrutiny. In this connection, 'ethical scrutiny' is again interpreted in economic terms regarding the capability of institutional rules to generate public good. Equally, cooperative win-win outcomes are not necessarily always viewed as ethically desirable; they are rejected if society at large loses as a result of cooperation at the interaction level (e.g. a monopoly situation). In contrast, behavioural ethics tends to generally view cooperative win-win outcomes in social interactions as ethically desirable and win-lose outcomes as ethically undesirable. In this respect, behavioural ethics has a more simplistic understanding of business ethics than economics: It is generally supportive of cooperation and adverse to competition (non-cooperation), not making the differentiations for socially acceptable cooperation versus socially unacceptable cooperation, on the one hand, and socially acceptable competition versus socially unacceptable competition, on the other, as illustrated by Fig. 1. These differentiations imply (1) that sometimes, at least from an economic, societal point of view, competition (non-cooperation) among individual agents—even if this means substantial losses to one party—may be socially highly desirable, and (2) that sometimes, at least from an economic, societal point of view, cooperation among individual agents—even if this benefits all agents—may be socially highly undesirable from an economic position (See also Wagner-Tsukamoto 2005).

In relation to this different and more complex understanding of morality as compared with behavioural ethics, economics differently conceptualises institutions that enact morality in social behaviour: *Incentive structures* reflect economics' understanding of institutions, as outlined by the New Institutional Economics (Coase 1984, 1992; Heyne 1999; Homann 1997, 1999; Homann and Suchanek 2000; Luetge 2005; North 1993a, b; Wagner-Tsukamoto 2003, 2007a; Williamson 1975, 1985). Moral problems are examined as a non-behavioural, situational condition of defective incentive structures. From a practical, normative perspective this implies that, if cooperation (competition) at the interaction level is viewed as morally desirable from the point of view of society, incentive structures are to be set up to make the same, to 'equilibrate' (disequilibrate) the self-interests of interacting choice-makers by allocating certain benefits and losses to the individual's different choice options (Williamson 1985, p. 84). In this way, it is to be ensured that cooperation and competition establish themselves at the interaction level on grounds of self-interested choice. An incentive logic is here to make individuals cooperate (not cooperate) in social interactions. Theoretically and practically, social problems are therefore *not* treated as the human condition, as a matter of inducing 'correct personal spirit' directly in the behavioural 'moves of the game' but as a matter of enacting morality through properly designed incentive rules. As a result, this approach makes small demands on like-mindedness and moral agreement among agents for cooperation to succeed.

Apparently, a behavioural understanding of morality and of institutions for enacting morality, as cherished by Quaker ethics, is thus at least partly incompatible with an economic reconstruction. This hints at the theoretical limitations of behavioural concepts for economic research on ethics, and inversely, it hints at the theoretical limitations of economic concepts for behavioural research on ethics. In this respect, the interesting question is which type of theoretical limitation is the more restrictive for understanding and solving problems of doing good in corporate behaviour. The next section argues that in social contexts in which the condition of modernity arises behavioural ethics, including institutionally oriented ones, is outperformed by an economic research program on ethics.

2 Practical Limitations of a Behavioural Business Ethics: Encountering Modernity

The subsequent discussion argues that probably only under very specific—'premodern'—conditions, as they can be derived, for instance, from a historic case study of Victorian Britain (Himmelfarb 1995), or from a contemporary case study of the Amish society in the USA, can behavioural ethics ensure the doing of good in social behaviour. However, when *modernity*—simply put, value pluralism, ethnic diversity, etc.—is encountered in social behaviour, behavioural ethics is likely to be not only ineffective and inefficient but even qualitatively inferior in terms of its concept of morality when compared with an economic approach to ethics. The discussion proceeds in two steps: Sub-section one interprets the condition of modernity, examining why and how value pluralism poses a theoretical and practical problem for behavioural ethics. Sub-section two examines the specific dilemmas religious managers face when encountering modernity.

2.1 The Condition of Modernity

The 'condition of modernity' can be diagnosed as the presence of value pluralism in social behaviour, or differently put, as the absence of a value, norm and belief consensus. Moral disagreement looms here as an interaction condition. Individuals then hold diverse, low or even no behavioural (pre)-dispositions regarding the doing of good in social behaviour (See Cochran 1957, pp. 128, 1972, p. 118; Gerecke 1997, pp. 9–20; Luhmann 1988, pp. 102–3; MacIntyre 1985, pp. 1–5; Williams 1988, p. 12). In the same way, the lost context to which leading moral philosophers and social scientists frequently refer when discussing behavioural ethics (e.g. Gambetta 1988; Homann 1990, 1997; Luhmann 1988, 1984; MacIntyre 1985; Popper 1957; Williams 1988, 1985) can be interpreted as the *pre-modern* context in which a value consensus, like mindedness and moral agreement in social interactions could be easily maintained. It is not generally questioned by this paper that in certain social contexts, especially tribal ones, the condition of modernity may be absent or could be easily remedied. However, a value-homogeneous context probably only survives in contemporary, industrialized, globalizing society in isolated instances, e.g. the Amish society. It can even be suggested that it widely disappeared as early as biblical times, as reflected by the social problems discussed in the Bible for inter-tribal scenarios and even for intra-tribal ones (See Wagner-Tsukamoto 2001, 2003). Still, behavioural research somewhat nostalgically laments the condition of modernity, clinging on to the ideal of the value consensus and the combating of value pluralism as a prime avenue for solving social problems in modern society (e.g. Collins 2000; Etzioni 1988, 1991; Küng 1999; also Cima and Schubeck 2001, when reviewing Catholic communitarianism).

For the firm, the onset of modernity could be first observed regarding interactions with external stakeholders (e.g. competitors, customers, suppliers). But from the late 19th century onwards and in the context of progressing industrialization, interactions 'within' the firm—amongst the internal stakeholders of the firm, such as managers, shareholders, employees, etc.—were caught up by modernity, too (Rathenau 1918, p. 143; similarly Berle and Means 1932; Vernon 1958, p. 93, also Chaps. "Boost up and Merge with. Order Ethics in the Light of Recent Developments in Justice Theory" to "Ethics and the Development of Reputation Risk at Goldman Sachs 2008–2010"). Documented as early as in Taylor's studies of Scientific Management (See Wagner-Tsukamoto 2003, 2007a), a different type of firm emerged as compared to the workshop or small family business: Ethnic diversity or heterogeneity began to arise in the organizational behaviour within a firm, and hierarchical structures, which induced competition even in intra-firm interactions, were installed (See also sub-section two below).

In modern interaction contexts such as the 'city' or the 'nation' and more so with regard to the 'multi-cultural society', the 'multinational enterprise', or the 'international community', where value pluralism and moral disagreement nearly always arise (and could even be ethically argued for; see below), the approach of behavioural ethics is likely to be theoretically and practically exhausted. Then, it is especially the *sharing* of perceptions of morality amongst interacting agents that yields ineffectiveness and inefficiency problems for behavioural ethics.[6] If diverse values, norms and beliefs are subscribed to by interacting individuals, intrinsic behavioural 'psychological', 'sociological', 'theological' contracting succumbs. The intrinsic behavioural self-sanctioning of violations of moral precepts through perceptions of guilt, a nagging conscience, etc. and social sanctions of peer group pressure, opinion leadership or social ostracism fail to work. Those who do not share a certain ethical code do not even realize that they have broken a behavioural contract and hence should suffer under conflicts of conscience or perceptions of guilt. Costs for remedying this problem in behavioural terms are likely to be higher than handling it in economic terms (further analysed below).

---

[6]As North's (1993a) institutional analysis hinted, the Coase theorem (Coase 1937, 1992) can in this respect be projected to effectiveness and efficiency assessments of 'psychological contracting'.

Adam Smith's exit from behavioural ethics, after decades of moral philosophical research on behavioural ethics, underlines this argument. Smith's and similarly Mandeville's turn to economics[7] was driven by their very attempt to conceptualise a viable ethics for handling social problems in their contemporary contexts. Their maxims that 'private vice' and 'self-love' (speak: self-interest) should yield 'public good' and the 'wealth of nations' formed the cornerstone of a new approach to ethics. Equally, Smith's (1976) famous suggestion that *not* the 'benevolence of the baker' (speak: business ethics understood in a behavioural way) should be relied upon for morality to materialize in social behaviour has to be read as the advice of a moral philosopher who was well aware of the condition of modernity and its undermining impact on behavioural ethics.

In general, behavioural ethics needs to conceptualise value pluralism and moral disagreement as a threat to a value consensus amongst interacting agents. From a practical, normative perspective, behavioural ethics must aim to overcome value pluralism, trying to (re)-moralize and (re)-harmonize the value, norm and belief structures of individuals. Psychological, sociological and theological techniques are applied and at times even physical force is advocated for restoring a value consensus. These considerations imply that certain moral 'costs' come with behavioural ethics and behavioural contracting in general. They have to be considered when the *quality* of morality of behavioural ethics is assessed and compared with that of an economic approach to ethics. Indeed, as Mill and similarly Hayek (1960, 1976) and Popper (1962) hinted, value pluralism could be viewed not only as morally acceptable but even as morally desirable since it tends to come with the behavioural autonomy of the individual, liberty, enlightenment, emancipation, tolerance, etc. Such ideals are likely to justify the promotion and protection of value pluralism on moral grounds. Hayek's concept of the 'great society' and Popper's concept of the 'open society' reflect this. In this respect, an economic approach to ethics may even outperform behavioural ethics with regard to the quality of morality.

2.2 The Institutional Enactment of Modernity and the Disillusionment of Behavioural Business Ethics

Institutional structures, which, for example, protect competition through business laws, are constitutionally, politically and legally imposed on business behaviour in a market economy. This intensifies the condition of modernity—and thus theoretical and practical limitations of behavioural ethics. For instance, a legal framework of business laws enforces self-interested and competitive ('conflict-oriented') behaviour on business interactions. The possibility is ever looming that 'unfit' firms

---

[7]It was probably no coincidence that moral philosophers like Adam Smith or Mill who seriously began to question the role of behavioural ethics had, in the wake of industrialization, intensively encountered modernity.

are eliminated from the competitive process. As Buchanan's (1975, 1987a, b) and Williamson's (1975, 1985) research demonstrated, such institutional, economic structures 'inside' and 'outside' a firm can be viewed as incentive structures (Fig. 2 illustrates what types of incentive structures had to be considered).

In this respect, the market economy not only tolerates the condition of modernity, but also actively draws upon the condition of modernity to organize social interactions as competitive processes—for larger moral reasons. Self-interested behaviour, which behavioural ethics might reject on behavioural grounds of 'pluralism', 'uncooperative predispositions' and 'benefiting at the expense of others', is here installed in the very 'rules of the game.' Also, interest conflict—a dilemma structure, in a methodological sense (Homann and Suchanek 2000; Wagner-Tsukamoto 2003)—is actively enacted. On these grounds, morality, understood in economic terms as the ideal of 'public good' and the 'wealth of nations' (and other ethical ideals; see below), is expected to emerge 'already' from self-interested choice and competitive social

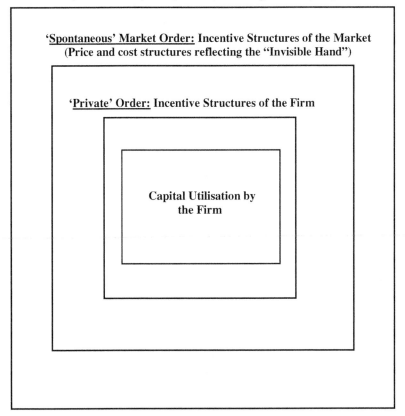

Fig. 2 Economic institutions (incentive structures). Adapted from Figure 2.1, p. 26 of Wagner-Tsukamoto (2003)

interactions. Thus, behavioural ethical ideals of social harmony and individual goodness are not drawn upon for analysing and enacting morality. If in the institutional setting of the market economy a behavioural approach to institutional ordering were favoured, severe conflicts of conscience and a clash of moral precepts of a behavioural ethics with institutionally enforced business objectives and constraints can be anticipated. Then behavioural measures as favoured by behavioural ethics are likely to be unsuccessful for inducing corporate social responsibility.

The Quakers' attempt to implement certain ideas of behavioural ethics in business practice here tells of a classic failure that compares to what Himmelfarb (1995) described as the de-moralization of Victorian society. Considering the condition of modernity and its institutional enactment in a market economy, it was hardly surprising that ultimately '... Quaker businessmen... called the title of Quaker employer... a flat contradiction in terms' (Child 1964, p. 297; similarly, Kirby 1984, pp. 117, 126)—although the underlying factors were not understood at the time. Most of the Quakers' field experiments in business ethics from 1900 to 1940 failed despite various factors being stacked in their favour. Firstly, the competitive environment of early 20th-century Britain was in certain respects rather benign. Globalisation and international competition, as we know it today, hardly existed. Secondly, Quaker firms like Cadbury or Rowntree were run by owner-managers, that means stockholder problems cannot illuminate why Quaker firms failed to implement their ethics in business life. And thirdly, weak moral predispositions of managers, as they are primarily targeted by behavioural business ethics, were no important factor that could explain the failure of Quaker firms: The Quaker managers were highly religious spiritual men (Vernon 1958; Windsor 1980).

As much as the practical ineffectiveness of the Quaker ethics was recognized, and despite Quaker firms holding numerous conferences on this issue between 1900 and 1940, Quaker managers were mystified as to why the implementation of their ethics had in certain respects failed. Institutional economics here explains that the implementation of Quaker ethics failed because institutional structures and mechanisms of the market economy were ignored. Institutional economics argues that the competitive environment ultimately constrained Quaker firms from enacting their beliefs. Specifically, 'modernity' can be diagnosed regarding self-interested competitors, who did not share Quaker values, norms and beliefs. Moral disagreement was here an ever-present interaction condition in competitive processes. In this respect the Quaker firm faced certain additional costs incurred by the implementation of their moral precepts. This put the Quaker firm at a cost disadvantage in—institutionally enacted and protected—competitive processes. This ultimately prevented the Quaker firm from engaging in—costly—behavioural business ethics in interactions with internal and external stakeholders (but not in behavioural business ethics that could be justified in economic terms, see below). Furthermore, anti-monopoly laws and cartel laws prevented Quaker firms from eliminating 'less moral' competition, e.g. through taking them over.

Ultimately, Quaker firms compromised and subordinated their ethical precepts to economic objectives and constraints. The principles of the Quaker ethics were only pursued if the costs of their implementation were covered by gains, e.g. a better treatment of employees, such as higher pay, yielded increases in productivity: '[A]ccommodation took the form of minimizing those Quaker maxims most in opposition to entrepreneurial interest... with counterbalancing emphasis on other precepts not so antithetical to this interest' (Child 1964, p. 299; also Vernon 1958, pp. 76, 95, 150, 164–166; Windsor 1980, pp. 85, 88, 90, 133, 137, 171). The precept of the promotion of the value of hard work proved least problematic in this respect. It focuses on the idea of productivity, of making good use of one's time, hinting at a capitalist work ethic of the Judeo-Christian tradition (See Weber 1974; also Gordon 1989, pp. 2–5; Himmelfarb 1995, p. 36; Windsor 1980, p. 166). The rich literature on Quaker firms (Child has a good overview) has highlighted such ethical achievements of Quaker businessmen, although the economic logic behind such achievements remains under-explored. Equally, this literature does not analyze in detail economic causes why Quaker employers failed to realize the reasons for their lacking implementation success of most of their other religious spiritual beliefs. The important point I want to make here is that Quaker employers tried with great sincerity and determination to implement their religious beliefs in business life but that these attempts, in very considerable degrees, failed and reasons for these failures remained not understood. A statement from Child, as already quoted above, is here indicative: 'Quaker businessmen ... called the title of Quaker employer ... a flat contradiction in terms' (Child 1964, p. 267). The present study here shed new light on—institutional, economic—reasons which illuminated the failure of Quaker employers and what can be learnt from these failures in more general terms.

In the period 1900–1940, processes of accommodation and compromise regarding precepts of Quaker ethics other than that based on the value of hard work left Quaker businessmen with awkward decision-making and conflicts of conscience regarding how to retreat from their religious spiritual principles. Conceptually, Quaker ethics offered little advice here: Like behavioural business ethics, it does not develop hypothetical, qualified imperatives to only obey moral precepts *if* this were compatible with the business requirements of maintaining profitability, the survival prospects of the firm, etc. Rather, Quaker ethics sets out categorical imperatives, as similarly done by Kantian ethics or religious ethics that draws on the Old Testament or New Testament, to always exercise 'correct personal spirit.'

It can be argued that Quaker firms may have stood a better chance to successfully implement their ethics if they had approached the implementation of their ethics in economic terms (For a conceptual overview of these three routes, see Wagner-Tsukamoto 2005, 2007b):

1. being content with the idea of unintended, 'indirect' moral agency;
2. laying moral precepts of Quaker ethics down in the institutional 'rules of the game' of the market economy, which are conventionally viewed by economics as the systemic place of morality in a market economy;
3. morality being conceptually located in the very 'moves of the game', as a matter of capital exchange with stakeholders (but in economic terms and not in behavioural ones).

The two latter routes imply a hypothetical qualification of categorical behavioural imperatives of behavioural ethics, and a prioritising of an economic approach to ethics over a behavioural one. To detail these three points:

1. Point one refers to the emergence of morality as an *un*intended outcome of self-interested choice in a market economy, specifically reflecting ideals such as mutual gains and the wealth of nations.
2. Up to a certain level, behavioural moral precepts can be laid down in the 'rules of the game' of the market economy which bind all firms in the same way. This implies cost neutrality of moral corporate behaviour for the single firm. Quaker firms could have lobbied for tougher constitutional and business laws that were more in line with their ethics. However, (i) in the face of global competition, a costly moral toughening of laws had to be internationally approached in order to succeed on a 'local'/national scale. Otherwise, over time morally less regulated and thus less costly markets are likely to attract firms from more highly regulated markets (Vanberg 2001; Wagner-Tsukamoto 2005). Also, (ii) a religious toughening of business laws raises questions regarding the effectiveness of the market mechanism being undermined by behavioural ethical codes. If undertaken in extreme form, a behavioural ethical toughening of the rules of the game can imply the exit from the market economy, for example, when self-interest as initiation and coordination mechanism of social interactions were partly or fully replaced by concepts of altruism, benevolence, compassion, etc. The comparatively unsuccessful field experiments of communism, Islamic banking or a 'social(ist) market economy' (e.g. the Swedish model of the 1960s and 1970s), provide warning examples. Furthermore, (iii) a religious toughening of business laws raises questions regarding cultural imperialism and the tolerance of value pluralism. Quaker firms like Cadbury or Rowntree here came under heavy criticism once they took over national newspapers in order to influence public life regarding Quaker beliefs (Vernon 1958; also Windsor 1980).
3. Most of the pioneering welfare advances in Quaker factories like Rowntree's or Cadbury's, such as a pension scheme, paid holiday, free medical services, profit-sharing arrangements, etc. (Vernon 1958; Windsor 1980), were only introduced once they had been 'tested' by Quaker employers in economic terms. As Vernon (1958, pp. 164–166) stressed, such advances were made not out of 'sentimental benevolence' but a seen need for economic success (similarly Windsor 1980, pp. 147–148). On the other hand, if such economic benefits did not exist, welfare programs were abandoned (e.g. Vernon 1958, p. 150). These implementation processes of behavioural ethics can be reconstructed in economic terms: With respect to the welfare programs introduced, Quaker employers created *ethical capital* in relation to the stakeholder 'employee,' both production capital (higher productivity, less wastage, less theft) and transaction capital ('trust' between employer and employee which stabilised and facilitated their interactions). Examples of ethical capital are generally reflected by cost/price differences between capital utilised in interactions in which stakeholders consider moral precepts and capital utilised in interactions in which

stakeholders do not consider moral precepts (apart form moral precepts enacted on grounds of self-interested choice through the rules of the game; Wagner-Tsukamoto 2005).

Since Quaker firms like Cadbury and Rowntree at least partly began to produce chocolate drinks in the 19th century for ethical reasons, namely to combat alcohol consumption which they viewed as evil, Quaker managers could have considered transforming their behavioural ethical precepts into ethical capital in another respect, as well: for instance, brand capital which could be traded and exchanged with ethically minded stakeholders, such as consumers.[8] Chocolate could have been marketed like fair trade coffee, environmentally friendly washing powder, organic cheese, free range eggs, etc. (See also Wagner 1997; Wagner-Tsukamoto 2005). In these cases, firms recoup from stakeholders costs of paying attention to higher moral standards than the ones set by the rules of the game (e.g. Wagner 1997, pp. 3–4, 206).

In contrast to the transfer of behavioural ethical precepts into the rules of the game, which implies that morality flourishes in the moves of the game as the *un*intended result of self-interested behaviour (as discussed under point 1) or as the intended result of law abiding behaviour (as discussed under point 2), a transformation of behavioural precepts into ethical capital implies highly active intent of ethical conduct in the moves of the game. Understood as ethical capital, morality can be intentionally created and utilised in interactions amongst the stakeholders of a firm. Here, economic advantages have to be identified so that a firm is capable of sustaining ethical stakeholder behaviour—and corporate social responsibility (For details, see Wagner-Tsukamoto 2003, Chap. 8; Wagner-Tsukamoto 2005). A key idea of Smith, as restated and explicated by Friedman (1970) and similarly Homann (1990, 1999), namely that morality in a market economy should and could only emerge either as the *un*intended outcome of social interactions or the intended outcome of behaviour that is driven by the rules of the game, can be qualified in this way.

It can be suggested the Quakers' *behavioural* experiments in business ethics, which related to precepts (1), (3) and (4) as discussed above, largely failed because their approach to handling morality in business behaviour was neither theoretically nor practically in tune with the systemic constraints and interaction logic of the market economy. Quaker firms neither attempted to codify the moral precepts of Quaker ethics in the rules of the game of the market economy nor did they attempt to transform their moral precepts into ethical capital that could be created, exchanged and utilised in interactions amongst the stakeholders of the firm. As indicated, for the stakeholder 'employee' they successfully introduced a number of welfare programs—because this was in tune with economic necessities and the creation of ethical capital. But as much as the transfer of morality into incentive structures and the transformation of morality into ethical capital outline effective

---

[8]Whether stakeholders were here conceptualised as utilitarians, religious believers, virtuous persons, etc. can be left to behavioural ethics and behavioural (economic) research.

and efficient routes for protecting and encouraging the doing of good in social behaviour in a market economy, they cannot be conceptually developed from within behavioural ethics. Institutional economics is required here for re-conceptualising morality, explicitly paying attention to the institutional systemic context that is constructed through incentive structures that govern capital exchange on grounds of self-interest. From such a suggestion, implications regarding the nature and feasibility of interdisciplinary collaboration are likely to emerge, namely regarding how to prioritise findings from different research programs for practically intervening with business behaviour in order to induce corporate morality.

3 Concluding Discussion: An Institutional Economic Platform for Business Ethics Theory and Practice

The paper did *not* interpret the economic approach in the tradition of behavioural economics, as is especially linked to Simon or similarly Sen, but in the tradition of classic, non-behavioural economics, as it emerged from Smith's and Mandeville's studies, and as it was connected to by economists like Hayek, Friedman, Buchanan, Becker, Homann, and to a considerable degree also by Williamson. In general, behavioural (ethics) research seems analytically ill-equipped and practically ineffective to handle social problems when value pluralism, ethnic diversity, moral disagreement or, in short, 'modernity' arises as an interaction condition. This is so because of the conceptualisation of behavioural ethics as a systemically *un*conditioned (moral) science of human nature. As noted, in a market economy, 'modernity' is even formally enacted—for moral reasons, as an economics of business ethics details—through incentive structures inside and outside a firm.

In the contemporary contexts of Smith and Mandeville in which value pluralism increasingly emerged, moral philosophers exited in force from behavioural ethics because of theoretical and practical problems of this types of ethics. Behavioural research may not have taken on board the counter-intuitive conclusions which moral philosophers with a deep understanding of behavioural ethics arrived at, such as MacIntyre (1985), Williams (1985, 1988) and early on Smith and Mandeville, or similarly religious owner-managers, like the Quaker industrialists, as reviewed in this paper.[9] In response to modernity, Mandeville's and Smith's programs of 'private vices, public good' and the 'wealth of nations resulting from self-love' set out a new approach for analysing and enacting morality.

It goes unquestioned that Quaker firms achieved very notable social innovations but it also goes unquestioned that many of their behavioural business ethics experiments failed. The paper here has reconstructed in economic terms why behavioural business ethics frequently runs into problems and why under certain

---

[9]The failure of communist societies to create the 'new good man' (Buchanan 1987b, p. 275, footnote 9) tells a similar story.

circumstances behavioural ethics works in a market economy. The study indicates that the analysis of questions of whether and how morality can thrive and can be made to thrive in a business context might benefit from

- a different conceptualisation of morality than the one suggested by behavioural ethics, focusing on an economic interpretation of morality and ideas like mutuality of gains and larger societal goals, such as the wealth of nations;
- a different conceptualisation of institutions for enacting morality, focusing on incentive structures and the assessment of situational conditions that constrain business behaviour in a market economy;
- a different conceptualisation of institutional behaviour, focusing on ethical capital and the interaction logic that drives business behaviour in a market economy.

On the basis of a classic, non-behavioural approach to economics, institutional economics, firstly, conceptualises morality on the basis of mutual gains (but in certain regards, also on the basis of mutual loss outcomes; see Fig. 1). Mutual gains at the interaction level of self-interested exchange needs to be projected to larger societal goals, such as the *un*intended emergence of social goals like the wealth of nations. Secondly, institutional economics *systemically* conceptualises morality with regard to the 'rules of the game' (incentive structures). They reflect the systemic place of corporate social responsibility and conventional practical, normative techniques of institutional economics for enacting corporate social responsibility. Less conventionally, the present paper outlines that there is room for conceptualising morality as the active, intended exchange and utilisation of *ethical capital* amongst the stakeholders of the firm (In more detail, Wagner-Tsukamoto 2003, Sect. 8.2; Wagner-Tsukamoto 2005). However, an economic conceptualisation of intended morality as ethical capital does not imply a re-entry into behavioural ethics or behavioural economics, the latter in the tradition of Simon (1993), Sen (1990), Frank (1988, 2003) or Margolis (1982).

In a value pluralistic context, behavioural research is probably only capable of solving an institutional 'rest-problem' where basic interaction problems have already been resolved in economic terms. That means, the economic approach—its concepts 'incentive structures' and 'capital utilisation' and its methods 'dilemma structure' and 'economic man'—may have to be drawn upon for setting out a design shell of practical, normative social science, which uses findings from various social science research programs by purposefully (re)-conceptualising behavioural concepts in economic terms. Morality is then (1) projected to economic ideals of public good (economic growth; wealth creation) and mutual gains; (2) it is codified in the rules of the game; and (3) morality is transformed into ethical capital. The idea of 'interdisciplinary' research is so strictly linked to a prioritising concept that is led by economics. Such leadership by economics is justified by its apparently higher viability to solve moral problems in a value pluralistic, competitive environment, as it characterizes so many 'modern', industrialized and globalizing societies. In addition, leadership of economics can be justified regarding the quality of its concept of morality: Behavioural contracting that aims at a value consensus and the elimination of moral disagreement frequently comes at the cost of an anti-pluralistic orientation and the application of certain indoctrination techniques which confine the behavioural autonomy of the individual.

Finally, on a methodological issue, which could not be further examined in this paper (for details, see Wagner-Tsukamoto 2003), an argumentation by behavioural ethics against economic ideas like 'economic man' and 'interest conflicts' may have to be discounted as a misunderstanding of the methodical nature of these ideas in economic research (as of equivalent ideas in behavioural research). If this is considered, a morally favourable image of man and of social life can be identified for economics, reflecting ideals such as public good (growth; wealth) and social justice; 'invisible', non-interfering, democratic rulers over social interactions; self-organizing social exchange (in which morality can emerge intentionally or unintentionally); the motivational and cognitive autonomy of the individual; tolerance of value pluralism; and the growth of knowledge and enlightenment. Only for purposes of behavioural theory building and behavioural consultancy are human nature and social behaviour to be modelled in an empirical, behavioural perspective. This is frequently overlooked by behavioural researchers when behavioural moral precepts regarding 'not to benefit at the expense of others' and the 'avoidance of social conflict' are viewed as being threatened by the economic approach. For instance, the Quaker managers seemed to rather negatively interpret self-interested choice in an empirical, behavioural way. In this respect, behavioural ethics researchers and practitioners may benefit from learning about the methodical nature of certain concepts in economic research (Wagner-Tsukamoto 2003). This also implies a rather different approach to teaching business ethics and to business ethics consultancy than a behavioural one, which focused on the re-moralization of managerial behaviour.

References

Argyris, C. 1992. *On organizational learning*. Oxford: Blackwell.
Berle Jr., A.A., and G.C. Means. 1932. *The modern corporation and private property*. New York: Macmillan.
Buchanan, J.M. 1975. *The limits of liberty. Between anarchy and leviathan*. Chicago/Ill: University of Chicago Press.
Buchanan, J.M. 1987a. *Economics: between predictive science and moral philosophy*. College Station, Texas: Texas A&M University Press.
Buchanan, J.M. 1987b. The constitution of economic policy. *American Economic Review* 77: 243–250.
Child, J. 1964. Quaker employers and industrial relations. *Sociological Review* 12(3): 293–313.
Cima, L.R., and T.L. Schubeck. 2001. Self-interest, love, and economic justice: a dialogue between classical economic liberalism and catholic social teaching. *Journal of Business Ethics* 30(3): 213–231.
Coase, R.H. 1937. The nature of the firm. *Economica* 4: 386–405.
Coase, R.H. 1984. The new institutional economics. *Journal of Institutional and Theoretical Economics* 140(1): 229–231.

Coase, R.H. 1992. The institutional structures of production. *American Economic Review* 82: 713–719.
Cochran, T.C. 1957. *The American business system*. Cambridge/Mass: Harvard University Press.
Cochran, T.C. 1972. *Social change in industrial society*. London: George Allen & Unwin.
Collins, D. 2000. Virtuous individuals, organizations and political economy. *Journal of Business Ethics* 26(4): 319–340.
Donaldson, T., and T.W. Dunfee. 1999. *Ties that bind. A social contracts approach to business ethics*. Cambridge: Harvard Business School Press.
Eggertson, T. 1993. Mental models and social values: north's institutions and credible commitment. *Journal of Institutional and Theoretical Economics* 149(1): 24–28.
Etzioni, A. 1988. *The moral dimension. Towards a New Economics*: Free Press, New York.
Etzioni, A. 1991. *The spirit of community. Rights responsibilities and the communitarian agenda*. London: Fontana.
Fort, T.L. 2000. A review of Donaldson and Dunfee's ties that bind: a social contracts approach to business ethics. *Journal of Business Ethics* 28(4): 383–387.
Frank, R.H. 1988. *Passions within reasons: the strategic role of the economics*. London: W. W. Norton & Company.
Frank, R.H. 2003. *What price the moral high ground? Ethical dilemmas in competitive environments*. Princeton: Princeton University Press.
Friedman, M. 1970, The social responsibility of business is to increase its profits, *New York Times Magazine*, 13 Sept 1970, pp. 32–33, 122–126.
Gambetta, D. 1988. 'Can we trust trust? In *Trust making and breaking cooperative relations*, ed. D. Gambetta, 213–237. Oxford: Blackwell.
Gerecke, U. 1997, *Soziale Ordnung in der modernen Gesellschaft*. Doctoral Dissertation, Eichstaett: Catholic University of Eichstaett at Ingolstadt, Germany.
Gordon, B. 1989. *The economic problem in biblical and patristic thought*. New York: E. J. Brill.
Gosling, J. C. B. 1973, *Plato*. London: Routledge & Kegan Paul.
Habermas, J. 1988, *Theorie des kommunikativen Handelns: Vol. 1 and 2*. Frankfurt, Germany: Suhrkamp.
Habermas, J. 1990. *Moral consciousness and communicative action*. Cambridge, UK: Polity Press.
Hayek, F. 1960. *The constitution of liberty*. London: Routledge & Kegan Paul.
Hayek, F. 1976. *Law, legislation and liberty: the mirage of social justice*, vol. 2. London: Routledge & Kegan Paul.
Heyne, P. 1999. *The economic way of thinking*. Upper Saddle River, NJ: Prentice-Hall.
Hill, A., and I. Stewart. 1999. Character education in business schools: pedagogical strategies. *Teaching Business Ethics* 3(2): 179–193.
Himmelfarb, G. 1995. *The de-moralization of society*. London: IEA Health and Welfare Unit.
Hodgson, G. 2006. What are institutions? *Journal of Economic Issues* 40(1): 1–25.
Homann, K. 1990, 'Ökonomik und Ethik'. *Conference Paper* (5th Symposium 'Kirche heute', 11–13 Oct 1990, Augsburg, Germany).
Homann, K. 1997, 'Sinn und Grenze der ökonomischen Methode in der Wirtschaftsethik', *Volkswirtschaftliche Schriften* 478, pp. 1–42.
Homann, K. 1999. Zur Grundlegung einer modernen Gesellschafts- and Sozialpolitik: Das Problem der Sozialen Ordnung. In *Soziale Marktwirtschaft im nächsten Jahrtausend*, ed. U. Blum, W. Esswein, E. Greipl, H. Hereth, and S. Müller, 119–148. Stuttgart, Germany: Schaeffer-Poeschel.
Homann, K., and A. Suchanek. 2000. *Ökonomik: Eine Einführung*. Tuebingen: Mohr Siebeck.
Izzo, G. 2000. Compulsory ethics education and the cognitive moral development of salespeople: a quasi-experimental assessment. *Journal of Business Ethics* 28(3): 223–241.
Key, S. 1997. Teaching managers to respond ethically to organizational crises: an inquiry into the case method. *Teaching Business Ethics* 1(2): 197–211.
Kieser, A. 1993. Human-relations bewegung und organisationstheorie. In *Organisationstheorien*, ed. A. Kieser, 95–126. Stuttgart, Germany: Kohlhammer.
Kirby, M.W. 1984. *Men of business and politics*. London: George Allen & Unwin.

Küng, H. 1999, 'Leitplanken für die Moral', *Der Spiegel* **51**, 20 Dec 1999, pp. 70–73.
Lampe, M. 1997. Increasing the effectiveness in teaching ethics to *undergraduate* business students. *Teaching Business Ethics* 1(1): 3–19.
Luetge, C. 2005. Economic ethics, business ethics and the idea of mutual advantages. *Business Ethics. A European Review* 14: 108–118.
Luhmann, N. 1984, *Soziale Systeme. Grundriss einer allgemeinen Theorie* (Suhrkamp, Frankfurt).
Luhmann, N. 1988. 'Familiarity, confidence, trust. Problems and alternatives. In *Trust making and breaking cooperative relations*, ed. D. Gambetta, 94–107. Oxford: Blackwell.
MacIntyre, A. 1985. *After virtue*. London: Duckworth.
March, J.G. 1978. Bounded rationality, ambiguity and the engineering of rational choice. *Bell Journal of Economics* 9: 587–608.
Margolis, H. 1982. *Selfishness, altruism and rationality*. Cambridge: Cambridge University Press.
Murphy, P.E. 1998. Character and virtue ethics in international marketing: an agenda for managers, researchers and educators. *Journal of Business Ethics* 18(1): 107–124.
North, D. 1990. *Institutions, institutional change, and economic performance*. Cambridge, UK: Cambridge University Press.
North, D. 1993a. Institutions and credible commitment. *Journal of Institutional and Theoretical Economics* 149(1): 11–23.
North, D. 1993b. Institutions and economic performance. In *Rationality, institutions and economic methodology*, ed. U. Mäki, B. Gustafsson, and C. Knudsen, 242–261. London: Routledge.
Popper, K. 1957. *The poverty of historicism*. London: Routledge & Kegan Paul.
Popper, K. 1962. *The open society and its enemies: the spell of plato*, vol. 1. London: Routledge & Kegan Paul.
Rathenau, W. 1918. *Von kommenden Dingen*. Berlin: S. Fischer.
Schanz, G. 1982, *Organisationsgestaltung. Struktur und Verhalten* Muenchen: Vahlen.
Schein, E. 1980. *Organizational psychology*. London: Prentice-Hall.
Sen, A.K. 1990. Rational fools: a critique of the behavioural foundations of economic theory. In *Beyond self-interest*, ed. J.J. Mansbridge, 25–43. Chicago/Ill.: University of Chicago Press.
Seshadri, S., G.M. Broekemier, and J.W. Nelson. 1997. Business ethics—to teach or not to teach? *Teaching Business Ethics* 1(3): 303–313.
Simon, H.A. 1976. *Administrative behavior*, 3rd ed. New York: Free Press.
Simon, H.A. 1993. Altruism and economics. *The American Economic Review Papers and Proceedings* 83(2): 156–161.
Siu, N.Y., J.R. Dickinson, and B.Y. Lee. 2000. Ethical evaluations of personal religiousness. *Teaching Business Ethics* 4(3): 239–256.
Smith, Adam. 1976. *An inquiry into the nature and causes of the wealth of nations, 2 Volumes*. Oxford: Clarendon.
van Oosterhout, J.H., P.P. Heugens, and M. Kaptein. 2006. 'The internal morality of contracting: advancing the contractualist endeavor in business ethics. *Academy of Management Review* 31: 521–539.
Vanberg, V. 2001. *The constitution of markets*. London: Routledge.
Vernon, A. 1958. *A quaker business man. The life of Joseph Rowntree 1836–1925*. London: G. Allen and Unwin.
Von Dran, G.M., E.S. Callahan, and H.V. Taylor. 2001. Can students' academic integrity be improved? Attitudes and behaviors before and after implementation of an academic integrity policy. *Teaching Business Ethics* 5(1): 35–58.
Wagner, S.A. 1997. *Understanding green consumer behaviour*. London: Routledge.
Wagner-Tsukamoto, S.A. 2001. Economics of genesis: on the institutional economic deciphering and reconstruction of the stories of the Bible. *Journal of Interdisciplinary Economics* 12(3): 249–287.
Wagner-Tsukamoto, S.A. 2003. *Human nature and organization theory*. Cheltenham: Edward Elgar.

Wagner-Tsukamoto, S.A. 2005. An economic approach to business ethics: moral agency of the firm and the enabling and constraining effects of economic institutions and interactions in a market economy. *Journal of Business Ethics* 60(1): 75–89.

Wagner-Tsukamoto, S.A. 2007a. An institutional economic reconstruction of scientific management: on the lost theoretical logic of taylorism. *Academy of Management Review* 32(1): 105–117.

Wagner-Tsukamoto, S.A. 2007b. Moral agency, profits and the firm: economic revisions to the Friedman Theorem. *Journal of Business Ethics* 70(2): 209–220.

Warner, M. 1994. Organizational behaviour revisited. *Human Relations* 47(10): 1151–1166.

Weber, M. 1974. *The protestant ethic and the spirit of capitalism*. London: Urwin University Books.

Williams, B. 1985. *Ethics and the limits of philosophy*. London: Fontana.

Williams, B. 1988. Formal structures and social reality. In *Trust making and breaking cooperative relations*, ed. D. Gambetta, 3–13. Oxford: Blackwell.

Williamson, O.E. 1975. *Markets and hierarchies. Analysis and antitrust implications*. New York: The Free Press.

Williamson, O.E. 1985. *The economic institutions of capitalism*. New York: Free Press.

Williamson, O.E. 1998, *Human actors and economic organization*. Conference Paper. Vienna: 7th Biannual Meeting of the International Joseph Schumpeter Society, June 1998.

Windsor, D.B. 1980. *The quaker enterprise. Friends in business*. London: F. Muller.

Part IV
Problems of Business Ethics from an Order Ethics Perspective

The Constitution of Responsibility: Toward an Ordonomic Framework for Interpreting (Corporate Social) Responsibility in Different Social Settings

Markus Beckmann and Ingo Pies

Abstract This article shows how taking a constitutional economics perspective can clarify the idea of responsibility. Applying constitutional economics, the authors distinguish between within-game (or sub-constitutional) responsibility when playing a game and context-of-game (or constitutional) responsibility for developing the conditions under which a game will be played. These two conditions are interpreted as comprising not only the institutions (rules of the game) but also discourse about the game, its deficiencies, and reform options. Accordingly, the authors' concept of "ordo-responsibility" distinguishes between "governance responsibility" and "discourse responsibility." This concept is used to critically discuss the conventional dichotomy between state and non-state actors. The authors examine the capacity of private actors to engage in political processes of rule-setting and rule-finding. The article thus provides important conceptual clarification for the debate on corporate social responsibility.

Keywords Responsibility · Constitutional economics · Ordo-responsibility · Social structure · Semantics · Corporate social responsibility · Global governance · Ordonomics

---

The authors thank two anonymous reviewers as well as the editor for constructive and very valuable comments. The authors also thank participants of the 2006 conference "Business Ethics, Social Integration and Corporate Citizenship" in Valencia, Spain, for comments on a conference paper that first developed some of the ideas of this article and that has been published as Beckmann and Pies (2008) in the according conference volume.

M. Beckmann (✉)
Corporate Sustainability Management, University of Erlangen-Nürnberg, Nuremberg, Germany
e-mail: markus.beckmann@fau.de

I. Pies
Economic Ethics, Martin Luther University Halle-Wittenberg, Halle, Germany
e-mail: ingo.pies@wiwi.uni-halle.de

> Responsibility is the product of definite social arrangements.
>
> Frankel (1955, p. 203)

In recent years, there has been intense debate, both in public and in academia, on the subject of "responsibility" and, especially, *corporate social responsibility* (CSR). The academic discussion has been truly interdisciplinary, and resulted in articles from a wide variety of fields, including philosophy, business ethics, management literature, economics, political science, sociology, and other social sciences. This article contributes to this interdisciplinary discussion by showing how the *constitutional economics* perspective can be applied and extended to an *ordonomic perspective*, resulting in conceptual clarification of the idea of responsibility. More specifically, the authors suggest that the notion of responsibility needs to be interpreted differently in different social settings. Three ideas are particularly central to the authors' argument.

First, the authors *apply* the perspective of constitutional economics to distinguish between responsibility at the sub-constitutional level, which is the "within-game responsibility" in playing a given game, and responsibility at the constitutional level, which is the "context-of-game responsibility." Second, the authors *extend* the perspective of constitutional economics to the ordonomic perspective, proposing that the constitutional "context-of-game responsibility" comprises not only a "governance responsibility" for the shared "rules of the game" but also a "discourse responsibility" for the shared "ideas of the game". Third, the authors *clarify* the perspective of constitutional economics by highlighting that "constitutional responsibilities" can be undertaken not only by state actors, but also by corporations and civil society organizations.

These ideas will be presented in more detail following the next section, which introduces and defines key terms and concepts.

1 Clarifying Key Concepts: Constitutional Economics and the Ordonomic Perspective

Nobel Laureate Buchanan (1987, 1990) as well as Brennan and Buchanan (1985) are the most notable voices in the field of constitutional economics. The insight of constitutional economics most relevant to this article is the way it distinguishes between two aspects of social interaction (or societal "games"), namely, the distinction between playing a given game (the basic game) and setting the rules for that game (the meta game).

Figure 1 illustrates how constitutional economics relates to conventional rational-choice analysis. *Conventional economic analysis* (lower left box in Fig. 1) is concerned with the first type of social interaction. The conventional rational-choice approach looks at a certain social setting (such as a market), takes the constraints of the situation as given, and then explains aggregate social

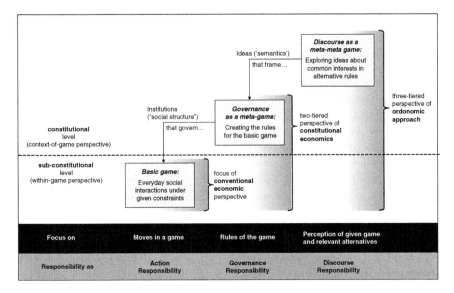

Fig. 1 An overview of key concepts and their relationship

outcomes by modeling how rational actors optimize their individual choices given these constraints (Becker 1976, 1993, 1996; Coleman 1990).

Constitutional economics, in contrast, adds the second type of social interaction (Fig. 1). From this perspective, the conditions constraining how actors interact are not inevitable, but can be changed and are thus themselves the result of choice. For example, in soccer, the constraints under which players interact are largely defined by the rules of the game. These rules specify the number of players, the size of the field, the duration of the game, the options available to the players, and the costs and benefits of certain moves (e.g., the sanctions for foul play or the points obtained by making a goal). Constitutional economics views such a set of rules as the "constitution" of a game. Of key importance is that this constitution is human-made and thus there are innumerable constitutions that could be designed and agreed upon, resulting, of course, in very different games.[1] Accordingly, Buchanan (1990, p. 2, emphasis in original) distinguishes two levels of choice: the sub-constitutional level of "choices made *within* constraints" (within-game perspective) and the constitutional level of "choice among constraints" (context-of-game perspective), that is, the choice between different games, or in other words: "What kind of game do we want to play?"

---

[1]For example, in soccer, the duration of the game could be changed from 90 to 60 min, the number of players could be changed from 11 to 5, or off-side positions could be made legal. Any such change in rules would basically result in a different game. The constitutional perspective takes this second level of choice into consideration.

With the aim of clarifying the concept of responsibility, the authors believe that this two-tiered approach of constitutional economics can be extended to a three-tiered framework (Fig. 1), which is the "ordonomic" approach put forward by Pies et al. (2009, 2010, 2011, 2013) and Beckmann et al. (2014). Drawing on the concept and terminology developed by sociologist and system-theorist Luhmann (1980, 1981, 1997, 1998), the *ordonomic perspective* uses the distinction between *social structure* and *semantics* to further elaborate the "context-of-game" domain as introduced by constitutional economics. The ordonomic perspective extends constitutional economics by interpreting the context or constitution that frames and defines social interactions as comprising not only formal and informal institutions (social structure) but also the ideas (semantics) that influence how the players perceive their interaction. Both terms, social structure and semantics, are briefly defined below.

The authors use Luhmann's term, *social structure*, to describe the properties of a social problem context. The social structure of an interaction thus includes the actors involved, their options, and the costs and benefits of these options. For social interaction that occurs repeatedly, the social structure includes above all formal and informal institutional arrangements. As North (1990, p. 3) states, "[i]nstitutions are the rules of the game in society or, more formally, are the humanly devised constraints that shape human interaction. In consequence they structure incentives in human exchange, whether political, social, or economic." What sociologists call social structure is thus very similar to what constitutional economists denote as the sum of institutional constraints, that is, the "constitution" for social interaction. With regard to a particular social interaction, the social structure thus defines what Popper (1966) calls the "logic of the situation," that is, the structure that channels how players act and interact.

For a definition of *semantics*, the authors draw on Luhmann (1980, p. 19, translated by Möller 2006, p. 51), who defines "semantics" as the "socially available sense that is generalized on a higher level and relatively independent of specific situations." While "social structure" refers to how the social sphere operates, "semantics" or "semantic structures," according to Luhmann, refers to how reality is observed and described. Semantics is thus more than just meaning; rather, semantics refers to the socially relevant ideas that are driven by conscious or unconscious theories held by individuals, alternatively called "mental models" (Denzau and North 1994), "framing" (Kahneman and Tversky 2000), "searchlights" (Popper 1972), "heuristics" (Lakatos 1978), or "paradigms" (Kuhn 1962). In this article, "semantics" is used to mean the socially constructed lenses through which actors observe and make sense of their environment.

Semantics is important because socially relevant ideas grounded in conscious or unconscious theories channel how actors perceive, describe, and evaluate social phenomena and, in particular, social interactions, conflict, and cooperation (cf. North 1994, 2005; Schelling 1980, 2006). Semantics thus enriches and complicates rational-choice analysis. The authors thus suggest extending the two-tiered rational-choice framework of constitutional economics into the three-tiered ordonomic model. Constitutional economics distinguishes the "within-game" sub-constitutional level (basic game) from the "context-of-game" constitutional level (meta-game), seeing the constitutional level as the level at which the institutional constraints or rules of the game are set. From the ordonomic perspective, such rule-setting does not occur in a vacuum; rather, semantic concepts—understood as socially relevant ideas grounded in conscious or unconscious assumptions—influence how the players perceive their situation, which understanding influences whether or not they will "enact" a specific rule and, if so, the specifics of it. As a third tier, the authors suggest adding the concept of *discourse*, defined to mean the social arena in which actors exchange ideas, identify common interests, and possibly come to a shared understanding of their situation, leading, in the best of possible worlds, to a win-win way of handling the situation.

Figure 1 illustrates the key concepts and their relationship; Table 1 provides brief definitions of key terms. As the figure illustrates, the ordonomically extended version of constitutional economics distinguishes three different "games" of social interaction. At the sub-constitutional level, the first level of the "basic game" comprises day-to-day interactions within a given frame, such as a market, a sports game, or academia. The constitutional "context-of-game" domain includes the two "meta games" that influence and frame how the basic game will unfold. At the second level, the "meta game of governance" involves rule-setting, that is, the creation and reform of institutions, or in Luhmann's terms, the social-structure properties of the basic game. Finally, at the third level is the "meta-meta game of discourse," which involves discursive processes of rule-finding, that is, the exchange of ideas or, again in Luhmannian terms, the communication of semantic lenses through which the actors perceive their given game as well as potential alternatives for playing a better game under reformed rules.

The authors suggest that the three-tiered ordonomic framework is a step toward overcoming the conceptual challenges posed by the notion of responsibility in general and corporate social responsibility in particular. The three social games described in Fig. 1 constitute three different social settings with rather dissimilar logics: the sub-constitutional basic game focuses on the actors' individual *moves in a game*, the constitutional meta-game of governance involves creating *rules of the game*, and the constitutional meta-meta game of discourse circles around the construction of shared *perceptions of possible games.* These three levels of social interaction are thus characterized by three very different social structures. Yet, to date, the notion of responsibility fails to distinguish between these different social settings. Instead, a "one-size-fits-all" idea of responsibility is used across all three levels.

Against this background, the authors claim that one reason the concept of corporate social responsibility is controversial, possibly even the major reason, is that the same semantics of responsibility is applied to widely different social settings. Therefore, the purpose of this article is to develop a conceptual framework for the notion of responsibility such that it can be fruitfully applied across all three levels of societal interactions. The conceptual framework developed in this article thus distinguishes three different kinds of responsibility: first, *action responsibility* for one's individual moves (basic game); second, *governance responsibility* for contributing

Table 1 Definitions of key terms

Concept	Definition	Terminology by	Relationship to other concepts
Game	Metaphor for interaction of different actors ("players") that unfolds under certain "rules" (constraints)	Buchanan (1987, 1990), Schelling (1980)	Social interaction; a game is defined by its players and the constraints under which they interact
Basic game	Everyday interaction under given constraints	(Buchanan, Schelling)	Interaction at the sub-constitutional level; within-game interaction
Meta-game	Higher-order game that defines or changes context of basic game	(Buchanan, Schelling)	Level of "choices among constraints"/interactions at the constitutional level that define the context-of-game
Sub-constitutional level	Interactions within a given context or constitution	Buchanan (1990), Brennan and Buchanan (1985)	Level of the basic game; within-game level
Constitutional level	Domain in which the context or "constitution" of a game is changed/defined	Buchanan (1987, 1990), Brennan and Buchanan (1985)	Context-of-game level; level of the meta-games; governance level
Governance	Processes that create constraints under which basic game interactions unfold	Williamson (1985, 2009)	Governance is provided through meta-games at the constitutional level; is similar to institutions and constitution
Discourse	Arena for sharing and exploring ideas (semantics)		Discourse can be interpreted as a meta-meta game that frames the available mindsets (semantics) for the meta-game and basic game
Social structure	Social constraints that define the properties of a given situation	Merton (1968), Luhmann (1980, 1997)	Social structure can be interpreted as the institutional context of a situation or the sum of institutional constraints that channel how interactions unfold

(continued)

Table 1 (continued)

Concept	Definition	Terminology by	Relationship to other concepts
Semantics	"Socially available sense" or socially relevant ideas with often unconscious assumptions	Luhmann (1980, 1997)	Socially available ideas are an important element of the context that frames how actors perceive their social setting; similar concepts are "mental models," "frames," "ideologies," "paradigms," etc.
Institutions	"the humanly devised constraints that shape human interaction" or "rules of the game" (North 1990)	North (1990)	Sum of institutions constitutes the constitution or social structure of a social situation; as "rules of the game," institutions can be changed through social meta-games
Constitution	Sum of constraints or institutions under which a game is played	Buchanan (1990)	Constitution of a game can be changed or reformed on the constitutional or meta-game Level

to shared rules of the game (meta game); and third, *discourse responsibility* for contributing to a discourse aimed at finding superior rules (meta-meta game).

Taking constitutional economics as its foundation, the conceptual framework introduces action responsibility as a sub-constitutional "within-game responsibility" and distinguishes it from a constitutional "context-of-game responsibility." This ordonomic framework then interprets the "context-of-game responsibility" as comprising two constitutional responsibilities: governance responsibility for the shared rules of the game and discourse responsibility for the shared ideas of the game. To highlight the difference between this three-tiered ordonomic approach and the two-tiered approach of constitutional economics, the authors use the term "ordo-responsibility" (Beckmann and Pies 2008), which is defined to include both governance and discourse responsibility.

The remainder of this article develops and substantiates this conceptual framework for interpreting responsibility in different social settings in three steps. The first step (2.-5.) is to explain why application of a standard understanding of responsibility to very different contexts creates problems. In the second step (6.-10.), constitutional economics is applied and extended to develop the three-tiered ordonomic concept of "ordo-responsibility." The third step (11.-12.) discusses theoretical implications of "ordo-responsibility," particularly with regard to the role of the state and corporate social responsibility. The article ends (13.) with a short summary and concluding remarks.

2 Diagnosing the Problem

The CSR debate provides ample evidence that the concept of "responsibility" is far from universally embraced or interpreted. Many corporations, scholars, and government actors (e.g., the European Commission) have eagerly embraced a CSR agenda, but critics have just as eagerly denounced CSR as "misguided virtue" (Henderson 2001). Indeed, when it comes to corporations, the very meaning of "responsibility" remains highly disputed.

One reason for this conceptual dispute lies in conflicting notions of "fitness to be held responsible" (Pettit 2007, p. 173). In fact, since the beginning of the CSR debate, critics have raised doubts as to whether corporations are able to be attributed responsibility in the first place because, as for example Friedman (1970) claimed, responsibility can only be ascribed to persons. Against this background, a rich discussion has explored how responsibility can be understood from the perspective of group agency (Mukerji and Luetge 2014) and as "collective responsibility" (French 1984) or "incorporated" responsibility (Pettit 2007).

The authors argue that there is a further reason for the responsibility controversy is that the same semantics of responsibility is applied to a wide variety of social settings. To substantiate this claim, the authors first differentiate paradigmatically between two situations; they then show that the notion of responsibility originally referred to only the first of these two situations; finally, the authors discuss why application of a general notion of responsibility to the second situation stretches it too far.

3 Action-Based Versus Interaction-Based Situations

As a well-established framework for the analysis of social structure, the rational-choice perspective helps decipher the logic of two different social settings. When one reflects on the connection between actions and their outcomes, two simplified situations emerge (cf. Beckmann and Pies 2008).

The first situation is *action-based*. Here, the outcome is the *result of individual action*. The key characteristic of this situation is individual outcome-control. As an example of an action-based situation, imagine that it is winter and your house is too cold for comfort. You take the action of turning up the thermostat. The direct consequence of this action is that the house becomes warmer. This outcome is controllable and intended—in fact, the result is the very reason for the action.

The second situation, the *interaction-based* one, is different in that the outcome is not determined by an individual actor but by the interplay between many actors. Individual control of the outcome is not possible. To illustrate, let us return to the thermostat example. If individuals warm themselves and their homes by turning up their thermostats, they contribute to global warming through emissions of greenhouse gases. Thus, global warming results from individual action, but the aggregate

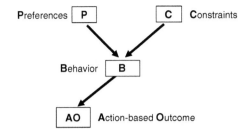

Fig. 2 The micro-level perspective of the rational-choice model focuses on action-based outcomes (adapted from Beckmann and Pies 2008, p. 93)

outcome—"climate change"—is neither controllable by any single individual nor was it intended; it is an unintentional outcome of the social behavior of many. To put it simply, it is a global side-effect of individual action.

Economic theory—or, more precisely, rational-choice social science—offers a framework that combines analysis of both action-based and interaction-based situations, thus distinguishing between a micro level of individual action and a macro level of aggregative group outcomes (Coleman 1990, pp. 1–23). Figure 2 illustrates this perspective on the micro level of individual action. Here, a representative actor is assumed to be trying to achieve his or her individual aims (or preferences, P) as efficiently as possible. He or she thus chooses the behavior B that—based on existing limited means, i.e., the constraints C—achieves the subjectively best possible outcome (the action-based outcome, AO). In other words, the rational-choice approach models the optimization of an individually controllable outcome, i.e., *action*-based consequences.

Figure 3 adapts Coleman's (1990) famous bathtub model to illustrate how the rational-choice perspective uses the micro-level analysis of action-based behavior to analyze *interaction-based* outcomes at the aggregative macro level. The idea is to explain how a change in a particular macro factor X (e.g., a decrease in the price of

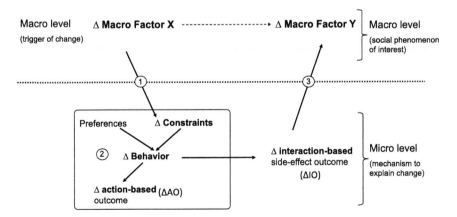

Fig. 3 The macro-level perspective of the rational-choice model focuses on interaction-based outcomes (adapted from Coleman 1990, p. 8 and Beckmann 2010, p. 110)

fuel) results in other changes (macro factor Y; e.g., a change in pollution) at the aggregative social level. Instead of explaining this effect directly, the rational-choice approach uses a three-step macro-micro-macro procedure. First, the changed macro factor X (e.g., cheaper fuel) is translated into changed constraints (ΔC) for individual behavior at the micro level (e.g., less incentive to save fuel). Second, assuming stable preferences ($\bar{P}$) (see Becker 1976, 1996; Stigler and Becker 1977), the rational-choice approach models how a representative actor would adapt his or her behavior to the changed constraints (e.g., turning up the thermostat). Note that for this cost-benefit calculus, the representative actor takes into account only his or her individual action-based outcome (e.g., a warmer house) but does not (fully) consider the marginal side-effects that this action contributes to aggregative interaction-based outcomes (ΔIO) (e.g., marginal increase in carbon emissions). This marginal side-effect is unintended. Third, the rational-choice model finally aggregates the marginal side-effects produced unintentionally by many individuals at the micro level to a social outcome at the macro level (e.g., global warming). Coleman's model thus demonstrates that while interaction-based outcomes such as global warming are ultimately caused by individual actors, a systematic determinant of these macro outcomes is the collective constraints under which individuals choose to act and interact.

4 Responsibility as a Concept Originally Tailored to Action-Based Situations

As Ricoeur (2000, p. 11) outlined in his seminal "Essay in Semantic Analysis," responsibility is a concept that "is not really well established within the philosophical tradition." He contends that with the current proliferation of the term, "a kind of vagueness invades the conceptual scene." For Ricoeur (2000, p. 19), the contemporary idea of responsibility is "a shattered concept." Historically, the term "responsibility" derives from classical juridical usage, where it is defined as responsibility "for the tort one has caused through one's own fault" (Ricoeur 2000, p. 11). Put differently, the original legal usage of the term responsibility was tailored to *action*-based situations characterized by *individual outcome-control* (Ricoeur 2000, p. 24). The authors hold that this individual outcome-control is an important condition that must be met before responsibility can be imposed meaningfully on someone, as a person can be made responsible only for that which he or she has in his or her own control.[2]

---

[2]There is a long tradition in ethics according to which it is wrong to hold someone responsible for something the person cannot influence. This idea can be traced back to the Roman Corpus Iuris Civilis. At around 100 A.D., Aulus Celsus Cornelius wrote in the Digest (50, 17, 185): "Impossibilium nulla obligatio est." Cf. Spruit (2001, p. 985). However, the classical Latin expression of this idea that nobody is bound beyond ability is much better known: ultra posse nemo obligatur (to say one should implies one can).

From the rational-choice perspective, the relevance of the responsibility semantics lies in its power to inspire prudent behavior in action-based situations. If one knows that one will be called to account for one's actions, one is more likely to consider the consequences of one's own actions. Acting "irresponsibly," as opposed to "responsibly," poses the risk of no longer being considered a trustworthy partner and thus, even worse, the loss of all future cooperation. In economic terms, failure to act responsibly carries depreciation costs, which occur when one forfeits one's ability to cooperate. Such long-term depreciation costs may include a guilty conscience, legal action by others, loss of trust, or a ruined reputation. As a socially available frame for one's actions, the responsibility semantics brings into focus such potential long-term costs so that the "responsible" foregoing of short-term advantage can be understood as a good investment. Therefore, under the original concept of action-based responsibility, an actor is not expected to sacrifice his or her self-interest; rather, the concept of responsibility can provide individual actors with a more enlightened and longer-term view of what is in their self-interest.

5 The Overextension of the Original Responsibility Concept

The conventional understanding of "responsibility" can lead to problems if is indiscriminately extended from action-based to interaction-based consequences. As succinctly stated by Ricoeur (2000, p. 12): "At the limit, you are responsible for everything and everyone." This unlimited responsibility not only falls on natural persons, but also on corporations when a single firm is held responsible for aggregative societal outcomes such as climate change. Such social interaction results, or aggregative outcomes, are neither controlled nor intended by single actors. In this sense, no *single* individual or corporate actor is or should be made responsible for such collective problems. If one transfers the *action*-based notion of individual responsibility to these *inter*action-based group problems, then the implicit assumptions (such as individual outcome control) on which conventional responsibility semantics rests no longer hold. As a consequence, the idea of responsibility loses its heuristic value in solving problems.

The ordonomic concept proposed here thus differs substantially from the morally charged notions of responsibility that are prominent in public and philosophical discourse. Critics of corporations may grant that no corporation can single-handedly bring about a solution to collective problems, and yet they insist that a "responsible" corporation must refrain, for example, from emitting any greenhouse gases. Similarly, in philosophical discourse, responsibility is discussed as a categorical moral duty to refrain from or engage in certain actions (cf., e.g., Jonas 1984)—a duty that does not depend on whether these individual actions are incentive-compatible or whether undertaking them will have any actual effect.

The authors agree with these morally charged notions of responsibility to the extent that, yes, there are urgent problems and, yes, the idea of responsibility provides an important perspective from which to think about how to solve these problems. Yet, in order to find and implement such solutions, the authors claim that a responsibility semantics is needed that is compatible with the actual social structure and incentive properties of the situation for which responsibility should be taken. Otherwise, the attribution of responsibility runs the risk of being misleading at best, counterproductive at worst.

If an undesirable situation derives as the outcome of a well-established and strong social system, appealing to individual "morals" is not going to be a very effective solution. Take, for example, the social structure of competitive markets. As argued by Baumol (1975, p. 49), "the competitive process ... leaves little up to the good will of individual managements." Expecting companies to forego profit for the sake of "being responsible" is infeasible: a company that—individually—agrees to realize continuously less profit than its competitors for the sake of some (individually) unobtainable goal will eventually be driven out of the market (Homann 2002), and thus will not be able to do anything about the problem at all and, indeed, quite possibly create another problem, such as unemployment. Against this background, Luhmann (1997, p. 133, translated by the authors) argues that the "call for responsibility" amounts to nothing but a futile "gesture of despair" and suggests not talking about responsibility in the first place. The present authors disagree and contend that the responsibility semantics is too valuable to be dismissed. Instead of rejecting the notion of responsibility, in the following section, the authors develop a conceptual framework of responsibility semantics that can be applied to both action-based outcomes and interaction-based outcomes.

6 Ordo-Responsibility as a Remedy Proposal

Endemic corruption, appalling labor conditions in entire industries, overfishing, and global warming are only a few examples of social problems caused by the interaction-based consequences of human behavior. To address such systemic social problems with a notion of responsibility tailored to action-based outcomes of individual behavior is problematic. However, as it is desirable to somehow solve these interaction-based problems, a concept of responsibility suitable to this type of problem is needed.

Taking constitutional economics as a basis, this article introduces the concept of "ordo-responsibility" as one that can be usefully applied to interaction-based outcomes. Ordo-responsibility argues for a change in perspective from taking responsibility *in* the game to a (constitutional) responsibility *for* the game. As the previous section showed, the idea of responsibility was originally focused on action-based outcomes of individual behavior. The authors suggest calling this conventional notion "action responsibility" or "within-game responsibility." The concept of ordo-responsibility, in contrast, refers to the constitutional "context-of-game responsibility" and builds on the following key insight: while action-based outcomes are determined directly by individual actions (or a single move in a game), interaction-based outcomes are determined by the constraints (or rules of the game) that define societal interaction. A concept of responsibility that can be applied to undesirable interaction-based outcomes therefore needs to be rooted in changing the context of the game.

The idea of a context-of-game or constitutional responsibility builds on the fundamental contribution of constitutional economics of distinguishing between the "choice within constraints" and the "choice among constraints" (Buchanan 1990, p. 2). However, constitutional economics says little about when and how a rational actor can accept constitutional context-of-game responsibility. With regard to this question, the above diagnosis shows that there is a context, a form, and a consistency requirement that any responsibility concept needs to meet in order to be applicable in interaction-based situations. (a) First, *contextually*, the responsibility concept needs to address the constraints of the shared interaction. (b) Second, in terms of *form*, it is important that the responsibility idea does not simply rest on moralistic appeals that call for self-sacrifice but that it aids in understanding how improving the constraints of a game can further one's self-interest. (c) Third, the concept must be *consistent*, meaning that an actor can be assigned responsibility only for those consequences for which individual outcome-control is possible.

The remainder of this section discusses when and how a context-of-game responsibility is possible. The authors elaborate on the idea of ordo-responsibility as a context-of-game responsibility that includes both governance responsibility and discourse responsibility.

7 Governance Responsibility for Improving the Rules of the Game

As Fig. 1 illustrates, constitutional economics views the social sphere as consisting of different levels of social interaction. At the level of the basic game, interactions take place within a given set of rules; the higher level—the "meta game"—is concerned with the processes that actually create these rules. To illustrate, if the "basic game" is the economy where market participants interact according to certain laws, then politics is the meta game that produces these laws. Since the meta game of rule-setting establishes the rules that govern the basic game, the authors call these processes *governance* processes.

Governance responsibility involves the idea that if the basic game has undesirable results, then ordo-responsibility can be engaged in by actively addressing the underlying problem by enacting better rules in a constructive governance meta game. Such a constructive governance contribution in the meta game can manifest as either an action-based or as an interaction-based consequence.

For example, improved rules can be an action-based outcome. That is, an individual actor can establish a better (or different) rule single-handedly. The one-sided prisoners' dilemma (or trust game) is the paradigm example. Here, mutual cooperation does not occur due to the *asymmetrical* opportunity for exploitation (Kreps 1990). Note that in the original game, failure to cooperate manifests as an interaction-based outcome. None of the players intends this outcome; to the contrary, each individual would prefer cooperation and its consequent advantages for all parties. However, no player can single-handedly create mutual cooperation; a rule reform through a meta game is necessary for successful cooperation. In the one-sided prisoners' dilemma, the player able to asymmetrically exploit the other can also change the rules. By means of an *individual self-binding commitment*, e.g., by paying a deposit, he or she can make the exploitation strategy so unattractive for himself or herself that the promise to cooperate becomes credible to others. A self-binding individual commitment thus establishes a jointly favorable new rule: cooperation becomes possible (cf. Pies et al. 2009).

On other hand, establishing a favorable rule may require the collective action of many actors; that is, it will be an interaction-based outcome that no player can deliver single-handedly. The classic many-sided prisoners' dilemma (Luce and Raiffa 1957, p. 95) is the paradigm example. The many-sided prisoners' dilemma involves *symmetrical* interaction between n players with $n > 1$ whose cooperation fails because of the reciprocal opportunity for mutual exploitation, so that the group never achieves its potential (Bowles 2004, pp. 23–55). The well-know tragedy of the commons (Hardin 1968) is a case in point. The collective self-damage caused by the failure to cooperate is an interaction-based outcome that is neither intended nor controlled by any individual player. To change this interaction result requires reforming the rules and thus the incentives for all players. An individual self-binding commitment is insufficient here. One player's commitment to unconditional cooperation would actually increase the others' incentive to exploit this contribution and withhold their own. For effective collection action, then, it is crucial that all players simultaneously commit to a rule that ensures the cooperation of each individual by instituting severe enough sanctions for refusal to do so that willingness to cooperate is credible. In short, what is needed is a *collective* commitment (Axelrod 1984; Ostrom 1990).

In a situation, however, where a collective commitment is needed, a particular player can only meaningfully be ascribed the individual responsibility to bring about this result as an action-based outcome if the exceptional case is given that all other players have already expressed their *conditional* willingness to cooperate and to commit themselves to a shared rule too. In this case where the other players' willingness to cooperate is conditional, i.e., based on the condition that the individual really cooperates, a mutually advantageous situation will occur only if the individual player actually cooperates and does not chose a free-rider strategy. Given this particular situation, a rational argument of enlightened self-interest can be made for the acceptance of individual responsibility where individual action is pivotal for tipping the entire group to a new outcome.

To summarize, the idea of governance responsibility clarifies how rational actors can take constitutional context-of-game or ordo-responsibility. The governance responsibility concept is focused on the meta game of rule-setting and thus fulfills the three requirements for being applicable to interaction-based situations. (a) *Contextually*, governance responsibility focuses on the institutional constraints (or social structures) that define an interaction and sheds light on how prudent self-commitments can improve these institutional constraints. (b) With regard to the *form*, governance responsibility does not involve moralistic appeals, but instead informs about the conditions under which individual and collective commitments can advance one's enlightened self-interest. (c) Finally, responsibility in this context refers strictly to action-based consequences and thus meets the *consistency* requirement.

However, there are some obvious limitations to governance responsibility when the social problem in the basic game is the result of a many-sided dilemma. In the field of CSR, sustainable solutions to such many-sided dilemmas require that not only a single company, but also its competitors, "get on board," e.g., to solve the problem of corruption, pollution, poor labor standards, etc. in a certain industry. Since only a collective commitment of all players can solve this type of dilemma, one's own action can bring about this solution with individual outcome-control and thus as an action-based consequence only if there is a conditional commitment to cooperate by all other players. Beyond this exceptional case, the collective self-commitment in the many-sided prisoners' dilemma manifests as an interaction-based outcome that no player can single-handedly control.

8 Discourse Responsibility for Creating a Shared Understanding of Common Interests

From a constitutional economics perspective, if social interaction leads to undesirable results, the rules of the game need to be changed. The ordonomic concept of discourse responsibility involves the idea that if the necessary better rules cannot be implemented effectively individually, but the other relevant players are not willing to cooperate, it is possible to initiate a discourse with these other players with the goal of reaching a shared understanding of how a rule reform could lead to a better game for all.

The idea of discourse responsibility thus focuses on how one can contribute to creating conditions under which constructive governance processes for setting better rules becomes possible. Collective action to establish better rules for joint interaction requires that the involved parties understand and agree that these new rules will benefit them individually. Otherwise, nobody would be willing to cooperate in setting such rules. There are two important aspects of achieving the necessary cooperation. First, every player needs to recognize the advantages of a collective commitment. They need to understand why the status quo is undesirable and how a different kind of "game" could improve the situation. To illustrate, corporations will not be motivated to fight endemic corruption in their industry if they do not understand why corruption is bad for them individually (e.g., bribery costs). Second, and equally important, every player needs to know that all other players are prepared and willing to commit themselves at least conditionally. For example, if Company A is convinced that a collective commitment is a great idea, but Company B is not, then collective action will be difficult. Moreover, each player needs to know that the others will not exploit his or her willingness to cooperate. Using again the example of endemic corruption in a particular industry, a company will be willing to accept a stricter anti-bribery industry standard only if it knows that its competitors will not free-ride, but abide by the standard, too.

Thus, the authors suggest that even if one cannot take governance responsibility directly, one can initiate a discourse by sending a signal comprised of two statements. The first statement is: "I have good reason to believe that the status quo is undesirable and that we could achieve a better situation if we agreed on a collective commitment to play under a different set of rules." The second statement sets out a conditional willingness to cooperate: "I am willing to accept a collective commitment as long as all others are willing to do so."

The authors suggest that such a two-part signal can initiate a new level of social interaction, namely, a rule-finding discourse that will both allow for recognizing shared problems and for exploring, discovering, and formulating better rules to address these problems. Since such a discourse can pave the way for subsequent rule reforms, the ordonomic perspective conceptualizes these rule-finding discursive processes as the *meta*-meta game (see Fig. 1).

To summarize, the concept of discourse responsibility further clarifies how rational actors can take a constitutional context-of-game or ordo-responsibility. If one cannot take governance responsibility directly because other players need to be on board before rules can be reformed, the discourse responsibility concept can be a way of creating the necessary awareness that one does need to get on board, and does so in a way that fulfills the three requirements for being applicable to interaction-based situations. (a) *Contextually*, the notion of discourse responsibility takes into account not only that there are constraints on social interaction, but also that these constraints include not only prevailing rules and institutions (in Luhmannian terms, social structures) but also socially available ideas, perceptions, and knowledge (in Luhmannian terms, semantics). Accordingly, the ordonomic perspective distinguishes two dimensions of ordo-responsibility: governance responsibility provides ways of accepting responsibility for joint rules (institutions); discourse responsibility involves shared awareness (ideas). (b) As for the *form*, discourse responsibility does not engage in moral appeals; instead, by means of the discussed two-part signal, it informs others that engaging in rule-finding discourse and subsequent rule-setting can be in their own interest. (c) The *consistency* of the responsibility concept remains unimpaired. Discourse responsibility is aimed at joint rule-finding discourse. If it is successful, that is, common interests are discovered and acted on, such is certainly an *interaction*-based consequence. No single person alone can determine the outcome of this discourse—one cannot dictate consensus. However, *initiating* the discourse by sending the signal *is* an individual act, and thus meets the requirement of having an action-based outcome for which responsibility can be appropriately assigned.

9 A Unified Framework for the Concept of Responsibility

Figure 4 illustrates the full concept of ordo-responsibility. A key condition for meaningful attribution of responsibility is individual outcome-control, which can be fulfilled only in the case of action-based situations. As indicated by the dotted arrows in Fig. 4, extending the original meaning of responsibility to cover interaction-based consequences leads, ultimately, to a situation in which no one takes responsibility and no solutions to the problem can be found. To restore the usefulness of the responsibility idea, the authors propose a conceptual framework for interpreting responsibility in different social settings such that in each instance a constructive attribution and acceptance of responsibility is possible (Fig. 4). For each social setting, the aim is to establish an action-based starting point in an interaction-based situation, thus identifying a basis for acceptance of responsibility. It is here that the concept of ordo-responsibility shows its value. The concept of ordo-responsibility sets out the conditions under which individual and collective commitments and participation in discourse can enable rational actors to play a better game.

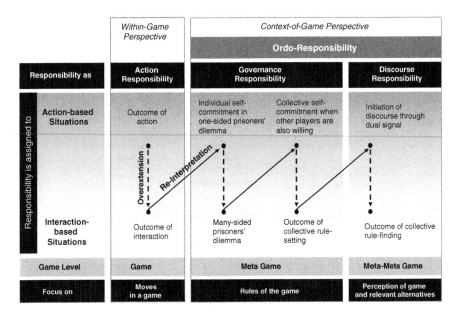

Fig. 4 A conceptual framework for interpreting responsibility in different social settings (adapted from Beckmann and Pies 2008)

10 Ordo-Responsibility, Discourse, and Rational-Choice

The concept of ordo-responsibility offers a fresh perspective on the importance of discourse. Perhaps this point is best made by comparing the ordonomic perspective on discourse to the perspective found in the literature on deliberative democracy (Dryzek 2001; Habermas 1996, 1998), political governance (Deitelhoff 2009; Risse 2000, 2004), or business ethics (Palazzo and Scherer 2006; Scherer and Palazzo 2007, 2011). Table 2 sets out the key differences.

As Table 2 indicates, *normative* approaches to discourse argue that there is a moral obligation to engage in deliberative discourse. Assuming that this moral obligation transcends self-interest, these theorists claim that deliberative discourse is incompatible with rational-choice theory (Elster 1986; Habermas 1998, pp. 241–243). From the ordonomic perspective, in contrast, discourse, though highly important, is not an end in itself but of importance for *pragmatic* reasons—as an instrument.

The pragmatic ordonomic approach is significantly different from normative notions of communicative rationality. To begin with, there is no need for the (counterfactual) presupposition of any Habermasian "ideal speech situation"; rather, the ordonomic perspective focuses on real-life discourse situations with real actors, their information asymmetries, tactics, and strategic interdependencies. The authors' position thus differs significantly from, for example, Palazzo and Scherer (2006, p. 83), who argue that civil society activists fail to participate in a real deliberate discourse if they make use of strategies such as public pressure. In contrast, the ordonomic perspective views *all* communicative behavior—including strategic behavior—as participation in the social meta-meta game of discourse.

With regard to the impact of discourse on behavior, there is a further difference. The authors fully concur with Risse (2000, 2004) and Deitelhoff (2009) that participation in discourse can result in a genuine change in behavior, yet interpret the underlying mechanism differently. Proponents of normative discourse theory argue

Table 2 Two ways of conceptualizing discourse

	Normative concept of discourse	Pragmatic concept of discourse
Motivation for participating in discourse	moral obligation	self-interested problem solving
Concept of rationality	transcends self-interested behavior	enlightened rational-choice paradigm
Discourse as …	(counterfactual) ideal speech situation	imperfect real-life situation
Behavioral change because of…	transformed individual preferences	altered informational constraints
Deliberation as…	true moral discourse	(social) learning process

that "truly" communicative action will (or should) transform the individual *preferences* of the actors involved in discourse. In contrast, following Becker's (1976, 1993, 1996) economic approach, the ordonomic approach models rational actors as having *given preferences* and then reacting to *changing constraints*—with information, knowledge, mental models, and perceptions being some of the most critical of these constraints.[3] Accordingly, the ordonomic rational-choice perspective does not reconstruct discourse as a mechanism through which actors transform their individual preferences but interprets discourse as an arena in which discursive practices change and expand these informational constraints in light of the bounded rationality of any rational actor (Simon 1955). In contrast to a notion of deliberation as "true moral discourse" in which actors are not allowed to follow their self-interest, the authors hold that discourse has a much more general importance as an arena for social and individual *learning processes*.[4]

The ordonomic rational-choice perspective also allows clarifying the limitations of the ordo-responsibility framework. *Conceptually*, the authors claim that there are, in principle, no limitations to applying the three-tiered conceptual framework; that is, to interpret interaction-based problems as resulting from a given basic game, then to analyze the possibilities for and difficulties in improving the rules of the game through appropriate strategies in the meta game, and finally to assess the options for initiating a rule-finding discourse if collective action is necessary for governance reform. *Substantially*, however, the ordonomic rational-choice perspective allows identifying the *practical* limitations to ordo-responsibility with regard to real actors in a specific problem context. As Frankel (1955, p. 203) argues, "[r]esponsibility is the product of definite social arrangements." The rational-choice perspective helps analyze these social structural conditions. Under the ordonomic concept laid out here, responsibility could be translated as "response-ability": the ability to respond to the interests of others in a prudent, mutually advantageous, way. For any actor, this capacity is not inevitable or unchangeable, but determined

---

[3]From this perspective, the given preferences do not refer to normal market goods but to "commodities" or "basic goods" such as "health," "the good life," etc. (cf. Becker 1996). Consequently, this approach does not look at a "preference" for, say, aspirin, but instead treats aspirin (its existence, its effects, its price, etc.) as one of the constraints that channel how rational actors try to best satisfy their desire for the basic good "health." If a rational actor learned about a new and better drug than aspirin and therefore changed his or her medication, the rational-choice perspective would not treat this as a case of transformed preferences but as a change in behavior triggered by altered information constraints.

[4]By this logic, even rational actors with strictly given meta-preferences have an interest in participating in discourse in order to learn about and adapt to the social constraints and interdependencies that determine the possibility space of their behavior. This is of particular importance when it comes to addressing the collective self-harm in a social dilemma. To overcome a social dilemma through collective action, the actors need to know how the others perceive and evaluate the situation. Here, it makes a huge difference whether the actors interpret their situation as one of pure conflict—a zero-sum game—or as a precarious positive-sum game (cf. Schelling 1980, 2006). To be sure, from a rational-choice perspective, discourse alone may be insufficient to solve a social dilemma, but far from simply being "cheap talk," discourse can help facilitate an agreement to (re-) form institutional incentives in a mutually advantageous way.

by situational factors: by the number of other players, by the costs and benefits of commitment strategies, and by the costs and benefits of participating in a rule-finding discourse.

As a consequence, there might well be situations in which the transaction costs of collective action or the costs of discourse are prohibitively high. Yet, the very perspective of ordo-responsibility reveals that these costs and benefits depend on societal arrangements that can themselves be made subject to reform. The key question then is: How can society enhance the capacity of self-interested actors to accept responsibility? Seen from this perspective, mechanisms for reducing the net costs of rule-setting and rule-finding could include, for instance, improving the negotiation capacities of poorer countries; protecting the openness and pluralism of public discourse; supporting new forms of cooperation through cross-sector partnerships; facilitating the formation of stewardship councils, roundtables, and policy networks; creating learning platforms; and—above all—fostering dialogue (Fung 2003).

11 Implications for Economic Theory, Constitutional Economics, and CSR

Mainstream neoclassical economics treats ordo-responsibility as exclusively reserved for the government (Friedman 1962, p. 15). According to this perspective, the state's primary role is to promote the common good through setting and enforcing appropriate rules and, moreover, state government is seen as the *only* legitimate rule-maker (Sundaram and Inkpen 2004, p. 355). Many economists thus are skeptical about companies becoming involved in public governance (Friedman 1970; Jensen 2001, p. 16) and argue that corporate influence on political rule-setting can only be understood as rent-seeking, as illegitimate lobbying at the expense of third parties.

Yet, there remains a puzzle. The rational-choice approach underlying neoclassical economics conceptualizes *all* actors as self-interested players—including politicians and government officials. Why is it, then, that the standard economic paradigm criticizes self-interested business and civil society actors for participating (or attempting to) in rule-setting but is apparently uncritical of self-interested nation-state actors?

Drawing on the ideas of governance and discourse responsibility developed here, the authors explain the economic nation-state paradigm by way of a cheapest-cost argument. If society's well-being hinges on functional governance and discourse processes, then two factors become relevant. First, it is necessary that the meta games of governance and discourse promote common interests instead of favoring rent-seeking behavior. Second, playing such welfare-increasing meta games needs to be as inexpensive as possible.

In light of both requirements, governments have a comparative advantage for taking ordo-responsibility through specialized rule-finding and rule-setting mechanisms. With regard to welfare-increasing win-win reforms, democratic states build on the democratic process as an inclusive feedback mechanism to legitimize governance reforms (Downs 1957; Schumpeter 2000). Institutional checks and balances, such as party competition, due process standards, parliamentary investigation committees, and a pluralist media, ensure that, in an ideal democracy, government actors have strong incentives to refrain from rent-seeking activities and to solve those societal problems that concern voters. To this end, states can use a sophisticated set of commitment technologies that facilitate taking governance responsibility: they can draw on the monopoly of force for—inexpensively—setting and enforcing rules and they can tax citizens to overcome the free-rider problem in providing public goods. Finally, state actors have access to the institutionalized discourse of parliamentary democracy, making it cheaper for them to initiate discourse processes for joint rule-finding. In sum, both the governance and the discourse costs are often lower for government actors than for corporate or civil society actors.

The ordo-responsibility concept thus provides a further explanation for why the nation-state paradigm has become so important. However, the ordonomic perspective also reveals that such a "methodological nationalism" (Smith 1983, p. 26) implicitly assumes fairly specific empirical conditions and thus may suffer from "blind-spots" when these boundary conditions no longer hold.

12 The Blind Spots of the Conventional Nation-State Paradigm

Figure 5 illustrates two blind spots of the conventional nation-state paradigm typically found in mainstream economics. Figure 5 is a two-by-two matrix showing four cases of how state and non-state actors can participate in political rule-setting. The row dimension distinguishes whether an actor's political influence in rule-setting leads to changes in the rules of the game that are mutually advantageous (win-win) or to the disadvantage of others (rent-seeking). The column dimension differentiates between state actors (government) and non-state actors (e.g., business corporations). Conventionally, neoclassical economics focuses almost exclusively on the upper-left and the lower-right boxes of this matrix, thus having two blind-spots regarding the remaining two boxes (upper-right and lower-left).

The upper-left box of Fig. 5 describes the ideal nation-state in which government promotes the public good. In the lower-right box, business corporations pursue private interests at the expense of the public. The underlying assumption is that companies have no or very little incentive to be "socially responsible" in rule-setting processes [a critical perspective already voiced by Smith (1976, pp. 145, 493)]. By this logic, the literature on corporate political action theorizes as

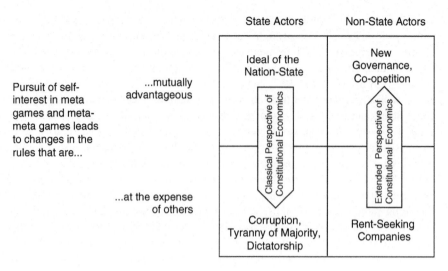

Fig. 5 The symmetry between state and non-state actors

to how companies can make use of their corporate political interest to best serve their profit interests (Shell 2004; Hillman et al. 2004).

Assuming an idealized democratic nation-state, such a strict separation between political and market actors may be a useful approximation for economic model building. Yet, in the debate about corporate social responsibility, this "separation thesis of economic theory" (Scherer et al. 2006, p. 508) has come under criticism. With regard to pressing challenges such as corruption, global warming, or appalling labor conditions, business increasingly operates in areas in which the assumption that governments are able and willing to set and enforce perfect rules of the game no longer holds (Pattberg 2005; Wolf 2008). If economic theory, however, nevertheless rests on a naïve dichotomy between self-interested corporations and public-interest-oriented state actors, then it is failing to see two relevant cases. The authors argue that an extended perspective of constitutional economics can illuminate *both* blind spots more clearly.

The first blind spot (lower-left box of Fig. 5) is the case that self-interested states and government actors may use rule-setting processes in a way that does *not* serve the general public good. Though mostly ignored by conventional economics, this phenomenon is at the forefront of constitutional economics research, most notably in the tradition of the Virginia school of political economy, i.e., in the public-choice theory advanced by Buchanan and Tullock (1962), Buchanan et al. (1980), and others. As illustrated by the left arrow pointing downward, public-choice theory calls attention to those cases—also within Western nation-states—in which government actors engage in rent-seeking or corrupt activities that do not promote the common good (Shleifer and Vishny 1999). For example, a familiar danger of democracies is the expropriation of a minority by a tyranny of the majority. Furthermore, economic theories of dictatorship have shed light on situations outside the ideal Western nation-state where state actors such as neopatrimonial rulers, military regimes, and warlords use political processes for domestic rent-seeking (Acemoglu and Robinson 2006; Olson 2000; Tullock 1989; Wintrobe 1998). Thus, constitutional economics illuminates one of the blind spots of conventional neoclassical economics.

In the context of the debate over CSR, this first blind spot suffered by economic theory is important because business firms, in particular multinational corporations, have been engaged for decades now in increasingly complex value chains that operate at least partially in areas where the ability and/or willingness of state actors to take ordo-responsibility for the public good is limited. As a consequence, companies can no longer rely on the state setting appropriate rules (Scherer et al. 2006).

The second blind spot shows up in the upper-right box of Fig. 5. This box illustrates the possibility that private actors can have an incentive to engage in rule-setting processes that are mutually advantageous. In other words, this box is about non-state actors' capacity to take ordo-responsibility. The authors claim that not only mainstream neoclassical economics but, by and large, constitutional economics as well have ignored this possibility. Yet, as illustrated by the right arrow pointing upward, there is—conceptually—no reason not to believe that under certain conditions private actors might engage in mutually advantageous forms of non-state governance. In fact, recent years have witnessed ample evidence demonstrating that business corporations as well as nonprofit civil society organizations can and already do contribute to creating better rules and institutions. To illustrate:

- Public-private partnerships have emerged as a new mode of governance. Here, actors from business and government not only pool resources, they create new procedures for (jointly) providing public goods (see Edwards and Zadek 2003; for a critical perspective on corporate engagement in public health, see Margolis and Walsh 2003).
- Traditionally, cooperation between companies has been viewed with suspicion as an attempt to form a cartel in order to limit competition. Yet the management literature on "competition" (Nalebuff and Brandenburger 1996) highlights that there are forms of cooperation that do not necessarily seek to limit but, instead, to actually empower market competition.
- When it comes to creating norms and standards, private actors are playing an increasingly important role. For example, in the absence of enforced government regulation, corporate codes of conduct play a crucial role in "upholding labor standards in third world countries" (Frenkel and Scott 2002, p. 30). Similarly, industry self-regulation can complement governmental regulatory regimes (King and Lenox 2000).
- Cross-sector new governance initiatives such as the Oslo-based Extractive Industries Transparency Initiative (EITI) have begun to create rules that regulate not only companies but that even seek to bind state actors. EITI aims to improve transparency and accountability in the extractives sector. Supported by leading

corporations, civil society groups, governments, and international organizations, EITI sets a global standard for companies to publish what they pay and for governments to disclose what they receive (Aaronson 2011; Eigen 2006; www.eiti.org).

In summary, the concept of ordo-responsibility contributes to at least two important fields. First, with regard to economics, the argument made here challenges the "separation thesis of economic theory" typically made by authors such as Baumol and Blackman (1991), Friedman (1962, 1970), Henderson (2001), Jensen (2001), and Sundaram and Inkpen (2004). The authors claim that neoclassical economic theory, to date based on a narrow nation-state paradigm, needs to broaden its perspective to capture the important new-governance phenomena described above and explore the potential for governance by nongovernmental actors (Hall and Biersteker 2002; Pattberg 2005; Scherer et al. 2009; Wolf 2008).

Second, the concept of ordo-responsibility makes an important contribution to the literature on CSR and, in particular, to the current discussion about the political role of the business firm. While there is a rich debate about the role of private firms as political actors (cf. Crane et al. 2008; Kobrin 2009; Matten and Crane 2005; Palazzo and Scherer 2006; Pies et al. 2013; Scherer et al. 2006; Scherer and Palazzo 2011), this work tends to call for an extended political role for the firm on normative grounds. For example, Scherer and Palazzo (2008, p. 414) argue that "in as much as the state apparatus does not work perfectly, there is a demand for business to be socially responsible." While this might be true, the present authors contend that simply identifying this societal demand does not explain why individual companies would step into meet it (see, similarly, Boatright 2011, p. 137). The literature on public goods is rife with examples of societal demands that have not been addressed, either by corporations or anyone else. The present authors are critical of the tendency found in the CSR literature to simply call for extended responsibility on the part of the business community without acknowledging the role of incentives and the issue of implementation. As Oosterhout (2005, p. 678) points out, "why should [corporations] … assume such extensive responsibilities if there is nothing in it for them?" It is against this background that the idea of ordo-responsibility makes an interesting contribution. Instead of arguing for a political role of the corporation on purely normative grounds, the ordonomic responsibility framework developed here provides a positive explanation as well as a valuable heuristics for the political participation of companies in new-governance processes.

13 Concluding Remarks

In his seminal article, "The Tragedy of the Commons," Hardin (1968, p. 1247) is sharply critical of using the word "responsibility" when addressing interaction-based problems such as the tragedy of the commons because such calls for individual responsibility ultimately amount to "trying to browbeat a free man in a commons into acting against his own interest." Hardin (1968, p. 1247) summarizes his criticism of the conventional responsibility semantics as follows: "Responsibility is a verbal counterfeit for a substantial *quid pro quo*. It is an attempt to get something for nothing."

The present authors both agree and disagree. The authors agree that there are many instances in which the word responsibility is used in a way so that its semantics—the implicit assumptions attached to it, such as individual outcome-control—does not fit with the social structure—the incentive properties—of the relevant situation. Such misleading use of the term is a problem. If notions of responsibility and, more specifically, corporate social responsibility, are incompatible with the workings of modern society and the market process, then the responsibility discourse runs the risk of being just empty talk with no constructive effect. At the same time, the authors disagree that "responsibility" necessarily needs to be "a verbal counterfeit" where the *quid* lacks the *quo* and so, as a consequence, one should refrain from using the term. The authors prefer a different strategy. Instead of warning against the responsibility semantics, this article clarified the concept of responsibility and suggested a way of restoring its applicability to social communication processes in modern society.

There is an analogy between the ordonomic argument presented here and Boatright's (1999) critical piece "Does Business Ethics Rest on a Mistake?" In this piece, Boatright criticizes what he calls the "Moral Manager Model." For him, the hallmark of the Moral Manager Model is to focus primarily on the individual manager within a given situational context. For the present authors, the mainstream CSR literature argues in a similar vein and focuses primarily on the moral responsibilities of a firm within a *given* situation. Accordingly, one could ask: "Does the responsibility debate rest on a mistake?" In his remarks on theorizing business ethics, Boatright (1999) argues for a new theoretical perspective that focuses not on the virtues of managers, but on the creation of *moral markets* (for a market failure perspective, cf. Heath 2004). He thus directs the focus toward understanding and, if necessary, changing the context in which managers and firms operate. Similarly, the present authors claim that the CSR debate would benefit from taking a constitutional "Moral Market" perspective that looks at how companies can contribute to changing the context—the "constitution"—that channels their behavior. However, companies will play a constructive role in transforming undesirable games only if they fully understand the difference between their "within-game responsibility" and their constitutional "context-of-game-responsibility." The authors hold that CSR concepts that fail to acknowledge this distinction risk overtaxing individual actors instead of helping them to behave ethically.

In terms of implications for corporate practice, the ordo-responsibility perspective has the following implications for CSR. First, CSR should not be aimed at emasculating the profit motive but at empowering it by identifying social win-win solutions—which requires extensive knowledge of one's stakeholders and the ability and willingness to communicate with them. Second, to create win-win outcomes, an often overlooked strategy is to contribute to better rules for the game—which often requires the ability and willingness to partner with others, including competitors. Third, however, this type of investment is not without costs, those of commitment devices and those of the discourse process itself. Therefore, a long-term CSR strategy might seek to lower these costs. With regard to collective action, public-private partnerships, cross-sector alliances, or business coalitions are potential mechanisms for lowering the net cost of commitment and discourse. Finally, a powerful and effective way of encouraging cooperation is to develop a culture of corporate integrity that is accompanied by good corporate governance. In effect, a company's integrity largely influences its capacity for social responsibility: the more credible a company is, the easier it is for the company to engage in inexpensive (self-)commitment and to cooperate with others in those discourses needed to identify common interests.

Finally, a short remark on methodology. This article demonstrates that taking a rational-choice perspective can reveal interesting insights for the debate about responsibility and CSR. However, the analysis also highlights the need for clarification and greater sophistication of the rational-choice methodology before this benefit can fully manifest. To this end, the authors applied and extended the constitutional economics perspective to achieve what they term an "ordonomic approach." Unlike constitutional economics, "ordonomics" focuses not only on the importance of institutions but also on the importance of ideas. The ordonomic approach thus distinguishes between two "constitutional" levels of social interaction and therefore suggests broadening rational-choice analysis to look systematically at institutions (social structure) *and* ideas (semantics). The authors believe there are substantial benefits to acknowledging, analyzing, and, if necessary, challenging the socially available conscious and unconscious theories that shape perceptions and are thus highly influential for institutional reform. Ideas matter. And thus, ideas of responsibility matter.

References

Aaronson, S.A. 2011. Limited partnership: Business, government, civil society, and the public in the extractive industries transparency initiative (EITI). *Public Administration and Development* 31: 50–63.

Acemoglu, D., and J.A. Robinson. 2006. *Economic origins of dictatorship and democracy*. New York: Cambridge University Press.

Axelrod, R. 1984. *The evolution of cooperation*. New York: Basic Books.

Baumol, W.J. 1975. Business responsibility and economic behavior. In *Altruism, morality, and economic theory*, ed. E.S. Phelps, 45–56. New York: Russell Sage Foundation.

Baumol, W.J., and S.A.B. Blackman. 1991. *Perfect markets and easy virtue: Business ethics and the invisible hand*. Cambridge, MA: Blackwell.

Becker, G.S. 1976. *The economic approach to human behavior*. Chicago, IL: University of Chicago Press.

Becker, G.S. 1993. Nobel lecture: The economic way of looking at behavior. *Journal of Political Economy* 101(3): 385–409.

Becker, G.S. 1996. *Accounting for tastes*. Cambridge, MA: Harvard University Press.

Beckmann, M. 2010. *Ordnungsverantwortung. Rational-Choice als ordonomisches Forschungsprogramm* [*Ordo-responsibility. Rational choice as an ordonomic research program*]. Berlin, Germany: Wissenschaftlicher Verlag Berlin.
Beckmann, M., and Pies, I. 2008. Ordo-responsibility. Conceptual reflections towards a semantic innovation. In *Corporate citizenship, contractarianism and ethical theory*, eds. J. Conill, C. Luetge, and T. Schönwälder-Kuntze, 87–115. Aldershot: Ashgate.
Beckmann, M., S. Hielscher, and I. Pies. 2014. Commitment strategies for sustainability: How business firms can transform trade-offs into win-win outcomes. *Business Strategy and the Environment* 23:18–37. doi: 10.1002/bse.1758.
Boatright, J.R. 1999. Does business ethics rest on a mistake? *Business Ethics Quarterly* 9: 583–591.
Boatright, J.R. 2011. The implications of the new governance for corporate governance. In *Corporate citizenship and new governance: The political role of corporations*, ed. I. Pies, and P. Koslowski, 133–146. Dordrecht, The Netherlands: Springer.
Bowles, S. 2004. *Microeconomics. Behaviors, institutions, and evolution*. New York: Russell Sage Foundation.
Brennan, G., and J.M. Buchanan. 1985. *The reason of rules: Constitutional political economy*. London, New York: Cambridge University Press.
Buchanan, J.M. 1987. The constitution of economic policy. *American Economic Review* 77: 243–250.
Buchanan, J.M. 1990. The domain of constitutional economics. *Constitutional Political Economy* 1: 1–18.
Buchanan, J.M., and G. Tullock. 1962. *The calculus of consent*. Ann Arbor, MI: University of Michigan Press.
Buchanan, J.M., Tollison, R.D., and Tullock, G. 1980. *Toward a theory of the rent-seeking society*. College Station, TX: Texas A & M University Economics Series.
Coleman, J.S. 1990. *Foundations of social theory*. Cambridge, MA: Harvard University Press.
Crane, A., D. Matten, and J. Moon. 2008. *Corporations and citizenship*. Cambridge, UK: Cambridge University Press.
Deitelhoff, N. 2009. The discursive process of legalization: Charting islands of persuasion in the ICC case. *International Organization* 63: 33–65.
Denzau, A.T., and D.C. North. 1994. Shared mental models: Ideologies and institutions. *Kyklos* 47: 3–31.
Downs, A. 1957. *An economic theory of democracy*. New York: Harper.
Dryzek, J.S. 2001. Legitimacy and economy in deliberative democracy. *Political Theory* 29: 651–669.
Edwards, M., and S. Zadek. 2003. Governing the provision of global goods: The role and legitimacy of nonstate actors. In *Providing global public goods*, ed. I. Kaul, P. Conceição, K. Le Goulven, and R.U. Mendoza, 200–224. New York: Oxford University Press.
Eigen, P. 2006. Fighting corruption in a global economy: Transparency initiatives in the oil and gas industry. *Houston Journal of International Law* 29: 327–354.
Elster, J. 1986. The market and the forum: Three varieties of political theory. In *Foundations of social choice theory*, ed. J. Elster, and A. Hylland, 103–132. Cambridge, UK: Cambridge University Press.
Frankel, C. 1955. *The case for modern man*. New York: Harper.
French, Peter A. 1984. *Collective and corporate responsibility*. New York, NY: Columbia University Press.
Frenkel, S.J., and D. Scott. 2002. Compliance, collaboration, and codes of labor practice: The Adidas connection. *California Management Review* 45: 29–49.
Friedman, M. 1962. *Capitalism and freedom*. Chicago, IL: University of Chicago Press.
Friedman, M. 1970. The social responsibility of business is to increase its profits. *New York Times Magazine*, September 13, 32–33, 122–126.
Fung, A. 2003. Deliberative democracy and international labor standards. *Governance* 16: 51–71.
Habermas, J. 1996. *Between facts and norms*. Cambridge, MA: MIT Press.

Habermas, J. 1998. Three normative models of democracy. In *The inclusion of the other. Studies in political theory*, pp. 239–252. Cambridge, MA: MIT Press.
Hall, R.B., and T.K. Biersteker (eds.). 2002. *The emergence of private authority in global governance*. Cambridge, UK: Cambridge University Press.
Hardin, G. 1968. The tragedy of the commons. *Science* 162: 1243–1248.
Heath, J. 2004. A market failures approach to business ethics. In *The invisible hand and the common good*, ed. B. Hodgson, 69–89. Berlin, Germany: Springer.
Henderson, D. 2001. *Misguided virtue. False notions of corporate social responsibility*. Wellington, New Zealand: New Zealand Business Roundtable.
Hillman, A.J., G.D. Keim, and D. Schuler. 2004. Corporate political activity: A review and research agenda. *Journal of Management* 30: 837–857.
Homann, K. 2002. Wettbewerb und Moral [Competition and morality]. In *Vorteile und Anreize [Advantages and incentives]*, 23–44, Tübingen, Germany: Mohr Siebeck (Original work published 1990).
Jensen, M.C. 2001. Value maximization, stakeholder theory, and the corporate objective function. *Journal of Applied Corporate Finance* 14: 8–21.
Jonas, H. 1984. *The imperative of responsibility: In search of an ethics for the technological age* (trans: Hans Jonas and David Herr). Chicago, IL: University of Chicago Press (Original work published in 1979).
Kahneman, D., and A. Tversky (eds.). 2000. *Choices, values, and frames*. New York: Cambridge University Press.
King, A.A., and M.J. Lenox. 2000. Industry self-regulation without sanctions: The chemical industry's responsible care program. *Academy of Management Journal* 43(4): 698–716.
Kobrin, S.J. 2009. Private political authority and public responsibility: Transnational politics, transnational firms and human rights. *Business Ethics Quarterly* 19: 349–374.
Kreps, D.M. 1990. Corporate culture and economic theory. In *Perspectives on positive political economy*, ed. J.E. Alt, and K.A. Shepsle, 90–143. Cambridge: UK Cambridge University Press.
Kuhn, T.S. 1962. *The structure of scientific revolutions*. Chicago, IL: University of Chicago Press.
Lakatos, I. 1978. *The methodology of scientific research programmes: Philosophical papers*, vol. 1. Cambridge, UK: Cambridge University Press.
Luce, D.R., and H. Raiffa. 1957. *Games and decisions*. New York: John Wiley.
Luhmann, N. 1980. Gesellschaftliche Struktur und semantische Tradition (Societal structure and semantic tradition). In *Gesellschaftsstruktur und Semantik: Studien zur Wissenssoziologie der modernen Gesellschaft. Vol. 1*, 9–71. Frankfurt a.M, Germany: Suhrkamp.
Luhmann, N. 1981. *Gesellschaftsstruktur und Semantik: Studien zur Wissenssoziologie der modernen Gesellschaft. Vol. 2 [Societal structure and semantics: Studies on the knowledge sociology of modern society]*. Frankfurt a.M, Germany: Suhrkamp.
Luhmann, N. 1997. *Die Gesellschaft der Gesellschaft [The society of society]*. Frankfurt a.M., Germany: Suhrkamp.
Luhmann, N. 1998. Modernity in contemporary society. *Observations on Modernity*, 1–22. Palo Alto, CA: Stanford University Press.
Margolis, J.D., and J.P. Walsh. 2003. Misery loves companies: Rethinking social initiatives by business. *Administrative Science Quarterly* 48: 268–305.
Matten, Dirk, and A. Crane. 2005. Corporate citizenship: Toward an extended theoretical conceptualization. *Academy of Management Review* 30: 166–179.
Merton, R. 1968. *Social theory and social structure*. New York: Free Press.
Möller, H.-G. 2006. *Luhmann explained: From souls to systems*. Chicago, IL: Open Court Publishing.
Mukerji, N., and C. Luetge. 2014. Responsibility, Order Ethics, and Group Agency. *ARSP. Archiv für Rechts- und Sozialphilosophie*. 100(2): 176–186.
Nalebuff, B.J., and A.M. Brandenburger. 1996. *Co-opetition*. New York: Doubleday.
North, D.C. 1990. *Institutions, institutional change, and economic performance*. New York: Cambridge University Press.

North, D.C. 1994. Economic performance through time. *American Economic Review* 84: 359–368.
North, D.C. 2005. *Understanding the process of economic change.* Princeton, NJ: Princeton University Press.
Olson, M. 2000. *Power and prosperity. Outgrowing communist and capitalist dictatorships.* New York: Basic Books.
Oosterhout, H. v. 2005. Corporate citizenship: An idea whose time has not yet come. *Academy of Management Review* 30(4): 677–681.
Ostrom, E. 1990. *Governing the commons. The evolution of institutions for collective action.* New York: Cambridge University Press.
Palazzo, G., and A.G. Scherer. 2006. Corporate legitimacy as deliberation: A communicative framework. *Journal of Business Ethics* 66: 71–88.
Pattberg, P. 2005. The institutionalization of private governance: How business and nonprofit organizations agree on transnational rules. *Governance* 18: 589–610.
Pettit, Philip. 2007. Responsibility incorporated. *Ethics* 117: 171–201.
Pies, I., S. Hielscher, and M. Beckmann. 2009. Moral commitments and the societal role of business: An ordonomic approach to corporate citizenship. *Business Ethics Quarterly* 19(3): 375–401.
Pies, I., M. Beckmann, and S. Hielscher. 2010. Value creation, management competencies, and global corporate citizenship: An ordonomic approach to business ethics in the age of globalization. *Journal of Business Ethics* 94: 265–278.
Pies, I., M. Beckmann, and S. Hielscher. 2011. Competitive markets, corporate firms, and new governance—An ordonomic conceptualization. In *Corporate citizenship and new governance: The political role of corporations*, ed. I. Pies, and P. Koslowski, 171–188. Dordrecht, The Netherlands: Springer.
Pies, I., M. Beckmann, and S. Hielscher. 2013. The political role of the business firm: An ordonomic concept of corporate citizenship developed in comparison with the Aristotelian idea of individual citizenship. *Business and Society.* doi:10.1177/0007650313483484.
Popper, K.R. 1966. The autonomy of sociology. In *The open society and its enemies. Vol. 2: Hegel and Marx*, 89–99. New York: Harper (Original work published 1945).
Popper, K.R. 1972. *Objective knowledge: An evolutionary approach.* Oxford, UK: Clarendon Press.
Ricoeur, P. 2000. The concept of responsibility—An essay in semantic analysis. In *The just* (trans: by David Pellauer), 11–35. Chicago, IL: University of Chicago Press (Original work published 1992).
Risse, T. 2000. "Let's argue!": Communicative action in world politics. *International Organization* 54(1): 1–39.
Risse, T. 2004. Global governance and communicative action. *Government and Opposition* 39(2): 288–313.
Schelling, T.C. 1980. *The strategy of conflict.* Cambridge, MA and London, UK: Harvard University Press (Original work published 1960).
Schelling, T.C. 2006. *Strategies of commitment and other essays.* Cambridge, MA, London, UK: Harvard University Press.
Scherer, A.G., and G. Palazzo. 2007. Toward a political conception of corporate responsibility: Business and society seen from a Habermasian perspective. *Academy of Management Review* 32: 1096–1120.
Scherer, A.G., and G. Palazzo. 2011. The new political role of business in a globalized world: A review of a new perspective on CSR and its implications for the firm, governance, and democracy. *Journal of Management Studies* 48: 899–931.
Scherer, A.G., G. Palazzo, and D. Baumann. 2006. Global rules and private actors: Toward a new role of the transnational corporation in global governance. *Business Ethics Quarterly* 16: 505–532.
Scherer, A.G., G. Palazzo, and D. Matten. 2009. Introduction to the special issue: Globalization as a challenge for business responsibilities. *Business Ethics Quarterly* 19: 327–347.

Schumpeter, J.A. 2000. *Capitalism, socialism, and democracy*. Introduction by R. Swedberg, London, UK: Routledge (Original work published 1942).

Shell, G.R. 2004. *Make the rules or your rivals will*. New York: Crown Business.

Shleifer, A., and R.W. Vishny. 1999. *The grabbing hand. Government pathologies and their cures*. Cambridge, MA: Harvard University Press.

Simon, H.A. 1955. A behavioral model of rational choice. *Quarterly Journal of Economics* 69(1): 99–118.

Smith, A. (1976). *An inquiry into the nature and causes of the wealth of nations*, eds. by R.H. Campell and A.S. Skinner. London, UK: Oxford University Press (Original work published 1776).

Smith, A. 1983. Nationalism and social theory. *British Journal of Sociology* 34: 19–38.

Spruit, J.E. (ed.). 2001. *Corpus Iuris Civilis, VI, Digesten 43-50 [Body of civil law, collection]*. Zutphen, The Netherlands: Walburg Pers.

Stigler, G.J., and G.S. Becker. 1977. De gustibus non est disputandum. *American Economic Review* 67(2): 76–90.

Sundaram, A.K., and A.C. Inkpen. 2004. The corporate objective revisited. *Organization Science* 15: 350–363.

Tullock, G. 1989. *The economics of special privilege and rent-seeking*. Boston, MA: Kluwer Academic.

Williamson, O.E. 1985. *The economic institutions of capitalism*. New York: Free Press.

Williamson, O.E. 2009. Transaction cost economics: The natural progression. http://nobelprize.org/nobel_prizes/economics/laureates/2009/williamson_lecture.pdf. Accessed 10 April 2013.

Wintrobe, R. 1998. *The political economy of dictatorship*. New York: Cambridge University Press.

Wolf, K.D. 2008. Emerging patters of global governance: The new interplay between the state, business and civil society. In *Handbook of research on global corporate citizenship*, eds. A.G. Scherer and G. Palazzo, 225–248. Cheltenham, UK: Edward Elgar.

Companies as Political Actors: A Positioning Between Ordo-Responsibility and Systems Responsibility

Ludger Heidbrink

The political role of private companies has changed greatly in recent decades. In the course of globalization, companies are increasingly expected to perform functions and services that until now have been the territory of nation states. Not only multinational corporations, but also medium-sized companies are seeing themselves confronted with responsibilities that only a short while ago still fell within the realm of state-provided public services and welfare policies.

This article is concerned with the question of what consequences the shifting distribution of responsibilities between the state and the private sector has for the political role of companies. The increase in assignments of political functions to companies and the acceptance of these functions not only requires that companies have the status of responsible actors and the capacity to perform public services. Shifts in the public-private structure of responsibilities also raise questions about the legitimacy and scope of companies' fulfilment of political duties.

With this in mind, I will examine in the following, first, the causes of this development, and then the systematic and pragmatic consequences that are essential for an adequate understanding of the political responsibility of companies in globalized marketplaces. My thesis is that companies bear not only *within-game responsibility* for the consequences of their business operations and *ordo-responsibility* for the co-determination and implementation of framework rules, but also a specific *systems responsibility* for maintaining the operating conditions of the social system that makes their operational activities possible. By taking a critical look at order ethics, I will show that the systemic responsibility of companies cannot be sufficiently justified with ordo-economic arguments, since these arguments rely on an incomplete understanding of morals and politics that does not do justice to the

---

L. Heidbrink (✉)
Lehrstuhl für Praktische Philosophie, Christian-Albrechts-Universität zu Kiel, Kiel, Germany
e-mail: heidbrink@philsem.uni-kiel.de

risks of discourse and regulatory failure in volatile and borderless markets. My conclusion is that it is in the long-term interest of companies to assume political co-responsibility, not only for economic benefits, but also to avoid social crises.

1 On the Changing Social and Political Role of Companies

The majority of companies are private organizations with the purpose of achieving a profit to fulfill the interests of legitimate stakeholders within the framework of existing basic systems. As legal entities, they are subject to state laws and regulations, by which they are afforded enforceable duties and rights that vary in scope according to country and culture. Whereas, in the USA, firms and corporations have a status as "legal persons" similar to that of citizens that permits civil and criminal sanctions,[1] companies in Europe, particularly in Germany, are not subject to criminal liability, which involves joint sanctions.[2] Depending on the legal culture and national constitution, companies represent "legal fictions," the purpose of which is value creation based on division of labor with cooperative resources within an existing social structure.[3]

The result is that there are fundamental difficulties in assigning responsibility to private companies within the social context. As a legal construction with its own rights, the company views itself as similar to natural persons in that it is confronted with the problem of being an actor in the market and in politics at the same time. As market actors, firms pursue the goal of increasing profits in the interest of their investors, while they are subject as political actors to the imperative to act in the public interest. As an organization embedded in both markets and in politics, the modern company must deal with what Kenneth Goodpaster has called the "stakeholder paradox"—namely, to fulfill societal norms and demands without thereby violating fiduciary duties.[4]

This challenge is exacerbated by the changing nature of the nation state with respect to hierarchical administration of public-sector processes. Changes in state activity due to global events related to the dissolution of borders and transnationalization do not constitute a clear development that can be reduced to a single phrase such as "demystification of the state" or "governance without government."[5] Rather, if one looks at environmental, social, and, most recently, financial market policies, state activity has in fact increased in quantity. The actual changes are primarily in the instruments and procedures of state management, which are no longer based on top-down strategies and command-and-control mechanisms, but

---

[1]Cf. Matys (2011), p. 42 et seq.
[2]Cf. Maurach and Zipf (1992), p. 187 et seq. See also Heine (1995), p. 201 et seq.
[3]Cf. Wieland (2009), p. 262 et seq.
[4]Goodpaster (1991), p. 63.
[5]Cf. Willke (1983); Rosenau and Czempiel (1992).

rather on principles of regulated self-regulation and of promotion of cooperative arrangements, as manifested in public-private partnerships, for example, or in the involvement of companies in standardization procedures.[6]

With the transition to heterarchical and contextual forms of governance, non-state actors have gained in importance, exercising politically significant influence on collective public processes in the form of transnational organizations and private companies. The politicization of firms and corporations is therefore less an expression of the abdication of the nation state than of a serious change of governance procedures, which present the democratic interventionist state in its classic form with a number of new challenges, for the overcoming of which it depends on the active involvement of companies.[7]

Of these new democratic policy challenges, which are situated at the intersection of state-provided public services and private-sector participation, three substantial areas of activities in particular can be pinpointed, following Michael Zürn and Helmut Weidner[8]: First, there is the unhindered flow of transactions in the markets, which is achieved by, e.g., eliminating trade barriers, stipulating tariffs and duties, designing trade agreements and determining competition rules. Second, negative consequences of markets that can appear in the form of self-endangering externalizations must be isolated. These include environmental policy measures of resource conservation and energy efficiency, but also financial policy instruments of bank supervision and capital guarantees, which serve to stabilize markets. The third point is the correction of socially undesirable market results, which can be carried out in the form of distributional policy interventions and include, among other things, the stipulation of minimum wages, welfare and unemployment assistance or tax increases to finance education and development measures.

In the creation, stabilization, and correction of market results, the nation state runs up against limits to its governance not only due to its limited reach, but also due to a global policy competition, which tends to lead to a spiral of deregulation, the risk of *levelling down* social and environmental standards and the weakening of national competitiveness.[9] Faced with these partially structural, partially homemade problems, the democratic intervention state has a number of possible countermeasures at its disposal. It can rely on market-based control mechanisms in order to keep a handle on undesirable and harmful effects of markets. This domain includes economic and legal mechanisms for increasing the prices of using public goods, toughening bans on pollution, or trade in emission certificates. Another tool is information and labeling strategies that lead to greater transparency and comparability of goods or consumer education and stakeholder communication. A similar path is found in the commitment to basic social and ecological standards, such as

---

[6]Cf. Schuppert (2007), p. 475 et seq.
[7]Cf. Mayntz (2007); Becker et al. (2007), p. 83 et seq.; Wolf (2005), p. 54 et seq.
[8]Cf. Zürn/Weidner (2009), p. 158 et seq.
[9]For a different perspective on the globalization-caused race-to-the-bottom diagnosis, cf. Noll (2010), p. 312 et seq.

ISO 26000, which refers to the social responsibility of organizations, or in public oversight of corporate behavior, as it is practiced through the EU strategy regarding corporate social responsibly and national CSR programs.[10]

In addition, more and more companies, societal actors and state institutions are banding together to form transnational public-private partnerships or multi-stakeholder initiatives, which, e.g., in the form of the Global Compact, the UN Guiding Principles on Business and Human Rights or the Global Business Initiative on Human Rights, produce public goods and perform political regulatory services of which the nation state is no longer capable on its own.[11]

This development toward "politicization without a state"[12] has fundamentally changed the societal and political role of companies. Particularly global corporations and market-listed transnational companies are finding themselves at the beginning of the 21st century again in a situation in which they, "willingly or not, become politically engaged."[13] Discussions of rules of global governance, corporate governance and public-private governance are evidence of a changing division of responsibilities between the public and private sectors, in which firms and corporations assume a new position between market-based and policy-strategy forms of governance, which they have to deal with whether they like it or not.[14]

Catchphrases such as the "politicization of the economy" and the "economization of politics" therefore paint an imprecise picture of this new type of situation, in which private companies are on the one hand assigned social duties and achievement of political goals from the outside, but on the other hand are actively taken over by them. The central challenge confronting companies, in view of the changing governance competencies of the democratic interventionist state, consists primarily in pursuing double value creation, in which market-driven and political purposes are connected with each other. This double value creation raises questions about the competence, legitimacy, and capabilities of the political company, which must be deduced from an adequate heuristics of corporate responsibility.

2 The Responsibility of Companies: A Heuristic Structuring Proposal

An adequate heuristics of corporate responsibility focuses on the special actor status and the particular organizational forms of companies. Private companies can be described from two basic perspectives, namely, methodological individualism and

---

[10]Cf. Schmidpeter and Palz (2008); Habisch and Brychuk (2011); Schmiedeknecht and Wieland (2012).
[11]Cf. Lukas (2007); Crane et al. (2008); Wettstein (2009).
[12]Zürn and Weidner (2009), p. 179.
[13]Scherer et al. (2006), p. 507.
[14]See, among others, the articles by Fuchs and Nölke in Schirm (2004).

methodological collectivism.[15] From the standpoint of methodological individualism, companies form higher-level acting units, whose operations result from the sum of individual actions and which, as corporate actors, do not bear an independent collective responsibility, but rather a derivative individual responsibility. The basis of the attribution of responsibility is the rational individual, who pursues goals related to his own interests in cooperation with other actors and within the company organization. In contrast, from the standpoint of methodological collectivism, companies represent corporate acting units that operate autonomously and bear independent collective responsibility, which cannot be attributed causally to individual actions. The basis of the attribution of responsibility is a collective intentionality of the company organization, which seeks to execute company objectives independent of individual decisions.[16]

Whereas methodological individualism views the company organization as a corporate actor to which responsibility can be ascribed only on the basis of and by analogy to natural persons, methodological collectivism views companies as autonomous social units that can bear responsibility without recourse to natural persons. This differentiation is not only of academic interest, but rather has immediate effects on the competence of companies for their operational consequences and their role as independent social and political actors. A heuristics of corporate responsibility that assumes that individuals are the ultimate bearers of responsibility in corporations has the advantage of being able to attribute the operation of companies to personal actors and to control it via individual incentives and the formation of preferences. However, the disadvantage of individualistic corporate responsibility is that responsibility deficits are not sufficiently appreciated on the organizational level and responsibility gaps in the company structure and governance are not adequately taken into account. In contrast, a collective heuristics of corporate responsibility has the advantage that a company can be understood as an independent unit of responsibility and can be directed through collective regulations and control mechanisms. The disadvantage is that responsibility deficits are not sufficiently understood on the level of individuals, the attribution of responsibilities to organizations has a significantly greater number of preconditions, and regulatory control of collective units is far more difficult.[17]

One sensible approach is to link the individualist and the collectivist perspectives with each other in order to achieve a heuristics of corporate responsibility based in reality, since private organizations must be described as a de facto combination of individual and collective acting elements. In addition, an action-theory view of companies must be expanded through a system-theory perspective which ensures

---

[15]Cf. historically Schumpeter (1970/1908), p. 88 et seq.; Hayek (1952), p. 15 et seq.; as well as Udehn (2001).
[16]Cf. Neuhäuser (2011), p. 133 et seq.
[17]Cf. Coleman (1985), p. 89 et seq.

that the internal operational and normative logic of companies is adequately considered within differentiated social subsystems.[18]

To cite Peter French and Patricia Werhane, companies can be described as "secondary moral actors,"[19] whose responsibility status results from the rights and duties of individual actors and can be attributed to them by analogy. The position of analogous responsibility between individuals and corporations has also been advanced by Kenneth Goodpaster, who derives the "responsible corporation" from the fundamental transferability of moral principles ("moral projection") from persons to companies.[20] Accordingly, corporations are subject to structurally equal normative obligations like individual actors. The prerequisite for this is that companies have internal decision-making structures that enable them to make sound decisions about actions, similar to persons. According to French, a "corporation's internal decision structure" (CID structure) such as this, which is based on the regulation of power relations and recognition conditions, is a central condition for treating companies as full-fledged responsible actors.[21]

Under these preconditions, companies can be viewed as high-level acting units that have not only legal, but also moral rights and duties, for the fulfilment of which they are responsible *sui generis*. It is essential for the attribution of responsibility that companies are characterized by structural homogeneity, which enables them to develop and execute intentional action processes. To what extent personal actors bear co-responsibility in these processes depends on the internal corporate organizational structures as well as on formal and informal rules of distributing responsibilities, which rely among other things on responsibility for tasks and fields, internal hierarchies and authority to issue instructions, areas of competence and power relations.[22]

Describing companies as secondary moral actors permits a connection of individualistic and collectivist action elements. Nonetheless, in this view corporations have only an analogous and derivative responsibility for their operations, which is derived from the interaction of primary single actions of individual actors in the corporation. The interplay of individual actions *in* the corporation depends on formal and informal rules as well as individual intentions of actions, which do not apply in the same way *for* the entire corporate organization. On the level of the corporation, the development of intentions and the normative regulation of behavior follow a different governance and attribution logic than on the level of individual actions.[23] It is precisely in the tradition of the *legal person* and the German *juristische Person*, where private companies are made morally and legally responsible, that accountability in the literal sense remains linked to the personal

---

[18]Cf. Heidbrink (2010a), p. 193 et seq.
[19]Werhane (1992), p. 330.
[20]Goodpaster (1983), p. 14 et seq.
[21]Cf. French (1992), p. 322 et seq.
[22]Cf. Lenk and Maring (1995), p. 276 et seq.
[23]On the debate surrounding collective intentionality, see Schmid and Schweikard (2009).

status. Even if a collectivist expansion of the individualistic organizational structure takes place and companies are treated as persons in their own right, the individualistic concept of action still represents the main benchmark of the evaluation, so to speak of corporate responsibility only makes sense if it can be identified with individual responsibility.[24]

Thus, in order to avoid the mistake of reductionism and, in the final analysis, to identify collective processes again with individual actions, a modified heuristics of corporate responsibility is required. The fact that corporations are characterized by their own operational and normative logic necessitates a systemic expansion of the model of corporate responsibility based on personalistic criteria. Drawing upon system theory, corporations can be described as autonomous acting units within the social subsystem of the economy,[25] which are characterized by specific forms of responsibility with respect to the environment of this subsystem. The necessity of a distinct concept of *systems responsibility* is a result of the fact that companies, as independent acting units within the economic system, are subject to the specific logic of complex social processes, "which may be contingent on actions and/or decisions (cultural processes), but which cannot be reasonably conceived as anyone's action (subjectless processes)."[26]

The object of systems responsibility are system processes, which result from action processes but which cannot be reduced to these, since they—in Hayek's words—cannot be ascribed to a "conscious plan," but instead are "the unforeseen result of the actions of individuals."[27] Systems responsibility therefore represents not only an expansion of actor-centric responsibility theories, but rather incorporates the unique dynamics and self-reproduction (autopoiesis) of social system processes, which are based on non-linear implementations of the emergent self-organization and the occurrence of unintended system consequences.[28]

Unlike actor-centric models of responsibility, systems responsibility is focused not only on responsibility *in* systems, but also on the responsibility *of* systems. Systems responsibility encompasses three main functions[29]: These are, first, the incorporation of *uncertainty processes* that result from the unique dynamics of systems and consist in system-typical factors of non-transparency (missing information), uncertainty (lack of planning and monitoring) and unintended risk consequences (social and ecological damage).[30] A second characteristic is the consideration of a specific *design responsibility*, which is directed towards the designing of organizational structures (employee and management processes),

---

[24]Cf. Seebaß (2001), p. 90.
[25]See Luhmann (1994). On the action status of systems, cf. Willke (2000), p. 167 et seq.
[26]Lübbe (1998), p. 15.
[27]Hayek (1952), p. 17.
[28]Cf. Bühl (1998), p. 92 et seq.
[29]Cf. for more detail on the following Heidbrink (2003), p. 244 et seq.; Heidbrink (2007), p. 46 et seq.
[30]Cf. Heidbrink (2010b), p. 4 et seq.

promotion of the company culture (e.g., through value management) and institutionalization of standards of conduct (such as through codes and mission statements), which contribute to the commitment of corporations to principles of responsive company organizations.[31] Third, systems responsibility relies on procedures of *context management*, which ensures through political and legal mechanisms of "regulation of self-regulating processes"[32] that companies comply with constitutional, social welfare and environmental goals in the public interest and are involved in providing public services for cooperative interests.[33] The mechanism of context management does not allow for direct intervention into market-based processes and companies, nor does it place incentives for corporate action through framework rules; rather, through "structural couplings" and the "interpenetration" of political and economic systems, companies are encouraged to develop and implement their own methods of socially compatible self-governance (e.g., environmental and social management programs).[34]

The system heuristics suggested here allows action and system processes to be connected with each other and for companies to be understood as *autonomous action systems* whose collective purposes do not have to be traced back to individual intentions, but certainly to personal actions.[35] Systems responsibility aims for the development of action systems with the autonomous willingness and ability to take on responsibility by connecting institutional governance of corporations with business practices of voluntary commitment.

3 From Ordo-Responsibility to Systems Responsibility

The systemic expansion of secondary corporate responsibility has the advantage that companies can also be addressed as organizations capable of morals if they are involved in transnational political processes and are exposed to disparate societal demands. As a heuristic approach, systems responsibility ensures that the heterogeneous forms of obligation resulting from the changing form of the nation state and the integration of companies into global multi-stakeholder networks can be taken into account with greater precision.

As described in the introduction, due to changes in state governance between corporations, NGOs, civil society actors and political institutions, overlapping responsibility sectors have evolved that require new procedures for sharing and

---

[31]Cf. Bühl (1998), p. 30 et seq.; Ortmann (2010), p. 253 et seq.; Küpers (2008), p. 319 et seq.
[32]Hoffmann-Riem (2001), p. 28; cf. also Hoffmann-Riem, (2000), p. 56 et seq.; Willke (1997), p. 72 et seq.
[33]Cf. Di Fabio (1999), p. 93 et seq.
[34]Cf. Münch (1996), p. 45 et seq.
[35]Cf. also Maring (2001), p. 318 et seq.

distributing responsibility.[36] Against this backdrop, the concept of a secondary actor that underlies collectivist approaches of corporate social responsibility runs up against systematic and pragmatic limits. The reason is that it is based on premises which, due to the transnational location of companies, are no longer fulfilled, because it presupposes "that we can hold institutions such as corporations responsible, morally and socially responsible, just as we hold individual people morally and socially responsible." And it assumes that "even if we can make a case for institutional responsibility (…) we then have to address the extent of that accountability."[37]

The concept of secondary corporate responsibility reaches its limits where "corporations are mezzosystems embedded in larger political, economic, legal, and cultural systems." The multidimensional embedding of corporations necessitates a "systems approach,"[38] which helps determine the functional and normative interconnectedness of companies with their social environment and define the resulting responsibilities. Against the backdrop of growing moral and political demands on companies articulated by governments and civil society, the advantage of the system approach is that it "takes into account what each party brings to the table, in terms of both claims and capabilities, and holds each to some measure of accountability."[39]

In the following I wish to explain the necessity of the systemic expansion of corporate responsibility against the backdrop of the concept of ordo-responsibility, as it has been developed from the standpoint of order ethics.[40]

3.1 The Concept of Ordo-Responsibility

The order ethics conception of corporate responsibility is based on an economic theory of morals, according to which individual or collective actors pursue moral goals for purposive-rational reasons in order to realize mutual benefits. The motive of self-interest as the foundation of moral action is not thereby attributed to individual dispositions, but is instead derived from socially observable behavior patterns. "The decisive criterion determining whether or to what extent self-interested behavior can be qualified as moral is found not within, but outside of the individual. Accordingly, the attribution of morals depends not on what an actor thinks, but rather how it behaves toward others in the social sphere. Thus, from an economic standpoint the decisive factor is the—empirically observable—differentiation

---

[36]For further on this, see Heidbrink (2007), p. 97 et seq.

[37]Werhane (2007), p. 461.

[38]Werhane (2007), p. 465. On the "systems approach" in an expanded evolutionary sense, cf. Laszlo and Knipper (1998), p. 54.

[39]Werhane (2007), p. 472.

[40]On the ordonomic approach, cf. Pies (2009), p. 2 et seq.

between a one-sided betterment at others' expense and a mutual betterment through the realization of common benefits."[41]

Corporate actors thus act morally when they resolve dilemmas through voluntary commitment in order to achieve mutual improvement.[42] On the basis of an expanded understanding of the *homo oeconomicus*, the purpose of morals is to realize individual benefits through collective cooperation. This benefit-oriented understanding of morals not only claims for itself the empirical merit of the observability of moral actions, but also the pragmatic merit of incentive compatibility, since actors can be induced through stimuli and sanctions to follow others' goals for their own interests.[43]

From an ordonomic perspective, companies in particular have the ability to do this, because as corporate actors they have a specific capacity for self-regulation which is superior in many respects to natural persons: "The superior capacity for self-regulation of corporate actors, and consequently their superior capacity for responsibility, is the result of two factors that reciprocally support and strengthen each other: First, corporate actors, in contrast to natural persons, have a fundamentally limitless time horizon. This makes it possible for them to make long-term investments that would not be worthwhile for individuals. Second, the 'character' of a corporate actor is constituted by an organizational structure that includes formal and informal rules. (...) Because of this, the 'character' of a corporate actor can be more easily programmed (...) than the character of a natural person. Corporate actors are more reliable, more predictable interaction partners. (...) Consequently, they are exceptionally qualified not only to passively ascribe responsibility to themselves, but also—by way of individual self-regulation—to actively assume responsibility."[44]

From an ordonomic standpoint, corporate competence for self-regulation is an essential reason that companies are not only capable, but also willing to resolve the "trade off"[45] between morals and self-interest which characterizes competitive market economies under conditions of action processes that follow the logic of interactions and the priority of a responsibility principle based on individual ethics. Whereas, under the guidance of individual ethics, there may be either a cynical disregard or moralistic transformation of responsibility resulting from a continued "discrepancy between social structure and semantics,"[46] i.e., the opposition of real social organization and ideal description, an expansion of the responsibility principle based on the logic of interactions and cooperation ethics ensures that facticity and normativity, social reality and moral reflection can be brought into accord. Guided by cooperation ethics, corporate actors follow a long-term win-win

---

[41] Pies (2001), p. 185.
[42] Cf. Vanberg (2000), p. 586 et seq.
[43] On the incentive structure, see Suchanek (2001), p. 31 et seq.
[44] Pies (2001), p. 187.
[45] Pies and Beckmann (2008), p. 35.
[46] Pies and Beckmann (2008), p. 32.

heuristics, according to which it may be wise to accept current disadvantages in favor of future advantages and to cooperate with competitors on a moral basis in order to achieve mutual returns.[47]

From the standpoint of order ethics, responsibility represents an investment in future action conditions for mutual benefit,[48] which requires an incentive-compatible design of rules of the game based on the logic of interactions, so that neither the effects of excessive demand nor those of exploitation arise among the cooperation actors. Designing rules of the game according to the logic of interactions follows consequently from the interests of corporate actors in mutually beneficial cooperation conditions, which are achieved by "changing the perspective from a responsibility *in* the game to a responsibility *for* the game."[49] In contrast to *within-game responsibility* for individual moves, the required *ordo-responsibility* based on cooperation goals according to the logic of interactions is aimed at changes in the rules of the game themselves, which must be implemented together with win-win ethical incentives and through monitoring of the results recognized under consistency requirements.[50]

Changes to the rules of the game occur at a higher level of play in the form of involvement of corporate actors in the collective design of rules. For this, companies assume *governance responsibility* for the framework under which they act in markets and in social contexts: "Governance responsibility designates the assumption of ordo-responsibility in the meta-game."[51] "This concerns the design of social structures through institutional reforms—from organizational codes of conduct to industry standards for companies to legislative initiatives and international agreements."[52]

Because joint rule-setting and individual compliance with the rules already assumes the participants' collective willingness to commitment—since otherwise, due to existing dilemma structures, there is no guarantee of an advantage for all—governance responsibility must be expanded through *discourse responsibility* for the determination of mutually valid framework rules. The purpose of discourse responsibility is to overcome existing dilemma structures through "discourse of common interests." It aims for the "shared knowledge of this interest" on the level of a "meta-meta game" and ensures the willingness of the participating parties to cooperate through procedures of discursive rule-finding, the result of which is the dismantling of information restrictions.[53]

Ordo-responsibility thus encompasses not only the design of the social structure through collective rule-setting (governance responsibility), but also processes of discursive rule-finding (discourse responsibility). Its heuristic goal consists in

---

[47]Cf. Homann and Blome-Drees (1992), p. 35 et seq.
[48]Cf. Suchanek and Lin-Hi (2008), p. 90 et seq.; Lin-Hi (2009), p. 73 et seq.
[49]Cf. Pies and Beckmann (2008), p. 44 et seq.
[50]See also Homann (2004), p. 3 et seq.; Beckmann (2010).
[51]Pies and Beckmann (2008), p. 48.
[52]Pies (2009), p. 296.
[53]Cf. Pies and Beckmann (2008), p. 49 et seq.

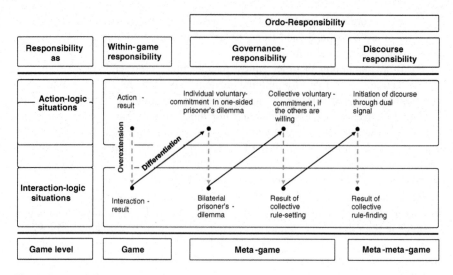

Fig. 1 Responsibility scheme based on win-win ethics. *Source* Pies, Beckmann (2008), p. 52

connecting the action logic responsibility for consequences of actions with the interaction logic responsibility for framework rules in such a way that both the individual monitoring of results and causal attributability of company operations are maintained and the co-design of mutually advantageous cooperation conditions grounded in incentive ethics is guaranteed (cf. Fig. 1).

On the sociopolitical level, the question is thus how individual calculations of advantage can be influenced such that they lead to desirable (advantageous) results for all of society. Three types of costs must be considered: "problem costs," which arise on the level of moves within the game and determine, as individually perceived disadvantages, the subjective need for rules and thus the advantage of ordo-responsibility; "commitment costs," which appear on the level of the rules of the game and are seen as disadvantages of collective rule-setting and/or assumed governance responsibility; "discourse costs," which occur on the level of reflection of the game and are felt as disadvantages of joint rule-finding and/or assumed discourse responsibility.[54] All three forms of costs delimit in their respective amounts the individual capacity for responsibility, since, from the point of view of order ethics, actors make their willingness to assume responsibility conditional on what benefits they draw from this. As a consequence, costs must be structured such that the advantages of assuming responsibility outweigh the disadvantages of exercising responsibility. This occurs on the level of moves within the game through the transformation of societal costs of social injustices into individual problem costs, which ensure, e.g., in the form of personal liability, that actors assume ordo-responsibility. On the level of the rules of the game, contractual agreements and voluntary

---

[54]Cf. Pies and Beckmann (2008), p. 54 et seq.

commitments provide support to actors involved in collective implementation of governance responsibility. On the level of game reflection, numerous mechanisms of deliberation and participation are available, e.g., in the form of stakeholder dialogues, operational co-determination or participation in social networks, that facilitate the joint exercise of discourse responsibility.

The implementation of ordo-responsibility thus proves to be a "decidedly sociopolitical (design) duty," in which the issue is to "systematically" identify "starting points for socially strengthening the individual capacity for responsibility of natural and corporate actors."[55] This strengthening takes place via institutional incentive arrangements, which ensure that actors better their own positions through mutually advantageous interactions and perpetuate the cooperation structures required for this. The key to this lies in actors' capacity for voluntary commitment and their capacity for discourse, by which they are able to help shape their spaces for action such that cooperative advantages thereby accrue to them. From the perspective of order ethics, for this conception of ordo-responsibility "a systematic difference between the responsibility of natural persons and the responsibility of corporate actors" is no longer necessary, since both can "wisely pursue their own self-interest and thus assume responsibility through voluntary commitment and participation in discourse."[56] Instead, compared to natural persons, companies have a significantly greater capacity for responsibility, since they are exposed to greater problem costs (which motivate them to change the rules), possess more effective commitment technologies, organize more professional discourse procedures, and, as already mentioned, can make long-term investments.

Due to these particular competencies for commitment and discourse, companies therefore also bear a specific co-responsibility in the transnational context for processes of rule-setting and rule-finding, which can no longer be accomplished by the nation state alone. Participation in tasks of global governance results from the self-interest of companies to assume active ordo-responsibility for the institutional governance of regulatory frameworks and the discursive clarification of regulatory knowledge in the face of dwindling state regulatory competencies, in order to achieve better conditions for economic actors: "In the face of poor regulatory frameworks, companies need to adopt a political role in new governance in order to better fulfill their role as economic actors. By participating in processes of new governance, business firms, as corporate citizens, conduct themselves in the political sphere just the same as they do in their day-to-day business: they engage in individual and collective commitments that improve the rules of the economic game. In a nutshell, the ordonomic understanding is that *the role of corporate citizens in processes of new governance is just win-win oriented value creation writ large.*"[57]

From the point of view of order ethics, companies are thus to be viewed as corporate citizens, which, for reasons of competitive advantage, commit themselves

---

[55]Pies and Beckmann (2008), p. 56.
[56]Pies and Beckmann (2008), p. 58 et seq.
[57]Pies et al. (2011), p. 184.

to socially expected codes of behavior and participate in tasks connected with the provision of public services. The concept of ordo-responsibility represents a model of the political corporate citizen based on incentive ethics and win-win heuristics, which assumes state governance tasks out of well-understood calculations of advantages by participating in collective procedures of rule-setting and rule-finding. In this way, motivational reasons can be cited for why companies become involved as private-sector actors in public functions and assume political responsibility without being subject to regulatory interference and normative demands from the democratic interventionist state and civil society stakeholders. The achievement of the *ordonomic approach* consists in being able to derive political corporate responsibility from the perspective of enlightened market actors that support the improvement of general market-policy conditions under actual competitive conditions and existing economic restrictions. Moreover, ordo-responsibility helps restrict corporate responsibility to the moral and political consequences of actions of corporate actors and thus guards against an expansion of the responsibility principle, which is reflected in a contradiction between the semantic demand and the socio-structural implementation. Subject to the requirement of consistent monitoring of success and institutional possibilities for influence, companies can be assigned governance and discourse responsibilities that result from their particular capabilities for self-commitment and discourse development. And not least, the cooperation ethics direction of ordo-responsibility generates a connection of market and political value creation that increases the chances for companies to realize social goals without violating fiduciary duties (cf. Fig. 2).

3.2 Limits of Ordo-Responsibility

In spite of these heuristic advantages, the order ethics approach comes up against a number of limits that necessitate an expansion through the concept of systems responsibility. Thus the principle of ordo-responsibility (1.) is still based on an *individualistic paradigm of corporate behavior*, which is reformulated collectivistically but is maintained in its methodological features. Adhering to methodological individualism is understandable for reasons of accountability and controllability of consequences of actions, but it ignores the unique dynamics and unintended consequences of corporate operations under functional system conditions and against the backdrop of network processes.[58] The same applies to neglect of the difference between natural persons and corporate actors, who, from an order ethics point of view, are treated similarly to persons as actor formations governable through incentive arrangements. This analogization does not sufficiently take into account the structurally independent character of organizations, which do not constitute higher-level collectives, but rather autonomous action systems that do not form any

---

[58] As a fundamental text, cf. Teubner (2009).

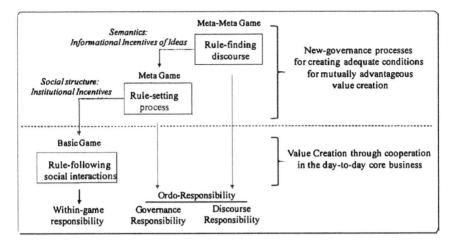

Fig. 2 The ordonomic perspective on the new governance. *Source* Pies et al. (2011), p. 181

direct moral or political intentions and therefore can be induced to assume responsibility only to a limited extent through win-win ethical calculations of advantages and self-regulatory commitment technologies.[59]

While the concept of ordo-responsibility overestimates the controllability of corporations through incentive ethics, at the same time it underestimates (2.) the *intrinsic significance of morals* for personal actors. Even if order ethics assumes an expanded understanding of the *homo oeconomicus* and the rational choice paradigm, which includes all objectives that actors subjectively wish to pursue,[60] the instrumentalist perspective of objective optimization and the economistic method of utility maximization remain unchanged. The *economic theory of morals* is based on a reductionist heuristics of moral reasons, which are identified with rational motives.[61] Under the primacy of calculation of advantages, morally preferable goals are pursued because they have rationally advantageous consequences. Whoever attributes the actions of persons to the overcoming of dilemma situations and the improvement of individual conditions confuses rational theory arguments with moral theory ones. The rationality conditions of creating mutually better solutions still do not guarantee any morality conditions of an equal and just distribution of cooperation benefits and burdens. Between the rationality discourse of advantage orientation and the morality discourse of production of equality, there are also categorial differences that cannot be overcome with enlightened economic moral justifications.[62]

In addition, the rational choice paradigm (3.) is based on an *empirically incomplete understanding of fairness*, which attributes ethical actions to

---

[59]On the example of criminal prevention measures, cf. Kyora (2001), 194 et seq.
[60]According to Pies (2009), p. 290.
[61]See also Chwaszsca (2003).
[62]Cf. Kersting (2008), p. 136 et seq.

Ordo-Responsibility	Systems Responsibility
- Individualistic paradigm of corporate actions	- Systemic paradigm of corporate actions
- Economic normativity	- Ethical normativity
- Theoretical moral understanding	- Empirical moral understanding
- Discursive cognitivism	- Situational realism
- Rational decision behavior	- Distorted decision behavior
- Discourse responsibility	- Design responsibility
- Rule management	- Context management
- Legitimation through cooperation interests	- Legitimation through public-welfare interests
- Externalization of market, rule, discourse limits	- Internalization of market, rule, discourse limits
- Elimination of competitive disadvantages	- Reduction of social risks
- Market-based value creation	- Societal value creation
- Cost orientation	- Damage orientation
- Regulating state	- Designing state
- Economic governance	- Political governance
- Responsibility as investment	- Responsibility as transformation

Fig. 3 Own source

interest-driven actions and reduces moral decisions to win-win reflections. From the perspective of the *homo oeconomicus*, it is not only unclear why actors pursue moral goals in day-to-day life without having a direct interest in them, and behave fairly even if there are no immediate benefits for them.[63] It is also unclear how, conversely, on the basis of enlightened self-interest, cooperation-relevant attitudes of reliability and trust are supposed to form and how, through the strategic pursuit of preferences, stable institutions can emerge that have a collectively binding force.[64] Where the assumption of ordo-responsibility is attributed primarily to corporate self-interest, an normative ideal type is made either from the methodological construct of the *homo oeconomicus*—which, in this form, does not exist empirically[65]—or ordo-responsibility is derived from a strategic interest in morals, which do not serve as the foundation for stable social interactions or institutions in the long run (Fig. 3).

---

[63] For more on the self-interest approach, see Ockenfels and Raub (2010).
[64] See Hartmann (2011).
[65] See already Schmölders (1973), p. 32 et seq.

Moral instrumentalism corresponds to (4.) a *discursive cognitivism*, which attributes the capacity of corporate actors for self-commitment to their capacity for discourse. It also makes a categorial difference whether mutual interests and the resulting behavioral norms are found and grounded in discourse ethics procedures and to what extent they are followed and implemented by the discourse participants.[66] The order ethics attribution of cooperative rule-setting to discursive rule-finding presupposes a willingness to cooperate that cannot be derived from clarification about shared knowledge and explicit information. Whoever deduces behavioral rules from knowledge of norms commits a cognitivist fallacy, since the explanandum of cooperative behavior is not in the knowledge of rules, but in the following of them. Furthermore, the transition from rule-finding to rule-setting to rule-following in a company's day-to-day life takes place not in a process of logical deduction on different levels of the game, in which actors agree to cooperative actions out of cognitive insight into the validity of norms, but rather is de facto subject to complex decision-making and implementation processes in which, in the end, not objective reasons, but situational demands are the deciding factor in most cases. From an ordonomic perspective, not only the *mind behavior gap* between consciousness and behavior is underestimated—according to which actors do not always do what they know[67]—but at the same time the discursively established competence of corporations for self-commitment is overestimated—which, under competitive conditions, resolve dilemma structures less through the assumption of governance and discourse responsibility than through decisionistic market choices.[68]

Therefore (5.) the *legitimation of political corporate responsibility* cannot be justified solely with recourse to adherence to market principles and competitive conditions.[69] Discursively-established acceptance of rules of the game that are advantageous from a cooperation ethics perspective is something different from the democratic justification of a liberal and human rights-oriented societal constitution. Interest in economically preferable rule-setting does not constitute a legitimation of political regulations. There is no direct path from ordo-responsibility motivated by win-win ethics to corporate responsibility grounded in democracy, since for this the corporate pursuit of interests and the political status of companies as corporate citizens themselves would have to be subjected to a democratic procedure of justification.[70] It is not sufficient to derive companies' competence for public functions from their competence for self-commitment and capacity for responsibility in an action logic analysis of conditions without clarifying the "democratic accountability"[71] of private companies in a higher-level legitimation procedure. At the same time, due to the insufficiently explained political embedding of companies in politics, there is a risk of

---

[66]Cf. for more on this topic Heidbrink (2003), p. 128 et seq.
[67]On this topic see Newholm and Shaw (2007).
[68]On dilemmatic decisions, cf. Heidbrink (2000), p. 285 et seq.
[69]Cf. Homann (2004), p. 7 et seq.
[70]Cf. Scherer et al. (2006), p. 519 et seq.
[71]Cf. Crane and Matten (2007), p. 67 et seq.

their deliberative overextension.[72] Since companies primarily have the status of economic actors from an order ethics point of view, there is not only a legitimation problem, but also a competence problem, because private organizations and their management are normally not trained to assume ordo-responsibility.[73] The "competence to take on ordo-responsibility" cannot be justified solely in "[that it] is increasingly important for managers to earn and secure their companies' license to (co-)operate and thus to foster successful value creation."[74]

The reason for this direct expectation and demand that companies provide public services (6.) is established in the indirect normativity of order ethics. The ordonomic approach is intended to avoid immediate ethical and political addressing of companies in order to reduce the risks of cynical disregard for the rules and moralistic dominance of the rules, as a consequence of which social structure and semantics collapse. But through an implicit normativity of utility maximization and calculation of advantages, economically effective competitive conditions can ultimately be realized only through a *regulating state*, since otherwise no cooperation-stabilizing structures are guaranteed. The economistic paradigm of interest-driven incentive ethics ensures that market-policy governance relies primarily on instruments of the state-designed order and companies' self- commitment. The faith of order ethics in regulatory governance mechanisms not only ignores behavioral psychology factors that lead even rational actors to systematically distorted decisions.[75] More significantly, in the implementation of corporate responsibility, strategies of regulation and standard-setting that include sanctions are pursued unilaterally, instead of more emphasis being placed on tactics of voluntary self-commitment and value-driven actions, which frequently produces more effective results in company practice than incentive-based order rules.[76]

Due to these limits, it is necessary to expand ordo-responsibility through systems responsibility. The systems ethics approach represents a heuristically sensible supplement to order ethics in a number of important points, which shall be explained in the following section with respect to the political role of companies.

4 Corporations as Political Actors from the Viewpoint of Systems Responsibility

From the viewpoint of ordo-responsibility, companies are treated as corporate actors in the tradition of methodological individualism that can be (self-)governed via ethical incentive arrangements. The political responsibility of companies is

---

[72]Cf. on this topic Willke and Willke (2008), 34 et seq.
[73]Reich (2007), p. 258.
[74]Pies et al. (2011), p. 182.
[75]See Etzioni (2011); Treviño et al. (2006).
[76]Cf. Wolff et al. (2009), p. 253 et seq.; Eigenstetter (2006).

primarily seen in their participation, out of enlightened self-interest, in designing order rules for improving the conditions of mutually advantageous value creation.

This goal is in accord with the market-based framework rules of globalized politics, which is characterized by the declining governance and integration power of democratic nation states, but it is not in accord with the societal framework of these states. Ordo-responsibility is primarily a principle of *market-based* governance. Moreover, the principle of ordo-responsibility relies on procedures of rational, goal-oriented rule formation and discursive self-regulation, which are not commensurate with the individual logical of organizations and the practice of communication processes. From the point of view of ordo-responsibility, win-win heuristic arguments can surely be made for companies' investment in the political improvement of economically relevant cooperation conditions, but not in answer to the question to what extent companies have the competence, legitimacy, and capability to perform genuinely political functions that do not bring any direct economic benefit, but instead pursue societal goals.

To put it another way, ordo-responsibility does not represent a sufficient *political* principle of governance to properly correct the deficits that may arise due to discourse, market, and regulatory limits. It is not only the risks of *discourse failure*, in the form of systematically deviating rationality decisions and lacking motivational and cognitive cooperation conditions, that are not adequately considered; rather, the risks of *market failure* in particular, which can occur due to the externalization of economically non-measurable costs, as well as the risks of *rule failure*, which can occur through globally limited instruments of incentive management and sanctioning rule violations.[77] The risk of discourse, market, and regulatory failure requires an expansion of ordo-responsibility through systems responsibility, which incorporates the marginal benefit of economic moral theory and provides heuristically expanded instruments for guidance of moral market behavior.

Such an expansion cannot be achieved only through a "complex governance mix"[78] that connects ordo-economic with system policy governance of corporate responsibility. From a system policy perspective, companies not only bear co-responsibility for improving mutually advantageous cooperation conditions, but also for guaranteeing the *normative system conditions* to which they owe their capacity for cooperation and value creation competencies and which are based on socio-ethical goals of providing public services. Whereas ordo-responsibility is primarily the result of economic interest in stable interaction relationships and structures of competition of market actors, systems responsibility is grounded in the political stabilization of the market system and the public interest-oriented monitoring of its own contingent dynamics. In contrast to ordo-responsibility, systems responsibility not only seeks to overcome dilemma structures through the reform of institutional rules of game, but is also directed towards the *socially and*

---

[77]Cf. Morner (2010), p. 341 et seq.
[78]Morner (2010), p. 347.

environmentally responsible transformation of existing institutions, which in the case of failing market processes must be implemented by changing the game process.[79]

Systems responsibility therefore means not only the responsibility *in* and *for* the game, but also the accountability *of* the game itself, whose control limits are incorporated in the game process. Systems responsibility represents a necessary complement to political governance, which is assumed by private companies beyond their ordo-responsibility in order to reduce the risks of discourse, market, and regulatory failure, which must be anticipated under the conditions of declining governance power of the nation state and a growing volatility and disappearance of boundaries of market processes.

The systemic perspective of corporate responsibility is seen especially in situations where firms take on political functions for reasons of *reflexive risk management* and provide public interest-oriented services. The performance of government functions, e.g., in the areas of environmental protection, labor and social standards, public safety and prevention of corruption, is only an ostensible result of economic benefit calculations, since the majority of the assumed functions and voluntary commitments involves no directly provable market-based advantages.[80] In this way companies participate in procedures of public discourse such as Germany's National CSR Forum or the development of the ISO 26000, not only for competitive reasons, but instead primarily for reasons of the *prevention of system crises*, which can arise from the growing scarcity of resources, demographic changes and problems of social integration.[81] Companies champion climate protection and incorporate sustainability goals in their business practices not only for reasons of cost and reputation, but to counteract social and political risks of migration or territorial conflicts due to lack of water or raw materials.[82] Multinational corporations back global regulations such as the Global Compact and support the observance of human rights in their supplier and production countries not for regulatory reasons alone, but to guarantee political stability in particular and the development of democratic institutions in crisis regions.[83]

Private companies thus emerge as co-producers of statehood, which are concerned with the socially relevant production of public goods and services through co-determination of norms and assumption of safety and educational tasks including infrastructure projects. They thus contribute to "co-performance of governance" that extends beyond traditional public-private partnership activities and involvement in state regulatory procedures.[84] When companies become political governance actors that take over quasi-governmental services of general

---

[79]Cf. Mirvis and Googins (2009), p. 19 et seq.

[80]On this topic, already Vogel (2006), p. 16 et seq.

[81]Cf. also Habisch and Brychuk (2011), p. 117 et seq.

[82]See Loew et al. (2011).

[83]Cf. Morrison (2011), p. 15 et seq.

[84]Cf. Schuppert (2008), p. 27 et seq.

interest, implementation of legislation, and conflict management, they help stabilize social conditions, which facilitate their own operating conditions.

Maintaining social conditions for company operations goes beyond ordo-responsibility insofar as systemic risks and the failure of discursive and regulatory procedures are integrated into the co-administration of market-based processes. From the standpoint of systems responsibility, it does not suffice to see the main moral criterion in advantage-oriented acceptance of the "market game,"[85] since neither the potential failure of market orders nor the externalization of costs to those who cannot participate in the market game are sufficiently taken into account. In contrast to ordo-responsibility, systems responsibility does not constitute a type of responsibility derived from individual preferences, but rather an independent procedural type, which allows it to attribute harmful consequences to companies especially if these have occurred due to mismanagement of the overall organization.[86] The heuristics of systems responsibility leads to an expanded corporate attribution practice, by which companies also take into account contingent factors in their self-organization such as operational disorganization, bad decisions, arbitrariness or aspiration for power, which cannot be explained solely from the perspective of rational choice behavior of benefit-oriented actors. Consideration of non-rational behavior and poor consequences for the social system is entirely in the interest of companies, since it allows them to be able to prevent risks of self-harm and contribute to long-term stabilization of their societal operating conditions.

Viewed this way, systems responsibility is a political mode of "meta-responsibility,"[87] which is required for *sustainable implementation* of market-based ordo-responsibility. Systemic meta-responsibility is a result of the fact that firms are confronted with residual risks with respect to their stakeholders, employees, competitors, and resources, which, in an operationally networked and territorially borderless corporate environment, cannot be solved with traditional instruments of order ethics governance and discourse responsibility, since on the micro-level these do not sufficiently consider the distorted decision rationale of actors or, on the macro-level, the social embedding of companies and the increase in extra-market relationships.[88]

At present, network-based and extra-market collaboration processes based primarily on "implicit contracts negotiated in a non-market public arena"[89] have taken the place of transactions and explicit contracts. The internationalization of the firm and its embedding in social contractual relationships necessitates a new understanding of political corporate responsibility, which relies on structures of competition but ultimately aims to provide public goods and services and to guarantee rights: "In consequence, the goods and services that accrue to individuals in society

---

[85]According to Vanberg (2000), 595 et seq.
[86]Cf. Kyora (2001), p. 207 et seq.
[87]Cf. Bayertz (1995), p. 60 et seq.
[88]Cf. Palazzo (2011), pp. 125–127.
[89]Boatright (2011), p. 143.

result from their separate roles as economic actors in a market and as citizens of a state. However, in the new competitive environment, the market no longer plays this distributive role to the same extent, and more goods and services become contestable in the public arena. Insofar as these goods and services are viewed as rights, their administration is no longer a matter purely for government but for corporate decision making as well."[90]

The provision of public services and the guarantee of social rights occur for reasons of systems responsibility, which leads to improvement of corporate policy operating conditions through a reflexive expansion of economic benefit calculations. The question, "why should (corporations) assume such extensive responsibilities if there is nothing in it for them,"[91] can ultimately be answered better with systems ethics than with order ethics arguments: Companies contribute in a particularly effective way to state co-governance—and thus to their own functional requirements—when they follow not only economic benefit calculations, but instead act for reasons of *socially relevant risk reduction* and with respect to *cross-border and cross-market network processes*. It is primarily societal changes of increasing non-market interactions and socio-ecological crisis potential that has led to private companies becoming involved in governmental functions of fulfilment, guarantee, and infrastructure responsibility. It is therefore more advantageous for companies in the long run to assume political co-responsibility, not only for market-based benefit reasons, but with the goal of avoiding social crisis processes.

5 Conclusion: Competence, Legitimacy, and Capability of Political Companies

It has become clear that companies bear not only within-game responsibility for the consequences of their business operations and ordo-responsibility for the co-creation and implementation of framework rules, but also a specific systems responsibility to maintain the functional conditions of the social system that makes their operational activities possible. The political role of companies consists in co-designing system conditions that are a prerequisite for the assumption of corporate ordo-responsibility and within-game responsibility. Due to the declining governance power of the nation state, co-responsibility for integrating market-based and political goals falls to private-sector companies so that *socially beneficial value creation* is guaranteed.

The competence, legitimacy, and capability of corporations to assume political co-responsibility is therefore measured not only by order ethics generation of competitive conditions relevant for the market economy, but instead primarily on

---

[90]Boatright (2011), p. 144.
[91]Oosterhout (2005), p. 678.

systems ethics inclusion of socially relevant risk and network processes and the return of accountability to the individual logic of corporate organizations:

Companies are *competent actors* if their operations can be attributed to them as autonomous action systems, for which an analysis of their organizational and intentional constitution is required that includes "responsivity as a system characteristic."[92] If companies have the constitution of a responsive action system, their operational consequences can also be attributed to them without direct fault if it can be shown that they have developed a "system character" that is unqualified to prevent typical operating risks.[93] From the point of view of systems responsibility, it is justified to expect that companies change their own systemic constitution if this has been proven to produce damage to the public interest and strain on public goods.[94]

Companies have the *legitimation* to exercise state co-governance if they are mandated to perform social functions within the scope of legal regulations and on the basis of democratic procedures. The legitimation and mandating of private regulation regimes is not only a result of interest-driven voting discourses about market rules and competitive conditions, but requires complex procedures of institutional distribution of responsibility, inclusion of stakeholders, and reference to recognized social norms.[95]

Finally, to be precise, companies only have the *capability* to participate as state co-actors in processes of public rule-finding and rule-setting if they have genuinely political action competencies and the effectiveness of private self-regulation is guaranteed. Whereas effectiveness requirements concern the reliability, sustainability, and accuracy of economic self-commitments and engagement activities,[96] political competencies make it necessary on the level of corporate management to implement greater professionalism in public governance and, e.g., strategies of responsible leadership in the company.[97]

By expanding ordo-responsibility through systems responsibility, the political role of companies can be appreciated more completely and thus more in line with reality. The three main dimensions of ordo-responsibility—incorporation of uncertainty processes, design of the organizational culture, and management of political context—make possible a heuristics of corporate responsibly that extends beyond the *ordonomic approach*. In times of declining governance power of the nation state, embedding of firms in social networks, and emergence of non-market collaborations, companies not only bear the political co-responsibility for competitive frameworks, but also for social system conditions. They are not only

---

[92]Ortmann (2010), p. 253.
[93]Kyora (2001), p. 213.
[94]Cf. French (1991), p. 138 et seq.
[95]Wolf (2005), p. 60.
[96]Cf. Embacher and Lang (2008), p. 357 et seq.
[97]Cf. Pless and Maak (2008); Voegtlin et al. (2010).

co-actors of the regulating state, but rather co-performers of the designing state.[98] From the standpoint of the *systemic approach*, it is therefore more advantageous for companies in the long term to assume political co-responsibility, not only for reasons of investment in future cooperation conditions, but also for reasons of sustainable transformation of socially relevant system processes.

Acknowledgments Der Beitrag ist ursprünglich erschienen unter dem Titel "Unternehmen als politische Akteure. Eine Ortsbestimmung zwischen Ordnungsverantwortung und Systemverantwortung", in: ORDO. Jahrbuch für die Ordnung von Wirtschaft und Gesellschaft, Bd. 63, Stuttgart 2012, S. 203-231. Mit herzlichem Dank für die Erlaubnis zum Wiederabdruck an den Verlag Lucius & Lucius sowie die Herausgeber Martin Leschke und Ingo Pies. Englische Übersetzung von Robert McCulloch.

References

Bayertz, Kurt 1995. Eine kurze Geschichte der Herkunft der Verantwortung. In *Verantwortung— Prinzip oder Problem?* ed. ibid, 3–71. Darmstadt.
Becker, Maren, John, Stefanie and Schirm, Stefan A. 2007. *Globalisierung und Global Governance*. Paderborn.
Beckmann, Markus 2010. *Ordnungsverantwortung: Rational Choice als ordonomisches Forschungsprogramm*. Berlin.
Boatright, John R. 2011. The implications of the new governance for corporate governance. In *Corporate citizenship and new governance. The political role of corporations,* eds. Ingo Pies and Peter Koslowski, 133–146. Heidelberg, London, New York.
Bühl, Walter L. 1998. *Verantwortung für Soziale Systeme*. Stuttgart: Grundzüge einer globalen Gesellschaftsethik.
Chwaszsca, Christine 2003. *Praktische Vernunft als vernünftige Praxis*, Weilerwist.
Coleman, James S. 1985. Responsibility in corporate action: A sociologist's view. In *Corporate governance and directors' liabilities. Legal, economic and sociological analyses on corporate social responsibility,* eds. Hopt, Klaus J. and Teubner, Gunther, 69–91. Berlin, New York.
Crane, Andrew and Matten, Dirk 2007. *Business ethics. Managing corporate citizenship and sustainability in the age of globalization*. 2nd ed. Oxford.
Crane, Andrew, Matten, Dirk and Moon, Jeremy 2008. *Corporations and citizenship*, Cambridge.
Di Fabio, Udo 1999. Unternehmerische Selbstbindung und rechtsstaatliche Fremdbindung. In *Unternehmerische Freiheit, Selbstbindung und politische Mitverantwortung. Perspektiven republikanischer Unternehmensethik,* ed. Peter Ulrich. 85–96. München, Mering.
Eigenstetter, Monika 2006. Ethisches Klima in Organisationen—Eine deutsche Übersetzung und Adaption des Ethical Climate Questionnaire. In *Mit Werten wirtschaften—Mit Trends trumpfen*ed, eds. B. Klauk and M.Stangel-Meseke, 51–78. Lengerich.
Embacher, Sergé, Lang, Susanne 2008. *Bürgergesellschaft. Eine Einführung in zentrale bürgergesellschaftliche Gegenwarts- und Zukunftsfragen*. Bonn.
Etzioni, Amitai 2011. Behavioural economics: Next steps. *Journal of Consumer Policy*. http://www.springerlink.com/content/mx4432622n017q18/(12.2.2011).
French, Peter A. 1991. Fishing the red herings out of the sea of moral responsibility. In *The spectrum of responsibility,* ed. Ders, 129–143. New York.

---

[98]On the designing state, see WBGU (2011), p. 215 et seq.

French, Peter A. 1992. Die Korporation als moralische Person. In *Wirtschaft und Ethik*, eds. Hans Lenk and Matthias Maring, 317–328. Stuttgart.
Goodpaster, Kenneth E. 1983. The concept of corporate responsibility. *Journal of Business Ethics* 2: 1–22, 14 et seq.
Goodpaster, Kenneth E. 1991. Business ethics and stakeholder analysis. *Business ethics quaterly* 1 (1): 53–73.
Habisch, André and Brychuk, Iryna 2011. Die europäische Diskussion um Corporate Social Responsibility zwischen staatlicher Regulierung und Freiwilligkeit: Ein Überblick. In *Finanzmarktakteure und Corporate Social Responsibility*, ed. Gotlind Ulshöfer and Beate Feuchte, 117–132. Wiesbaden.
Hartmann, Martin 2011. *Die Praxis des Vertrauens*. Berlin.
Hayek, Friedrich August 1952. *Individualismus und wirtschaftliche Ordnung*. Erlenbach-Zürich.
Heidbrink, Ludger 2000. Moral und Konflikt. Zur Unvermeidbarkeit sprachlicher Gewalt in praktischen Entscheidungssituationen. In ed. *Sprache und Gewalt*, Ursula Erzgräber und Alfred Hirsch, 265–310. Berlin.
Heidbrink, Ludger. 2003. *Kritik der Verantwortung*. Weilerswist: Zu den Grenzen verantwortlichen Handelns in komplexen Kontexten.
Heidbrink, Ludger 2007. Systemverantwortung, Selbstbindung und Ethik der wirtschaftlichen Organisation. In *Unternehmensverantwortung aus kulturalistischer Sicht*, eds. Thomas Beschorner, Patrick Linnebach, Reinhard Pfriem and Günter Ulrich, 45–66. Marburg.
Heidbrink, Ludger. 2007b. *Handeln in der Ungewissheit*. Berlin: Paradoxien der Verantwortung.
Heidbrink, Ludger. 2010a. Der Verantwortungsbegriff der Wirtschaftsethik. In *Handbuch Wirtschaftsethik*, ed. Michael S. Aßländer, 188–197. Stuttgart.
Heidbrink, Ludger 2010b. *Nichtwissen und Verantwortung. Zum Umgang mit unbeabsichtigten Nebenfolgen*. Workingpaper No. 8, Center for Responsibility Research. www.responsibility-research.de (12.2.2012).
Heine, Günter 1995. *Die strafrechtliche Verantwortung von Unternehmen. Von individuellem Fehlverhalten zu kollektiven Fehlentwicklungen, insbesondere Großrisiken*, Baden-Baden.
Hoffmann-Riem, Wolfgang 2000. Verantwortungsteilung als Schlüsselbegriff moderner Staatlichkeit. In *Staaten und Steuern. Festschrift für Klaus Vogel zum 70. Geburtstag*, ed. Paul Kirchhof, 47–64, Heidelberg.
Hoffmann-Riem, Wolfgang. 2001. *Modernisierung von Recht und Justiz*. Frankfurt am Main: Eine Herausforderung des Gewährleistungsstaates.
Homann, Karl 2004. *Gesellschaftliche Verantwortung der Unternehmen. Philosophische, gesellschaftstheoretische und ökonomische Überlegungen*, Diskussionspapier No. 04-6, Wittenberg-Zentrum für Globale Ethik.
Homann, Karl and Blome-Drees, Franz 1992. *Wirtschafts- und Unternehmensethik*. Göttingen.
Kersting, Wolfgang. 2008. Der *homo oeconomicus* und die Moral. Zur Kritik des Ökonomismus. In *Moral und Kapital*, ed. Wolfgang Kersting, 129–150. Grundfragen der Wirtschafts- und Unternehmensethik: Paderborn.
Küpers, Wendelin 2008. Perspektiven responsiver und integraler ‚Ver-Antwortung' in Organisationen und der Wirtschaft. In *Verantwortung als marktwirtschaftliches Prinzip. Zum Verhältnis von Moral und Ökonomie*, eds. Ludger Heidbrink and Alfred Hirsch, 307–338. Frankfurt, New York.
Kyora, Stefan 2001. *Unternehmensethik und korporative Verantwortung. Begriffliche Unterscheidungen, rechtliche Regelungen, praktische Schlussfolgerungen*, München, Mering.
Laszlo, Alexander and Krippner, Stanley 1998. Systems theories: Their origin, foundations, and development. In *Systems Theories and Priori Aspects of Perception*, ed. J. Scott Jordan, 47–74. Amsterdam.
Lenk, Hans and Maring, Matthias 1995. Wer soll Verantwortung tragen? Probleme der Verantwortungsverteilung in komplexen (soziotechnischen-ökonomischen) Systemen. In *Verantwortung – Prinzip oder Problem?* ed. Kurt Bayertz, 241–286. Darmstadt.
Lin-Hi, Nick. 2009. *Eine Theorie der Unternehmensverantwortung*. Berlin: Die Verknüpfung von Gewinnerzielung und gesellschaftlichen Interessen.

Loew, Thomas, Jens Clausen, and Friederike Rohde. 2011. *CSR und Risikomanagement*. Berlin, Hannover: Gesetzliches und freiwilliges Risikomanagement und die Rolle von Corporate Social Responsibility.
Lübbe, Weyma 1998. *Verantwortung in komplexen kulturellen Prozessen*. Freiburg, München.
Luhmann, Niklas 1994. *Die Wirtschaft der Gesellschaft*. Frankfurt am Main.
Luhmann, Niklas 1999. *Funktionen und Folgen formaler Organisation*. 5th ed. Berlin.
Lukas, Karen, Menschenrechtliche Verantwortung von Unternehmen 2007. In *Politik mit dem Einkaufswagen. Unternehmen und Konsumenten als Bürger in der globalen Mediengesellschaft*, eds. Sigrid Baringhorst, Veronika Kneip, Annegret März and Johanna Niesyto, 207–221. Bielefeld.
Maring, Matthias. 2001. *Kollektive und korporative Verantwortung*. Technik und Alltag, Münster: Begriffs- und Fallstudien aus Wirtschaft.
Matys, Thomas 2011. *Legal Persons—"Kämpfe" und die organisationale Form*. Konstanz.
Maurach, Reinhart, and Heinz Zipf. 1992. *Strafrecht*. Heidelberg: Allgemeiner Teil.
Mayntz, Renate 2007. Die Handlungsfähigkeit des Nationalstaats in Zeiten der Globalisierung. In *Staat ohne Verantwortung? Zum Wandel der Aufgaben von Staat und Politik*, eds. Ludger Heidbrink and Alfred Hirsch, 267–282. Frankfurt, New York.
Mirvis, Philip H. and Googins, Bradley K. 2009. *Neue Rollen und Aufgaben für Unternehmen in der Gesellschaft: auf dem Weg zur nächsten Generation von Corporate Citizenship*. ed. The Centrum für Corporate Citizenship Deutschland, Berlin.
Morner, Michèle. 2010. Funktionsbedingungen für Regeln und Diskurs zur Beeinflussung von moralischem Handeln: Implikationen organisatorischer Steuerung für Unternehmens- und Wirtschaftsethik. *Jahrbuch für Recht und Ethik* 18: 335–348.
Morrison, John 2011. An overview of current practice and policy relating to business activities and human rights: Some oft he implications for corporate,rule-making. In *Corporate citizenship and new governance. The political role of corporations*, eds. Ingo Pies and Peter Koslowski, 7–17. Heidelberg, London, New York.
Münch, Richard 1996. *Risikopolitik*. Frankfurt am Main.
Neuhäuser, Christian 2011. *Unternehmen als moralische Akteure*, Frankfurt am Main.
Newholm, Terry, and Deirdre Shaw. 2007. Studying the ethical consumer: A review of research. *Journal of Consumer Behaviour* 6: 253–270.
Noll, Bernd. 2010. *Grundriss der Wirtschaftsethik*. Stuttgart: Von der Stammesmoral zur Ethik der Globalisierung.
Ockenfels, Axel and Raub, Werner 2010. Rational und Fair. In *Soziologische Theorie kontrovers. Sonderheft. Kölner Zeitschrift für Soziologie und Sozialpsychologie,* eds. Gert Albert and Steffen Sigmund, 50: 119–136.
van Oosterhout, Hans. 2005. Corporate citizenship: An idea whose time has not yet come. *Academy of Management Review* 30(4): 677–681.
Ortmann, Günther. 2010. *Organisation und moral*. Weilerswist: Die dunkle Seite.
Palazzo, Guido 2011. Konsequenzen der Globalisierung für die Theorie der Firma. In *Die Zukunft der Firma*, ed. Josef Wieland, 115–130. Marburg.
Pies, Ingo 2001. Können Unternehmen Verantwortung tragen?—Ein ökonomisches Kooperationsangebot an die philosophische Ethik. In *Die moralische Verantwortung kollektiver Akteure*, ed. Josef Wieland, 171–199. Heidelberg.
Pies, Ingo. 2009. *Moral als Heuristik*. Berlin: Ordonomische Schriften zur Wirtschaftsethik.
Pies, Ingo and Beckmann, Markus 2008. Ordnungs-, Steuerungs- und Aufklärungsverantwortung —Konzeptionelle Überlegungen zugunsten einer semantischen Innovation. In eds. *Verantwortung als markwirtschaftliches Prinzip. Zum Verhältnis von Moral und Ökonomie*, Ludger Heidbrink and Alfred Hirsch, 31–68. Frankfurt, New York.
Pies, Ingo, Beckmann, Markus and Hielscher, Stefan 2011. *Competitive markets, corporate firms, and new governance—An ordonomic conceptualization*. In *Corporate citizenship and new governance—The political role of corporations*, eds. Ingo Pies and Peter Koslowski, 171–188. Dordrecht.

Pless, Nicola M. and Maak, Thomas 2008. Responsible leadership. Verantwortliche Führung im Kontext einer globalen Stakeholder-Gesellschaft. In *Zeitschrift für Wirtschafts- und Unternehmensethik* 9(2): 222–239.

Reich, Robert. 2007. *Superkapitalismus*. Frankfurt, New York: Wie die Wirtschaft unsere Demokratie untergräbt.

Rosenau, James N. and Czempiel, Ernst Otto eds. 1992. *Governance without government. Order and change in world politics*. Cambridge.

Scherer, Andreas, Guido Palazzo, and Dorothée Baumann. 2006. Global rules and private actors: Toward a new role of the transnational corporation in global governance. *Business Ethics Quaterly* 16(4): 505–532.

Schirm, Stefan A. ed. 2004. *New rules for global markets. Public and private governance in the world economy*, Hampshire, New York.

Schmid, Hans Bernhard and Schweikard, David P. eds. 2009. *Kollektive Intentionalität. Eine Debatte über die Grundlagen des Sozialen*. Frankfurt am Main.

Schmidpeter, René and Palz, Doris 2008. Corporate social responsibility in Europa. In *Handbuch corporate citizenship. Corporate social responsibility für manager*eds, eds. André Habisch, René Schmidpeter and Martin Neureiter, 493–500. Berlin, Heidelberg.

Schmiedeknecht, Maud H. and Wieland, Josef 2012. ISO 26000, 7 Grundsätze, 6 Kernthemen. In *Corporate social responsibility. Verantwortungsvolle Unternehmensführung in Theorie und Praxis*, eds. Andreas Schneider, René Schmidpeter, 259–270. Berlin, Heidelberg.

Schmölders, Günter 1973. *Sozialökonomische Verhaltensforschung*. Berlin.

Schumpeter, Josef 1970/1908. *Das Wesen und der Hauptinhalt der theoretischen Nationalökonomie*, 2nd ed. Berlin.

Schuppert, Gunnar Folke 2007. Staatstypen, Leitbilder und Politische Kultur. In *Staat ohne Verantwortung? Zum Wandel der Aufgaben von Staat und Politik*, eds. Ludger Heidbrink and Alfred Hirsch, 467–495. Frankfurt, New York.

Schuppert, Gunnar Folke 2008. Von Ko-Produktion von Staatlichkeit zur Co-Performance of Governance. Eine Skizze zu kooperativen Governance-Strukturen von den Condottieri der Renaissance bis zu den Public Private Partnerships. SFB-Governance Working Paper Series, No. 12.

Seebaß, Gottfried 2001. Kollektive Verantwortung und individuelle Verhaltenskontrolle. In *Die moralische Verantwortung kollektiver Akteure*, ed. Josef Wieland, 79–99. Heidelberg.

Suchanek, Andreas 2001. *Ökonomische Ethik*. Tübingen.

Suchanek, Andreas and Lin-Hi, Nick 2008. Die gesellschaftliche Verantwortung von Unternehmen in der Marktwirtschaft. In *Verantwortung als markwirtschaftliches Prinzip. Zum Verhältnis von Moral und Ökonomie*, eds. Ludger Heidbrink and Alfred Hirsch, 69–96. 90 et seq. Frankfurt, New York.

Teubner, Gunther. 2009. 'So ich aber die Teufel durch Beelzebub austreibe, …': Zur Diabolik des Netzwerkversagens. In *Ungewissheit als Chance*, ed. Ino Augsberg, 109–134. Perspektiven eines produktiven Umgangs mit Unsicherheit im Rechtssystem: Tübingen.

Treviño, Linda K., Gary R. Weaver, and Scott J. Reynolds. 2006. Behavioral ethics in organizations: A review. *Journal of Management* 32: 951–990.

Udehn, Lars 2001. *Methodological individualism. Background, history and meaning*. London, New York.

Vanberg, Viktor 2000. Ordnungsökonomik und Ethik—Zur Interessensbegründung von Moral. In *Freiheit und wettbewerbliche Ordnung. Gedenkband zur Erinnerung an Walter Eucken*, eds. Bernhard Külp and Viktor Vanberg, 579–605. Freiburg, Berlin, München.

Vogel, David. 2006. *The market for virtue*. Washington: The Potential and Limits of Corporate Social Responsibility.

Voegtlin, Christian, Patzer, Moritz and Scherer, Andreas G. 2010. *Responsible leadership in global business. A contingency approach*. IOU Working Paper No. 106, Zürich.

Werhane Patricia H. 1992. Rechte und Verantwortungen von Korporationen. In *Wirtschaft und Ethik*, eds. Hans Lenk and Matthias Maring, 329–336. Stuttgart.

Werhane, Patricia H. 2007. Corporate social responsibility/Corporate moral responsibility. Is there a difference and the difference it makes. In *The debate over corporate social responsibility*, eds. Steve May, George Cheney, Juliet Roper, 459–474. Oxford.
Wettstein, Florian. 2009. *Multinational corporations and global justice*. Stanford: Human Rights Obligations of a Quasi-Governmental Institution.
Wieland, Josef 2009. Die Firma als Kooperationsprojekt der Gesellschaft. In *CSR als Netzwerkgovernance—Theoretische Herausforderungen und praktische Antworten. Über das Netzwerk von Wirtschaft, Politik und Zivilgesellschaft*, ed. ibid, 257–287. Marburg.
Willke, Helmut 1983. *Entzauberung des Staates. Überlegungen zu einer sozietalen Steuerungstheorie*, Königstein i. Ts.
Willke, Helmut 1997. Supervision des Staates, Frankfurt am Main.
Willke, Helmut 2000. Systemtheorie I: Grundlagen, 6th revised ed. Stuttgart.
Willke, Helmut, and Gerhard Willke. 2008. Corporate moral legitimacy and the legitimacy of morals: A critique of palazzo/scherer's communicative framework. *Journal of Business Ethics* 81: 27–38.
Wissenschaftlicher Beirat der Bundesregierung Globale Umweltveränderungen (WBGU). 2011. *Welt im Wandel*. Berlin: Gesellschaftsvertrag für eine Große Transformation.
Wolf, Klaus Dieter. 2005. Möglichkeiten und Grenzen der Selbststeuerung als gemeinwohlverträglicher politischer Steuerungsform. *Zeitschrift für Wirtschafts- und Unternehmensethik* 6(1): 51–68.
Wolff, Franziska, Bohn, Maria, Schultz, Irmgard and Wilkinson, Peter 2009. CSR and public policy: Mutually reinforcing for sustainable development? In *Corporate social responsibility in Europe*, eds. Regina Barth and Franziska Wolff, 249–268. Cheltenham/Northhampton.
Zürn, Michael and Weidner, Helmut 2009. Politisierung der Ökonomisierung? Zum gegenwärtigen Verhältnis von Politik und Ökonomie. In *CSR als Netzwerkgovernance – Theoretische Herausforderungen und praktische Antworten*, ed. Josef Wieland, 155–184. Marburg.

Is the Minimum Wage Ethically Justifiable? An Order-Ethical Answer

Nikil Mukerji and Christoph Schumacher

Abstract Is the minimum wage ethically justifiable? In this chapter, we attempt to answer this question from an order-ethical perspective. To this end, we develop two simple game theoretical models for different types of labour markets and derive policy implications from an order-ethical viewpoint. Our investigation yields a twofold conclusion. Firstly, order ethicists should prefer a tax-funded wage subsidy over minimum wages if they assume that labour markets are perfectly competitive. Secondly, order ethics suggests that the minimum wage can be ethically justified if employers have monopsony power in the wage setting process. As it turns out, then, order ethics neither favours nor disfavours the minimum wage. Rather, it implies conditions under which this form of labour market regulation is justified and, hence, allows empirical science to play a great role in answering the ethical questions that arise in the context of the minimum wage debate. This illustrates one of order ethics' strengths, viz. the fact that it tends to de-ideologize the debate about ethical issues.

Keywords Minimum wage · Wage regulation policies · Ethics · Efficiency

---

This chapter reproduces some material that has previously been published in Mukerji and Schumacher (2008). We thank A B Academic Publishers for their permission to reproduce it here.

N. Mukerji (✉)
Faculty of Philosophy, Philosophy of Science, and the Study of Religion,
Ludwig-Maximilians-Universität München, Munich, Germany
e-mail: nikil.mukerji@lmu.de

C. Schumacher
School of Economics and Finance, Massey University, Auckland, New Zealand
e-mail: C.Schumacher@massey.ac.nz

1 Introduction

Ethicists widely disagree on the justification of the minimum wage. Cordero (2000), e.g., says that a wage that is "[...] too low for a good life is extremely hard to defend on the basis of moral principles that could be endorsed by benevolent rational beings" (p. 207), while Gaski (2004) argues that it is unethical and immoral. Some theorists hold "in-between" views. That is, they believe that "[...] at worst, the minimum wage is a mistake and, at best, something to be half-hearted about." (Wilkinson 2004, p. 351). Though the arguments put forwarded by these authors are rather different, most of them share a common trait. They are usually based on a *Conflict Paradigm* that sees ethics and economics as two inherently conflicting ways of thinking (e.g. Okun 1975). Order ethicists believe that this view of the relationship between ethics and economics is fundamentally flawed. On their view, ethics and economics are not in conflict, but two sides of the same coin. Hence, order ethicists believe that minimum wage legislation can only be *ethically* justified if it is at the same time *economically* efficient. In this chapter, we explore the implications of that view.

We develop two simple game theoretical models for different types of labour markets and derive policy implications from an order-ethical viewpoint. Our investigation yields a twofold conclusion. Firstly, order ethicists should prefer a tax-funded wage subsidy over minimum wages if they assume that labour markets are perfectly competitive. Secondly, order ethics suggests that the minimum wage can be ethically justified if employers have monopsony power in the wage setting process.

Our analysis relies on the order-ethical methodology that we laid out in Chap. "Order Ethics, Economics, and GameTheory" of this volume. The present chapter can be read separately, however, since we briefly reprise and explain the five basic propositions of the order-ethical methodology in the next section (though we shall not attempt to justify them here). After that, we develop the general structure of the minimum wage model before we review key findings in labour market economics in the ensuing section. In the following two sections, we then specify two interpretations of our general model. We first look at the *Standard Model* which is based on the assumption that labour markets are perfectly competitive. We show that order ethics implies the illegitimacy of minimum wages in such a market. Then, we introduce what we call the *Renegade Model*. It assumes that there are market imperfections in the labour market. We show that, on that assumption, order ethics may suggest that wage floors are justified under certain conditions. In the final section, we sum up and conclude with a brief note on an interesting aspect of the order-ethical framework, viz. the fact that it allows empirical investigation to play a great role and tends, therefore, to de-ideologize ethical debate.

2 The Order-Ethical Methodology

In the present chapter, we assume that the order-ethical methodology can be characterized by the five propositions we have discussed in Chap. "Order Ethics, Economics, and GameTheory". A brief explanation should suffice in each case.

The first proposition instructs us about the nature of ethical problems. It says that

(1) Overcoming Dilemma Structures (DS) in pursuit of efficient outcomes is *the* fundamental problem of ethics.

To explain, DS are, roughly put, situations in which two or more individuals interact and where the rational pursuit of self-interest by each leads to a situation that is dispreferred by all. Order ethicists assume that individuals generally follow incentives and expect, therefore, that DS will predictably lead to ethically undesirable, i.e. Pareto-inferior, outcomes. These outcomes are ethically undesirable because there are alternative outcomes under which everyone would be better off. Order ethicists conclude, therefore, that DS should be overcome. They also believe that DS are omnipresent in human interactions, such that more or less every ethical problem has a DS at its root.

The second proposition of order ethics suggests how DS can be overcome. It says that

(2) The problem of DS is to be solved at the institutional level through a change to a Pareto-superior rule.

In other words, we should not rely on individuals to make any sacrifices. Rather, we should expect that they will act in their own self-interest (at least in the long run) and change the institutional structure in which they interact in order to enforce a behaviour that benefits all. To illustrate, consider the well-known *Tragedy of the Commons* popularized by Hardin (1968). A number of herdsmen share a common pasture to graze their animals. If there is no rule that limits the number of animals that each herdsman may put on the pasture, each will have an incentive to overuse their common resource. Why? Because the entire proceeds from putting an additional animal on the pasture go to one herdsman. The costs of his doing so, however, are shared by all herdsmen collectively. In this situation, order ethics calls for the implementation and enforcement of a rule that limits the number of animals that each herdsman is permitted to put on the pasture. This rule will help the herdsmen to overcome their DS and improve everybody's lot.

While Propositions (1) and (2) tell us, respectively, what ethical problems are and how they can be overcome, they do not tell us how we can detect them. Proposition (3) fills this gap. It says that the

(3) The concept of a DS is to be used as a *heuristic*. Every interaction that is subject to ethical investigation has to be modelled in terms of a DS, if possible.

To explain, ethical problems are often not apparent. E.g., the costs from corrupt dealings in public administration may not be obvious at all. Nevertheless, they are ethically problematic because they harm all citizens. At the same time, certain situations may strike us as being ethically problematic when, in fact, they are not. E.g., many of us perceive the market economy as morally questionable since it is based on the idea of competition between market participants. Superficially, this appears to be the opposite of solidarity. However, there is a good ethical justification for the market economy since it produces efficient results that benefit everyone. In order to avoid both types of mistake, order ethics recommends that we try to construct every interaction in society as a DS. If we succeed in doing this, we are faced with an ethical problem. If not, all is well.

Proposition (4) is implicit in Propositions (1) and (2). But it is worth stating separately. It says that

(4) An existing institutional arrangement is ethically justified, if and only if there is no Pareto-superior alternative.

This means that policy makers should examine a given institutional arrangement along with all feasible alternative arrangements. If none of them would make everyone better off, the *status quo* is ethically justified. Otherwise, it is not and one of the alternatives ought to be implemented.

Finally, Proposition (5) establishes a link between the well-known Kaldor-Hicks criterion for efficiency (Kaldor 1939; Hicks 1939) and the Pareto-efficiency criterion. It says that

(5) If we do not find a Pareto-better state of affairs, we should look for a Kaldor-Hicks-superior state. If we can find one, there is a potential for a Pareto-improvement under a suitable redistributive rule.

To explain, on the Kaldor-Hicks efficiency criterion, one outcome, B, is better than another, A, if those who are better off under B than under A could, in theory, compensate those who are worse off and still be better off. Another way to put this is to say that B is Kaldor-Hicks-better than A if the aggregate benefits to all individuals are greater under B. To be sure, Proposition (5) does not say that the Kaldor-Hicks criterion has any intrinsic relevance. In fact, order ethicists reject it as a normative principle. What Proposition (5) does say is that it is a useful *heuristic*. In economic ethics, we are often faced with situations where it is not obvious how a Pareto-improvement can be accomplished. In these situations, Proposition (5) instructs us to analyse whether a Kaldor-Hicks improvement is possible. In a next step, it says that we should attempt to transform this Kaldor-Hicks-superior outcome into a Pareto-superior outcome via a suitable redistributive rule. Further below, we will use this methodological tack to analyse the ethical justification of the minimum wage.

3 The General Structure of the Minimum Wage Model

Having stated the five propositions that make up the order-ethical methodology, let us proceed to the question whether the minimum wage is ethically justified. As a first step, we shall develop a concrete model for evaluating the economic-ethics of minimum wage legislation. In Mukerji and Schumacher (2008), we used game theory to analyse the potential conflict between economic and ethical goals. Using the above propositions, we transformed the minimum wage game into a game with a Pareto-superior outcome. We reprise this general approach here.

First, we have to analyse the interactive structure that underlies our ethical question. That is, we have to identify an appropriate game structure in terms of the players involved as well as their strategies and preferences. Then we are to diagnose whether or not a dilemma structure exists and, if so, look for rules which are potentially Pareto-superior. We designate player 1 to be the group of low-wage workers and player 2 the group of firms which employ these workers. We furthermore premise that all workers have the same productivity, preferences and strategies and will, thus, behave like *one* player.[1] This justifies their aggregation into one group. The same stipulation is made in regards to firms. It is furthermore assumed that workers seek to maximize utility and firms profit. Workers' utility, we assume, depends only on their expected wage which, in turn, depends on the labour demand chosen by firms and whether or not a minimum wage is in place. We stipulate that workers have two strategies. They can either choose to lobby for a minimum wage (W) or not (W). For simplicity, it shall be assumed that they have enough political influence to pull off the minimum wage lever alone. Firms are also assumed to have a discrete choice between two strategies. They can either employ all workers who are willing to work at the current wage or they can employ a smaller number. Of course, firms actually face a continuous choice. For the sake of formal tractability, however, it shall be assumed that firms can either choose to employ Q_W or $Q_{\underline{W}}$, where Q_W is the optimal amount of labour if there is no minimum wage and $Q_{\underline{W}}$ is the optimal amount of labour if there is a minimum wage. These premises lock in the rough structure of our interaction model (Table 1).

In a further step, we need to determine the preferences of both workers and firms in regards to the quadrants I–IV in order to fully identify the game and predict the parties' choices. This might seem like a straightforward task. However, the theory of the economic dynamics of minimum wages has, in fact, become quite complex. We, therefore, provide a short overview over the most important theoretical and empirical findings in the literature.

4 The Economics of the Minimum Wage

The economic literature about minimum wages predominantly discusses the question how employers will respond to wage floors. The *Standard Model*, which assumes a perfectly competitive labour market, provides the following familiar sounding

---

[1]For simplicity, we neglect the fact that low-wage workers may differ in productivity. Differences in productivity have, however, played a role in the empirical investigation of the economic consequences of minimum wage laws for some time, particularly in regards to the impact of minimum wages on unemployment amongst youths (e.g. Moore 1971).

Table 1 Labour market interaction—General structure

		Firms	
		$Q_{\underline{W}}$	Q_W
Workers	W	I	II
Workers	$\underline{W}$	III	IV

answer. The establishment of a wage floor above the competitive rate will induce perfectly competitive firms to reduce employment (Stigler 1946). The reason is simply that, if the minimum wage exceeds the marginal product of labour, firms will lose their incentive to employ as many people. Thus, labour demand is a decreasing function of wage with the proportional reduction in employment being equal to the proportional wage increase times the elasticity of demand. In a two-sector model, the disemployment effects from minimum wages are less drastic. Unemployed workers, it is claimed, may find work in sectors that are not covered by minimum wage legislation (i.e. wage floors have been negotiated by unions in a specific sector only). Other factors that impact on the disemployment effects are the level of homogeneity of workers and potential substitution of other production factors. Neglecting these as well as the implications of the two-sector model may result in overestimating the disemployment effects of the minimum wage.[2] Nonetheless, economists generally agree that wage floors cause net job losses. Wessels (1980), Brown et al. (1982), and Brown (1988) each provide literature reviews that support this consensus. Empirical studies generally find that a 10 percent increase in the minimum wage has a disemployment effect of 1 to 3 percent (Brown 1988).

The consensus, however, is not unanimous. Several influential studies have failed to detect this negative employment effect predicted by the Standard Model (Katz and Krueger 1992; Card 1992a, b; Card and Krueger 1994, 1995). Each of these studies finds either an insignificant or even positive impact of wage floors on employment. Katz and Krueger (1992) detect higher employment after an increase in the minimum wage in the Texan fast-food industry. Card (1992a), using Current Population Survey data, concludes that there is no evidence of a disemployment effect on teenagers after the 1990 increase in the minimum wage. He also finds no significant negative employment effect after a rise in minimum wages in California

---

[2]The theoretical extensions to two-sector economies have been developed by Welch (1974), Gramlich (1976), and Mincer (1976).

(Card 1992b). Card and Krueger (1994) examine the impact of minimum wages on employment in the fast-food industry in New Jersey and Pennsylvania. The authors not only find no indication that the rise in the minimum wage reduced employment. They suggest, furthermore, that the rise in the minimum wage in New Jersey may have increased employment in the fast-food industry. To explain these findings, which seem to contradict the conclusions of the *Standard Model*, the authors point towards what we shall refer to as the *Renegade Model* of labour markets (see also Burdett and Mortensen 1998; Manning 2003, 2004). The *Renegade Model* assumes that labour markets are best approximated by a monopsonistic structure and challenges the hypothesis of the *Standard Model* that the wage elasticity of the labour supply curve is infinite (i.e. the smallest of wage cuts will cause all workers to leave the firm). Several reasons are suggested why this may not be the case. It may, for instance, be costly for workers to change jobs. Furthermore, employees may have imperfect information about alternative jobs or non-wage job attributes may convince staff to stay. It is, therefore, conjectured that employers have some monopsony power over their workers and they are expected to use it. As a consequence of the employer's monopsony power, employees are paid less than their marginal productivity in equilibrium. Thus the introduction of a minimum wage between the original monopsony wage and the competitive wage will increase both employment and efficiency. Similar results are obtained by an equilibrium search model in which firms announce wages and employees search among posted offers (see e.g. Mortensen 1988). More recently, several studies have provided additional empirical support for the monopsony model. Bell (1997) found that a very low value of the minimum wage had no impact on employment in Mexico in the 1980s. Feliciano (1998) identified strong differentiated impacts of minimum wages in Mexico between 1970 and 1990. A reduction of the minimum wage increased employment of women aged 15–64 but reduced employment of older male workers. Saget (2001) concluded that minimum wage had only an insignificant effect on the level of employment in Latin America in the 1990s. A cross-section study in France conducted by Bruno and Cazes (1997) found no impact of minimum wage on youth unemployment.

The *Renegade Model*, however, has not gained wide recognition in political and economic circles and several empirical studies have challenged the findings by Katz and Krueger (1992), Card (1992a, b) and Card and Krueger (1994, 1995). For example, Neumark and Wascher (1992, 2000) and Deere et al. (1995) use data similar to Card (1992a, b) and find a negative employment effect of wage floors in the US. Kim and Taylor (1995), using a different data set, could not confirm the findings by Card (1992b) and find negative employment effects after an increase in the minimum wage in California in 1988. Finally, Neumark and Wascher (1995, 2000) analyse the same event as Card and Krueger (1994) with a similar data set. The authors detect a decline in employment after a raise in the minimum wage in the fast-food industry in New Jersey.[3]

---

[3]Since then, Card and Krueger (2000) have confirmed their initial findings using a different data set.

This said, the Standard Model generally seems to fit the empirics of the labour market better than the Renegade Model. On occasion, however, the latter may be more appropriate than the former. It all depends on the empirical conditions that we are dealing with in a given situation. We proceed by examining how these empirical conditions impact the implications that order ethics implies regarding the ethical legitimacy of the minimum wage.

5 The Standard Model

Assuming we deal with a labour market structure that can be approximated by perfect competition, our interaction model can be further specified as follows. Workers prefer firms to employ a higher quantity of labour, as the degree of unemployment negatively influences their expected wage through an increase in unemployment risk. If a minimum wage is in place, firms will employ fewer workers, thus $Q_{\underline{W}} < Q_W$. Therefore workers prefer quadrant II over I and IV over III. Trivially, since the minimum wage is higher than the competitive market wage, $\underline{W} > W$, III is preferred over I and IV over II. In addition, we shall assume that the wage floor induced unemployment risk is outweighed by the difference between $\underline{W}$ and W. Otherwise workers would be quite unlikely to lobby for a minimum wage and the latter would become irrelevant as a policy measure. Thus, we arrive at the complete preference order for workers: IV > III > II > I.

Firms always prefer workers to play W, thus I > III and II > IV. If workers choose W, they prefer Q_W. Therefore, we have II > I. And if workers choose $\underline{W}$, firms prefer $Q_{\underline{W}}$. Thus, we have III > IV. This yields the complete preference order: II > I > III > IV.

We can now attach numbers to the quadrants in accordance with the players' preferences from 1 to 4, where a high number indicates a high preference (Table 2).

The outcome of this game is quadrant III. The workers' decision to play $\underline{W}$ is not dependent on the firms strategy choice. Given the workers' strategy, firms will play $Q_{\underline{W}}$ which is the profit optimizing quantity to employ.

Now let us proceed to the order-ethical analysis of the case. First, we should clarify, along the lines of Proposition (1), whether the present interactive situation poses an ethical problem. Proposition (1) holds that the fundamental problem of ethics lies in overcoming DS in pursuit of efficient outcomes. The present interactive situation does pose an ethical problem, then, if and only if we are dealing with a DS here. At first glance, however, this is not the case. There is no Pareto-superior quadrant, as would be required to answer this question in the affirmative. Moving to any quadrant where workers are better of, i.e. IV, would make firms worse off. And moving to any quadrant where firms would be better off, i.e. I and II, would make workers worse off.

Note, however, that, on order ethics, the concept of a DS is to be used as a *heuristic*. As Proposition (3) says, every interaction that is subject to ethical investigation has to be modelled in terms of a DS, if possible. Plainly though, it is

Table 2 Labour market interaction—Standard model

		Firms	
		$Q_{\underline{W}}$	Q_W
Workers	W	I (1,3)	II (2,4)
	$\underline{W}$	III (3,2)	IV (4,1)

not possible to model the above situation as a DS since the relevant assumptions that we used to construct the interactive structure follow from the Standard Model.

In fact, in the present situation it is necessary to draw on Proposition (5) before we can proceed. It states that, if we do not find a Pareto-better state of affairs, we should look for a Kaldor-Hicks-superior state. If we can find one, there is a potential for a Pareto-improvement under a suitable redistributive rule. Note, then, that the total surplus of quadrant II is greater than the surplus of quadrant III with the difference being the deadweight loss from wage floors. According to the Kaldor-Hicks-efficiency criterion, quadrant II is superior to quadrant III and it should therefore be possible to achieve an outcome that makes everyone better off. In order to reach quadrant II, workers obviously have to forego their demands for a wage floor. If and only if they do so, it is optimal for firms to employ the efficient quantity of labour which clears the market. But why would workers do that? We cannot expected them to cooperate in this way. And we cannot expect firms to voluntarily share their increase in profits with workers. In line with Proposition (2), we should devise an institutional solution that ensures this outcome. In exchange for their choosing W, workers will obviously call for an appropriate compensation that is at least as high as the difference in expected utility between quadrant III and quadrant II. In order to make an outcome possible that is Pareto-superior to quadrant III, we need, hence, to implement a policy measure that redistributes some of the economic potential which is unlocked as we go from III to II. Obviously, such a Pareto-superior rule cannot entail a direct compensation of workers through firms. If it did, it would not change the status quo and firms would still employ the same number of workers as if the minimum wage was still in place.

The solution looks, rather, like this: We need a mediator who guarantees workers compensation conditional on their choosing W and requires firms to pay an incentive-compatible lump-sum tax independent of their subsequent employment decisions. The level of the tax should be set as high as is necessary in order to collect sufficient funds for workers' compensation. Since a lump-sum tax does not influence firms' employment decisions, under such a rule, firms will choose to employ an efficient amount of labour. Such an alternative regulatory scheme will realize the productive potential that is lost through minimum wages and will make everyone better off. Levying the tax will not force any firm to leave the market which would have stayed in under a minimum wage policy. Rather, it will enable firms to increase profits and will furthermore increase the aggregate income of low-wage workers. (In Mukerji and Schumacher (2008) we survey a number of concrete policy measures that may be seen as rough approximations of the solution that we have just outlined. These include cuts in social security contributions as an indirect wage subsidy to employers and tax credits which serve as a direct wage subsidy, e.g. the American style 'earned income tax credit' or the UK's 'working tax credits'.)

At this stage, then, we can complete the order-ethical evaluation of the minimum wage by applying Proposition (4). According to Proposition (4), the minimum wage is ethically justified if and only if there is no Pareto-superior alternative. As we have just shown, however, there is such an alternative, viz. the solution we have just laid out. Thus, we conclude that, according to order ethics, the minimum wage is not ethically justifiable if labour markets are approximated by the Standard Model.

6 The Renegade Model

Let us now examine how order ethics judges the justification of the minimum wage as we adopt the *Renegade Model*. If we assume that labour markets are better approximated by this theoretical alternative, we need a slightly different model specification. Evidently, firms' preferences do not change at all. Firms still prefer workers to play W rather than $\underline{W}$ in conjunction with every quantity of labour they choose to demand and *per definitionem* they prefer to play Q_W if workers play W and $Q_{\underline{W}}$ if workers play $\underline{W}$. This gives us the complete preference order: II > I > III > IV.

We shall now assume that workers have a choice between a free market wage W and minimum wage $\underline{W}$. Note that we stipulate the latter to be exactly equal to the workers' marginal productivity when markets are cleared and when there is no excess supply of labour. $\underline{W}$ thus maximizes employment at employment level $Q_{\underline{W}}$. We furthermore premise that workers prefer a situation with minimum wages and less than full employment, i.e. IV, over a situation with full employment and without minimum wages, i.e. I.[4] In comparison with the above model, workers' preferences change slightly. Whereas they still prefer $\underline{W}$ over W, they now favour $Q_{\underline{W}}$ over Q_W since now $Q_{\underline{W}}$ is the maximum employment level and optimizes their job security. The complete preference order is: III > IV > I > II (Table 3).

Let us proceed once again to the ethical analysis of the case. According to Proposition (1), we are faced with an ethical problem here if and only if the game

---

[4]Note that we set this premise only for the sake of completeness. It does not influence the outcome since the alternative preference order III > I > IV > II for workers leads to the same outcome.

Table 3 Labour market interaction—Renegade model

		Firms	
		$Q_{\underline{W}}$	Q_W
Workers	W	I (2,3)	II (1,4)
	$\underline{W}$	III (4,2)	IV (3,1)

between workers and firms constitutes a DS. Does it? A Pareto-improvement over III is not obviously possible since every move away from III that would benefit firms, i.e. towards I or II, would harm workers. And there is no quadrant that workers value at least as highly as III. Hence, we apparently do not have a DS here. Perhaps Proposition (5) is of use then? As we discussed above, the possibility of a Kaldor-Hicks improvement may indicate a potential for a Pareto improvement. But in the present situation a Kaldor-Hicks-improvement is equally impossible because, in the Renegade Model, an abolition of the wage floor would induce firms to employ *fewer* workers. Under the minimum wage, the efficiency condition that marginal productivity has to equal wage is *qua premise* fulfilled and thus every departure from the wage regulation policy $\underline{W}$ (i.e. increasing or lowering the minimum wage or its abolition) will necessarily lead to a decrease in production and to someone being worse off. There is, thus, no alternative regulatory scheme that can make all parties involved better off. By Proposition (4), the minimum wage is, hence, ethically justified if we are dealing with a labour market that is approximated by the Renegade Model.

Note, however, that this conclusion is to be handled with caution. It should be stressed that the minimum wage can only be justified if and as long as the conditions of the *Renegade Model* prevail. As mentioned before, the empirical adequacy of the model may be called into question. And even though it is conceivable that particular labour markets exhibit a monopsonistic structure, the ethical justification of minimum wages might well be merely temporary. An instance that illustrates this is a telecommunication market in which a single state-owned company is the only player. In such a market, the *Renegade Model* might be appropriate if one assumes that workers in that market have very specific skills and no choice but to work for the only telecom firm. We entertain certain doubts that such a situation might in fact arise because skill-requirements in low-wage jobs can be assumed to be quite little. But we accept the premise for argument's sake. This telecom firm might exploit its negotiation power over workers, thereby influencing the market price of labour. But as we know, such markets are subject to dynamic liberalization processes in most countries, as history has proven. As soon as competition for workers is intensified and the firms' monopsony status vanishes, minimum wages seem out of place—at least on the order-ethical view. Therefore, if order ethicists draw the conclusion that minimum wages are justified in a particular labour market, they should be ready to revise their judgement, as the underlying economic conditions change. Furthermore, it should be stressed that our model does not justify minimum wages in general. It only justifies an *efficient* minimum wage which satisfies the condition that wage equals marginal productivity.[5]

7 Conclusion

In this chapter, we applied the order-ethical methodology in order to answer the question whether minimum wage laws are ethically justified. We drew a twofold conclusion. If we assume that labour markets are best described by what we called the *Standard Model*, a model that assumes perfect competition for labour, we can reconstruct the interaction between workers and firms in terms of a DS. Workers prefer minimum wages and firms, thus, choose a smaller number of workers than they would in the absence of a wage floor. The outcome involves a deadweight loss from minimum wages which, in turn, implies the possibility of a Kaldor-Hicks-improvement through the abolition of the minimum wage. We reasoned that in this situation a Pareto-improvement is conceivable and might be generated through a redistributive rule. Such a rule would (over) compensate workers for sacrificing the difference in expected utility between the minimum wage and the market wage. Since the rule would require that workers bind themselves to not lobbying for minimum wages, it would be able to stabilize a Pareto-superior outcome. The quintessence of our analysis was that, on order ethics, minimum wages are not justifiable under the *Standard Model* since a Pareto-superior solution is conceivable. If we assume, however, that the *Renegade Model* of minimum wages, a model that assumes a monopsonistic labour market structure, mirrors the facts better than the *Standard Model*, the minimum wage seems to be without alternative and is, hence, ethically justified. In the renegade case, no potential for a Pareto-improvement exists. It is generally doubted, however, that the renegade view is an adequate way of looking at the labour market. As is consistent with the standard view, we, therefore, conclude that order ethicists are likely to doubt the ethical legitimacy of the minimum wage.

We would like to conclude with two brief observations about the order-ethical approach to public policy issues. Firstly, we would like to emphasize that economic and ethical considerations coexisted peacefully in our investigation. This is worth noting because many ethicists subscribe to the so called *Conflict Paradigm*, as we pointed out initially. They believe that the aims of ethics and economics are

---

[5]For a discussion of a minimum wage which fulfills this requirement, see Manning (2003).

inherently conflicting. On order ethics, this is not so. As we made clear, the minimum wage is ethically justified, according to order ethics, only if it is economically efficient. Hence, there need not be a contradiction between an ethically desirable and an economically desirable outcome. In Mukerji and Schumacher (2008), we framed this into a slogan. We said that when it comes to the ethicality and efficiency of the minimum wage, *we can have our cake and eat it too*. On order ethics, this idea applies to all issues in public policy.

The second point that we would like to highlight is this. On order ethics, the ethical justification of a given policy measure, e.g. the minimum wage, depends entirely on its *empirical* properties. We stress this, because we would like to contrast our approach once more with the way in which the discussions about social and economic ethics are usually led. The debate about the minimum wage is a good illustration of this. Both employers' representatives and trade unionists tend to base their opinions on ideological positions. It is, for instance, argued that minimum wages are impermissible because they interfere with the employers' right and liberty to negotiate their own terms with employees. Another ideological view mostly uttered by workers' representatives is simply that labour has to pay! A minimum wage is justified because it is right *as a matter of principle*—not for its desirable economic effects. Order ethics offers an alternative to these positions in asking: If we can make everyone better off, why should we not do it? Note that, in doing this, it makes the answer to the question about the ethical legitimacy of minimum wages depend on the answer to the empirical-economic question of whether everyone actually is better off due to minimum wages. The order-ethical approach has thus the advantage that it makes the answer to an ethical question ("Is the minimum wage ethically justified?") depend on the answer to an empirical-scientific question ("What are the economic effects of the minimum wage?"). This shift in focus, we believe, may play an important part in de-ideologizing many ethical debates and may conceivably lead to progress on many fronts.

References

Bell, L.A. 1997. The impact of minimum wages in Mexicao and Colombia. *Journal of Labour Economics* 15(3): 102–135.
Brown, C., C. Gilroy, and A. Kohen. 1982. The effects of the minimum wage on employment and unemployment. *Journal of Economic Literature* 20(2): 487–528.
Brown, C. 1988. Minimum Wage Laws: Are They Overrated?, *Journal of Economic Perspectives* 2(3): 133–145.
Bruno, C., and S. Cazes. 1997. La chômage des jeunes en France: Un état des lieux. *Revue de l'OFCE* 62: 75–107.
Burdett, K., and D.T. Mortensen. 1998. Wage differentials, employer size, and unemployment. *International Economic Review* 39(2): 257–273.
Card, D. 1992a. Using regional variation in wages to measure the effects of the federal minimum wage. *Industrial and Labor Relations Review* 46: 22–37.
Card, D. 1992b. Do minimum wages reduce employment? A case study of California, 1987–1989. *Industrial and Labor Relations Review* 46: 38–54.
Card, D., and A.B. Krueger. 1994. Minimum wages and employment: A case study of the fast-food industry in New Jersey and Pennsylvania. *American Economic Review* 84(4): 772–793.

Card, D., and A.B. Krueger. 1995. *Myth and measurement*. Princeton University Press: Princeton.
Card, D., and A.B. Krueger. 2000. Minimum wages and employment: A case study of the fast-food industry in New Jersey and Pennsylvania: Reply. *American Economic Review* 90(5): 1397–1420.
Cordero, R.A. 2000. Morality and the minimum wage. *Journal of Social Philosophy* 31(2): 207–222.
Deere, D., K.M. Murphy, and F. Welch. 1995. Employment and the 1990–1991 minimum wage hike. *American Economic Review* 85(2): 232–237.
Feliciano, Z.M. 1998. Does the minimum wage affect employment in Mexico? *Eastern Economic Journal* 24(2): 165–180.
Gaski, J.F. 2004. Raising the minimum wage is unethical and immoral. *Business and Society Review* 109(2): 209–224.
Gramlich, E. 1976. The impact of minimum wages on other wages, employment, and family incomes. *Brookings Papers on Economic Activity* 2: 409–451.
Hicks, J.R. 1939. The foundations of welfare economics. *The Economic Journal* 49(196): 696–712.
Hardin, G. 1968. The Tragedy of the Commons, *Science* 162: 1243–1244.
Kaldor, N. 1939. Welfare propositions of economics and interpersonal comparisons of utility. *The Economic Journal* 49(195): 549–552.
Katz, L.F., and A.B. Krueger. 1992. The effect of the minimum wage on the fast food industry. *Industrial and Labor Relations Review* 46(1): 6–21.
Kim, T., and L. Taylor. 1995. The employment effect in retail trade of California's 1988 minimum wage increase. *Journal of Business and Economic Statistics* 13(2): 175–182.
Manning, A. 2003. Monopsony and the efficiency of labour market interventions. *Labour Economics* 11: 145–163.
Manning, A. 2004. *Monopsony in motion: Imperfect competition in labour markets*. Princeton University Press: Princeton.
Mincer, J. 1976. Unemployment effects of minimum wages. *Journal of Political Economy* 84: 87–105.
Moore, T.G. 1971. The effects of minimum wages on teenage unemployment rates. *The Journal of Political Economy* 79(4): 897–902.
Mortensen, D.T. 1988. Equilibrium wage distribution: A synthesis. Center for Mathematical Studies in Economics and Management Science, *Discussion Paper 811*, Northwestern University.
Mukerji, N., and C. Schumacher. 2008. How to have your cake and eat it too: Resolving the efficiency-equity trade-off in minimum wage legislation. *The Journal of Interdisciplinary Economics* 19(4): 315–340.
Neumark, D., and W. Wascher. 1992. Employment effects of minimum and subminimum wages: Panel data in state minimum wage laws. *Industrial and Labor Relations Review* 46: 55–81.
Neumark, D., and W. Wascher. 1995. *The effect of New Jersey's minimum wage increase on fast-food employment: A re-evaluation using payroll records*. Mimeograph: Department of Economics, Michigan State University.
Neumark, D., and W. Wascher. 2000. Minimum wages and employment: A case study of the fast-food industry in New Jersey and Pennsylvania: Comment. *American Economic Review* 90(5): 1362–1396.
Okun, A. 1975. *Equality and efficiency—The big tradeoff*. Washington, D.C.: The Brookings Institution.
Saget, C. 2001. Poverty reduction and decent work in developing countries: Do minimum wages help? *International Labour Review* 140(3): 237–269.
Stigler, G.J. 1946. The economics of minimum wage legislation. *American Economic Review* 36(3): 358–365.
Welch, F. 1974. Minimum wage legislation in the United States. *Economic Inquiry* 12(3): 285–318.
Wessels, W.J. 1980. *Minimum wages, fringe benefits and working conditions*. Washington, D.C.: American Enterprise Institute.
Wilkinson, T.M. 2004. The ethics and economics of the minimum wage. *Economics and Philosophy* 20(2): 351–374.

Sustainability from an Order Ethics Perspective

Markus Beckmann

1 Introduction

Over the past decades, sustainability has emerged as a prominent and widely shared concept in public, civil society, corporate, and academic debates. The speed and breadth of this development is quite astounding. Within a few years, governments around the world have embraced the goal of sustainability at international conferences and through national sustainability strategies. Civil society organizations have framed environmental, social, cultural, economic, and human rights objectives as part of a shared sustainability agenda. In business, companies have created dedicated sustainability departments internally while at the same time measuring and reporting their sustainability performance to the outside. Finally, in academia, sustainability science is evolving as a new discipline that bridges the natural and social sciences (Kates et al. 2001), with sustainability also emerging as a key concept in established disciplines including, most notably for this chapter, the field of (business) ethics.

The purpose of this chapter is to examine the emergence of the sustainability concept and its societal relevance from an order ethics perspective. As a distinct theoretical paradigm, order ethics departs from individualist approaches to ethics by highlighting the importance of the social order in which individuals and organizations interact. While individualist approaches to ethics focus on individual *actions* and the ethical quality of their underlying *intentions* (such as altruism or self-love), "order ethics" or "institutional ethics" highlights that many pressing societal issues such as unemployment, climate change, financial crises, pervasive corruption, or environmental degradation are collective challenges that largely arise from the *un*intended consequences of the *interactions* of individuals in a particular

M. Beckmann (✉)
Chair for Corporate Sustainability Management, University of Erlangen-Nürnberg, Nuremberg, Germany
e-mail: markus.beckmann@fau.de

institutional context. As a consequence, order ethics shifts the focus towards the ethical quality of those *institutions* or "rules of the game" (Brennan and Buchanan 2000; Buchanan 1987) that channel how individuals interact and that govern whether the involved individuals (can) realize ethically desirable or undesirable group outcomes.

As shown in the following, there are substantial commonalities and areas of overlap between the sustainability concept and the order ethics approach. In fact, a key claim of this chapter is that the very notion of sustainability can best be fully understood from an order ethics perspective. At the same time, the development of the sustainability concept also provides insights for learning in the order ethics domain.

To explore this potential for mutual learning, the argument of this chapter proceeds in five steps. The first step explores the origin of the sustainability concept and discusses important milestones in how sustainability evolved as a novel, yet widely accepted regulative idea. Seeking to explain this remarkable career, the second step then analyzes the sustainability concept as a semantic innovation. Taking an order ethics perspective, the argument illustrates how sustainability differs in several regards from conventional normative categories such as justice, virtue, or solidarity—and why these distinct features render the sustainability notion particularly fruitful for the kind of learning processes of interest in order ethics. The third and fourth step then examine two important fields for implementing sustainability. Applying the order ethics perspective to the level of the societal macro order, the third step spells out implications of the sustainability agenda for (global) governance and the changing interplay between governments, companies, and civil society actors in the age of globalization. Then, the fourth step applies the order ethics approach to the level of the organizational order of the individual firm and discusses corporate sustainability management from an institutional perspective. In the fifth and last step, the chapter concludes and discusses implications for how sustainability can inspire future learning for the research program of order ethics.

2 Origins of the Sustainability Concept and Milestones of the Sustainability Debate

While the current sustainability debate is fairly young, the term itself has much older roots (Wiersum 1995). The first documented use of the word "sustainable" goes back more than 300 years when Hans Carl von Carlowitz (1713) published his book *Sylvicultura oeconomica,* the first comprehensive treatise on forestry. As the mining administrator at the court of the German state of Saxony, von Carlowitz reacted to a looming resource crisis by publishing his book. At the time, Saxony's economy relied heavily on its silver mines, which, in turn, depended on a steady supply of timber. To provide this timber, trees were cut at unsustainable rates, consuming most of the region's old growth forests. The resulting timber scarcity threatened the survival of Saxony's wealth and power.

In light of this looming ecological and economic collapse, von Carlowitz's book not only pioneered the forestry principle of cutting only as much timber as the forest can regrow within the same time period. He also laid out how to increase regrowth through systematic reforestation and cultivation measures. Von Carlowitz called this approach of using the forest in a way that avoids collapse and can be continued perpetually as "sustainable use" (*nachhaltende Nutzung*). Within a few decades, these novel principles of modern "sustainable yield" forestry were quickly adopted not only in Saxony but also throughout Europe and even in some North American colonies.

Some key components of the modern sustainability concept (see below)—the idea of avoiding collapse, taking a long-term perspective, and living off interests instead of consuming the capital base—thus go back to its origins in 1713. Nevertheless, for most of the following three centuries, "sustainability" was used only as a technical term to discuss 'sustainable yields' in the narrow field of forestry and, as of the early 20th century, in the fishery domain as well. Why and how, then, did sustainability evolve from such a narrow technical term into a widely held societal concept? To understand this development requires an examination of the second half of the 20th century when two important debates first emerged and then converged: the ecological movement and the debate on the social and economic development in the global south.

As of the 1950s and 1960s, a number of events paved the way for the modern environmental movement. In the 1952 Great Smog of London, for instance, air pollution in London was so bad that within a few days 4000 people died and more than 100,000 were ill in the city according to contemporary estimates. [Recent research suggests that the number of fatalities was even higher reaching about 12,000 (Bell and Davis 2001)]. Ten years later, Rachel Carson's (1962) book *Silent Spring* drastically warned that the use of pesticides such as DDT had devastating effects on the environment, particularly on birds to the point that song birds could no longer be heard during spring. Events like these gave momentum to the birth of the environmental movement and its claim that the intensive industrialized economic growth patterns endangered not only nature but also the future of human well-being. The founding of the World Wildlife Fund for Nature (WWF) in 1961 marked the emergence of national and international environmental organizations in civil society, while the 1970s saw the advent of the first green parties at a national level.

In 1969, responding to such growing environmental concerns on a local level, Sweden obtained a mandate to convene the first UN conference addressing environmental concerns, the 1972 *United Nations Conference on the Human Environment*. Despite its important contribution of creating global awareness for the environment, the conference, however, struggled to reconcile two seemingly competing demands. On one side of the aisle, many rich, industrialized countries of the global North stressed the urgency of protecting nature and called for more environmental protection. On the other side of the aisle, however, many poorer, developing countries of the global South questioned the priority of environmental concerns as long as their population still suffered from the social ills of poverty, low life-expectancy, and underdevelopment. Although the conference tried to sponsor

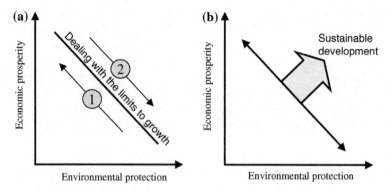

Fig. 1 Limits to growth versus sustainable development perspective

the idea that underdevelopment can cause environmental deficiencies (UNEP 1972), the perception that environmental protection and economic development were conflicting goals prevailed—with poorer countries asserting their right to economic growth and social development.

Throughout the 1970s, the view of a fundamental conflict between what is good for the economy/development and what is good for nature continued to shape the debate. An important milestone in this regard was the influential report to the Club of Rome in which Meadows et al. (1972) urgently highlighted "Limits to Growth." Assuming that economic development cannot be separated from increasing resource consumption, the report concluded that modern levels of economic wealth are necessarily per se linked to a drastic deterioration in environmental quality (Arrow 1 in Fig. 1a). As Porter and Linde (2008, p. 347) state, "the prevailing view [was] that there is an inherent and fixed trade-off: ecology versus economy." Given this perceived trade-off, economic, social, and ecological objectives seemed to be conflicting. While environmentalists claimed that in order to conserve nature, it was necessary to abstain from growth and accept lower levels of economic wealth (Arrow 2 in Fig. 1a), people concerned about economic growth and social development took an opposing stance.

To overcome the aforementioned frontlines, the UN decided at the beginning of the 1980s to establish a new commission. As explicitly expressed by its official title, this *World Commission on Environment and Development* (WCED) placed equal emphasis on both ecological *and* development concerns. Headed by former Norwegian prime minister Gro Harlem Brundtland, the so-called Brundtland Commission started its work in 1983. The commission soon departed from the previous either-environment-or-development dichotomy and emphasized the interdependence of the two dimensions.[1]

---

[1] As Gro H. Brundtland maintained in her foreword to "Our common future," "the 'environment' is where we live; and 'development' is what we all do in attempting to improve our lot within that abode. The two are inseparable."

It was only when the Brundtland Commission's work brought together concerns for the environment and for development that the sustainability idea started shaping the broader societal debate. Throughout the 1950s, 1960s, and 1970s, the term sustainability remained confined to its technical usage in the fields of forestry and fishery. This changed quite remarkably with the publication of the WCED's report *Our Common Future* in 1987. This so-called "Brundtland Report" contains probably the most well-known and widespread definition within the sustainability debate.[2] (Take note of the title of the report.) By taking the shared interests of all people in our common future as an integrative lens, the report introduces the concept of "sustainable development" as a "development that meets the needs of the present without compromising the ability of future generations to meet their own needs" (Brundtland 1987).

The Brundtland definition contains the following noteworthy elements. With its focus on needs, it acknowledges the diverse interests of human beings, in particular with regard to development but also in view of the need to live in an intact environment. Furthermore, the idea of intergenerational justice (between present and future generations) introduces the time dimension that allows reconciling short-term conflicts between development and the environment. Note how the Brundtland definition of sustainable development thus incorporates the three aspects already implied in Carlowitz's sustainability concept: first, "our common future" refers to the shared interest in avoiding collapse of ecological or social systems. Second, the idea of living off the interests without consuming capital is mirrored by the principle that present generations do not erode future generations' ability to satisfy their needs. Third, just as von Carlowitz stressed the possibility of increasing a forest's productivity through advanced reforestation and cultivation methods, the Brundtland Report stresses that the "limitations ... on the environment's ability to meet present and future needs" are "imposed by the state of technology and social organization." In other words, these limitations are not invariably given but can be changed. The Brundtland Report thus departs from a static "limits to growth" perspective (the limits are fixed) and highlights that with innovation a dynamic "growth of limits" perspective (the limits can expand) makes "sustainable development" possible (see Fig. 1b).

The impact of the Brundtland Report was significant. With sustainability being specified as an umbrella for development, environmental considerations, and global cooperation, the former technical term was soon embraced as a regulative idea at the international level that brought together government leaders and heads of state from all over the world at conferences such as the 1992 Rio Earth Summit

---

[2]While the Brundtland report contains the most well-known definition of "sustainable development," it did not provide the first. A few years earlier, in 1980, the "World Conservation Strategy" (WSC) had already coined "sustainable development" as "the integration of conservation and development to ensure that modifications to the planet do indeed secure the survival and well-being of all people." The WCS, however, was largely driven by Northern environmentalists (including the WWF) and criticized for being too biocentric—and less concerned about the needs of the global poor (Adams 2003).

[UN Conference on Environment and Development (UNCED)], the 2002 World Summit on Sustainable Development in Johannesburg, the 2012 UN Conference on Sustainable Development and the Sustainable Development Goals (SDGs) in late 2015. At the same time, programs like the Agenda 21 (a product of the 1992 Earth Summit) provided an action plan for applying the idea of sustainable development not only to the global but also to the national and local level.

However, the rapid diffusion of the sustainability idea was not restricted to the political sphere but quickly entered civil society and the business world. At the Earth Summit in 1992, CEOs of multinational companies formed a group that then became the World Business Council for Sustainable Development (http://wbcsd.org/). Businesses soon started to apply the sustainability idea to the organizational level of the firm. Only a few years later, John Elkington (1997) and his think-tank "AccountAbility" coined and popularized the concept of a "triple bottom line" (TBL). The TBL builds upon the *three-pillar model* whereby sustainability seeks to combine the economic, social, and ecological dimension (also known as "profit, people, planet").

In the attempt to further operationalize sustainability at the organizational level, the past ten years have witnessed the advent of the "ESG" criteria, a concept advanced and popularized largely by the "Global Reporting Initiative" (Global Reporting Initiative 2009). ESG stands for the 'ecological,' 'social,' and 'governance' dimensions of sustainability. Taking for granted that economic success in the long-term is simply a must for any company, the ESG criteria replaces the economic dimension of the TBL with the governance dimension, thus focusing on the institutional arrangements within a company that seek to guarantee the integrity of the organization as well as the integrity of its internal management processes. The ESG approach, then, highlights that not only ecological and social but also governance factors are relevant, even crucial, to the economic success and sustainability of a company.

In short, after being confined to a merely technical usage in forestry for more than two centuries, sustainability has emerged rapidly as a widespread regulative idea in politics, civil society, and business in less than two decades. Taking an order ethics perspective, the following section discusses some specific features that have qualified the sustainability semantics for this remarkable career.

3 The Distinctive Heuristic Quality of the Sustainability Semantics

As the previous section demonstrated, sustainability has emerged within less than two decades as a novel and influential normative category in societal discourse. Yet, why is it that a fairly technical term from forestry could gain societal relevance on a wide scale? How do the sustainability semantics differ from the perspective of more conventional normative categories such as justice, virtue, or solidarity? And how can these distinctive features of the sustainability semantics explain its remarkable career in societal discourse?

The key claim of this section is that the sustainability concept—popularized by the Brundtland Report's definition of sustainable development—provides a semantic innovation that has a distinctive heuristic quality not only for a broad range of current societal challenges but also for the perspective of order ethics. The following eight aspects may serve to illustrate this distinctive heuristic quality (cf. in part to Beckmann et al. 2014):

1. *Sustainability is a cosmopolitical term of its own kind.* As a normative category for societal discourse it was literally '*born global*' as it emerged in global debates between nations before diffusing to the national (i.e. within nations) and corporate level. Note the difference from traditional concepts such as justice or solidarity. These normative categories were first used to provide guidance in the microcosm of the small group such as the Greek polis. Scaling up such small-group semantics to the national or even global level is, however, not trivial. Take the case of "global justice" (Pogge 2001). As Nagel (2005, p. 113) points out, it is far from "clear what, if anything, justice on a world scale might mean." In contrast to this challenge of adapting a small-group category to the world scale, the societal concept of sustainable development has its very roots in a global debate and was then translated down to the national, local, and organizational level.

2. The sustainability semantics *shift the focus from actors and actions to processes and systems*. Note again the difference from traditional normative categories. A supervisor can be just or show solidarity. A decision can be fair or unfair. A person can have responsibility or virtue. In contrast, it would sound less natural to argue that a supervisor has no sustainability or is sustainable, or that a particular behavior of how he/she treated you was sustainable or unsustainable. Rather, the focus of sustainability semantics lies on the outcomes and qualities of continuing processes or systems. Just like the perspective of order ethics, sustainability thus departs from a mere individualist ethics paradigm.

3. Sustainability uses an *internal process criterion to define its normative perspective*. Again, note the difference from a concept like justice. To decide whether an act is just or unjust necessarily requires an (implicit or explicit) ethical theory that provides an external normative yardstick. In a modern, globalized world, however, "the fact of reasonable pluralism" (Rawls 1993, p. 114) highlights that there is not one, but many, competing and sometimes incommensurable ethical standpoints. By asking whether a process or system can be sustained or might collapse, sustainability shifts the focus from such competing external ethical perspectives to internal process properties. This can explain how the sustainability perspective was able to reframe the controversial debate between environmentalists and people interested in growth and development.

4. Sustainability seeks to *transcend perceived (value) trade-offs* by introducing a win-win perspective on shared interests. Like the Brundtland Report's title *Our*

Common Future expresses, sustainability focuses on the shared interest of avoiding collapse and safeguarding an open future that allows for the realization of diverse interests (Suchanek 2004). To illustrate, people can have a shared interest in the sustainable management of fish stocks without necessarily sharing the same values and individual interests in economic (maximize long-term profits), social (save jobs), or environmental (protect fish) objectives.

5. Sustainability is a *constructivist perspective for institutional reform*. Just as the order ethics perspective, sustainability does not assume that win-win solutions are automatically given. Rather, sustainability provides a searchlight for exploring and, if necessary, inventing win-win solutions (Beckmann et al. 2014). And just as the order ethics perspective shifts the focus from individual intentions to the institutional order, the sustainability semantics does not focus on reforming people but on reforming processes and systems. The sustainability perspective therefore directs its attention automatically to those institutions and rules of the game that govern societal processes and that channel system dynamics. It is thus not surprising that the global sustainability debate almost immediately turned into a discussion about global governance (see below) while the corporate sustainability perspective quickly embraced the governance dimension, too (see the ESG discussion above).

6. From its very beginning, the sustainability semantics implies *a pronounced long-term orientation*. Note again the difference to conventional normative categories such as justice whose initial focus was rather on intragenerational relations at a specific point in time. In contrast, the sustainability semantics is not only inherently open to look at long-term, even intergenerational challenges, it also takes this long-term perspective on the future as the starting point for reconciling diverse objectives that seem to be conflicting when only viewed in an isolated point in time.

7. Sustainability calls for *continuous learning processes*. With its focus on processes and the long-term future, sustainability is not a static goal that can be achieved once and for all. Sustainability is rather a moving target. The value of the sustainability semantics thus does not lie in its ability to provide blueprint answers but to stimulate relevant questions.

8. Finally, sustainability promotes and necessitates—the *cooperation and discourse of diverse stakeholders and theoretical perspectives*. Integrating ecological, economic, and social criteria requires not only the interdisciplinary exchange between the natural and the social sciences. Rather, as sustainability challenges are often so complex that no single actor has the knowledge and the resources to address them alone, sustainability also calls for dialogue between diverse stakeholders, the transdisciplinary cooperation between researchers and practitioners (Hirsch Hadorn et al. 2006), and cross-functional teams within corporations (Schaltegger et al. 2013).

In summary, the remarkable career of the sustainability semantics rests on a number of features that distinguish sustainability from traditional normative categories. As a societal concept, sustainability is a 'born global' cosmopolitical term with a long-run perspective that shifts the focus from individual actors to shared processes. Instead of taking sides within a perceived trade-off between the ecology and the economy, sustainability aims at transcending trade-offs through institutional reforms. Sustainability semantics is therefore in many ways closely related to the order ethics perspectives. Both viewpoints refrain from prescribing individual values but rather focus on how governance reforms can allow a pluralist society to reach their diverse needs through societal cooperation. The next two sections discuss the implications of such an institutional sustainability concept for the domain of global governance and for managing corporate sustainability.

4 Sustainability and the Need for (New Forms of Global) Governance

In 2009, the scientific journal *Nature* published an article that quickly gained prominence in the sustainability debate. Entitled "A safe operating space for humanity" (Rockström et al. 2009), this piece examines the Earth's ecological systems and then discusses nine planetary boundaries that define the natural preconditions for the development of humankind. One of these nine dimensions is the issue of climate change, which has received considerable public attention. As the authors highlight, however, the other dimensions, including issues such as loss of biodiversity, ocean acidification, or changes in the nitrogen cycle, are no less critical for human survival although they are hardly talked about in public. Yet, just as in the case of climate change, overstepping any of these planetary boundaries threatens to have devastating effects on human development.

Rockström et al.'s (2009) work provides a vivid illustration of global interdependence. Regardless of nationality, level of wealth, religion, gender, ethnicity or political ideology, all humankind faces the same challenge of avoiding the breakdown of Earth's ecological carrying capacity. Ensuring sustainability is thus in the interest of each individual. At the same time, however, sustainability challenges such as climate change amount to what Hardin (1968) described as the "tragedy of the commons." In such a situation, each individual uses a shared resource (such as fish stocks, grazing land, etc.) more than would be sustainable at the group level in the long-term. Put in the language of sustainability, individuals unintentionally deplete a shared capital stock by taking out collectively more than the capital stock yields in terms of interests. An individual change in behavior cannot solve this tragedy. If the other individuals kept consuming what is available, they would eventually extract what a moral first mover refrained from consuming. Consequently, since the tragedy of the commons and, for that matter, virtually any sustainability challenge involve a *collective* dilemma, the solution also needs to be a collective one that brings all relevant actors on board.

Sustainable development thus requires arrangements to align the short-term incentives of individuals with the shared long-term interests of the group. This is why a critical key to sustainability lies in creating adequate forms of *governance*. As Williamson (2010, p. 456) put it, "governance is the means by which to infuse order, thereby to mitigate conflict and realize mutual gain." From an order ethics perspective, this is precisely what sustainability is about, namely to (re-)design institutional arrangements such that conflicting (short-term) interests can be managed in a way that allows realizing shared long-term objectives. The question then is: who provides governance solutions?

Throughout most of the 20th century, the default provider of societal governance solutions, at least in the rich developed countries, was nation-state governance that relies on a clear division of labor between government, business, and civil society. In this model, states are the political rule-*makers* who define the "rules of the game," while other actors such as businesses or civil society organizations (CSOs) are merely rule-*takers*. In their respective domains, businesses then engage in economic activities while CSOs focus on charitable activities or act as watchdogs for governments and firms.

For a number of reasons, the provision of governance solutions by specialized nation-state institutions has been a remarkable success story. In functioning Western democracies, government institutions have special *resources* to set and enforce collective rules through the legislative and judicial process. Based on the consent of the voters, governments also have the *legitimacy* to establish collective solutions. Finally, government actors have *incentives* to solve governance problems and create productive solutions in order to ensure their (re-) election. Against this background, many economists have treated the Western nation-state governance model almost exclusively as the only legitimate way to address those collective action problems that define societal sustainability challenges (Friedman 1970; Jensen 2002).

However, while sustainability issues like the ecological ones highlighted by Rockström et al. (2009) as well as social ones such as the spread of infectious diseases or poor labor standards in supply chains have globalized, adequate global governance arrangements are only beginning to emerge. Mitigating climate change, protecting global fish stocks, ensuring labor standards in transnational supply chains, preventing corruption in the extractive industries in developing countries, or dealing with conflict diamonds in failed states are just a few instances in which there is no state governance body that could handle these challenges at the national level. Yet, at the transnational or even global level, there is no world government either that has the resources, the legitimacy, or the incentives to provide functional governance solutions for the global public good. At the same time, in many parts of the world, effective state governance is missing where local governments fail to set or enforce adequate rules that promote social and ecological sustainability.

This gap between the demand for functional governance solutions for sustainability and the limited ability of traditional state governance to provide such solutions has created the need for "new governance" (Boatright 2011; Scherer and Palazzo 2011). Following the idea of "governance without governance" (Rosenau and Czempiel 1992), new governance means that not only nation-state governments but also corporations, civil-society organizations, and supranational bodies can collaborate in order to jointly provide governance solutions for sustainability.

The example of the Marine Stewardship Council (MSC) illustrates how such forms of new governance can contribute to addressing sustainability challenges. The MSC is an international labeling scheme for sustainable fish production. Due to overfishing, fish stocks all over the world face the risk of depletion and collapse. Yet, individual action by fishermen to protect fish stocks fails to solve the overfishing problem if other fishers keep catching as much as they can. As a classic "tragedy of the commons," the challenge of overfishing thus requires a collective governance solution. Frustrated by the inability of national and supranational government institutions to provide such a governance solution through setting and enforcing adequate catch-quotas, the WWF (World Wildlife Fund), the Anglo-Dutch corporation Unilever, and other non-state actors joined forces in 1996 to create a standard that monitors where and how fish are caught in order to enforce sustainable fishing (www.msc.org).

The MSC illustrates how non-state actors can bring together resources, legitimacy, and incentives to provide a governance solution where governments fail to do so. As the world's largest fish buyer, Unilever provided enough bargaining power to exert influence on its fish producing suppliers. By including the WWF as one of the world's most well-known environmental NGO, by allowing other actors to join, by making the process transparent, and by providing a tangible improvement for the sustainability challenge of overfishing, the MSC also created both input and output legitimacy. Finally, Unilever and the WWF had incentives to create and provide a governance solution. While the WWF had the ecological objective of protecting aquatic wildlife, Unilever followed the economic objective of securing critical supplies. This example thus shows again how the goal of sustainability can create consensus despite diverging individual interests.

New governance for sustainability thus questions the conventional division of labor between the state, business, and civil society. In cases like the MSC, non-state actors such as businesses and CSOs stop being mere rule-takers but actively engage in collective rule-setting processes as well, thus taking "ordo-responsibility" (see Beckmann and Pies 2016, in this book). These changing actor roles can facilitate novel governance solutions for sustainability. At the same time, however, they are not without friction but create new ambiguities. Take CSOs for example. On the one hand, CSOs remain important as watchdogs to criticize government and corporate misconduct. On the other hand, when jointly creating new governance arrangements, CSOs increasingly need to partner with companies and governments. CSOs thus face the challenge to build up trust and partnerships with the same actors that they need to be able to criticize with independence and credibility if necessary. Similarly, companies need to learn to cooperate not only with CSOs but also with their competitors and with governments—without crossing the line to unfair cartels or illegitimate forms of lobbying. Finally, governments need to learn to use a mix of subordinating business to government regulation where appropriate (and possible) —and coordinating and promoting modes of self-regulation where the latter is the superior form of governance (Pies et al. 2010).

In short, systemic sustainability challenges are eventually governance challenges. Consequently, addressing global sustainability requires improving global governance. As conventional state governance has its limits, new forms of global governance are needed that bring together businesses, states, and civil society to improve the institutional order on both the national and global level.

5 Corporate Sustainability Management from an Order Ethics Perspective

The order ethics perspective highlights that achieving sustainability at the global level is above all a (global) governance challenge. This section now shifts the focus from the global to the organizational level of the business firm. What is the role of companies for sustainability? And how can the order ethics perspective provide guidance for better understanding and managing this role? From an order ethics perspective (the key claim to be developed here), corporate sustainability management is also a governance challenge: namely to link the company's stakeholders through a business model that creates a win-win outcome by combing the creation of value with the avoidance or reduction of negative impacts.

(1) Companies can contribute to sustainability through two fundamental and complementary roles. As sustainability in its essence is about meeting present and future needs of people, the *primary sustainability function* of companies is to *satisfy diverse needs through value creation*. Imagine a world without companies. How could we possibly satisfy the multiplicity of needs ranging from food, water, housing, sanitation or energy to communication, health, mobility, and entertainment without ventures that organized dense webs of cooperation and complex value chains? By bringing together diverse stakeholders (Freeman 1984), companies transform available inputs (such as labor, raw materials, and energy) into outputs (products and services, attractive jobs, return to investors) that have higher value in terms of their ability to satisfy our needs. Given an adequate institutional framework, profits then signal and reward a company that is fulfilling its primary sustainability function. Granted that prices express real scarcity, profits are only possible if society's willingness to pay is higher for the produced outputs than for the consumed inputs (Jensen 2002). Profits, in other words, then signal that a company has improved society's ability to satisfy human needs. Given the scarcity of resources and the diversity of our needs, the value creation function is therefore a fundamental contribution of corporations for sustainability. Value creation allows for sustainability.

(2) Most, if not all processes of value creation, however, can cause negative externalities. These negative side effects can be physical and impact the natural environment such as in the case of air pollution, wastewater, destructed habitat, land use or the consumption of energy. And they can affect the social

sphere be it through noise, negative health effects, discrimination, abuse or even violation of human rights. Such side effects of value creation processes negatively impact both present and future generations and undermine their ability to satisfy diverse needs. As a consequence, a company's creation of negative impacts reduces sustainability.

As negative environmental and social impacts affect people and reduce their present and future ability to meet diverse needs, the *secondary function* of companies for sustainability is *to avoid or reduce negative impacts*. From a sustainability perspective, negative impact reduction is a secondary function not because it is less important but because it comes second logically. Any business needs a positive purpose first. Just avoiding negative impacts would fail to provide a raison d'être for the company (why found a firm if "no firm" would be the most effective way to avoid all negative impacts). It is only through its primary function that a firm can begin contributing to needs satisfaction and thus sustainability. It is then the secondary function that decides whether a company's eventual net contribution to sustainability is largely positive, mixed, or even negative.

(3) Corporate sustainability management thus seeks to realize two complementary goals: to increase value creation and to reduce negative impacts (Schaltegger and Burrit 2005). Figure 2 illustrates both objectives as two independent dimensions. How, then, do these two objectives relate to each other? Mirroring the origins of the sustainability debate, two competing approaches have emerged to address this question. The order ethics perspective can help put them into context.

The first approach understands sustainability management as a *reactive win-lose management*. As illustrated by the negatively sloped line in Fig. 2a, this approach assumes that the reduction of negative impacts—e.g. through the installation of expensive filters—creates extra costs meaning there is an essential tradeoff between the goal of value creation and impact reduction. The role of sustainability management is then to carefully analyze these tradeoffs and react to them by identifying

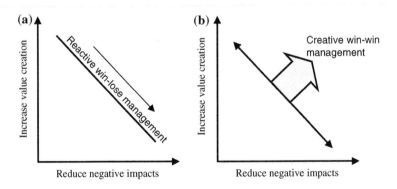

Fig. 2 Reactive win-lose versus creative win-win corporate sustainability management

a compromise that balances the gains and losses for the different stakeholders (e.g. balance product costs and external costs of environmental pollution) (Hahn et al. 2010; Winn et al. 2012).

In contrast, as illustrated by the arrow pointing to the Northeast, the *creative win-win management approach* does not perceive value creation and impact reduction as a necessary trade-off but aims at win-win solutions in which the reduction of negative impacts *increases* the firm's ability to create value.

There has been a longer debate as to what corporate sustainability management *"really"* is about—the management of either trade-offs or of win-win situations (Dyllick and Hockerts 2002). Seen from an order ethics perspective, this question, if understood ontologically, is misleading. Whether trade-offs exist or win-win outcomes are possible is not an invariable quality of the objectives of value creation and impact reduction. Rather, it depends on the situational order that links both dimensions. From the order ethics perspective, both situations—trade-off *and* win-win—are possible. However, management does not have to take a given situation at face value but can seek to change the situation and thus render win-win outcomes feasible (Beckmann et al. 2014). Viewed from the order ethics perspective, the key to such solutions lies, most prominently, at the level of the *business model* where the company can change or redefine more than just isolated measures.

The business model lens offers a useful framework for analyzing value creation processes (Zott et al. 2011). Combined with the order ethics perspective, it also helps to put the reactive win-lose and creative win-win approach to corporate sustainability management into context. The reactive win-lose approach refers to those situations where companies address situational conflicts between value creation and impact reduction within a *given* business model. One reason for such a reactive approach can be that companies are forced to do so. In the 1970s and 1980s, for example, government regulation mandated that companies use certain "end-of-pipe technologies" to curb environmental impacts. Adding expensive filters while the underlying process remains the same, however, just adds additional costs in a given business model. With no extra revenues or cost savings created, end-of-pipe technologies necessarily resulted in a trade-off between value creation (cheaper products, more jobs, higher dividends) and environmental impact reduction (less pollution) (Hart 2010, p. 23).

The end-of-pipe-technology example illustrates that a company may end up in a situation facing short-term trade-offs if it can only react within a given situation or business model. The role of strategic sustainability management, however, is to avoid such tradeoffs by proactively re-engineering and creating new business models. A simple example is the strategy of process re-engineering. While end-of-pipe technologies accept that a process produces negative outputs such as contaminated wastewater that then needs to be filtered, a process-redesign solution might implement a closed-loop system in which wastewater treatment allows using the same water as input for the production process. Ecological impact reduction then reduces costs (canalization fees, freshwater inputs), thus increasing value creation through eco-efficiency (Schaltegger and Synnestvedt 2002).

The key idea of the business model lens is that stakeholders are ultimately not interested in certain technical features of a product but in how they can meet a specific need (Zeyen et al. 2014). To satisfy such a need, multiple governance configurations are possible. While eco-efficiency measures are often rather technical, genuine business model innovations demonstrate that a much more potent lever for combining impact reduction and value creation lies in the institutional order—the underlying rules and mechanisms—that defines how value is created for the participating stakeholders (Osterwalder and Pigneur 2011). A prominent example in this regard is the difference between satisfying a need by selling a product or by providing a service (Tukker and Tischner 2006). Depending on such business model choices, companies can face radically different options for reducing negative impacts and increasing their value creation capacity.

Take the example of a firm that produces pesticides. Pesticides can create value for farmers by increasing crop productivity and for chemical companies who produce them. The use and, above all, the overuse of pesticides, however, also cause negative environmental impacts. A chemical firm whose business model rests on selling pesticides as a product to farmers will experience a trade-off between impact reduction and its own value creation. With its expertise regarding the pesticides, the chemical firm could educate and support the farmers to use as little pesticides as possible for effective pest control. This would reduce negative environmental impacts; yet it would also reduce the company's revenues. The business model then creates a trade-off. In contrast, the same company could use the same technical product in a business model that does not sell a product but the service to provide effective pest control for farmers. With a fixed price for providing effective pest control to a field, the firm can then increase its profits by using its expertise to cut down pesticide use to the lowest level necessary. Reducing negative environmental impacts and increasing corporate value creation then go hand in hand. Even without any technological innovation, the business model innovation makes win-win possible.

For an order ethics approach to sustainability management, the business model perspective substantiates that trade-off or win-win relationships are not invariably given but can be reformed through creative management. Just as sustainability at the societal level requires adequate forms of societal governance, the institutional order that governs the interaction between diverse stakeholders is critical for how corporations can contribute to sustainability and benefits from doing so. Managing the primary and secondary function of companies for sustainability thus requires creative governance innovations.

6 Conclusion and Avenues for Future Learning

This article has used the order ethics perspective to examine the concept of sustainability. These reflections have shown that sustainability is a semantic innovation with a powerful heuristic value for guiding institutional reform processes, that such learning processes require new forms of (global) governance at the societal level, and that companies can constructively manage their primary sustainability role of value creation and secondary role of negative impact reduction at the organizational level of the business model that defines how value is created and how stakeholders cooperate.

After illustrating the usefulness of the order ethics approach for the sustainability debate, the remainder of this article now changes the perspective to ask: How can the sustainability debate stimulate learning for the order ethics approach?

If only looked at superficially, order ethics can be misunderstood as a fairly abstract, simplistic, and static approach: Societal problems are reconstructed as a deficient game such as a social dilemma; to solve the dilemma, the institutions are then changed and the problem is easily solved for good. The sustainability concept challenges this simplified outlook in at least three ways.

First, sustainability highlights the need for *continuous learning processes*. Sustainability is not about reaching a static end-point but about managing permanent change. When a new functional rule is implemented, unintended consequences may surface that create novel challenges. To illustrate, take the example of biofuels where new rules were meant to tackle climate change by subsidizing plant-based energy sources, yet led to the destruction of primary rain forests. As a consequence, further changes of the institutional order are necessary to react to novel developments and unintended consequences. While this idea is of course not new for the order ethics perspective, the sustainability discussion helps to better understand the institutional order not as a static phenomenon but a much more dynamic process.

Second, the *complexity* of many sustainability challenges *underlines* the importance of *bringing together diverse and dispersed knowledge* (Hirsch Hadorn et al. 2006). This is ultimately an epistemological argument. An important value of the order ethics approach is to reduce complexity by analyzing social phenomena for example as a social dilemma and to then derive a rule that helps realize so-far unrealized shared interests. In the face of complexity, however, understanding shared long-term interests is not trivial. In fact, many sustainability issues such as climate change demonstrate the need to bring together a broad spectrum of perspectives that range from atmospheric chemistry and ecology to law, sociology, economics, and political science. Order ethics can benefit from such inter- and transdisciplinary cooperation to refine its analysis.

Third, and closely related, the sustainability debate makes the case for the *transdisciplinary integration of diverse stakeholders* to improve the odds for successful implementation. If misunderstood as a mostly academic discipline, order ethics focuses on win-win solutions *for* actors in a social dilemma. The emerging sustainability sciences, however, highlight that the best theoretical analysis of the researcher will fail to guide successful implementation if the proposed solutions do not build on "socially robust" knowledge. This means that not only the researchers but also the actors affected by a certain proposal need to understand its benefits and have ownership for it. Similarly, order ethics can benefit from developing win-win solutions *with* the relevant stakeholders. Transdisciplinary exchange between diverse disciplines, practitioners, and other stakeholders is thus crucial not only for improving the quality of analysis but also for successful implementation.

The importance of continuous learning processes that bring together diverse actors raises a number of interesting questions. How can such processes be organized? What are appropriate mechanisms for participation and transparency? What kinds of incentives are needed to participate constructively and to refrain from rent-seeking activities? What these questions boil down to, is, ultimately, that learning processes for sustainability do not happen in an institutional vacuum. Rather, adequate rules are needed to promote the sustainability of these processes. The order ethics approach and the sustainability debate thus share further areas for mutual learning.

References

Adams, W.M. 2003. *Green development: Environment and sustainability in the third world*. London: Routledge.
Beckmann, M., and I. Pies. 2016. *The Constitution of Responsibility: Toward an Ordonomic Framework for Interpreting (Corporate Social) Responsibility in Different Social Settings*, in this book.
Beckmann, M., S. Hielscher, and I. Pies. 2014. Commitment strategies for sustainability: How business firms can transform trade-offs into win-win outcomes. *Business Strategy and the Environment* 23: 18–37. doi:10.1002/bse.1758.
Bell, M.L., and D.L. Davis. 2001. Reassessment of the lethal london fog of 1952: Novel indicators of acute and chronic consequences of acute exposure to air pollution. *Environmental Health Perspectives* 109(February): 389–394.
Boatright, J.R. 2011. The implications of the new governance for corporate governance. In *Corporate citizenship and new governance. The political role of corporations*, eds. I. Pies and P. Koslowski, 133–146. Dordrecht: Springer. doi:10.1007/978-94-007-1661-2.
Brennan, G., and J.M. Buchanan. 2000. *The reason of rules*. Indianapolis, IN: Liberty Fund.
Brundtland, G.H. 1987. *Our common future: report of the world commission on environment and development*. Geneva. Retrieved from http://www.un-documents.net/ocf-ov.htm.
Buchanan, J.M. 1987. The constitution of economic policy. *The American Economic Review* 77(3): 243–250.
Carson, R. 1962. *Silent spring*. Boston: Houghton Mifflin.
Dyllick, T., and K. Hockerts. 2002. Beyond the business case for corporate sustainability. *Business Strategy and the Environment* 11(2): 130–141. doi:10.1002/bse.323.
Elkington, J. 1997. *Cannibals with forks: the triple bottom line of 21st century business*, 417. Chichester: Capstone Pub.
Freeman, E. 1984. *Stakeholder management. A strategic approach*. Marchfield, MA: Pitman Publishing.
Friedman, M. 1970, September 13. The social responsibility of business is to increase its profits. *The New York Times Magazine* 32–33 and 122–126, New York.
Global Reporting Initiative. 2009. *Reaching investors. Communicating value through ESG disclosures*. Global Reporting Initiative: Amsterdam.
Hahn, T., F. Figge, J. Pinkse, and L. Preuss. 2010. Editorial trade-offs in corporate sustainability: You can't have your cake and eat it. *Business Strategy and the Environment* 229: 217–229. doi:10.1002/bse.
Hardin, G. 1968. The tragedy of the commons. *Science* 162(3859): 1243–1248.
Hart, S.L. 2010. *Capitalism at the crossroads: Next generation business strategies for a post-crisis world*, 3rd ed. Upper Saddle River, NJ: Prentice Hall.
Hirsch Hadorn, G., D. Bradley, C. Pohl, S. Rist, and U. Wiesmann. 2006. Implications of transdisciplinarity for sustainability research. *Ecological Economics* 60(1): 119–128. doi:10.1016/j.ecolecon.2005.12.002.

Jensen, M.C. 2002. Value maximization, stakeholder theory, and the corporate objective function. *Business Ethics Quarterly* 12(2): 235–256.
Kates, R.W., Clark, W.C., Corell, R., Hall, J.M., Jaeger, C.C., Lowe, I., Svedin, U. 2001. Sustainability science. *Science* 292(5517): 641–642. doi:10.1126/science.1059386.
Meadows, D.H., D. Meadows, J. Randers, and W.W.I. Behrens. 1972. *The limits to growth*. New York: Universe Books.
Nagel, T. 2005. The problem of global justice. *Philosophy & Public Affairs* 33: 113–147. doi:10.1111/j.1088-4963.2005.00027.x.
Osterwalder, A. and Pigneur, Y. 2011. Aligning profit and purpose through business model innovation. In *Responsible management practices for the 21st century* eds. G. Palazzo and M. Wentland, 61–75. Pearson International.
Pies, I., von Winning, A., Sardison, M., and Girlich, K. 2010. Sustainability in the petroleum industry: Theory and practice of voluntary self- commitments. Halle.
Pogge, T. 2001. Priorities of global justice. *Metaphilosophy* 32: 6–24. doi:10.1111/1467-9973.00172.
Porter, M.E., and Linde, C. van der. 2008. Green and competitive. Ending the stalemate. In *On competition*, ed. M. Porter ,347–371. Boston: Harvard Business School Publishing.
Rawls, J. 1993. *Political liberalism*. New York: Columbia University Press.
Rockström, J., Steffen, W., Noone, K., Persson, A., Chapin, F.S., Lambin, E.F, Foley, J. 2009. A safe operating space for humanity. *Nature* 461(September): 472–475.
Rosenau, J.N., and E.-O. Czempiel (eds.). 1992. *Governance without goverment: Order and change in world politics*. Cambridge: Cambridge University Press.
Schaltegger, S., M. Beckmann, and E.G. Hansen. 2013. Transdisciplinarity in corporate sustainability: Mapping the field. *Business* 229: 219–229. doi:10.1002/bse.1772.
Schaltegger, S., and R. Burrit. 2005. Corporate Sustainability. In *The international yearbook of environmental and resource economics 2005/2006*, ed. H. Folmer, 185–222. Cheltenham: Edward Elgar.
Schaltegger, S., and T. Synnestvedt. 2002. The link between 'green' and economic success: Environmental management as the crucial trigger between environmental and economic performance. *Journal of Environmental Management* 65: 339–346. doi:10.1006/jema.
Scherer, A.G., and G. Palazzo. 2011. The new political role of business in a globalized world: A review of a new perspective on csr and its implications for the firm, governance, and democracy Andreas Georg Scherer and Guido Palazzo. *Journal of Management Studies* 48(June): 899–931. doi:10.1111/j.1467-6486.2010.00950.x.
Suchanek, A. 2004. Überlegungen zu einer interaktionsökonomischen Theorie der Nachhaltigkeit. Lutherstadt Wittenberg.
Tukker, A., and U. Tischner. 2006. Product-services as a research field: past, present and future. Reflections from a decade of research, *Journal of Cleaner Production* 14(17):1552–1556. doi:10.1016/j.jclepro.2006.01.022.
UNEP. 1972. *Declaration of the United Nations conference on the human environment*. Retrieved from http://www.unep.org/Documents.Multilingual/Default.asp?DocumentID=97&ArticleID=1503&l=en.
Von Carlowitz, H.C. 1713. *Sylvicultura Oeconomica. Anweisung zur wilden Baumzucht*. Freiberg.
Wiersum, K.F. 1995. 200 years of sustainability in forestry: Lessons from history. *Environmental Management* 19(3): 321–329.
Williamson, O.E. 2010. Transaction cost economics: The natural progression. In *Les prix nobel*, 455–476.
Winn, M., J. Pinske, and L. Illge. 2012. Editorial case studies on trade-offs in corporate sustainability. *Corporate Social Responsibility and Environmental Management* 19(January): 63–68. doi:10.1002/csr.293.
Zeyen, A., Beckmann, M., and Akhavan, R. 2014. Social entrepreneurship business models: Managing innovation for social and economic value creation. In *Managementperspektiven für die Zivilgesellschaft des 21. Jahrhunderts,* eds. C. Müller and C.-P. Zinth, 107–132. Wiesbaden: Springer Gabler.
Zott, C., R. Amit, and L. Massa. 2011. The business model: Recent developments and future research. *Journal of Management* 37(4): 1019–1042. doi:10.1177/0149206311406265.

An Ordonomic Perspective in Medical Ethics

Nikolaus Knoepffler and Martin O'Malley

1 Introduction

We begin with three case studies:

I. A series of scandals in 2012 and 2013 radically shook transplantation medicine in Germany. Whether referred to as the "organ-donation scandal" or the "transplantation scandal", the publicity about the irregularities in transplantation medicine has significantly affected public confidence in the doctors practicing this medicine. And despite a modification of the laws regulating organ donation intended to increase the number of available organs for transplantation, post-mortem donations were down 25 % in the first quarter of 2013. Media sources have treated this matter with harsh scrutiny, claiming medical malpractice due to the violations of relevant regulations and the falsification of patient information.

II. Another form of medical scandal in recent years involves deficiencies in hospital patient care. This case study is from a personal experience and it illustrates the interpersonal dilemmas of both care-givers and patients in critical nursing care situations. A nurse makes the bed of a patient suffering from amyotrophic lateral sclerosis (ALS—also called Lou Gehrig's disease). The patient is barely able to move her limbs or raise her voice, and so the patient is optimally provided with a call button to alert medical personal of

---

N. Knoepffler (✉)
Chair of Applied Ethics and Director of Ethics Centre, Director of the Department of Ethics of Sciences of Jena University, Jena, Germany
e-mail: n.knoepffler@uni-jena.de

M. O'Malley
Ethics Centre, Departement of Ethics of Sciences of Jena University,
Jena, Germany
e-mail: martin.omalley@uni-jena.de

urgent needs. Yet when the nurse preparing the patient for the night forgets to place the electronic button in the patient's hand, the patient's limited breathing is further restricted by the panic of not being able to contact anybody to help her. In the morning, after an entire night of pain and distress, the caregivers face the criticism from the patient and her family.

III. The third case study deals with the structure of health care in Germany—a system that is financed by German citizens and organized according to social principles characterized by solidarity and human dignity. Health providers in this system are incentivized not to offer the best care for the patients, but rather the most lucrative from a list of permitted treatments. And healthcare recipients have no incentive to monitor the costs of treatments, but rather demand the best care regardless of costs.

The following discussion uses these three brief case studies to illustrate first the inadequacy of classic bioethical approaches and the basic reasons why approaches that rely on moralistic rules, shaming, and ethics as the setting of limiting rules are unable to efficiently guide medicine in avoiding the dilemmas of the cases. The paper then examines how structural misalignments and institutional incentives are relevant for medical ethics. Finally, the paper offers an argument for an ordonomic approach for medical ethics analogous to the ordonomic approach in business ethics (Pies et al. 2009).

2 Classical Medical Ethics Approaches and Their Limits

While there are a handful of distinct approaches to medical ethics, the most prominent ones are alike in locating the basic focus of ethics on the level of interaction among individuals. For example, they focus primarily upon the individual moral choices and actions of medical administrators, physicians, nurses, patients and patients' family members. The following section demonstrates this with brief outlines of the most prominent approaches.

2.1 Medical Ethics in the Tradition of the Hippocratic Oath

Medical ethics in the tradition of the Hippocratic Oath focuses specifically upon the physician-patient relationship. The fundamental idea of this approach is *salus aegroti suprema lex*, the patient's well-being is the highest law. The central concern of the physician is thus the health of the patient as understood in an objective medical sense. And the physician, as expert, stands as the focal point in this determination. The principle of non-maleficence, do no harm, is a corollary point. This medical ethics approach has had wide influence upon medical practice (cf Orr et al. 1997) and includes a list of concrete rules relevant to the physician-patient level. For example, the physician is bound to confidentiality and is prohibited from assisting the patients in ending their own lives.

Considerations of wider issues of justice are not excluded from this approach; they are simply not addressed. Thus the focus on the physician-patient level and the emphasis upon the well-being of patients is potentially compatible with and even incentivizes actions of misconduct. With regard to the irregularities that led to the transplantation scandals, doctors were prioritizing certain patients, their own patients, on organ-recipient lists in order to benefit their well-being. Their incentives were consistent with the Hippocratic Oath. Regarding the patient with ALS, the disproportionate focus upon the physician-patient relationship leaves a vacuum of ethical responsibility for the rest of medical care. The care provider almost certainly does not want to harm the patient and has an interest in the patient's well-being, but pressures of limited resources leave nurses and other care providers in sub-optimal situations. Despite high medical costs, nurses and other care providers are often over-burdened with responsibilities. Their incentives within the system are focused upon their achieving compliance with only general standards of care. It would certainly help to set and enforce protocols specific to ALS patients, like insuring they are able to alert medical staff and also checking on them in regular intervals. But it is worth noting that employee compensation and job security are not strongly linked to actions of care that exceed minimum standards.

On a system-wide level, we see how the individual actors in the medical system are suboptimally incentivized to use the significant resources allotted to medical care to actually benefit the population being served by the medical community. In many ways, physicians are being entirely rational in choosing medical procedures with expenses disproportionate to the benefits they provide. And patients are being entirely rational in their sky's the limit demand for medical services. The problem, which lies in the disordered incentives, is one that is not adequately addressed within this medical ethics approach.

2.2 Medical Ethics in Christian Ethical Tradition of Natural Law

Medical ethics in the Christian natural law ethical tradition (cf USCCB 2009) is open to a similar critique. This approach begins with a basic anthropological understanding —human dignity and human nature as given by God—and it builds a system of ethical principles, norms and values relevant to medicine. *Salus aegroti secundum naturam suprema lex.* The most basic principle of natural law ethics is *bonum est faciendum, malum est vitandum*, do good and avoid evil. The teleological structure of natural law ethics should in principle address the difficulties (cited above) of the Hippocratic Oath approach because the principle of justice plays such a prominent role in natural law. Personal, interpersonal and social ethics are ordered to the "good", and there is ideally no inherent conflict in the successively more complex social good all the way up to the common good. Yet in practice the natural law approach tends to prioritize non-negotiable ideals, intrinsic evils, and limits to medical practice and research. The dignity of the human person and the absolute prohibitions on IVF fertilization or physician-assisted euthanasia are a few examples. There are reasons to support those positions, of course, but as an ethical system, this natural law approach is strongly paternalistic and devalues the self-determination of the patient. Adapting its own motto, it stresses the "do no evil" over and above the "do good". Its rule orientation sets limits and it recognizes the importance of individual moral virtues, but the approach does not necessarily address the importance of the inherent rule-settings of structures and systems.

2.3 The Modern 4—Principles Approach to Medical Ethics

The modern four-principles approach to medical ethics developed by Beauchamp and Childress (2013 [1979]) resolves significant defects of the previous two ethical approaches. The principle of patient autonomy addresses the health of the patient, the *salus aegroti*, and this is complemented by a concern for the patient's own *voluntas* or will. In the first edition of their classical text their ethical approach could be described in the following way: *Voluntas aegroti suprema lex*, the will of the patient is the supreme law. Yet even with this approach, the foreground concern is on the level of relationship between patient and medical-care provider. The physician-patient relationship is characterized in this way: The physician educates the patient so that the patient can make informed decisions ("informed consent"). Having the patient's informed consent, the physician is empowered to treat the patient under the guidance of the principle to act according to the patient's own welfare and doing no harm (non-maleficence).

Medical treatment is constrained not only by the patients' informed consent, but also by the principle of justice—where the particular treatment for an individual patient, for whatever reason, would create an unfair or unjust situation for other individuals. In the first of the cases presented above, this would restrain a physician from manipulating the organ donor lists to give unfair or non-transparent priority to one patient over others. However, this approach does not resolve the fundamental problem that a physician would be under constant pressure to benefit some patients to the disadvantage of donor recipients. The physician's interests, incentives and well-being, as well as those of their patients, are at odds with the interests and incentives of other physicians, patients and the common good. The principle of justice should ideally function in this system to coordinate practices so that individuals are treated fairly across the medical system, including within organ transplantation programs. The principle of justice is supported by social conventions and laws, but nevertheless lacks a realistic strategy for dealing with some incentives in the medical system leading to suboptimal treatments. Physicians, other care providers, institutions, governments and patients continue to have incentives with cross purposes and unwanted consequences.

2.4 A Utilitarian Perspective on Medical Ethics

One might think that a utilitarian medical ethics (cf Singer 1994) would offer solutions to the issues posed above because the utilitarian approach is ordered precisely to the overall good: Act in such a way to benefit the most possible people to the greatest degree possible: *Utilitas suprema lex*. It might seem that the trade-offs would be acceptable for individual patients, the larger pool of potential patients, and society in general because physicians would consider and choose those medical treatments that generate maximum benefits. Indeed it is precisely this argument that has been used by some of the physicians involved in the transplantation scandals. They have argued that their actions of manipulating patient data were done with the intention of multiplying the utility of the donated organs. They argued further that existing criteria for awarding organs were suboptimal and that they were, so to speak, answering a higher call to justice. Yet this example also demonstrates the great limitation of utilitarianism on the level of patient-physician interaction.

2.5 Medical Ethics in the Human Rights Tradition

One can speak also about a rights-based ethical approach for medicine. This approach bases its fundamental claims upon the broader tradition of the Universal Declaration of Human Rights (UDHR 1948). This approach underscores the individual, the unique dignity of each patient and their basic human rights. A concrete example of this approach can be seen in the International Council of Nurses' Code of Ethics for Nurses (ICN 1953 [2012]). The preamble of the code includes the explicit responsibility of nurses to respect their patients' human rights: "Inherent in nursing is a respect for human rights, including cultural rights, the right to life and choice, to dignity and to be treated with respect." And the implementation of this responsibility is stated this way in §1.1: "The nurse's primary professional responsibility is to people requiring nursing care." The ethics code is quite comprehensive in the sense that it addresses the personal needs of the nurses themselves, their patients, professional environment, their profession and the larger society. And it is also comprehensive in the sense that it addresses emotional and physical aspects of care, but also the values of all of those people of the medical community and those being served by it. The point here is that this is a very well thought out and comprehensive code of ethics.

So the question we must ask is: What could we do to avoid the experience of the ALS patient of our example above? Is there some way that the code could be altered so that a nurse would not forget to properly place the call button? There are already laws and hospital codes dealing with the necessity for such devices and outlining their proper use (See DIN VDE 0834-1:2000-04 Rufanlagen in Krankenhäusern, Pflegeheimen und ähnlichen Einrichtungen). The above example is illustrative of a deeper issue that cannot be addressed by appealing to individual nurses to amend their personal values or be subject to additional moralistic directives. Rather, this situation and others like it are best diagnosed as the effect of suboptimal incentive structuring on the systems or institutional level. Codes of conduct that utilize rights-based principles and arguments are ill-conceived—the error is a categorical one. Take, for example, another clause from the code (1.6): "The nurse practices to sustain and protect the natural environment and is aware of its consequences on health." This shows how the very reasoning of the code is directed at a social level much more general than that appropriate for managing the relationship of nurses and their patients.

3 The Necessity of a Change in Perspective

The very brief and selective overview of bioethical approaches above is meant to draw attention to a very basic point regarding a common limitation shared by many ethical approaches. The three case studies mentioned above were selected to illustrate this limitation. And the present section makes the systematic argument for this point.

3.1 The Concept of Ordonomics

Pies et al. (2009, 2010) introduced the term "ordonomics" into the international debate on the societal role of business. Pies and his collaborators rely heavily on Becker's economic "imperialism", Buchanan's normative constitutionalism, so called "constitutional economics" (Buchanan 1990) and Homanns "ethics in terms of economics" (Homann and Lütge 2004). According to Pies et al. (2010) "[t]he basic concern of ordonomics is the systematic exploration of the interdependencies between social structure and semantics. To this end, ordonomics makes uses of elementary game theory and a rational-choice-based analysis of institutional arrangements" (ibid., p. 267). Ordonomics is distinctive in its realistic skepticism that ethical actions can be achieved with moralistic appeals that challenge persons to act against their own best interests. An ordonomic ethics differentiates the interpersonal level of action from more systematic and structural levels. It focuses upon those levels and, with the aid of empirically-based social sciences, attempts to achieve insight about how to order rules regimens to optimally align personal interests with socially beneficial actions. Ordonomics explores the social structure, i.e. "the institutional framework of society, including its incentive properties; 'semantics' has to do with the terminology of public discourse and the underlying thought categories that determine how people perceive, describe and evaluate social interactions and, in particular, social conflicts" (ibid., p. 267). Ordonomics is an ethical position that draws from philosophical contractualism and places emphasis upon the role of the particular conditions under which actors are asked to act morally. Specifically, it examines the structure of rules, the "order", within which persons are acting, i.e., on the level of institutional social ordering (cf Lütge 2012, p. 89).

3.2 An Ordonomic-Ethical Perspective Surpassing the Limits of Classical Individualistic Ethics

How does one implement moral rules or influence moral decision-making? The answer is that one must structure institutions so that the actors in those institutions will be incentivized to act in ways that are socially beneficial. Creating mutual benefit scenarios on the rule level may not seem very much like classical moral theories where morals often means acting without any self-interest (subjective preferences in a broad sense, e.g. the subjective preference of a physician for *his* or *her* patient instead of other patients unknown to him or her). The ordonomic approach has made strides in developing ethics in ways that combine self-interest with societal expectations. The approach is using advances of economic modeling for working out optimal scenarios, and for recognizing sub-optimal situations that are not ordered to sustainable value-creating practices.

Thus, behind this general ordonomic program are two basic convictions:

1. morality and self-interest must not be pitted against one another, and
2. ordonomics can achieve a great deal of good on the level where people actually act by focusing on the more system-level of rules that govern the level of action.

This should certainly not be misunderstood as a retreat from morality on the level of action. This approach is concerned with morality, but wishes to avoid non-effective moral platitudes when structural issues are largely to blame. In the transplantation scandal case, physicians were faced with a system for conferring donated organs that they believed was not adequately serving them or their patients. For such dilemma situations, Pies recommends an ordonomic approach using a diagram of orthogonal positioning (Pies et al. 2009, p. 380) (Fig. 1).

Fig. 1 Ordonomic approach

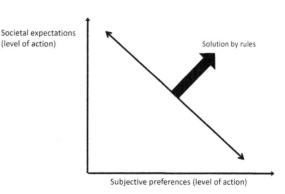

The use of economists' tools for ethics reflects an ancient philosophical respect for the context of moral action. Intentionality and moral culpability are precisely the subject of ethics and this culpability is mitigated in suboptimal situations of conflicting interests. This seems to be the case for the physicians who interpreted the situation as one calling for them to prioritize the well-being of their own patients over the need to respect official protocols. This is the reasoning of Homann's consistency postulate: Expectations of interpersonal action must be consistent with the level of rules (Homann and Lütge, pp. 30 f.).

The question remains, how is consistency achieved and why is it important? The answer begins with a realization that people only feel themselves bound by such rules that are in their interest to follow. This is a basic contractarian point. "The credible collective commitment to a system of moral rules is achieved only when those rules serve their self-interests" (ibid., p 51). In other words: "This is the incentive-compatible condition for the implementability of normative validity" (p. 51). The basic conviction is that morality is not an individual but a collective enterprise (cf. ibid, p 51).

Once this point is established, particular situations can then be addressed with the goal of reforming the level of rules. This approach thereby differentiates itself from the classic medical-ethics approaches. The ordonomic approach also differentiates itself by integrating concerns for the common good vis-à-vis the utility achieved with reform of rules or conditions.

Lütge describes the difference between the ordonomic approach and classical individualistic ethics systems: Individualistic ethics are recognizable because "in morally questionable situations, the immoral motives and preferences of the actors receive the blame" (Lütge 2012, p. 94). In our examples, such approaches place the burden of ethical action squarely and exclusively upon physicians, nurses or patients. This tends also to be the case in terms of the ways that the media tend to report ethics violations. The underlying structural causes do not receive necessary scrutiny, blame, or most importantly, attention for reform.

A game-theory analysis of this situation substantiates the value of the ordonomic approach for the case of the transplantation scandals. This analysis abstracts essential elements of the case within the framework of a decision diagram. Specifically, it attempts to distill the subjective perspective of the actors in the ethically-conflicted situation, in this case the physician facing the choice to cheat the system to obtain a transplanted organ for their own patient. The key insight of this analysis is that a good rule system can align individual interests with more generally beneficial practices. Conversely, this approach can highlight social traps —unwinnable or fundamentally disordered structures that leave the actor without good choices.

In the scenario described in the diagram below, two organ-transplantation physicians have critically-ill patients needing organ transplants. Transplants are awarded on the basis of points describing the patient's health, age and other factors which represent their worthiness to receive a scarce organ for transplantation. Both physicians are aware of a common practice of cheating the system by deceitfully raising a patient's points. The diagram below shows simply that the

	Doctor A (cheats) raises points for patient A	Doctor A plays by the rules for Patient A
Doctor B plays by the rules for Patient B	Patient A gets organ/Patient B cheated, minimal risk of scandal for doctor A	Fair situation for both patients
Doctor B (cheats) raises points for Patient B	Scenario of cheating – no respect for rules, elevated risk for scandal for both doctors	Patient B gets organ/Patient A cheated, minimal risk of scandal for Doctor A

Fig. 2 Organ-transplantation physicians follow the rules or cheat the rules

organ-transplantation physicians in this scenario have two options: Either follow the rules, which leaves their patient without a chance for an organ, or cheat the rules, bringing risk of scandal (Fig. 2).

A well-established and properly run organ-transplantation system would be best for all the physicians and patients because physicians would not have such a high incentive to cheat and, in the absence of scandals, patients would benefit by the greater availability of donated organs. The key is reducing incentives to cheat and raising rewards for compliance. Physicians will be much less likely to cheat a system that they know is fair and thus it gives their patients a predictable chance to obtain an organ. Patients too would be less likely to single out doctors with a reputation for gaming the system if there was a broad confidence that physicians were objective in assessing patients' points for organ eligibility. And the wider public would be more like to be organ donors if they respected the integrity of the whole transplantation system. This would obviously reduce the scarcity of organs and likewise reduce the incentive for cheating.

The case of the ALS patient presents a different structural problem. The limitation of the system is that it methodologically assumes that compliance with general standards is adequate for providing nursing care. The reality of medical illness is that every patient presents unique needs. It is conceivable that standards could be generated for every disease at every stage of its development, though such standards must be adapted to each patient's personal medical history. And the nurses must have the motivation in the first place to generate and follow such standards. In the case of ALS patient, good nursing care would involve knowing the patient's specific needs presented by the disease's rapid onset of nerve paralysis. The patient had very recently lost the capacity to move her limbs and her lungs were unable to effectively expel mucus. A caring nurse would have known this and not only placed the call button in the patient's hand, but also checked on her during the night. Care is a simple but immensely valuable element of the nursing vocation, but it is not simply reducible to basic standards. The ordonomic approach cannot provide a recipe for "care", but it can recognize its worth and understand the ways that structures either provide incentives for it, or mitigate against it, as will be shown below.

The ordonomic structural analysis is especially applicable to the case study on the German healthcare system. The following diagram abstracts the basic dynamic on the interpersonal level. It is simplified by limiting the system to two actors, patients A and B. Both understand that the healthcare system is:

(a) built upon the principle of solidarity,
(b) a social good available for public utilization,
(c) responds to individuals' healthcare claims on "first come—first served" basis,
(d) treats patients discretely (no public knowledge of healthcare utilization), and
(e) involves no (or minimal) economic penalty for the specific services provided.

The diagram shows that when all the actors in a health care system make unlimited demands upon the system, all the actors suffer adverse consequences. They receive less adequate care and pay more for it (Fig. 3).

The diagram shows that by remaining simply on the interpersonal level, a healthcare system depending solely upon the restraint of those using its services will be at the mercy of those utilizing its services. Moreover, the discrete or anonymous nature of medical care implies that there is no public shame involved in its use. The only limitation of such services is the moral restraint of those individuals—a restraint that places such "moral" persons at significant disadvantage by those exercising no such moral restraint. Using economic analysis of the context described above, we could even say that actors are being rational in showing no restraint, given that there is no economic or other penalty for such choices. Thus the moral norms and appeals of classical medical ethics for restraint are of little help here.

A more proportionate and effective approach must consider more aspects of medical-ethical action, including individual, institutional, systematic, legal and also theoretical. The ordonomic approach attempts to do this by differentiating the sphere of ethical action into three distinct levels. These levels are, using Pies' terminology (2012, 25):

	Patient B demands limitless healthcare resources	Patient B claims limited healthcare resources
Patient A demands limitless healthcare resources	System pushed to limits, thus healthcare is both rationed and more expensive	A is advantaged, B is disadvantaged
Patient A claims limited healthcare resources	B is advantaged, A is disadvantaged	Best overall situation: System allocates adequate healthcare at reasonable cost

Fig. 3 Actors in health care system make unlimited demands upon the system damaging themselves

(1) Rule Following: the interpersonal level of individual ethical decision making
(2) Rule Setting: the meta-level of systems, institutions, and organizations
(3) Rule Finding: the meta-meta-level of ideas or theory.

This paper's three case studies illustrate the quandary faced by medical ethics primarily focused upon the rule-following level, i.e., the personal choices of individual actors (physicians, nurses, patients). The case studies show that rule violations cannot be effectively avoided by focusing primarily upon interpersonal action: upon codes of ethics, on professional ethics oaths, on moral pleas, or upon compliance with guidelines. Thus, there is a need to examine and reform the rule-setting process. And this means dealing with ethical problems within the systematic, institutional and even political domains where rules are set.

Setting rules requires ethical understanding and it is clear that the classical medical-ethical discourse traditions have a great deal to offer the rule-setting process. The ordonomic approach does not seek to displace these traditions, but to optimally achieve their goals of fostering ethical action within social institutions.

4 Towards an Integrative Medical Ethics (IME)

An "Integrative Medical Ethics" integrates the ordonomic ethical approach with classical medical ethics approaches. In doing so, it recognizes that there are deep-seated disagreements among classical theories. Nevertheless, it pragmatically seeks overlapping consensus on matters of potential mutual agreement and action.

4.1 Rule Finding: The Meta-Meta Level of Ideas

The fundamental purpose of medicine is fostering the health of persons. Physicians, nurses and other people in medical professions take appropriate pride in their work and the great benefit they provide society. An Integrative Medical Ethics (IME) recognizes that their "self-interest" includes not only compensation and material benefits, but also their sense of identity, self-worth, and the confidence that they are providing a great help for their patients. Thus, the term "self-interest" should be understood in a very broad sense here.

This self-evident point must be kept in mind, because it is ultimately the measure of effective rules—even as we recognize that healthcare is only one aspect of the "common good", which includes many other social goods (such as safety, education, leisure, family life, and so on). The "good" of the common good is fostered by moral ideals, principles and practices that order all of social life—medicine included. Despite the fact that there are contemporary debates about some aspects of moral ideals, principles and practices, those debates should not mask the broad social consensus on fundamental moral matters that undergirds social action. We do not live in Hobbes' state of nature.

IME sees the value of the ordonomic ethics as potentially compatible with many classical ethical theories, despite the fact that medical ethics must understand the limited value of specific ethical demands in situations where they will inevitably contradict with the perceived self-interests of individual actors. Ordonomic ethics therefore systematically considers the subjective interests of patients, physicians, doctors, nurses, and other medical officials and care-givers. It also respects that these self-interests involve much more than simply financial, status and personal health matters.

With this background, the essential task of IME is to participate in structuring the rules that will effectively lead to persons acting in ways consistent with moral ideals. Stated differently, IME seeks to reform rules that incentivize persons to act in ways that are contrary to moral norms and thereby socially destructive. Rule-setting is more than just an exercise in efficiency, it is properly a scientific endeavor focused upon right action, i.e., ethics. Included in this endeavor is the search for the overlapping consensus necessary for effective rule-setting. This search often demands more abstract theoretical discourse that ordonomics describes as "rule-finding". Rule-finding discourse is what classical ethical theories have often taken to be the whole of ethics.

Effective rules require the basic consensus of all stakeholders. Human rights represent important consensus principles, especially as they are articulated in the Universal Declaration of Human Rights and in subsequent international developments of those rights with respect to specific populations at risk (minority groups, refugees, women, disabled persons, and others). These rights are complemented and undergirded by the principle of human dignity declaring the inestimable value of every human person. Because humans have dignity, they must be considered as a subject themselves—and not merely an instrument for some purpose, including the common good. The dignity principle claims the fundamental equality of all human beings, with an implied right to at least basic access to adequate healthcare. This is the best possible safeguard for the right to life and to physical integrity.

These foundations are shared with most ethical systems, including utilitarian medical ethics, when the greatest happiness of the greatest number is understood to require the rule of respecting the dignity and rights of every person. Rights and dignity need not be understood universally as based upon metaphysical principles or deontological standards of pure rationality (Knoepffler and O'Malley 2010). Pragmatic ordonomic reflection seeks rather consensus on the level of practice, and it is no stretch for utilitarians and others to recognize the great good that rights and dignity provide society.

The four-principled approach of Beauchamp and Childress is also potentially within a broad consensus on the principles of rights and dignity, as well as with an ordonomic approach to medical ethics. Rights and dignity find functional equivalences in the principles of patient autonomy, beneficence, non-malevolence and justice. And ethical perspectives characterized by the Hippocratic Oath or Christian natural law can likewise be included in this broad consensus as they too are willing to incorporate the self-determination of patients.

Deeply contested ethical questions such as abortion and euthanasia will continue despite overlapping consensus on broader medical issues. Ordonomic ethics can accept the reality of particular disagreements without jeopardizing the larger project of finding consensus on the basic rules that should govern practices in medicine.

Interestingly, the Hippocratic Oath adds an important element to the rule-finding process that is often neglected in classical medical ethics. The oath begins with an invocation to the gods, and then the oath recognizes the great value of and respect due to the teacher of medicine. The rule-finding process has to take into account the self-interests of medical professionals, that they be treated with respect and compensated fairly. Hippocrates knew well that worries about livelihood compromised care for patients. The right to a fair wage has been widely recognized internationally. This is thus a point of consensus relevant to generation of rules.

An IME proposes the following moral principles as relevant for overlapping consensus:

- The principle justice: Justice is understood in the sense of fair pay and decent working conditions for medical professionals. For patients, it entails the responsibility of societies to treat patients with respect to their dignity and which does not injure their basic equality regardless of their gender, religion, social status, ethnicity or nationality). The principle of solidarity is part of the principle of justice. Solidarity reflects a basic obligation of members of society to each other, especially during times of sickness, and prevents medical situations from leading to financial or existential ruin. The principle of justice also calls for the careful stewardship of public resources; that resources are wisely allocated and benefits are shared fairly.
- The principle of patient autonomy: A patient must be treated only with patient's clear informed consent to that treatment.
- The principle of non-maleficence: The patient has a right to appropriate medical treatment that does not impose unreasonable harm.
- The beneficence principle: The patient has a right to be treated with care.

4.2 Rule Setting: The Meta-Level of Systems, Institutions, and Organization

There is a dynamic relationship between all three levels of rule finding, rule setting and rule following, as experience and theory are intimately related in a pragmatic ethical approach. Nevertheless, there is a logical priority to the rule-finding theoretical level of discovering and developing the theoretical principles for guiding the setting of rules. Rule setting involves a complex and often technical process of putting the theory into practice within the relevant matrix of legal, professional, institutional and customary rules. Conceptually, ordonomic ethics attempts to be more than a critical voice, pointing out ethical violations and the limits for scientific research and practice. Rather, ordonomic ethics seeks to generate understanding and proposals for systematic reform on the level of rules—offering implementable strategies for political, professional and institutional leaders.

In the German federal government during the past decade, there have been myriad legal reforms of the healthcare system—the so-called healthcare reform laws. However, the basic problem of paradoxical incentives for healthcare providers remains. For example, physicians and their medical institutions have the incentive to provide the most treatment possible with minimal concern for cost, and patients have no counter-incentives to limit themselves in their claims for treatment.

A rule-setting solution might involve increasing patients' personal costs for therapeutic measure that go beyond a certain minimal standard of treatment. Here, there would be measures to insure that such financial participation does not put in jeopardy the patient's health or financial wellbeing. With respect to providers, an obvious measure is to have increased control measures and effective penalties for unnecessary medical treatments. This efficiency approach is a matter of justice, but it is hardly unique to ordonomic ethics. And patients also have no incentive to receive unnecessary and wasteful treatments.

A more creative ordonomic approach would seek to shift the incentive structure such that the medical providers have incentive to provide appropriate services at minimal cost. One measure with promise is providing medical-provider groups agreed-upon sums for taking care of a designated group of people—however this is done. The underwriting amount would correspond to probabilities relevant to the potential patients' demographics. When necessary, patient-treatment costs would deplete the medical provider's own resources. Care would have to be taken, of course, to protect the patient from the self-interests of the providers. Nevertheless, the key is to shift the incentives so that the basic medical-ethical principles are fostered, that everyone benefits from a healthy population, and that there are integrated and self-regulating controls for medical expenditures.

Shifting the incentives to medical providers introduces inherent dangers, of course, which also need to be anticipated and controlled. For example, providing a lump sum to a nursing home for the comprehensive care of its patients incentivizes the nursing home to provide as little care as necessary for those patients. Similarly with the case of the ALS patient in a hospital where the hospital is receiving a standard payment per overnight stay. The hospital is incentivized to provide as little nursing care as medically necessary without putting itself in jeopardy of generalized hospital regulations and laws. Here there might be a solution by introducing competition among medical groups providing services, and requiring that measures of care quality be available publically. If a hospital is sparing costs with minimal nursing staff, this would be a shaming point that would be publically available. Patients would be incentivized to find medical groups with good reputations for providing adequate services with outstanding nursing care. And the measures for judging this would be relevant, publically available, and provided by independent auditors. To maintain a healthy incentive for medical groups, patients would also need the option to switch from poorly-run groups.

The role of minimal standards continues to be relevant for and compatible with ordonomic ethics. An example from modern aviation is relevant here. Jet aircraft are immensely complex machines and yet there are astoundingly few incidents of their failures resulting in personal casualties. How can this be? Gigerenzer (2013, 72–77) argues that this safety record is achieved with a comprehensive and standardized system of checklists. Preflight checks are mandatory and inflight crises are also addressed with crisis-response protocols to isolate the problem and deal with it. Such discovery and remedy management can and is utilized to some extent in medical care. Though this management approach is also not unique to ordonomic ethics, it may be combined with it. For example, treatment of critical-care patients like the ALS patient in the case above should include care checklists that include reasonable access to the call button. This management tool could be incentivized in three ways. First, the hospital would be incentivized not to overburden their nursing staff because nursing-care quality would be publically available. Second, blatant nursing mistakes would be grounds for a refund of the patient co-pay, as judged in a relatively non-bureaucratic patient advocate acting indecently from the hospital. Such a refund might be only a symbolic measure in terms of the cost to the hospital, but it would present a third option. Namely, the number of patient co-pay refunds in the hospital would also be publically available. And the hospital would have an incentive to avoid these as well.

The organ-transplant scandal was motivated in large part by scarcity. Recognizing this, an ordonomic approach could propose rule-setting changes on the Eurotransplant-level to address this scarcity as a way of minimizing the incentive for ethical misconduct. The "Spanish model" offers insights to an alternative that provides nearly three times the number of organs for transplantation than in Germany (cf. the classical paper by Johnson and Goldstein (2003) on how defaults save lives). Spain has succeeded by a coordinated effort of greater public information, increased medical-staff training regarding organ donation, and the implementation of an "opting-out" legal framework where informed consent for organ donation is presumed absent an explicit contrary wish. Increased available organs reduces the need and incentive for cheating and at the same time increases the respect for the system. Together with stronger rules and enforcement to deter cheating, the whole system should function dramatically better. This dynamic is demonstrated in the chart below (Fig. 4).

The ordonomic measures would raise the rate of available organs, increase the incentive for compliance, and reduce the incentive for cheating. It continues to be true that cheating the system would marginally increase a patient's chance for an organ, but the increased danger of exposure and associated penalties mitigates against cheating.

	Doctor A (cheats) raises points for Patient A	Doctor A plays by the rules for Patient A
Doctor B plays by the rules for Patient B	Patient A has marginally better chances to receive organ, but Doctor A has significant risk of exposure	Fair situation for both patients and favorable chance for organ for both
Doctor B (cheats) raises points for Patient B	Scenario of cheating – no respect for rules, elevated risk for scandal for both doctors	Patient B has marginally better chances to receive organ, but Doctor B has significant risk of exposure

Fig. 4 Increased available organs reduces the need and incentive for cheating and at the same time increases the respect for the system

4.3 Rule Following: The Interpersonal Level of Individual Ethical Decision Making

The rule-following level is the level at which the theory and rules meet reality. As with any truly practical science, the rules need to be constantly monitored for effectiveness using objective measures and, to the extent possible, empirical data. And they need to be continually reformed to achieve optimal performance. With respect to this paper's three case studies, these objective measures would include, for example: (a) rates of organ transplantation and scandals involving transplantation; (b) measures of hospital-patient care satisfaction; and (c) measures of per capita healthcare expenditures, overall average health insurance rates, and measures of general satisfaction with healthcare system. Ideally, scientists should be able to follow trends in comparative markets to recognize policies and practices that are most effective in achieving desired objectives. Included in these desired objectives are norm-compliance, but also moral values to the extent that they can be measured. It may be easiest to measure infractions, but even compliance and flourishing can be monitored in the form of satisfaction surveys and social psychological studies. These monitoring attempts have varying levels of meaningfulness, but the point is that ethics can and should utilize empirical measures to monitor effectiveness.

4.4 Conclusion

Integrative Medicine Ethics (IME) integrating the ordonomics approach offers solutions to social traps in medicine. Such an integrated approach respects and fosters the essential principles of medical ethics and long-cherished moral traditions. Here, the health and well-being of every person in society remains a central concern—as articulated in the principles of autonomy, human rights and human dignity. But the approach advocated in this paper integrates these concerns for the person with the long-term and sustainable concern for all persons in society—the common good. Thus another central concern of ethics is the context of moral action, and not merely the moral action of individuals. The context of moral action can be enriched with effective rules that foster virtuous personal and institutional practices. That is in everyone's interest.

References

Buchanan, James M. 1990. The domain of constitutional political economy. *Constitutional Political Economy* 1: 1–18.
Beauchamp, Tom L., and James L. Childress. 2013. *Principles of biomedical ethics*, 7th ed. Oxford: Oxford University Press.
Gigerenzer, Gerd. 2013. *Risk savvy. How to make good decisions*. New York: Penguin.
Homann, Karl, and Christoph Lütge. 2004. *Einführung in die Wirtschaftsethik*. Münster: LIT.
ICN (International Code of Nurses).1953. (revised 2012): International Code of Nurses (see:http://www.icn.ch/images/stories/documents/about/icncode_english.pdf).
Johnson, Eric and Goldstein, Daniel. 2003. Do defaults save lives? *Science* 302: 1338f.
Knoepffler, Nikolaus, and Martin O'Malley. 2010. Human dignity: Regulative principle and absolute value. *Journal international de bioéthique* 21: 63–76.
Lütge, Christoph. 2012. Ordnungsethik als philosophischer Entwurf. In *Ders.: Wirtschaftsethik ohne Illusionen*. Mohr Siebeck, Tübingen, 89–110.
Orr, Robert et al. 1997. Use of the hippocratic oath: A review of twentieth century practice and a content analysis of oaths administered in medical schools in the U.S. and Canada in 1993. *Journal of Clinical Ethics* 8: 377–388.
Pies, Ingo. 2012. Wie kommt die Normativität ins Spiel? – Eine ordonomische Argumentationsskizze. In *Ders.: Regelkonsens statt Wertekonsens: Ordnomische Schriften zum politischen Liberalismus*. wvb, Berlin, 3–53.
Pies, Ingo, et al. 2009. Moral commitments and the societal role of business: An ordonomic approach to corporate citizenship. *Business Ethics Quarterly* 19: 375–401.
Pies, Ingo, et al. 2010. Value creation, management competencies, and global corporate citizenship: An ordonomic approach to business ethics in the age of globalization. *Journal of Business Ethics* 94: 265–278.
Singer, Peter. 1994. *Rethinking life & death. The collapse of our traditional ethics*. Melbourne: The Text Publishing Company.
UDHR (Universal Declaration of Human Rights). 1948. Universal Declaration of Human Rights (see: http://www.un.org/en/universal-declaration-human-rights/).
USCCB (United States Conference of Catholic Bishops). 2009. Ethical and religious directives for catholic health care services, 5th ed. http://www.usccb.org/issues-and-action/human-life-and-dignity/health-care/upload/Ethical-Religious-Directives-Catholic-Health-Care-Services-fifth-edition-2009.pdf.

Ethics and the Development of Reputation Risk at Goldman Sachs 2008–2010

Ford Shanahan and Peter Seele

> *Substantial legal liability or a significant regulatory action against us, or adverse publicity, governmental scrutiny or legal and enforcement proceedings regardless of the ultimate outcome, could have material adverse financial effects or cause significant reputational harm to us, or adversely affect the morale and performance of our employees, which in turn could seriously harm our business and results of operations (Goldman Sachs 2010, p. 38) (1d).*

1 Introduction

1.1 Aim of the Article

This paper explores the role that allegations of unethical behavior played in the development of reputation risk in the case of Goldman Sachs from 2008 to 2011. While the role of ethics in business hasn't always been universally understood, it is becoming increasingly clear that failure to comply with certain ethical norms such as trustworthiness can and may have a serious impact on corporate performance if not corporate survival. In particular, in the service industry where no physical goods are produced, trust can be critical, and to the degree that reputation is an intangible asset, a decline in reputation could have financial implications in the form of reputation risk. In 2008, Goldman Sachs was accused of misleading investors and government in its business dealings. These allegations not only had a material impact on Goldman Sachs' bottom line via multi-million dollar settlements with the U.S. government and private parties, but society's changing impression of the corporation likely did harm to business prospects as well.

F. Shanahan · P. Seele (✉)
Corporate Social Responsibility and Business Ethics, Università della Svizzera italiana, Lugano, Switzerland
e-mail: peter.seele@usi.ch

This paper is an offshoot of a separate paper that discusses the role of Aristotelian *ethos* and the role of persuasion in corporate reputation management (Shanahan and Seele 2015). It reviews the role of ethics, specifically trustworthiness, and the development of reputation risk in the Goldman Sachs case as a means of demonstrating the connection between ethical standards and market forces. Finally, the paper proposes that awareness of such a link may help change market behavior via the mechanics of obligational norms, potentially helping repair what has become known as the "fractured contract" (Brigley 1995, p. 225) between the marketplace and society.

1.2 Timeline of the Goldman Sachs Case 2008–2010

In 2008, Goldman Sachs was one of the largest and most successful investment banks in the world with annual revenues exceeding $39 billion, offering investment banking and investment service globally. In 2009, the firm's vaunted reputation as a global leader was challenged via numerous public allegations of fraudulent behavior including the firm's tendency to benefit at the expense of various stakeholders. Negative press stemming from these allegations made by regulators, investors and the public in general began to accumulate, chipping away at Goldman Sachs' reputation.

By mid 2009, with frustration mounting as the U.S. and global economy was going into a second year of economic recession, Goldman Sachs continued to be was the target of allegations from multiple sources. In May 2009, the New York Times announced that Goldman Sachs agreed to pay $60 million to settle an investigation and charges by the Massachusetts Attorney General alleging that the firm promoted unfair home loans in the state (Wayne 2009).

In July 2009, the magazine Rolling Stone published an article that characterized Goldman Sachs as a "giant vampire squid" wrapping its tentacles around the "face of humanity" (Tiabbi 2009). According to the article, the firm was shameless in its pursuit of self-gain regardless of whom it took advantage. In December 2009, the New York Times reported that the U.S. Securities and Exchange Commission (SEC) was investigating the firm's role in fraud regarding its own investors (Morgenson and Story 2009).

In February 2010, Goldman Sachs acknowledged that public scrutiny and bad press may have an impact on its business in the form of reputation risk. The disclosure was unique in that it was made in the Form 10k, an annual disclosure made to the U.S. Securities and Exchange Commission, designed to ensure financial transparency for the investing public. Likewise in the 2010 annual report to shareholders, Goldman Sachs acknowledged adverse publicity and governmental scrutiny may have an adverse financial effect. As such, the reputational damage became clearly linked to Goldman Sachs' financial prospects.

While it may seem self-evident that negative press may have an impact on finances, these disclosures were unique and different from previous years. In the 2008 Form 10-k annual report to the SEC and the annual report to investors, Goldman Sachs disclosed in the section entitled "risk factors" that generally, legal and regulatory action could have an impact on reputation and business prospects (Table 1). The 2009 Form 10k filed 26 February 2010) included language from previous years; however, there was a new paragraph describing the impact that governmental or regulatory scrutiny and negative publicity might have on the firm's finances (Table 1). The 2009 Annual Report to investors also used similar language as in the 2008 report; however, new language was feathered in acknowledging the impact that adverse publicity might have. (Table 1) This language in the 2009 report noted that the reputational risk could be based on the allegations alone, "regardless of the ultimate outcome" (Goldman 2010).

Three months after the 2009 reports were released, the SEC filed a federal complaint on 15 April 2010, alleging that Goldman Sachs had mislead investors by omitting and misstating important facts (Securities and Exchanges Commission 2010a, b). The same complaint alleged that Goldman Sachs had then bet against the investments it was selling to clients. Thereafter, Goldman Sachs was widely perceived to have acted in its own self interest often at the expense of its own clients and investors. As one article characterized it, Goldman Sachs became "one giant piñata to whack" (Elson cited in Bel Bruno 2010, paragraph 4).

At the annual shareholders meeting on 7 May 2010, Goldman Sachs announced its intent to create the new "Business Standards Committee" (Goldman Sachs Annual 2011a). The Committee's mandate was to conduct a review of Goldman Sachs business standards to ensure that they are of the "highest quality, that they meet or exceed the expectations of our clients, other stakeholders and regulators; and that they contribute to overall financial stability and economic opportunity." (Goldman Sachs 2011a).

In February 2011, Goldman Sachs released the 2010 Form 10k which was similar to the 2009 report with respect to reputational harm (Table 1). The 2010 annual report to shareholders; however, differed in that there was a much greater emphasis on reputation. In one section entitled, "Certain Risk Factors that May Affect Our Business," the report enumerate specific types of risk including:

- Conflicts of interest are increasing and a failure to appropriately identify and address conflicts of interest could adversely affect our business.
- We may be adversely affected by increased governmental and regulatory scrutiny or negative publicity.
- Substantial legal liability or significant regulatory action against us could have material adverse financial affects or cause us significant reputational harm, which in turn could seriously harm our business prospects.[1]

---

[1] Page 87.

Table 1 Comparison of the 2008–2010 10k and annual reports

	2008	2009	2010
Form 10k	**Substantial legal liability or significant regulatory action against us could have material adverse financial effects or cause us significant reputational harm, which in turn could seriously harm our business prospects** We face significant legal risks in our businesses, and the volume of claims and amount of damages and penalties claimed in litigation and regulatory proceedings against financial institutions remain high. See "Legal Proceedings" in Part I, Item 3 of our Annual Report on Form 10-K for a discussion of certain legal proceedings in which we are involved. Our experience has been that legal claims by customers and clients increase in a market downturn. In addition, employment-related claims typically increase in periods when we have reduced the total number of employees There have been a number of highly publicized cases involving fraud or other misconduct by employees in the financial services industry in recent years, and we run the risk that employee misconduct could occur. It is not always possible to deter or prevent employee misconduct and the precautions we take to prevent and detect this activity may not be effective in all cases. (Goldman Sachs 2009, p. 38) (1a)	**Substantial legal liability or significant regulatory action against us could have material adverse financial effects or cause us significant reputational harm, which in turn could seriously harm our business prospects** We face significant legal risks in our businesses, and the volume of claims and amount of damages and penalties claimed in litigation and regulatory proceedings against financial institutions remain high. See "Legal Proceedings" in Part I, Item 3 of this Annual Report on Form 10-K for a discussion of certain legal proceedings in which we are involved. Our experience has been that legal claims by customers and clients increase in a market downturn and that employment-related claims increase in periods when we have reduced the total number of employees There have been a number of highly publicized cases involving fraud or other misconduct by employees in the financial services industry in recent years, and we run the risk that employee misconduct could occur. It is not always possible to deter or prevent employee misconduct and the precautions we take to prevent and detect this activity have not been and may not be effective in all cases. (Goldman Sachs 2010, p. 37) **We may be adversely affected by increased governmental and regulatory scrutiny or negative publicity** Governmental scrutiny from regulators, legislative bodies and law enforcement agencies with respect to matters relating to compensation, our business practices, our past actions and other matters has increased dramatically in the past several years.	**Substantial legal liability or significant regulatory action against us could have material adverse financial effects or cause us significant reputational harm, which in turn could seriously harm our business prospects** We face significant legal risks in our businesses, and the volume of claims and amount of damages and penalties claimed in litigation and regulatory proceedings against financial institutions remain high. See "Legal Proceedings" in Part I, Item 3 of this Form 10-K for a discussion of certain legal proceedings in which we are involved. Our experience has been that legal claims by customers and clients increase in a market downturn and that employment-related claims increase in periods when we have reduced the total number of employees. There have been a number of highly publicized cases, involving actual or alleged fraud or other misconduct by employees in the financial services industry in recent years, and we run the risk that employee misconduct could occur. This misconduct has included and may include in the future the theft of proprietary software. It is not always possible to deter or prevent employee misconduct and the precautions we take to prevent and detect this activity have not been and may not be effective in all cases **We may be adversely affected by increased governmental and regulatory scrutiny or negative publicity** Governmental scrutiny from regulators, legislative bodies and law enforcement agencies with respect to matters relating to compensation, our business (continued)

Table 1 (continued)

2008	2009	2010
	The financial crisis and the current political and public sentiment regarding financial institutions has resulted in a significant amount of adverse press coverage, as well as adverse statements or charges by regulators or elected officials. Press coverage and other public statements that assert some form of wrongdoing, regardless of the _factual basis for the assertions being made, often results in some type of investigation by regulators, legislators and law enforcement officials or in lawsuits. Responding to these investigations and lawsuits, regardless of the ultimate outcome of the proceeding, is time consuming and expensive and can divert the time and effort of our senior management from our business. Penalties and fines sought by regulatory authorities have increased substantially over the last several years, and certain regulators have been more likely in recent years to commence enforcement actions or to advance or support legislation targeted at the financial services industry. Adverse publicity, governmental scrutiny and legal and enforcement proceedings_ can also have a negative impact on our reputation and on the morale and performance of our employees, which could adversely affect our businesses and results of operations. (Goldman Sachs 2010, p. 34) (1c)	practices, our past actions and other matters has increased dramatically in the past several years. The financial crisis and the current political and public sentiment regarding financial institutions has resulted in a significant amount of adverse press coverage, as well as adverse statements or charges by regulators or other government officials. Press coverage and other public statements that assert some form of wrongdoing often result in some type of investigation by regulators, legislators and law enforcement officials or in lawsuits. Responding to these investigations and lawsuits, regardless of the ultimate outcome of the proceeding, is time consuming and expensive and can divert the time and effort of our senior management from our business. Penalties and fines sought by regulatory authorities have increased substantially over the last several years, and certain regulators have been more likely in recent years to commence enforcement actions or to advance or support legislation targeted at the financial services industry. Adverse publicity, governmental scrutiny and legal and enforcement proceedings can also have a negative impact on our reputation and on the morale and performance of our employees, which could adversely affect our businesses and results of operations. (Goldman Sachs 2010, p. 27) (1c)

(continued)

Table 1 (continued)

	2008	2009	2010
Annual report to investors	*Substantial legal liability or a significant regulatory action against us could have material adverse financial effects or cause significant reputational harm to us, which in turn could seriously harm a business prospects. (Goldman Sachs 2009, p. 24) (1b)*	*Substantial legal liability or a significant regulatory action against us, or <u>adverse publicity</u>, governmental scrutiny or legal and enforcement proceedings regardless of the ultimate outcome, could have material adverse financial effects or cause significant reputational harm to us, <u>or adversely affect the morale and performance of our employees</u>, which in turn could seriously harm our business and results of operations (Goldman Sachs 2010 , p. 38) (1d)*	*Substantial legal liability or a significant regulatory action against us could have material adverse financial effects or cause significant reputational harm to us, which in turn could seriously harm a business prospects. (Goldman Sachs 2011a, p. 88)* *We may be adversely affected by increased governmental and regulatory scrutiny or negative publicity. (Goldman Sachs 2011a , p. 87)*

The report also included a new section entitled, "Our Business Standards" with a subsection entitled, "Strengthening Reputational Excellence" (Goldman Sachs 2011a). It begins,

> Goldman Sachs has one reputation. It can be affected by any number of decisions and activities across the firm. Every employee has an equal obligation to raise issues or concerns, no matter how small, to protect the firm's reputation. We must ensure that our focus on our reputation is as grounded, consistent and pervasive as our focus on commercial success.

As a company with a global market cap of over $50 billion, such reputational damage could potentially have a multi-million, if not multi-billion, impact on the stock price and market capitalization. Following the public scrutiny, two analysts downgraded to their ratings of Goldman Sachs stock, and the stock price tumbled. As quoted in a April 2010 article,

> How much trouble is Goldman Sachs really in? One answer, $21 Billion. That is how much the vaunted Wall Street bank has lost in market value since it was engulfed in a fraud accusation a week ago".

In July 2010, Goldman Sachs agreed to pay $550 million to settle the lawsuit alleging fraud brought by the SEC (Harper 2010).

By September 2010, Goldman Sachs initiated a new, and relatively novel (for the firm) public relations campaign. As opposed to targeted communications to specific investors and customers which were more common for the firm, the firm launched a broad general awareness campaign to the broader population of the US. With it's slogan, "Progress is what we do" the initial advertisement showed a worker in a windfarm, explaining how Goldman Sachs helped with job creation. The advertisement appeared to link Goldman Sachs to broader issues in society such as the environment, job creation and energy. In contrast, Goldman Sachs' logo was understated, very small in the corner of the page. Goldman Sachs CEO Lloyd Blankfein explained on the Charlie Rose show in April 2010, "We have a lot of work to do explaining to people what it is that we do, and we're starting from a hole." Nonetheless the campaign was criticized by some as failing to offer evidence that the firm had in fact changed any of its troubling practices, and was merely an attempt to improve its image.

2 Reviewing Literature for the Case

In the following section we present a literature review on the most important theoretical concepts in reputational risk. First, we look at corporate reputation and profitability, then at reputation risk, and finally at approaches to reputational repair management.

2.1 Corporate Reputation and Profitability

Similar to other service industries such as education and legal services, reputation plays a significant role in the success of financial institutions, (Atchinson 2005). A reputation is generally understood to be an "opinion, or social evaluation, of the public towards a person, group or organization" (Walter 2010, p. 105). It is a set of assumptions or beliefs based upon experience, relationship, and knowledge gained through personal knowledge and other sources including mass media (Barnett 2002; Kewell 2007). A reputation is less reflective of individual acts, but rather a generalization of cumulative behavior and is a "simplification" of complex behavior patterns over time as perceived by the various interest groups (Clardy 2005). Fombrun and Shanley (1990) define a corporate reputation as a "cognitive representation of a company's actions and results that crystallizes the firm's ability to deliver outcomes to its stakeholders" (1990, p. 235) Stakeholders are defined broadly as, a "group or individual who can affect or is affected by the achievement of the organization's objectives" (Freeman 1984, p. 46), anyone who can affect the organizations performance or goals (Bland 1998) or anyone in the organization or outside of the organization in the public sphere that can be affected by the organization (Ray 1999). Following Freeman et al. (2010), primary stakeholders likely include employees, suppliers, financers, communities and customers while secondary stakeholders include competitors, government, media, NGOs and consumer interest groups. As a corporation has different relationships with each of their various stakeholders, they may in fact not have one reputation, but many reputations (Dowling 2006).

Reputations are developed through people's perception of previous behavioral patterns, however, their value is in the predictability of future behavior (Clardy 2005; Scott and Walsham 2005). A good reputation can be based on a track record of quality service or products, or in its managerial code of conduct. A good reputation gives customers and other stakeholders the framework to believe that because a corporation has a good track record of meeting various expectations, and it likely will do so in the future (Fombrun 1996). Trust plays a large role in the development of business relationships (Kapstein 1998), and as such can play a key role in the identity of a corporate reputation such as Goldman Sachs. It is the value upon which business relationships are built, (Kapstein 1998), and serves to encourage behavior within socially accepted norms and discourage behavior outside of these norms (Granovetter 1985). In the finance industry in particular, trust plays a large role in corporate reputations (Atchinson 2005). Financial companies such as Goldman Sachs do not sell hard goods but rather a service that requires an increased amount of trust due to the nature of the service and the potential consequences of poor decisions. Financial firms that are successful at developing relationships with their stakeholders are more likely to develop increased loyalty (Fombrun 2001).

In general, corporations strive to develop good reputations (Eccles et al. 2007; Rayner 2001) which are considered to be valuable and strategic assets (Fombrun 2001;

Economist 2005). Better reputations can lead to higher pricing (Klein and Leffler 1981; Shapiro 1983) and greater sales (Shapiro 1983). Customers of reputable corporations are often more inclined to buy products across a broader spectrum. (Eccles et al. 2007) A good reputation can attract more qualified employees and investors, leading to more sustainable growth with higher price to earnings ratios and lower cost of capital, keeping expenses down (Fombrun and Shanley 1990; Eccles et al. 2007; Rayner 2001). A poor reputation on the other hand can send customers to competitors and increase expenses (Fombrun 2001; Hammond and Slocum 1996).

While reputations are clearly valuable, Fombrun (2001) explains that the value of a reputation can be difficult to determine, and Heugens et al. (2004) indicates that the relationship between corporate reputation and overall market value is neither simple nor static. It has been estimated that up to seventy percent of corporate value may be attributed to non-tangible assets including reputation (Eccles et al. 2007; Neufeld 2007; Weber Shandwick 2006).

2.2 Reputation Risk

Like other forms of risk, the concept of "reputation risk" is founded generally in the potential for this valuable asset to be compromised or diminished in value. Most definitions of reputation risk revolve around potential for an organization to fail to meet an expectation (reputation), leading to an adjustment of that expectation. Walter (2010) defines reputation risk as the "risk of loss in the value of a firm's business franchise that extends beyond event related accounting losses and is reflected in a decline of share performance metrics" (p. 105). The Office of the Comptroller of the Currency (OCC) in the United States defines reputation risk as follows,

> Reputation risks threaten the current and prospective impact on earnings and capital arising from negative public opinion that may expose the institution to litigation, financial loss or a decline in its consumer base (Eisenberg 1999a, b).

Rayner (2001) however contends that reputation risk is not an independent risk, but rather a compilation of various risks that may impact reputation. According to Rayner (2001) "reputation risk" is a convenient catch-all phrase for the various sources of risk involving that may have an impact on a corporate reputation including; financial, regulatory, ethical, and customer expectations.

Reputation risk involves the potential for a gap to develop between an expectation and a reality (Eccles et al. 2007). Whether it be a financial expectation, a belief regarding environmental practices, a service provided, or compliance with other social norms; if there is a difference between an expectation that is widely held by stakeholders and actual practice, there is potential for the existing reputation to be in jeopardy. According to Eccles et al. (2007) "when the reputation of a company is more positive than its underlying reality, this gap poses a substantial risk. Eventually the failure of a firm to live up to its billing will be revealed and its reputation will decline until it is more closely matches the reality" (p 107).

Reputational risk also stems from the difficult task of reaching financial benchmarks in market performance and expectations of corporate conduct at the same time (Walter 2010). Corporations such as Goldman Sachs need to meet performance benchmarks, including short term benchmarks like quarterly results, lest they risk the loss of investors as their reputation for profitable returns decline. At the same time they need to meet corporate conduct benchmarks as measured by the laws and regulations of a particular society, as well as the social values that often form the basis of the laws or regulations (Walter 2010). Their reputation is based on a measurement of the corporate character against these standards. Managers are often challenged to meet both expectations at the same time, and failure to do so can contribute to reputation risk. Making things even more difficult, societal standards and expectations can change or be unclear (Walter 2010). Nonetheless, when corporate behavior is inconsistent with stakeholder perception or social expectations, a consensus can emerge within the various stakeholders groups challenging the current perception and reputation of the corporation (Walter 2010).

To the degree that trustworthiness plays a role in reputation, risk would be present when there is a misalignment with the perception of their trustworthiness and stakeholders perception of it. For example, if the firm was perceived as business savvy but not trustworthy, there would be little risk if it were discovered that they breached trust among a group of stakeholders. Likewise there would be no risk if they were perceived as trustworthy, and acted consistently with such impression. Risk, particularly substantial risk, would develop primarily if an important element of the reputation, such as trust, and it was discovered that the actual behavior did not meet that expectation.

A primary source of reputation risk stems from compliance issues. In a survey of 269 corporations, the compliance failure and the failure to meet legal obligations were the most commonly cited sources of reputation risk among the respondents (Economist 2005). Exposure of unethical practices was second, failure to meet minimum standards of product/service was the fourth most common source, and the failure to meet financial expectations was sixth (Economist 2005).

A lack of internal coordination contributes to the risk, where various units of a large corporation may be acting inconsistently, creating inconsistent perceptions (Eccles et al. 2007). In some cases, the nature of the board may contribute to reputation risk. (Dowling 2006) Board's members often only contribute several hundred hours to their governance responsibility, and their effectiveness in that capacity is reduced by the fact that they often receive filtered information, have personal blind spots and operate in a group decision making environment (Dowling 2006).

When expected outcomes are not delivered, however, the result can lead to the decline of corporate reputation. The decline of corporate reputation often manifests itself in impoverished revenues, decreased ability to attract financial capital, and reduced appeal to current and potential employees. This adjustment can come in the form of a slow decline in the reputation however it often involves a triggering event or sudden awareness among the stakeholders and takes the shape of an acute crisis.

2.3 Managing Reputation Risk

In the absence of a crisis, addressing reputation risk requires a coordinated two-prong approach, managing both the actual character of the firm and the expectation stakeholders have of it. From a proactive approach, managing the character starts with an accurate assessment of the firm's character and practices (Eccles et al. 2007; Fombrun and Foss 2004). Managing the perception should also start with an assessment of the corporate reputation or perception that stakeholders have of the corporation (Eccles et al. 2007). If there is a difference between the character of the firm and the reputation, Eccles et al. (2007) recommends "closing the gap" (p. 106). If the reputation supersedes the actual character, the clear preference is to bring the character of the firm up to a level that is consistent with the reputation. Alternatively, the firm could attempt to reduce the reputation the firm has among stakeholders, however that path is not recommended due to the value that good reputation has. (Eccles et al. 2007). Feedback loops can help match the behavior to the expectation through increased communication and assessment.

Public relations and corporate communications play a strategic role in managing relationships with stakeholders and their perception (Steyn 2003; Fombrun 2001). Positive and frequent visibility in the press lead to better reputations, and companies with extensive negative publicity suffer from a poor reputation (Heugens et al. 2004). Companies must not only remain on the public's radar screen to maintain awareness, at least 20 % of the stories regarding the firm must be positive, and less than 10 % negative, with the rest neutral (Fombrun 2001).

Most corporations address reputation risk once a crisis draws attention to the issue. Pearson and Mitroff (1993) define a crisis as an event that has a small likelihood of occurring, however a potentially large and negative impact on the organization. According to Coombs and Holliday (2001) corporate crisis often involve a violation of a social expectation. Such crises are often outside the immediate control of the organization, but require a direct response (Pearson and Mitroff 1993; Stephens et al. 2005).

Corporate response during a crisis requires coordinated response and dialogue with stakeholders to maintain and rebuilt reputational legitimacy (Allen and Caillouet 1994; Ray 1999). In terms of image repair, efforts often focus primarily on modifying the perception that stakeholders have of the firm in terms of responsibility and the crises, and attempt to modify these impressions (Coombs 1999). Stakeholder response to such efforts can have a material impact on the organizations ability to restore the reputation (Sims 2009), and failure to rebuilt legitimacy within a critical window of opportunity can potentially jeopardize organizational survival (Erickson et al. 2011).

A well-known theory regarding organizational responses to crises is Benoit's theory of restoration (1995) (see also Erickson et al. 2011). Also Coombs (1995) builds on Benoit's theory of restoration and offers an outline regarding various response strategies commonly employed by corporations in crisis. The responses include:

- Nonexistence: convincing stakeholders that there is no crisis via denial, intimidation or clarification
- Distancing: minimizing the corporate connection to the crisis
- Ingratiation: augmenting the reputation
- Mortification: soliciting forgiveness
- Suffering: describing the corporation as a victim of the crises as well.

Following this framework Stephens et al. (2005) found that mortification and ingratiation, were employed in 63 % of corporate crises with rectification (subcategory of mortification), convincing the audience that similar crises would not happen again, being very common (p. 407). Stephens et al. (2005) also found there to be a surprising lack of consistency in the message to the various stakeholders that may appear disenfranchising among some of the stakeholder groups.

Mortification in the form of accommodation, can be very influential for regaining trust (Benoit 1995). However accommodation, such as a full apology, can also invite greater liability. Coombs and Holladay (2002) developed the "Situational Crisis Communication" theory provide guidance in the determining the appropriate response, including accommodation. As described by Coombs and Holladay (2002) there is little reputational threat where the corporation is perceived to be the victim. As such little to no accommodation should be employed. An accident that involves the corporation deserves more accommodation. Accommodation such as corrective action and apology should be considered where a corporation is perceived to be responsible for a preventable crisis, as such a situation involves the greatest threat to reputation (Benoit 1995).

Heugens et al. (2004) identified four distinct types of responses that firms employ in reputational crises;

- Dialogue: employing cooperative dialogue to understand stakeholder issues, express understanding thereof, communicate key information, and build trust.
- Advocacy: employing persuasion in communications to characterize organizational views favourably, including "persuasion oriented public affairs plans" (p. 1363).
- Corporate silence: limiting organizational responsibility through minimal communication.
- Crisis communication: coordinating communication across the organization with stakeholders.

Messages varied based on the stakeholder, using different impression management strategies with the most effecting strategy being ingratiation; using belief, values and attitude similarity to persuade the recipient of the organizations positive traits and gain approval. (Allen and Caillouet 1994).

The overarching theme in the above literature, particularly in relation to reputational crises is the need to shape public perception of responsibility and influence the audience (Coombs 1999). The purpose of communication during a crisis is to persuade stakeholders to maintain positive image of organization or restore a damaged perception (Ray 1999). This is purportedly time-critical and the future of the organization can depend on the initial steps it takes.

3 Reputational Risk at Goldman Sachs

In this paper we review secondary data from the Goldman Sachs case including the annual report to investors, the form 10k to the SEC, public relations announcements and advertisements from 2009 to 2011, along with media coverage of Goldman Sachs during this timeframe to review the development of reputation risk and Goldman Sachs' response, in comparison with the prevailing literature.

As the world's largest investment banking firm, Goldman Sachs reputation likely preceded itself, conveying confidence in the firm's abilities. As a firm with a global market cap of $74 billion in June 2009, the value of the reputation would have been difficult to establish with certainty; however, according to Eccles et al. (2007) research, Goldman Sachs intangible assets including reputation may have constituted 70 % of that market cap, or $51 billion. As elaborated by Kapstein (1998) trust is an important component of reputations in the service sector, and as such the perception of trust would have played an important role in the value of Goldman Sachs reputation.

Goldman Sachs reputation among investors and clients was probably different than the reputation it has among employees, the government and society in general. Following Clardy (2005) above, Goldman Sachs reputation among each of these subgroups was likely a "simplification" of complex behavior displayed over time, and not the result of a single event. Among clients and investors, their reputation likely involved a measure of perceived trustworthiness.

To the degree that Goldman Sach's reputation was positive in 2009, it would have lead to higher pricing (Klein and Leffler 1981; Shapiro 1983) and greater sales (Shapiro 1983). With a positive reputation, Goldman Sachs customers were likely inclined to buy products across a broader spectrum (Eccles et al. 2007), attract qualified employees and investors, leading to more sustainable growth with higher price to earnings ratios and lower cost of capital, keeping expenses down (Fombrun and Shanley 1990; Eccles et al. 2007; Rayner 2001).

The allegations being made against Goldman Sachs and bad press challenged the reputable firm's reputation. The settlement in May 2009, whereby Goldman Sachs agreed to pay $60 million resolve allegations that it had taken advantage of customers in home loans, the article in the Rolling Stone in July 2009 painting Goldman Sachs as a "giant vampire squid wrapped around the face of humanity" (Bel Bruno 2010), the announcement of the S.E.C. investigation in December 2009 regarding fraud, and then the complaint filed in U.S. Federal Court in April 2010 all contributed to the changing perception of Goldman Sachs.

Financial performance is clearly a component of reputation within the financial industry, and a portion of Goldman Sachs reputation was likely suffering from the global financial recession in 2009 independently. Nonetheless, with trust being an important component of reputation in the financial industry, allegations of fraud and self-serving behavior from numerous stakeholders (including customers, investors, government and broader society) likely contributed to the development of reputation risk. These revelations exposed the gap between the corporate reputation and the actual character of the firm. As described by Walter 2010, it is unclear what precipitates change; however, the consensus leading to a different perception of a firm can suddenly form. Consistent with the Economist (2005), compliance and ethical issues relating to fraud and trust were at the source of Goldman Sachs reputation risk issues. The lack of internal coordination within Goldman Sachs business units allegedly led to conflicts of interest at the customer's and investor's expense.

Analysis of the 10k reports filed by Goldman Sachs below (Table 1) reveals the unique acknowledgement of this risk. While the annual report to investors also shows the same organizational concerns, it was the disclosure in the Form 10k that was most revealing in light of the forms emphasis on financial performance and corporate transparency. The sections added into the disclosure from year 2008 (filed in February 2009) to the 2009 report (filed in February 2010) reveal a marked acknowledgement (Seele 2010; Seele and Zapf 2011) that negative press regardless of the factual basis, might have a material impact on the firms performance.

An analysis of the annual reports to investors reveals the same disclosure, where Goldman Sachs took the extraordinary step in feathering in additional language stating that *"adverse publicity, governmental scrutiny or legal and enforcement proceedings regardless of the ultimate outcome, could have material adverse financial effects or cause significant reputational harm to us, or adversely affect the morale and performance of our employees."* Whereas the previous annual reports discuss the potential for reputational harm in a more generic sense.

Likewise, the annual report revealed an attempts to manage this reputational risk consistent with the recommendations by Eccles et al. (2007) to "close the gap" (p. 107) between the reputation and reality, or the perceived character and the real character. The advent of the "Business Standards Committee" was a notable first step to address the actual character of the firm. The reports recognized that various business units within the firm may be creating different perceptions, and gave the Standards Committee the authority to identify and manage sources of conflict of interest within the firm.

Goldman Sachs also took notable steps to shore up the firms withering reputation. Such steps were consistent with Allen and Caillouet's (1994) recommendation to use strategic communication and corporate discourse to rebuild reputational legitimacy. While the information available to this study does not reveal actual steps taken internally within critical initial response period; however, the unique and again extraordinary step Goldman Sachs took in September 2010 via the national PR campaign is consistent with the recommendations by Benoit (1995) and Coombs (1995). The widely released public relations campaign, reaching broadly out to society as opposed to specific target markets which it was more known for, attempted to convey Goldman Sachs in a positive light. It attempted to characterize the firm as a benefit to society via its involvement in environmentally friendly energy projects and job creation. The understated Goldman Sachs logo in the corner revealed the self-depreciating nature of the effort to re-characterize people's impression of the firm, using ingratiation and mortification, the most common approaches to crisis management according to Stephens et al. (2005).

Communicating these efforts and the mandate of the new Business Standards Committee to shareholders in the 2010 Annual Report was consistent with rectification, previously being recognized as the most common subcategory.

By September 2011, Goldman Sachs' market cap had shrunk from $74 billion (June 2009) down to $47 billion, just over half of its previous market cap. Clearly the global financial crises and downward financial pressure on banks played a significant role in the depreciation of the firm's value. Nonetheless, it appears clear from the acknowledgements made by Goldman Sachs and the literature on reputation risk, that the allegations of unethical behavior had a material impact on the corporate performance. Similarly, these observations contribute to the "business case" for ethics, and lead to the final section briefly discussing why awareness of the business case for ethics may be necessary for change in the marketplace.

4 Ethical Implications for Goldman Sachs in the Light of Eisenberg's Obligational Norms

There has been tremendous growth in the subject of business ethics in academia over the past thirty years, yet at the same time a frustrating increase in the number of ethical scandals with little abatement in the number and impact these scandals have had (Heugens et al. 2004), bringing even further attention to what has been characterized as a "fractured contract between business and society" (Brigley 1995, p. 225). This raises questions regarding the role that ethics play in the commercial context; which factors foster ethical compliance and which serves as a detriment. Although the "business case," or profitable justification, for ethics may seem to be at odds with traditional justifications for ethical behavior, research into the "business case" for ethical behavior in the corporate context may provide insight into why the relationship between society and business continues to appear "fractured," and why noticeable scandals continue to influence the perception of the corporate world.

Eisenberg (1999a, b) provides one theory regarding the influence that social norms have on managers. In his article entitled "Social Norms and Corporate Law" Eisenberg (1999a, b) describes obligational norms as unwritten rules in a society that are widely expected to be followed. Failure to comply with obligational norms results in either self-criticism or criticism by others, as opposed to other norms that are less compulsory in nature. (Eisenberg 1999a, b) Both individuals and organizations are expected to abide by social norms and expectations alike (Allen and Caillouet 1994). Obligational norms, however, are perceived and internalized by individuals.

Obligational norms can be either "internalized" or "non-internalized" depending on individual perspectives. A norm is "internalized" by those who perceive it as the "right thing to do" regardless of other considerations. (Eisenberg 1999a, b) For those who have not "internalized" a given obligational norm, compliance requires additional reasons to do so (maintained or improved reputation, social acceptance, financial benefit) (Basu 1998). Telling the truth is an example of an obligational norm. Many tell the truth simply, and only, because it is the right thing to do. Many others recognize that telling the truth is by and large an expectation, however, doing so may be more situationally dependent. For example, a person who stands to gain from a lie may consider the likelihood that they will be exposed, and the consequences to reputation, shame or sanctions. Thus, according to Eisenberg (1999a, b), compliance with any given obligational norm will be dependent on the extent that it is "internalized" relevant actors, and for some, the degree that alternative reasons to do so can be appreciated.

A corporate environment, such as Goldman Sachs', may play a role in how obligational norms from the broader society are perceived and internalization within the corporate context. Efforts to promote ethical standards within various sectors of the business community through education and policy often face an "uphill battle" (Dobson 2003). Dobson (2003) argues that behavior and morals in the financial industry are heavily influenced by implicit education on neoclassical economic theory. In one survey in the financial industry, nearly one quarter of participants stated that they experienced or witnessed unethical behavior in the previous twelve months (Viet et al. 1996). Although this can not be quantified, it is likely that the unwritten expectation of the broader society regarding trust may not have been reflected within the Goldman Sachs trading department and boardrooms where pressure for profitability may have played a dominant role.

According to Eisenberg (1999a, b) obligational norms will be complied with by those who have internalized them as the proper thing to do regardless of other considerations. For others, however, compliance may require a clearer understanding of the associated benefits. An increased awareness of the benefits of compliance and the consequences of non-compliance on reputation stemming from unethical behavior may therefore have an impact on behavior in the corporate context.

Reputation risk management requires a two-prong approach addressing the perception of the corporation, and the actual character of the corporation as described above. This analysis provides another framework to understand the link between ethics and business profitability. As the link between unethical behavior and profitability may demonstrate the "business case" for ethics, this paper starts by discussing why the "business case" may be relevant. According to Eisenberg (1999a, b) there are varying degrees of compliance with obligational societal norms depending on the degree to which norms are internalized. With regard to a particular norm, many individuals may have internalized it and as such believe that compliance with the norm is expected regardless of any other influences. Other individuals, however, may have not internalized the norm, and as such will comply with the norm only when the perceived benefits of compliance outweigh the perceived benefits of noncompliance.

As such, any evidence that demonstrates the long term benefit of compliance may have an impact on behavior. In the case of Goldman Sachs, any evidence that shows that compliance with social obligatory norms has positive benefits, and non-compliance has negative reputational consequences that can be quantified, may be beneficial for in terms of the operation, tactical and strategic decision-making process. If this became the case, we may be close to addressing the "fractured contract" between business and society (Brigley 1995, p. 225).

Bibliography

Allen, M.W., and R.H. Caillouet. 1994. Legitimation endeavours: Impression management strategies used by an organization in crisis. *Communication Monographs* 61: 44–62.
Atchinson, B.K. 2005. Ethics after Enron: The Next 10 Years in the Financial Services Profession. *Journal of Financial Service Professionals* 59(1): 56–60.
Basu, K. 1998. Social norms and the law. In *New encyclopedia of law and economics*, ed. P. Newman.
Barnett, M. 2002. From me to we ... and back again: Returning to business as usual. *Journal of Management Inquiry*, 11(3): 249–252.
Bel Bruno, J. 2010. Goldman risks new "risk': bad press. *The Wall Street Journal*. Retrieved April 25, 2011, from http://finance.yahoo.com.
Benoit, W.L. 1995. *Accounts, excuses and apologies: A theory of image restoration strategies*. Albany: State University of New York Press.
Bland, M. (1998) Communicating Out of a Crisis. London: Macmillan Business.
Brigley, S. 1995. Business ethics in context: Researching with case studies. *Journal of Business Ethics* 14: 219–226.
Clardy, A. 2005. Reputation, goodwill, and loss: Entering the employee training audit equation. *Human Resource Development Review* 4: 279–284.
Coombs, W.T. 1995. Choosing the Right Words: The Development of Guidelines for the Selection of the Appropriate Response Strategies. Management Communication Quarterly 8: 447–475.
Coombs, W.T. 1999. *Ongoing crisis communication: Planning, managing and responding*. Thousand Oaks, CA: Sage.
Coombs, W.T., and S.J. Holladay. 2002. Helping crisis managers protect reputational assets. *Management Communication Quartely* 16(2): 165–186.
Coombs, W.T., and S.J. Holladay. 2001. An extended examination of the crisis situations: A fusion of the relational management and symbolic approaches. *Journal of Public Relations Research* 4: 321–340.
Dowling, G. 2006. Reputation risk: It is the board's ultimate responsibility. *The Journal of Business Strategy* 27(2): 59–67.
Dobson, J. 2003. Why ethics codes don't work. *Financial Analysts Journal* 59(6): 29–34.
Eccles, R.G., Newquist, S.C., Schatz, R. 2007. Reputation and its risks. *Havard Business Review* 104–114.
Eisenberg, M.A. 1999a. Corporate law and social norms. *Columbia Law Review* 99(5): 1253–1292.
Eisenberg, S.A. 1999. Broader horizons. Financial institutions must consider all forms of risk: Fiscal, economic and reputation. *Credit Union Management* 38.
Economist. 2005. *Reputation: risk of risks*. London, U.K.
Erickson, S.L., M. Weber, and J. Segovia. 2011. Using communication theory to analyze corporate reporting strategies. *Journal of Business Communications* 48(2): 207–223.
Fombrun, C.J. 2001. Reputations: Measurable, valuable, and manageable. *American Banker*
Fombrun, C.J. 1996. *Reputation: Realizing the value from the corporate image*. Boston: Harvard Business School Press.
Fombrun, C.J., and C. Foss. 2004. Business ethics: Corporate responses to scandal. *Corporate Reputation Review* 7(3): 284–288.

Fombrun, C.J., N.A. Gardberg, and M.L. Barnett. 2000. Opportunity platforms and safety nets: Corporate citizenship and reputation risk. *Business and Society Review* 105(1): 85–106.

Fombrun, C.J., and C.B.M. Van Riel. 1998. The reputational landscape. *Corporate Reputation Review* 1(1): 5–13.

Fombrun, C.J., and M. Shanley. 1990. What's in a name? Reputation building and corporate strategy. *Academy of Management Journal* 33(2): 233–248.

Freeman, R.E. 1984. *Strategic management: A stakeholder approach*. Boston: Pitman.

Freeman, R.E., J. Harrison, A. Wicks, B. Parmar, and S. Colle. 2010. *Stakeholder theory, the state of the art*. Cambridge, MA: Cambridge University Press.

Goldman Sachs Annual Report. 2008. Accessed 20 July 2011 from http://www.goldmansachs.gs/investor-relations/financials/archived/annual-reports/2008-annual-report.html.

Goldman Sachs Annual Report. 2009. Accessed 20 July 2011 from http://www.goldmansachs.gs/investor-relations/financials/archived/annual-reports/2009-annual-report.html.

Goldman Sachs. 2011a. Business Principles and Standards Committee report. Accessed 10 November 2011 from http://www2.goldmansachs.com/who-we-are/business-standards/committee-report/business-standards-committee-report.html.

Goldman Sachs Annual Report 2010. 2011b. Accessed 20 July 2011 from http://www2.goldmansachs.com/investor-relations/financials/current/annual-reports/2010-annual-report.html.

Goldman Sachs Annual Report 2010. Published 28 February 2011, Accessed 20 July 2011 fromhttp://www2.goldmansachs.com/investor-relations/financials/current/annual-reports/2010-annual-report.html.

Granovetter, M. 1985. Economic Action and Social Structure: The Problem of Embeddedness. *American Journal of Sociology* 91(3): 481–510

Harper, C. 2010. Goldman Sachs runs U.S. ad campaign emphasizing job creation. Bloomberg News. Retrieved 21 January 2011 from http://www.bloomberg.com/news/2010-09-29/goldman-sachs-runs-u-s-advertising-campaign-emphasizing-job-creation-role.html.

Hammond, S.A., and J.W. Slocum Jr. 1996. The impact of prior firm financial performance on subsequent corporate reputation. *Journal of Business Ethics* 15(2): 159–165.

Heugens, P.M., C.B. van Riel, and F.A. van den Bosch. 2004. Reputation management capabilities as decision rules. *Journal of Management Studies* 41(8): 1349–1374.

Kapstein, M. 1998. *Ethics Management: Auditing and Developing the Ethical Content of Organizations*. Boston: Kluwer Academic Publishers.

Kewell, K. 2007. Linking risk and reputation: A research agenda and methodological analysis. *Risk Management* 9(4): 238–254.

Klein, B., and K.B. Leffler. 1981. The role of market forces in assuring contractual performances. *Journal of Political Economy* 89: 615–641.

Morgenson, G., and Story, L. 2009. Banks bundled bad debt, bet against it and won. The New York Times. Retrieved 10 November 2011 from http://www.nytimes.com/2009/12/24/business/24trading.html?_r=4andref=business.

Neufeld, G.A. 2007. Managing reputation risk. *Risk Management* 54(9): 38–40,42,44.

Pearson, C.M., and I.I. Mitroff. 1993. From crisis prone to crisis prepared: A framework for crisis management. *Academy of Management Executive* 7: 48–59.

Pulliam, S., and Perez, E. 2010. Criminal probe looks into Goldman trading. Retrieved 10 Nov 2011 from http://online.wsj.com/article/SB10001424052748703572504575214652998348876.html.

Ray, S.J. 1999. *Strategic communication in crisis management lessons from the airline industry*. Westport, CT: Quorum.

Rayner, J. 2001. *Risky business: Towards best practice in managing reputational risk*. London: Institute of Business Ethics.

Scott, S.V., and G. Walsham. 2005. Reconceptualizing and managing reputation risk in the knowledge economy: Toward reputable action. *Organizational Science* 16(3): 308–322.

Seele, P. 2010. Goldman Sachs als Geburtshelfer der Wirtschaftsethik, Neue Zürcher Zeitung, 28.04.2010: 23.

Seele, P. and Zapf, L. 2011. Just a banker doing god's work. In *Ethica* 4/11. 259–278.

Shanahan, M.F., and P. Seele. 2015. Shorting Ethos: Exploring the relationship between Aristotle's ethos and reputation management. *Corporate Reputation Review* 18(1): 37–49.

Shapiro, C. 1983. Premiums for high quality products as returns to reputations. *Quarterly Journal of Economics* 98: 659–679.

Sims, R. 2009. Toward a better understanding of organizational efforts to rebuild reputation following an ethical scandal. *Journal of Business Ethics* 90: 453–472.

Stephens, K.K., P.C. Malone, and C.M. Bailey. 2005. Communicating with stakeholders during a crisis. *Journal of Business Communication* 42(4): 390–419.

Steyn, B. 2003. From Strategy to Corporate Communication Strategy; A Conceptualization. *Journal of Communication Management* 8(2): 168–183.

Tiabbi, M. 2009. From tech stocks to high gas prices, Goldman Sachs has engineer every major market manipulation since the great depression—and they are about to do it again. *Rolling Stone*. Retrieved April 25 2011, from http://www.rollingstone.com.

U.S. Securities and Exchange Commission. 2010a. Securities and Exchange Commission vs. Goldman Sachs and Co. & Fabrice Tourre. Retrieved 10 Nov 2011 from http://www.sec.gov/litigation/complaints/2010/comp21489.pdf.

U.S. Securities and Exchange Commission. 2010b. Goldman Sachs to pay record $550 million to settle SEC charges related to subprimed mortgage CDO. Retrieved 10 Nov 2011 from http://sec.gov/news/press/2010/2010-123.htm.

Viet, T., M. Murphy, and H.K. Baker. 1996. Ethics and the investment profession: An international survey. *Financial Analysts Journal* 53(1): 9–14.

Walter, I. 2010. Reputation Risk. In *Finance ethics: Critical issues in theory and practice*, ed. J. Boatright, 103–123. Hoboken, NJ: Wiley.

Wayne, L. 2009. Goldman pays to end state inquiry into loans. The New York Times. Retrieved 10 Nov 2011 from http://www.nytimes.com/2009/05/12/business/12lend.html?_r=1.

Weber Shandwick and KRC Research. 2006. Safeguarding Reputation. November 17. http://governancefocus.blogspot.com/2006/11/nearly-80-percent-believe-reponsible.html. Accessed 4 Dec 2008.

Executive Compensation

Christoph Luetge

1 Introduction

Executive compensation is the payment of top executives. This type of compensation is frequently under moral pressure in public discussions. The pivotal question is whether *high* payment of top executives, especially of CEOs, can be ethically justified, and if so, under which conditions.

2 Forms of Executive Compensation

Executive compensation can take different forms. It can have fixed and variable portions. The base salary is a fixed portion. Usually, it is only a smaller fraction of a CEO's total income, rarely more than €1 million. All other portions are variable in principle, consisting in the following four: Annual bonuses, stock options, stock grants, and long-term incentive plans.

Annual bonuses depend on the company's performance. During the years a company does well, these bonuses can reach quite high levels. In the public view, they are under particularly close scrutiny, as it is not always made clear that large incomes of €10 million and higher are tied to performance at all. Their level is usually determined by a bonus plan that links performance and payment.

This chapter reproduces revised material that has previously been published in C. Luetge, "Executive Compensation", In *Encyclopedia of Applied Ethics*, ed. Ruth Chadwick, 2nd ed., Oxford: Elsevier, vol. 2, pp. 243–249. We thank the publisher for their permission to reproduce it here.

C. Luetge (✉)
Chair of Business Ethics, Technical University of Munich,
Munich, Germany
e-mail: luetge@tum.de

© Springer International Publishing Switzerland 2016
C. Luetge and N. Mukerji (eds.), *Order Ethics: An Ethical Framework for the Social Market Economy*, DOI 10.1007/978-3-319-33151-5_20

Stock options and stock grants usually constitute the largest share in executive compensation. They are chiefly responsible for the vast increases in executive compensation since the 1970s.[1] Stock can be directly granted to top executives.[2] Stock options handed to employees (not necessarily only to top executives) allow them to buy stock in the future at a given rate. If the stock price rises above that rate, the employee can make additional money by buying stocks at the given rate and then selling them at the higher market rate. They may, however, also choose to hold the stock.

Long-term incentive plans are less common. They are established to provide incentives for executives to work in the company's *long-term* interest. As average years in office of CEOs have dropped to 5.7 years in Europe in 2007,[3] for example, long-term incentive plans are not always very effective.

Special forms of executive compensation are the so-called *golden handshakes* which are compensation packages a CEOs receives when he or she leaves the company. Golden handshakes often include contracts for long-term services like consulting, and also *golden parachutes* in case the company decides to end the CEO's office term.[4]

3 Ethical Problems Concerning Executive Compensation

There are several ethical problems commonly associated with executive compensation, in the press, in public discussions, but also in scientific discourse. The first is the general problem of whether high compensation in a market economy can be justified at all. While few believe that all employees should be paid the same regardless of their position, there are regular outcries over high total payments for CEOs. The level necessary to cause such an outcry varies by country. For example, the earnings of Deutsche Bank's CEO, Josef Ackermann, have regularly been the cause of outrage in Germany. In the US, however, managers like Lawrence Ellison, CEO of Oracle, earn more than ten times of Ackermann's pay.[5] The *average* payment of CEOs, even in the US, is however much less, US$ 4 million for mid-cap 400 companies.[6]

A second perceived problem is the question whether executive compensation is adequately related to executive performance.[7] In particular, there has been outrage

---

[1] Cf. Boatright (2009).

[2] For example, in 2009, the top executives of Deutsche Bank held 0.08 % of the company's shares (*Der Spiegel*, 24.03.2009).

[3] *Die Zeit* 22/2007, p. 29.

[4] Cf. Cochran and Wartick (1984).

[5] According to Forbes Executive Pay 2008 (www.forbes.com).

[6] Estimation by Bebchuk and Grinstein (2005, fn. 28).

[7] Cf. for empirical results Tosi et al. (2000).

over high compensation for executives of companies that are not doing very well at all.[8]

A third problem is the concern about proportion of payment: CEO pay—especially in the US, but elsewhere too—has increased far more than the average worker's pay.[9] Including stock options, the ration has increased from 30 to 1 in 1970 to 210 to 1 in 1996. Sometimes, even figures of up to 500 to 1 are given.[10] P. Drucker demanded—already in 1984—that there should be a maximum ratio of 20 to 1 between CEO and average worker's payment.[11] In ethical perspective, these statements are often tied to concerns about greed. To many people, the enormous increases seem to promote greed as a dangerous ethical ideal.

A fourth problem is the question of incentives: Does high executive compensation set the right incentives? One view is that these incentives are unnecessary and that CEOs would be motivated just as much if they were not paid millions, but only hundreds of thousands.[12] Another view is that the incentives might be counterproductive, in keeping CEOs' eyes fixed on short-term gains instead of the company's long-term interest. According to a similar criticism, stock options do not work as incentives at all, as, in many cases, stock prices rise without CEOs contributing to this.

A fifth question raises more detailed concerns about the process itself which determines CEO pay. These critics argue that CEOs and other executives exert too much influence on the pay-determining process, at the shareholders' expense. I will discuss this further in Sects. 7 and 8.

These are serious concerns. However, the nature of these problems requires some background discussion: First, of the relevant ethical background, including the very fundamentals of an ethics in a market economy, and second, of the relevant economic theories. I will start with the first one.

4 Ethical Background

The question of whether high executive pay is justified *in general* hinges on other, overarching ethical questions. Therefore, some basic issues of business ethics must be discussed here, namely those that concern the normative criteria according to which ethical judgments can be sensibly made.

There are two different ways of dealing with normativity: Either all possible normative criteria from all strands of ethics are listed and examined for their consequences regarding the evaluation of high executive compensation. Here, one

---

[8] See Iyengar (2000).
[9] See, for example, Murphy (1999), Weinberg (2000).
[10] Bebchuk and Fried (2004, 1).
[11] R. Wartzman, Put a Cap on CEO Pay, *BusinessWeek*, September 12, 2008.
[12] Cf. Bok (1993, 102).

ends up with a list of criteria and consequences and leaves it to the actors, i.e. the managers and shareholders, to decide among them.[13]

The second possibility is to disregard normative criteria for the moment and ask for their conditions of implementation in a market economy. Normative criteria are important, but equally important is that ethical justification in business ethics is tied to the rule or order framework of a society (cf. Luetge 2015, 2016, and Luetge et al. 2016). For the question of executive compensation and for ethically justifying decisions in this matter, it seems more fruitful to give some overview of social background theory. The normative criteria are being discussed in many other articles.

A fundamental distinction in business ethics is the one between actions and conditions of actions (rules). Traditional ethics concentrates on actions. Its norms require individuals to change those parameters they are able to control through their actions. The conditions of these actions have in traditional ethics often been taken as 'given', which is understandable since they have remained stable for centuries. These conditions include laws, constitutions, social structures, the market order, and also ethical norms.

In the modern world, however, this situation has changed dramatically. The rule framework like constitutions, the market order and others, has increasingly come under control. Smith (1776/1982) recognised this and introduced systematically the difference between actions and conditions of actions in order to link competition and morality together.

Morality (incorporated in the normative idea of the solidarity of all, for example) can be found on the level of the conditions, the *rules*. Only then can competition be made *ethically* productive. The individuals' moves are rendered moral-free *in principle*. With the aid of rules, of adequate conditions of actions, competition is directed at realising advantages for all people involved. In this way, moral behaviour of individuals cannot be exploited by others, as rules are the same for everybody.

Thus, under modern conditions, ethics is sensibly conceptualised on two different levels, as an ethics of actions and as an ethics of conditions of actions, most notably of rules or institutions. We can expect ethical behaviour on the level of actions only if it is not punished on the level of institutions. The relevant model here is the prisoners' dilemma:[14] In their individual actions, the prisoners cannot compensate for the lack of a co-ordinating institution and thus end up with an inferior outcome.

For any ethical problem in a market economy, it is thus most important not to let rules and actions get in opposition to each other. For example, an institutionalised import ban on goods manufactured with child labour leads to such a situation: It is—in very poor countries—counteracted on the level of the individuals' actions—as it

---

[13]For this approach see, for example, Rodgers and Gago (2003).
[14]Cf., for a wide range of literature, Axelrod (1984).

may lead to child labour being shifted into other, more hazardous areas (cf. Luetge 2005).

Actions are governed by rules, and rules themselves are governed by other rules of higher order. Higher order means that there is a greater degree of consent needed to put these rules in effect or to change them—as is the case with laws and constitutional rules, for example.[15]

Getting back to the normative question: Ultimately, the only normative criterion that is needed here is consent. This criterion has been the core of social contract theory from Hobbes and Spinoza to Rawls. Other normative criteria, such as justifying norms by reference to the will of God, to the law of nature, to reason or to intuition cannot count on acceptance in the modern pluralistic world anymore.

Keeping this perspective in mind leads to several conclusions about morality which are relevant to executive compensation.

First, only rules can be sensibly called moral or immoral—not individual actions. Rules are chosen by the members of a society, by the citizens,—but not particular distributions of goods or of income.[16]

Second, a sensible approach to business ethics needs to focus on incentives for implementing a moral norm, and not primarily on moral motivation. And a sensible ethical assessment of executive compensation should aim for changes in *incentives*, not rely primarily on changing individual *motivation* by means of morally appealing to the actors.

5 Economic Background

While executive compensation has quite a number of economic aspects, three of these are necessary to mention here:

1. The *labor market* determines not only executive pay, but every employee's payment. This has two implications: First, a CEO should be paid her marginal product. She should receive no more than what she adds to the total profits of the company. Second, the payment is tied to the supply of potential other CEOs on the labor market. When there are few individuals handy who can "do the job", the pay of CEOs will rise.
2. Within a company, there are however *agency problems*, which complicates the supply-demand oriented payment situation:[17] According to the principal-agent approach, the separation of ownership and control is the cause of special incentive problems: The shareholders—as principals—cannot have all information that would be needed to control or supervise the behaviour of the agents—the executives. Thus, executive compensation is designed to overcome an agency

---

[15]Cf. Buchanan (1975), Brennan and Buchanan (1985). For the ethical dimension of Buchanan's work, see Luetge (2006).

[16]Cf. Hayek (1976).

[17]For the principal-agent approach, cf. for example Jensen and Meckling (1983).

problem: In fixing a high payment, the shareholders secure not just a CEO's "work-to-rule", but, more important, her loyalty in questions where she has vital information. The payment can then be regarded as an *agency cost*. In Sects. 7 and 8, I discuss further problems associated with the agency problem.

3. An important aspect should be mentioned that is relevant for executive compensation in other countries than the US or UK: Does not the German system of the "Social Market Economy" highlight other values than just 'economic' ones? This system is indeed often justified—or equally criticised by others—by saying that the role of the 'social', of other values than economic ones, is to *correct* the 'anti-social' consequences of the market. In this picture, the market in itself is regarded as morally dubious. Another view however, is that the social market economy is intended to be a better, economically more productive *and* ethically more desirable market economy. This argument proceeds by showing that people—as market competitors—can take more risks if they know that the social system will support them.[18]

6 Bad Arguments for High Executive Compensation

Some arguments for high compensation, that are frequently used in public, are clearly insufficient:

1. "In a democracy, there is no need to justify one's actions." While that may be "true" in principle, there is still public discussion going on in a democracy. CEOs and other managers of large companies are under public observation—whether they like it or not. And good reputation is a key to economic success. So this argument does not take the problem of justification in a democracy seriously.
2. "Those who work harder than others deserve to earn more." It was already Hayek (1976) who pointed out that in a market economy, what one 'deserves' (according to what criterion ever) is not what one actually gets. In a market economy, there is no one who decides on a certain distribution of goods. Instead the distribution is the result of an anonymous process of competition within rules for which no one can be held responsible in any meaningful sense. Brennan and Buchanan's remark sums it up: "What emerges from a process is what emerges and nothing more."[19] In this process, skill and capabilities play a role, but also luck. And the distribution that emerges can be called just because it came into being according to the rules. It is not just *because* someone gets what she *deserves*. So this argument misses the point of a market economy.
3. "People just are like that—they are looking to maximize their income." This is not intended as a justification to begin with, but as an empirical claim. Leaving aside the empirical aspect—experimental economics is only one of several

---

[18]Cf. Sinn et al. (2006), Luetge (2009).
[19]Brennan and Buchanan (1985).

approaches that have cast doubts on the validity of this claim[20]—this argument assumes that things would become better if people did *not* seek to maximize their utility. If people were nice to each other, if they were to temper themselves, this would be best for all. But that is not the way a market economy works. It delivers the goods—the benefits for all—not via direct moral or altruistic motivation, but as a system of rules which benefit all. Income maximization is not only a necessary, but a desired part of this system.
4. The same holds for the argument used by managers looking for an excuse in the rule framework only: "We are playing according to the rules, but we did not invent them." While this is not in doubt, it still does not say anything about the *ethical* dimension of their behaviour, namely about its place within the logic of the market economy.

7 Refined Arguments for High Executive Compensation

There are however more serious arguments that can be used to defend high executive compensation:

1. It is not possible to hire good executives without adequate, which means market-based, compensation. And, even more important: Especially for top executives, there must be incentives not just to do work-to-rule, but to put all effort into working for their company and its shareholders. And trade union officials agree: The then head of the Porsche workers' council once said: "We already had inexpensive directors. They were so inexpensive we almost went bankrupt."[21]
A good example of this is the case of Klaus Esser, former CEO of Mannesmann who in 2000 sought to "defend" his company against the eventually successful takeover by British competitor Vodafone. Esser got €30 million as a "golden parachute"—which was the subject of much morally motivated uproar. Neither by law nor by company rules had Esser been obliged to battle against the takeover. However, his efforts raised the stock value of Mannesmann by €60 billion, which went to the shareholders. And approx. €10 billion of it went to small investors. From an ethical standpoint, it would be difficult to find this problematic. The golden parachute of €30 million seems rather small in comparison: Not many real-estate agents would work for a commission of 0.3 % (0.05 % if gains for institutional shareholders are considered too).
In the Esser case, another ethical objection was that the extra payment had not been negotiated in advance. However, extraordinary cases like fierce takeover battles cannot all be negotiated in advance. Such a view would be solely

---

[20]Cf. Smith (1991).
[21]*Tagesspiegel*, 16.12.2007.

focusing on the past. From another point of view, focusing on future cases, the question is whether other CEOs will conclude from the Esser case that value-increasing takeover battles will not be applauded but might instead lead to judicial prosecution. In future cases, this could result in CEOs just doing work-to-rule and leaving out on chances and gains for their shareholders. This is ethically not desirable, either.

What should be changed according to the critics? Most frequent are calls for either limits to executive compensation or for higher taxation. But both measures have side effects which can make them counterproductive: First, as I already pointed out, the largest part of executive compensation is tied to performance. And bad performance quickly leads to CEOs getting fired: The average length of time in office for a CEO in Germany had been 8.3 years by the end of the 1990s—but it dropped to 4.7 years by 2007[22] (this figure is 5.7 years in Europe, 7.8 years worldwide). CEOs who are hired quickly to cope with a crisis are often fired as fast.

The pressure for success is enormous, and success must be achieved quickly. But this has not always been the case. Until the early 1980s, CEOs everywhere were regarded (and paid) mostly as top bureaucrats who had to steer a large organisation like a government administration. In some countries like France, this has changed little. Especially in the US, however, major changes began in the 1980s. CEOs started to be treated and paid mostly as entrepreneurs who work in the shareholders' interest and need to maximise the shareholders' returns. This development was not welcomed by all CEOs at that time and, in several cases, it took considerable shareholder action to change the status of a company's CEO.[23] But eventually, top executives found that they could secure much higher compensation: Entrepreneurs need to be paid as such. They take higher risks and may make higher profits as bureaucrats. This has been the major cause for the dramatic increase of CEO payment, especially in the US.

Thus, when asking whether high executive compensation can be justified, it needs to be explained what CEOs are getting paid for. If they are regarded as bureaucrats, a case can be made for large fixed salaries. But if they are regarded as entrepreneurs, large variable portions make more sense.

2. Regarding taxation, the second point is that corporations, in a growing number of sectors, compete internationally for the best CEOs. There is an international labor market for top executives. These employees have more options than others in choosing their country to work in. High taxation is not the best way to succeed in hiring the best people. Higher taxation tends to raise emigration.

A famous example was taxation in Sweden during the 1970s. Extremely high tax rates forced not only the traditional type of rich people out of the country, but even famous artists: Writer Astrid Lindgren and director Ingmar Bergman

---

[22]*Die Zeit* 22/2007, p. 29.
[23]Cf. Boatright (2009).

were the most known examples who left Sweden because of tax issues. (Shortly afterwards, this situation was changed, following an election.)

Generally, high tax rates always carry a danger with them to make people look for new possibilities of investing money in other countries. Since the beginning of the financial crisis, tax loopholes are being put under closer scrutiny—whether these can be closed entirely is however unclear. There will most probably continue to be grave differences among tax rates, globally.

3. Whenever compensation is deemed excessive in absolute terms, it needs to be pointed out that soccer players or top Hollywood actors usually earn as much, if not more, yet they are not criticised nearly as much as CEOs in public discussions. In 2009, Michael Ballack earned nearly €10 million—which is in the same category as many CEOs.

 It seems that the performance of professional athletes is more evident to many people or can be judged more easily by the public at large. It is true that most soccer players and other athletes can earn these large sums only for a limited period of time during their career, while CEOs have this opportunity for a longer time. Many top actors, however, also have this chance. So the case of high compensation for executives is, while certainly no common, not a singular case either.

4. Sometimes another ethical issue is tied to the problem of executive compensation: Here, the difficulties do not arise from the compensation as such, but from a company's communication policy. There are cases in which the salaries of a company were raised significantly while large groups of employees were dismissed. This has frequently been cricitised as immoral.

 Here, a point is at issue that is very different from the ones mentioned above: Its background is clearly the idea that if a company is doing well and if its executives earn a lot of money in the course, then the number of employees should be increased or at least not lowered. This idea is mistaken from the beginning, under conditions of globalisation in any case: It was adapted to the conditions of large, bureaucracy-like companies of the 1950s and 60s, often (at least partly) in public hands which received their first blow during the 1973 oil crisis and have been declining ever since.

 According to a somewhat weaker version of this argument, mass dismissals should at least not announced at the same time as increases in executive compensation or huge company profits. This is termed bad style. Whether a different policy of communication would do anything about the actual situation of people getting dismissed, is in doubt. But it certainly is in the own interest of many companies to improve their public image. Many of them are not yet used to their new role as political actors[24] in the limelight. In this regard, the critics touch a sore spot that is important for the economic well-being of a company, too. The fundamental criticism, however, is mistaken: In a market economy, dismissals are a necessary tool for companies which has both an economic as well as an

---

[24]See the corporate citizenship approach, for example Matten and Crane (2005).

ethical rationale: It would be unethical to keep unprofitable employees and tie resources that could be used in other, mutually more beneficial positions.

8 The Independence of the Board in Fixing Executive Compensation

Traditionally, top executives—more often than not—were themselves directly or indirectly in charge of fixing their own compensation. This has long been seen critically from both ethical and economic standpoints, as it leaves not only the moral integrity, but also the economic performance of executives for their company in doubt. Therefore, a number of arrangements have been invented and set up in most countries to deal with this problem.

The process of determining executive compensation, especially the level of bonuses, varies in detail, depending on the country in question. In general, however, it is some special body of the company that fixes the level of compensation. In the one-tier-system, common in the US and UK, for example, there usually is a compensation or remuneration committee of the board of directors. In the two-tier system, common in parts of Continental Europe (but also in Japan and in three of the four BRIC states, namely China, Brazil and Russia), the supervisory board (Aufsichtsrat) determines the payment of the executive board. In Germany, until recently, this could be done by a subcommittee, however, new legislation introduced in March 2009 determined that the entire supervisory board must take these decisions.

In both systems, however, some measures have been taken to ensure that it is not the directors themselves that set their own compensation. The question is whether these measures are enough. Do CEOs maybe exercise still too much control over their own compensation? It is this viewed lack of independence from the part of the board of directors that can be seen as responsible for many ethical concerns about executive compensation.

9 The Managerial Power Thesis

Bebchuk and Fried have been exploring this line of argument further. In their book "Pay without Performance",[25] they are not against high executive compensation, but argue that the process of determining this compensation is very often flawed. Basically, Bebchuk and Fried claim that CEOs exercise too much power in this

---

[25]Bebchuk and Fried (2004).

process, which results in CEOs getting paid more than their performance justifies. In more detail, the following evidence for this claim is being quoted:

First, CEOs often have very direct control over the members of a board. While some committees have a majority of outside directors, this is not true in general for the committees that nominate board members. Thus, board members who have been appointed with the explicit consent of the CEO are often unlikely to oppose him or her. Such control may also be exercised in much more indirect ways, when CEOs and board members know each other from various kinds of social networks. In these cases, there are likely to be a number of indirect incentives that will induce the board members to vote for higher CEO payment. Sometimes, those members may even be CEOs themselves and will likely have the same opinions about appropriate levels of executive pay.

Second, even if board members were sufficiently independent of the CEO and other top executives, several practical obstacles might still prevent effective control of CEO payment. Board members may not have the necessary information, time and bargaining skill to effectively bargain with a CEO. Similar, shareholders usually have little influence on executive compensation as well. And even institutional regulatory bodies like the Securities and Exchange Commission (SEC) in the US (or the Bundesanstalt für Finanzdienstleistungsaufsicht (BaFin) in Germany) usually have only very limited possibilities to take action in this regard.

Bebchuk and Fried argue that all these factors contribute to the process of determining CEO pay being severely flawed. Their arguments have however been criticised in several ways: Empirically, first, it can be shown for example that a greater number of independent directors does not lead to a reduction in CEO payment.[26]

Second, it can be argued that granted there is an excess of CEO power, the result of the bargaining process over compensation is still optimal because transaction costs, i.e., costs of contracting, must be taken into consideration, too. It may not be desirable to just hire the cheapest CEO—because it is very doubtful that such a person would act in the best interest of the shareholders and the board.

Most important however, third, the question is what the ethical implications of the managerial power thesis are. If there is no unlawful activity, such as fraud or a breach of fiduciary duty, then it is difficult to see anything unethical about a CEO trying to maximise his or her compensation. Certainly, boards may make mistakes in the bargaining process, and might not reduce compensation as far as theoretically possible. But this cannot be seen as unfair in itself.

However, what could be called for is greater transparency, i.e. an improvement of the order framework. Rules for disclosure of executive compensation have been put into practice in several countries—and this can in principle lead to increased public acceptance of high CEO payment. It would have to be accepted however, that *high* payments, if disclosed, *must* be called just by definition, too.

---

[26] A number of references can be found in Boatright (2009, fns. 101 and 102).

Thus, the upshot of the discussion concerning the managerial power thesis is that Bebchuk's and Fried's arguments must be taken seriously, but that they cannot be seen as decisive points against the entire compensation-setting process.

10 Conclusion

There are good and bad arguments for high executive compensation. Some arguments can be easily dismissed, while others must be taken seriously. The tentative conclusion is that high executive compensation is generally justified, provided certain conditions are met: No fraud or breach of fiduciary duty must be involved. Also, the ethical rationale behind the market economy must be accepted. However, changes in rules can be ethically and economically desirable. For example, greater disclosure of executive payment is a desirable rule. By way of rules, ethical norms can be implemented. But this requires both ethical deliberation and economic competence regarding executive compensation.

References

Axelrod, R. 1984. *The evolution of cooperation*. New York: Basic Books.
Bebchuk, L., and J. Fried. 2004. *Pay without performance: the unfulfilled promise of executive compensation*. Cambridge: Harvard University Press.
Bebchuk, L., and Y. Grinstein. 2005. The growth of executive pay. *Oxford Review of Economic Policy* 21(2): 283–303.
Boatright, J. 2009. Executive compensation. In *Oxford handbook of business ethics*, ed. G. Brenkert, and T. Beauchamp. Oxford: Oxford University Press.
Bok, D. 1993. *The cost of talent: How executives and professionals are paid and how it affects america*. New York: The Free Press.
Brennan, G., and J.M. Buchanan. 1985. *The reason of rules: Constitutional political economy*. Cambridge: Cambridge University Press.
Buchanan, J.M. 1975. *The limits of liberty: Between Anarchy and Leviathan*. Chicago: University of Chicago Press.
Cochran, PhL, and S.L. Wartick. 1984. 'Golden parachutes': A closer look. *California Management Review* 26(4): 111–125.
Hayek, F.A. 1976. Law, legislation and liberty, Vol. 2: The mirage of social justice. Chicago: University of Chicago Press.
Iyengar, R.J. 2000. CEO compensation in poorly performing firms. *Journal of Applied Business Research* 16(3): 97–111.
Jensen, M.C., and W.H. Meckling. 1983. Theory of the firm: Managerial behavior, agency costs, and ownership structure. *Journal of Financial Economics* 3: 305–360.
Luetge, C. 2005. Economics ethics, business ethics, and the idea of mutual advantages. *Business Ethics: A European Review* 14(2): 108–118.
Luetge, C. 2006. An economic rationale for a work and savings ethic? J. Buchanan's late works and business ethics. *Journal of Business Ethics* 66(1): 43–51.
Luetge, C. 2009. Business engagement, mental models and philosophy in the globalized world. In *Elements of a philosophy of management and organisation*, ed. P. Koslowski. Berlin: Springer.

Luetge, C. 2015. *Order ethics vs. moral surplus: What holds a society together?*. Lanham, Md.: Lexington.

Luetge, C., 2016. Order ethics and the problem of social glue. *University of St. Thomas Law Journal* 12(2): 339–359.

Luetge, C., Armbrüster, T., and Müller, J. 2016. Order Ethics: Bridging the Gap Between Contractarianism and Business Ethics. *Journal of Business Ethics*, forthcoming.

Matten, D., and A. Crane. 2005. Corporate citizenship: Towards an extended theoretical conceptualization. *Academy of Management Review* 30: 166–179.

Murphy, K.J. 1999. Executive compensation. In *Handbook of labor economics*, ed. O. Ashenfelter, and D. Card. New York: Elsevier.

Rodgers, W., and S. Gago. 2003. A model capturing ethics and executive compensation. *Journal of Business Ethics* 48: 189–202.

Sinn, H.-W., et al. 2006. *Redesigning the welfare state, Germany's current agenda for an activating social assistance*. Cheltenham: Elgar.

Smith, A. 1776/1982. An inquiry into the nature and causes of the wealth of nations. Harmondsworth: Penguin.

Smith, V.L. 1991. *Papers in experimental economics*. Cambridge: Cambridge University Press.

Tosi, H.L., et al. 2000. How much does performance matter? A Meta-Analysis of CEO Pay Studies. *Journal of Management* 26(2): 301–338.

Weinberg, C. 2000. CEO compensation: How much is enough? *Chief Executive* 159: 49–62.

Index

A
Altruism, 11, 39, 40, 210, 293

B
Bargaining, 69, 140, 141, 303, 359
Behavioural approaches to business ethics, 195–199, 204, 206, 208, 209, 212
Behavioural ethics, 196–199, 203, 204, 206, 210, 212, 214
Bible, 121, 205
Biology, 14, 40
Bounded rationality, 61, 239
Business ethics, 6, 7, 10, 14, 21, 30, 37, 41, 171, 196, 198, 212, 312, 343, 352, 353

C
Capabilities, 132, 144, 259, 264, 354
Capitalism, 22, 38
Categorical imperative, 99, 209
Collective responsibility, 255
Competition, 8, 9, 12, 14
Consent, 3, 6, 10, 22, 80, 302, 314, 325, 353
Consequentialism, 14
Constitutional economics, 44, 110, 111, 113, 120, 222, 224, 242, 246, 316
Constructivism, 45, 49, 51, 300
Contractarian business ethics, 5, 7, 14
Contractarianism, 3, 8, 13, 80, 128
Contractualism, 4, 316
Corporate citizenship, 11
Corporate governance, 246, 254
Corporate social responsibility (CSR), 213, 222, 225, 259
Corruption, 9, 24, 87, 89, 235, 242, 293, 302
Counter-defection, 41, 47, 68
Creating shared value, 235

D
Deconstruction, 182

Deliberative democracy, 238
Democracy, 241, 267, 354
Deontology, 322
Developing countries, 295, 302
Development economics, 71
Difference principle, 62, 156–161, 165, 168
Dignity, 135, 182, 315, 322
Dilemma situations, 23, 48, 68, 88, 129, 265, 317
Dilemma structures, 42, 49, 50, 101, 102, 151, 267, 269
Discourse ethics, 4, 128, 129, 267
Distributive justice, 164
Dualism and monism in ethics, 110, 121

E
Economic ethics, 176, 282, 291
Economic growth, 22, 295, 296
Economics, 5, 7, 21, 37, 39, 43, 48, 51, 60, 61, 76, 94, 95, 97, 105, 110, 111, 121, 196, 201, 203, 212, 241, 280, 290, 316
Economy, 8, 31, 38, 45, 57, 76, 113, 254, 257, 296, 330
Efficiency, 14, 38, 43, 60–62, 67, 74–76, 97, 100, 104, 118, 120, 157, 159, 160, 164, 253, 282, 285, 289, 291, 322, 324
Egoism, 11
Empathy, 140
Equality of opportunity, 131, 155, 164
Equilibrium, 23, 59, 60, 68, 141, 285
Ethics, 280–282, 286, 288, 290, 291
Ethical principles, 6
Ethical theory, 94, 299
Evolution, 5, 23, 140
Executive compensation, 350, 351, 353, 357, 360
Experimental economics, 73, 354
Experimental ethics, 74, 75
Experimental Ethics Lab (EEL), 74

Exploitation, 14, 48, 129, 234, 261

F
Face-to-face society, 14, 143, 189
Fairness, 12, 13, 62, 63, 265
Financial crisis, 12, 357
Fraud, 330, 341, 359, 360
Freedom, 22, 30, 64, 68, 182, 187, 192
Free riding, 70, 79

G
Game theory, 5, 14, 23, 44, 80, 94, 97, 98, 105, 128, 283, 316
Global compact, 254, 270
Global governance, 254, 263, 294, 300–302, 304, 307
Globalisation, 357
Global Reporting Initiative, 298
Good life, 20, 280
Governance, 23, 111, 112, 118, 119, 121, 144, 145, 225, 227, 233, 236, 240, 243, 253, 255, 263, 268, 269, 272, 298, 301, 302, 304
Greed, 42, 112, 351
Growth, 8, 23, 29, 44, 120, 214, 296, 297, 343

H
Heuristics, 71, 86, 145, 174, 178, 244, 255, 258, 271, 273
Homo economicus, 40, 43, 47, 48, 109–115, 117, 119
Honest businessman, 12, 83
Human capital, 31
Human dignity, 312, 313, 327
Human rights, 40, 254, 270, 293, 315, 322, 327
Hunger, 42

I
Implementation, 10, 14, 40, 41, 48, 73, 99, 104, 138, 142, 145, 162, 163, 174, 177–179, 208, 210, 257, 267, 271, 308, 352
Incentives, 5, 9, 13, 21, 24, 32, 33, 73, 77, 85, 89, 100, 128, 130, 132, 142, 145, 156, 157, 173, 199, 241, 258, 301, 303, 312, 313, 319, 324, 351, 353, 359
Incentive structures, 47, 67, 68, 73, 76, 115–117, 119, 128, 144, 195, 198, 203, 207, 211–213
Income redistribution, 160, 164
Incomplete contracts, 7, 8, 11, 12
Individual ethics, 32, 33, 41, 45, 49, 52, 143, 260
Individualism, 254, 268
Inequality, 161, 170

Innovation, 22, 31, 156, 212, 297, 307
Institutional economics, 63, 65, 119, 199, 208, 213
Institutional ethics, 63, 293
Institutions, 7, 13, 21, 32, 49, 67, 70, 74, 79, 88, 89, 91, 130, 131, 139, 145, 153, 158, 197, 199, 203, 221, 236, 259, 308, 323, 352
Integrative social contract theory, 6
Interaction, 11, 13, 42, 47, 48, 69, 84, 86, 95, 101, 105, 110, 111, 114–116, 119, 128, 144, 173, 196, 200–202, 205, 214, 234, 235, 261, 263, 269, 281, 286, 290, 312, 316
Internet, 104, 240, 246, 284, 305
Intuitions, 38, 41, 50, 51, 72, 79, 102
Investment, 10, 44, 60, 173, 200, 231, 246, 261, 274, 331, 341

J
Justice, 4, 8, 23, 63, 65, 99, 131–136, 141, 142, 145, 149, 150, 152, 154, 157, 162–164, 167–179, 214, 251, 294, 297–300, 313–315, 322–324
Justice, theory of, 4, 168, 175
Justification, 11, 40, 102, 103, 105, 129, 139, 150, 171, 178, 179, 267, 282, 291, 352, 354

K
Kaldor-Hicks-criterion, 104

L
Legal theory, 320, 323
Liberalism, 134
Liberty, 4, 30, 77, 153, 291

M
Market economy, 7, 59, 102, 110, 156, 198, 203, 207–209, 211, 213, 282, 352, 354, 357, 360
Market failure, 27, 60, 61, 65, 245, 269
Maximin principle, 62
Medical ethics, 312, 313, 320–322, 327
Mental models, 224, 239
Methodology, 7, 38, 42, 44, 45, 49, 51, 76, 94, 101, 104, 105, 151, 246, 280, 281, 282, 290
Minimum wage, 104, 160, 280, 283–285, 288–291
Modern societies, 8, 14, 45, 71, 72, 127, 143, 144
Morality, 4, 5, 20, 21, 38, 40, 45, 48, 50, 52, 88, 137, 141, 151, 196, 199, 201, 204, 208, 210, 211, 213, 214, 317, 318, 353
Moral surplus, 127, 130, 138, 141, 145, 146

Motivation, 8, 40, 49, 83, 87, 89, 129, 130, 154, 319, 355
Multi-national corporations, 12, 205, 243, 251, 298
Mutual advantages, 11, 110
Mutual gains, 95, 109, 111, 114–120, 146, 210, 213

N
Naturalism in ethics, 14
Normativity, 7, 14, 181, 260, 268, 351

O
Old testament text, 109, 111, 112, 115, 116, 120
Open contracts, 144
Opportunity cost, 59, 61
Order ethics, 4, 5, 7–11, 14, 15, 21, 45, 68, 72, 76, 80, 87, 97, 104, 110, 112, 143, 144, 150, 156, 161, 164, 165, 171, 176, 179, 261, 265, 268, 280, 288, 291, 293, 298, 304, 307, 309
Ordonomics, 27, 33, 246, 316, 317, 326
Ordo-responsibility, 199, 221, 227, 232, 233, 235–241, 243–245, 251, 258, 259, 261–273, 303
Original position, 4, 131, 143
Orthogonal position, 19, 21, 24–29, 33, 317

P
Pareto, 58–62, 103, 289
Pareto-efficiency, 97–99, 282
Pareto superiority, 61
Paternalism, 41
Philosophy, 5, 15, 23, 37, 44, 77, 127, 139, 160, 199
Philosophy of economics, 175, 199, 201, 222
Pluralism, 7, 15, 22, 120, 127, 131, 143, 172, 196, 198, 205, 207, 212, 214, 299
Politics, 26, 27, 58, 233, 251, 252, 269, 298
Positive sum games, 8
Poverty, 42, 102, 169, 295
Practical philosophy, 175
Pre-modern societies, 8
Prisoners' dilemma, 9, 80, 128, 151, 234, 352
Profits, 8, 31, 43, 252, 287, 300, 304, 307, 353, 357
Protestant ethics, 28
Psychology, 40, 73, 76, 81, 90, 164, 268
Public good, 24, 29, 60, 70, 117, 206, 213, 241, 243, 253, 271, 302

Q
Quaker industrialists, 212

R
Rational choice, 48, 265
Rationality, 68, 94, 181, 182, 238, 265, 269, 322
Rawls, 4, 23, 40, 44, 45, 50, 62, 65, 95, 98, 99, 128, 131–135, 141, 149–163, 167–169, 172, 196, 299, 353
Rawlsian order ethics, 99, 149, 150, 164, 165
Reporting, 293
Reputation, 13, 139, 231, 319, 324, 330, 331, 335–342, 354
Responsibility, 30, 49, 182, 211, 213, 222, 225, 228, 231, 232, 236, 239, 244, 246, 252, 255, 257, 260, 261, 263, 264, 268, 271, 272, 313, 340
Rights, 4, 30–32, 40, 60, 99, 110, 112–114, 116–118, 131, 134, 150, 153, 154, 156, 164, 177, 190, 191, 252, 254, 256, 267, 270–272, 293, 305, 315, 316, 322, 327
Risk management, 344
Rules, 3, 5–7, 9, 10, 13, 23, 65, 72, 81, 116, 130, 134, 144, 150, 173, 198, 210, 213, 225, 233, 235, 243, 258, 261, 267, 269, 302, 312, 318, 322, 324, 352, 353, 360

S
Self-interest, 4, 5, 8, 11, 24, 26, 42, 94, 105, 113, 128, 145, 157, 210, 233, 259, 269, 321, 323, 324
Semantics, 30, 73, 141, 145, 146, 224–228, 231, 232, 236, 245, 260, 268, 298–301, 316
Shareholders, 11, 12, 205, 330, 331, 343, 352, 354, 356, 359
Signaling, 13, 115, 236, 304
Situationism, 79, 81, 83
Social capital, 119
Social contract, 5, 7, 89, 118, 120, 138, 140, 141, 143, 144, 168, 353
Social dilemma, 19, 21, 23, 24, 25, 28, 30, 31, 33, 70, 71, 73, 239, 308
Social glue, 127
Social market economy, 31, 354
Social networks, 263, 273, 359
Social structure, 23, 138, 199, 224–228, 232, 235, 236, 245, 246, 252, 260, 261, 268, 316, 352
Solidarity, 9, 31, 39, 102, 282, 294, 299, 312, 320, 323, 352

Stakeholders, 11, 197, 198, 203, 208, 209, 211, 213, 245, 264, 273, 304, 306–308, 330, 336, 338–340
Stakeholder theory, 195–197
Sustainability, 23, 30, 44, 270, 273, 294, 298–306, 308, 309

T
Temperance, 8
Trade-offs, 85, 98, 299, 301, 306, 315
Transaction cost, 118, 120, 240, 359
Trust, 13, 200, 231, 266, 329, 336, 338, 341, 344

U
Utilitarianism, 14, 98, 315

V
Virtue ethics, 197–199
Virtues, 20, 39, 72, 245, 314

W
Wage regulation policies, 289
Welfare economics, 57–59, 61–63, 65
Well-being, 57, 82, 98, 295, 312, 314, 327, 357
Win-win situations, 9, 11, 13, 306

Z
Zero sum game, 25, 201
Zero sum society, 8, 201

Printed by Printforce, the Netherlands